A Debonair Scoundrel

Books by Lately Thomas

THE VANISHING EVANGELIST

A DEBONAIR SCOUNDREL

A Debonair

Scoundrel

*An Episode in the Moral
History of San Francisco*

By Lately Thomas

ILLUSTRATED WITH PHOTOGRAPHS

HOLT, RINEHART AND
WINSTON / NEW YORK

Designer: Ernst Reichl
88408-0112
Printed in the United States of America

To Frustration

"From strict justice, O Lord, preserve us!"

—THE PREBENDARY

To the Reader   Among glamor cities of the globe, San Francisco has received a documentation as copious as any, more minute than some. The great chapters of its flamboyant history—the Gold Rush, the Vigilantes, the earthquake and fire—have been told and retold. But one chapter, perhaps the most turbulent of all, has lain relatively neglected, as if it were an uneasy memory, primly swept under the carpet of civic consciousness. This is the full story of the so-called graft prosecutions of 1906–1910 and the city's resultant virtual civil war. Here is that unforgotten, avoided chapter. The author cannot pretend that it is the whole story, for that would fill a library; nor is it the only story, because each of the embattled partisans had a separate account, few of which agreed. This is the record, drawn scrupulously from the voluminous, contemporary, original sources. No fact, and no direct quotation, has been invented or knowingly distorted. Whatever omissions or errors of detail may have crept in unintentionally are chargeable solely to the author.

Contents

Second Book

The City at War

PART ONE

PART TWO

PART THREE

PART FOUR

First Book

"The Unspeakable Ruef"

A FABLE

An Assassin being put on trial in a New England court, his Counsel rose and said: "Your Honor, I move for a discharge on the ground of 'once in jeopardy'; my client has already been tried for that murder and acquitted."

"In what court?"

"In the Superior Court of San Francisco," the Counsel replied.

"Let the trial proceed—your motion is denied," said the Judge. "An Assassin is not in jeopardy when tried in California."

AMBROSE BIERCE, 1908

PART ONE

1   The City and a Citizen

During the opening years of this century, the world's startled attention was drawn to a place on the western shore of the United States which had attracted global interest more than once before,—the fledgling, raucous, rich, and passionately opinionated town of San Francisco. Odd and wayward behavior had seemed normal to that city, a latecomer among great ports; but the current goings-on were so extraordinary, so unseemly, contradictory, and complex, they ran so counter to accepted rules of civic conduct, that observers at a distance could only surmise what issues or truths underlay the muddled farce-tragedy. So fair-minded a spectator as *The Nation* magazine shook its head reprehensively,—but admitted that it did not fully understand the rights and wrongs of the matter, and doubted whether San Franciscans did, either.

The drama *was* different. The antagonists were both individuals and segments of the community, personified in leaders of daring and ability, and in epitomes of the obscure. The stakes were at once tangible and intangible, ethical and material: a city's preservation, and the vindication of fundamental law. But to retain the threads of the action became all but impossible—everybody talked at once! The gallery of the world looked on with shock and aversion, then with perplexity, then doubt, then suspicion and resentment, and at last disgust. San Francisco, the verdict was, had become lost to honor and its people were delivered over to a hoodlum mob committing indecencies in a sepulchered ruin.

What kind of city was this San Francisco of, say, 1900 to 1906, which could generate such appalling japeries? Not the city of today certainly; and already in its few decades of existence it had in turn been several cities. Spawned in the chaos of the Gold Rush of 1849, it had expanded abruptly amid sporadic violence. It was destroyed again and again, and sprang up rejuvenated and irrepressible. By the dawn of the twentieth century, it had grown both urban and urbane; but underneath the opulence and glitter of sophistication persisted a residue of frontier crudity, and its temperament retained vestiges of the improvident recklessness and daring of its mining-camp origin. The people of San Francisco were cosmopolitan, energetic, noisily self-reliant, hot in dispute, tolerant of the gaudier vices, and always ready to egg on a diverting brawl. Toward friends they were notoriously open-handed, and they took nostalgic pride in the rank lustiness of their infant-Gargantua metropolis. Two traits which above all distinguished the dwellers by the Golden Gate were their exuberance and a boundless zest for living.

In size, the city ranked sixth in the United States, numbering nearly half-a-million inhabitants. It was the West's only real city: Los Angeles, for example, which stood twenty-sixth on the national roster, was just emerging from the dust of a pokey cow-town. And in 1900 San Francisco was launched upon a boom period which seemed to hold promise of illimitable growth. Its bustling port, in a bay that is a dream of poets, contributed vastly to its wealth, and it stood preeminently the social, commercial, cultural, and financial capital of the agricultural empire which California had become. Gold, silver, and wheat were its exports; its imports comprised the costliest luxuries of the globe.

Much of this metropolitan wealth and power was concentrated in a select society dominated by second-generation millionaires, patrician sons of pioneer fathers, who had inherited princely fortunes amassed by their forebears, often with ruthless rapacity. Next below this confraternity of gold was a numerous, substantial, intelligent middle class, strongly endowed with go-ahead push. Lower in the scale there was poverty, but not the demeaning squalor of the industrial slums of Eastern and Old World cities: high wages, cheap food, and superabundant space and sunlight precluded real misery. And the spirit of the town was neither poor nor static: San Francisco had been born of gambler's luck and its people had never lost the gambler's optimism. Every man, however trivially employed today, felt that, with sufficient will and a bit of luck, he might, tomorrow or the day after, scramble to the top of the glittering heap.

In one significant aspect San Francisco was in the van of events: it was a stronghold of organized labor, the foremost in the nation. No other city in the world was as firmly knit by unionism; in no other city were labor unions so influential. This condition had come about as a result of the concurrence of geographical and sociological factors too complex to enter into here, and had been attained only after protracted and bitter struggle. Time and again the unions and the capitalists had battled each other with hearty ferocity, and their deep-rooted, still unresolved rivalry was one of the forces which, in conjunction, were to produce a civic explosion.

In 1901 San Francisco was paralyzed by a great transportation strike; for the first time, a coalition of employers, investors, and agriculturists lined up against a united labor front. Farmers whose harvests rotted for want of conveyance to shipping points joined the "money interests," and the unions were whipped into sullen submission; principally, they contended, because city policemen had been used to smash picket lines and "club men back to work." The battle cost several lives and inflicted millions of dollars of damage, and it left a legacy of mutual distrust and rancor that was to smoulder for decades. Both the belligerent parties felt that the settlement (the exact terms of which the public never learned) was only a truce.

One ardent champion of the unions was a Catholic priest, Father

Peter C. Yorke, who acted as spokesman and fiery mentor of the strikers. After their humiliating defeat, he said bluntly that labor would never win a strike in San Francisco as long as the "money interests"—property owners, merchants, employers—controlled the city government. Therefore, let labor form its own political party and through the ballot box install its representatives in the City Hall, Father Yorke repeated tirelessly; then no future strike would be broken by policemen's clubs.

Many workingmen listened sympathetically to this radically aggressive advice. And thus hope of political domination was added to the tensions at work in the populace.

Politics in San Francisco were carried on, like most activities, with torrid enthusiasm; it was a rough-and-tumble game. At that period, municipal elections were conducted on a party basis (the outlawing of party labels coming later), and voters were sharply divided between Republicans and Democrats. A city election was to be held in November of 1901: a ground swell set in favoring the adoption of Father Yorke's bold program.

The incumbent mayor was James Duval Phelan, a native of the city, a millionaire, son of a wealthy father, a leading property holder, and a social luminary of the first magnitude. A bachelor, he managed to be both popular and respected. He had been elected by the Democrats in 1895 and re-elected for two succeeding terms of two years each; and his administration was a refreshing change from the venality of those preceding it, compiling a record of progressive accomplishment without incurring any scandal. The strike of 1901, however, drew down on Mayor Phelan the enmity of both factions, the unions denouncing him for supposedly ordering the police to club strikers, and the employers excoriating him for assertedly having encouraged bloodshed. Both accusations were unwarranted, and in time the union spokesmen admitted that Phelan had never instigated the police brutality, but had done his best to safeguard life and rights impartially. But at the time they were made, the charges were widely credited. Phelan realized that his popularity was compromised, and having large personal interests requiring his attention, he was content to retire.

This left the Democrats with no outstanding candidate for mayor. The Republicans also had no proved vote-getter to put forward, and talk of forming a separate political party of workingmen gained strength. Suddenly a number of lesser union leaders circulated a formal call for a convention of delegates, to be chosen by trade unions, for the purpose of organizing the Union Labor Party, adopting a platform upholding labor's rights and nominating candidates for city offices. Nowhere in the world, at that time, had union labor entered politics as a separate, self-cognizant party.

This ambitious prospectus aroused no alarm among old-line, experienced politicians: the men issuing the call were naïve and inept, and the really powerful unions, dominated by Patrick Henry McCarthy, adroit and able president of the Building Trades Council, held themselves aloof or expressed disapproval. Only one professional politician—an astute little lawyer who for ten years had bossed the polyglot North Beach district for the Republicans—saw in the development a possibility for self-aggrandizement. He had no special sympathy with unions (he was a bourgeois landlord and investor himself), but he had been thwarted in several attempts to grasp control of the machinery of his own party, and power, with the excitements attendant upon the exercise of power, was what he craved.

That man was Abraham Ruef, who was to become the peg upon which the forthcoming civic convulsion would turn.

Abraham Ruef was a typical product of his city and era—able, ambitious, and accommodating. He had been born in San Francisco on September 2, 1864, the son of Meyer Rueff, a French mercantile Jew who emigrated to California in 1862. (The name was pronounced "roof," and the family gradually dropped the second "f.") Meyer Rueff prospered in the new milieu, and by 1892 was listed, among a profusion of catering and champagne advertisements, in the *Jewish Elite Directory and Society List of San Francisco* as maintaining a home at 316 Lombard Street, a quietly genteel address.

Abe (so he was universally called) grew up with two sisters in a family tightly linked in the French tradition. He never knew privation. He attended the public schools of San Francisco, and, proving prodigiously clever, at the age of fourteen matriculated at the University of California, situated in the pleasant town of Berkeley on the opposite shore of San Francisco Bay. At the mature age of eighteen he was graduated from the university with highest honors. While a student, he helped to found the students' co-operative, organized to provide textbooks at prices the students could afford, and in recognition of this and other beneficial activities, he was elected permanent secretary of his class of 1883. He had majored in classical languages and became a brilliant Latinist, but his true bent was indicated by the topic of his senior thesis: "Purity in Politics."

Enrollment at Hastings College of the Law in San Francisco followed, and in 1886, when he was twenty-one, Abe was admitted to the California bar. That also was the first year he could vote.

Like many young men of that generation, profoundly stirred by revulsion against the cynicism and degradation prevalent in political life, Ruef dabbled in exploring schemes for reform; with several young friends he organized a discussion club, which they rather pompously called the Municipal Reform League, for the purpose of studying civic government. Two members of the group were Franklin K. Lane (subsequently Secretary of the Interior in President Wilson's cabinet) and John H. Wigmore (who was to become the revered Dean of Northwestern University Law School and author of the monumental *Treatise on Evidence*). As club secretary, Ruef corresponded with representatives of similar groups elsewhere, including (he was to recount) a political greenhorn in New York City named Theodore Roosevelt.

From his downtown law office, advantageously located first at the corner of Sutter and Montgomery streets, but shortly moved to nearby Kearny and California streets, Abe registered as a voter at the first opportunity; and when a meeting of the Republican club of his district was announced, in preparation for a forthcoming primary election, he eagerly made his way to the address listed. This proved to be a sailors' lodging house at the foot of Telegraph Hill, on the edge of the sinister Barbary Coast. It was a murky evening, and shanghaiing was a relatively common mishap befalling trespassers in that area; Ruef was thoroughly uneasy when he knocked at the closed door.

Inside, all was still. Then came the clump of feet slowly descending a staircase. Ruef's heart pounded. The door opened a crack, and a man holding a lighted lantern peered out sourly. Abe explained his mission. The man with the lantern replied gruffly that the meeting was all over, but he could come in.

With increasing trepidation Ruef followed this uninviting guide up the dark stairs and into a room where two individuals sat at a bare table; one proved to be a saloonkeeper nearby, the other was the operator of the lodging house. The latter confirmed that the meeting had adjourned, after electing the three men on hand as president, secretary, and treasurer.

Ruef was turning away when the saloonkeeper asked: "Young man, can you write?"

Ruef gave assurance that he was moderately literate and was invited to compose a report of the meeting for the newspapers. Under dictation, he set down a glowing account of a gathering of one hundred and fifty enthusiastic Republicans and their unanimous election of his companions, there present, as the keepers of their political consciences. Obeying instructions, he carried this to a newspaper office, and the next morning basked in the dual refulgence of successful authorship and awareness of a real political connection, when he read the report printed in full.

Not until long afterward did he learn that the three "officers" had convened their meeting unhampered by the intrusion of outsiders and unanimously elected themselves, and that the time and place of the meeting had purposely been selected with a design to frighten away honest citizens.

As a reward for his contribution in the line of publicity, Abe was made a captain of two precincts, the lowest grade of practical politician; and for a couple of years he assiduously ran errands for ward heelers and "rockrollers"—toughs hired to influence balloting and overawe upstart rivals, generally by the use of brass knuckles and slingshots. This noisy and unsavory gang was also known as "the push."

Young Ruef, haunting the back rooms of saloons with horrified fascination and hopefully angling for legal clients, presented a striking contrast to the plug-uglies with whom he perforce associated. His speech, manners, and dress were those of gentility. He was prepossessingly good-looking: he had the head of an artist or connoisseur, with finely molded ears, darkly arched eyebrows, virile nose, humorous, mobile mouth, and sensitive chin. Although five feet, eight inches in height, he was so delicately framed he appeared smaller; in tights he might have passed for a French acrobat. He had sported a wisp of black mustache in college (it made him look older, he thought), and in conformity with the whisker fashion of the decade this bloomed into the handlebar luxuriance that was that age's outward symbol of proper manhood.

His quick intelligence soon grasped that the façade of free popular elections, erected for the beguilement of the citizenry, was a sham. He saw candidates for public office nominated and elected by a combination of wheedling, barter, intimidation, and bribery. Two Republican bosses shared party sway in the city—Phil Crimmins and Martin Kelly, both rough, uneducated men. The Democratic boss was a blind man, equally rough-and-tough—Chris Buckley. Above these petty satraps was the political overlord of California, the Southern Pacific Railroad.

To California there was only one Railroad, and it had been an incubus upon the economy of the state for many years; by subvention, chicanery, and pressure, contriving to corrupt public authority at every level; its influence was potent even in the Congress in Washington. Public agencies, other corporations, the banks, the press, agriculture, commerce, and industry,—all of these it had succeeded in manipulating to swell its profits, and for forty years every attempt to break this predatory squeeze had failed. The California Legislature was its puppet, and the courts were largely packed with judges subservient to its wishes.

These political realities the agile-minded Ruef quickly assimilated. The study excited him; it was like a course in applied social science; and in his eagerness he often forgot to eat. His cleverness marked him as a comer, and in 1888, when he was twenty-three, the roustabout Martin Kelly tapped him to boss the North Beach district, or Latin Quarter. Kelly hoped that Abe's culture, fine manners, and gentlemanly diction would give the machine a polish it totally lacked.

The Quarter, so called for short, was exceptionally cosmopolitan even for melting-pot San Francisco. It included the rowdy Barbary Coast, and its streets swarmed with Italians, Greeks, Lascars, Chinese, Irish, Scandinavians, French, Germans, Kanakas, Aleuts, and other outlandish races and nationalities. Ruef spoke several languages, five or six fluently, and he swiftly mastered the finesse required to harmonize antagonistic viewpoints. His law practice increased measurably, and he began to be known around the courts as an able strategist, perhaps over-crafty, but visibly on his way to wealth and position. Meanwhile, he lived simply, with his parents and a married sister, not far from Telegraph Hill, which overlooked his political bailiwick. His personal habits were frugal: he neither smoked nor gambled, and seldom drank more than one glass of wine with meals in the temperate French fashion, with possibly a liqueur afterward. He dressed neatly and unobtrusively, was regular in religious observances, contributed to worthy causes, and had no amours. "The ladies? I love them all, married and single!" he would laugh. Socially, he nursed no consuming ambitions: he was contentedly middle class, and enjoyed watching the vagaries of the restless rich without aspiring to ape them. His by no means inconsiderable legal earnings he invested thriftily, mainly in real estate.

All during the Nineties, Ruef remained small-time in the political swirl, primarily a lawyer with a political avocation. He was ambitious politically, but during that decade the Republicans in San Francisco were in eclipse. In 1891 the Democratic boss, blind Chris Buckley, venal and vulnerable, had been toppled by a faction of reform Democrats; he fled to Canada temporarily, and the reformers clamped a hold on the city government which they were able to maintain for ten years. During their tenure, Phelan was elected mayor. Early in 1901 Ruef had tried to wrest control of the Republican city machine from his sponsor, Kelly, and had been soundly whipped; somewhat contemptuously, Kelly allowed his underling to remain party boss in North Beach.

It was precisely while Abe was recovering from this rebuff that the call for the formation of a labor party was promulgated. The action provoked guffaws from Martin Kelly, but Ruef scented an opportunity. Canvassing his precinct workers, he found that a number were members or officials of labor unions, and these men he ordered to get themselves elected by their unions to the organizing convention. For such practised professionals, this was an easy assignment; and before the inexperienced delegates had fairly settled into their chairs, Abe's clique had taken command, installed their chairman, infiltrated committees, and engineered the adoption of a platform and slate of candidates drawn up by Ruef. Overnight the North Beach politician found himself the actual, although hidden power behind a new political force, the Union Labor Party, while retaining his strategic position in Republican councils. Riding these two horses, he headed into the riskiest race of his spectacular career.

2 "Red Riot and Anarchy"

Heading the list of Union Labor Party candidates was Ruef's carefully considered choice for mayor, Eugene Edwards Schmitz.

Tall, thrillingly masculine, with arrogant head set off by a fierce black beard, flaring mustaches, flashing dark eyes, and a shock of jet black, wavy hair, "Handsome Gene" possessed one advantage over some other men whom fate has marked for a piratical role—he looked like a swashbuckler of romance.

Schmitz was thirty-seven: he was born in San Francisco in the same year as Ruef. His mother was a Dubliner, daughter of a Captain Hogan in the British Army, who migrated to Charleston, South Carolina, and later to New York; there, in 1848, Miss Hogan was married to an immigrant German musician, Joseph L. Schmitz. In the early Fifties, the couple joined the stampede to California. As a boy, Eugene sold newspapers on Montgomery Street, wistfully wondering whether he would ever be as rich as the flashily dressed men who tossed him pennies. He was reared in an artistic atmosphere, and by 1901 had acquired some local distinction as a violinist and composer of occasional ballads and marches, and he was regularly employed as conductor of the orchestra in the fashionable Columbia Theater on Powell Street at a salary of $40 a week. His work threw him into the company of actors, from whom he learned the importance of gesture and poise, and nightly observation of elegantly got-up audiences had taught him deportment and taste in dress.

"A commanding figure of a man," Ruef described him, "of natural ability, good intelligence, keen perceptions. He possessed a tenacious memory and unsurpassable nerve. He could put up a better front than any man I knew; I had often seen him assume a pretense which covered up all deficiencies. His face could completely mask his feelings."

Schmitz seemed providentially suited to Ruef's purposes. He was president of the musicians union, but in no way resembled the popular notion of a labor leader; hence he could appeal to the conservative middle class, who rated musicians almost on a professional par with lawyers, doctors, and teachers. Schmitz was gregarious and had a multitude of friends; he was active in the politically potent fraternal order, the Native Sons of the Golden West (of which Ruef was a grand trustee), and like Ruef was a joiner of many social organizations. He lived with his wife and two daughters in irreproachable domesticity, and his German-Irish ancestry would appeal to the two largest segments of foreign-born voters. Moreover, he was a Catholic, another strong asset.

Subconsciously, perhaps, Schmitz's "commanding presence" was what most stirred Ruef's admiration. Western men as a breed are tall and rangy; Ruef was physically insignificant, although conscious of mental stature above the average. He always disliked being called "the little boss," although he was too intelligent and well bred to betray his irritation often. An observation he made years later revealed the fascination which tall, physically striking males held for him.

"The psychology of the mass of voters," he philosophized, "is like that of a crowd of small boys or primitive men. Other things being equal, of two candidates they will almost invariably follow the fine, strongly built man."

Schmitz ideally fulfilled this subjective yearning: if diminutive Abe could not be king, he would be king-maker,—a Svengali to Schmitz's Trilby.

When first tapped for nomination to City Hall, Schmitz was incredulous.

"I have no ability to act as mayor," he protested. "I have no experience. I don't know anything about municipal affairs. I couldn't go through a campaign. I never made a public address. Besides, I haven't the means to fight. The whole thing is preposterous!"

Ruef reassured him on all points. "You have as much experience and information as many men who have been nominated and more than some who have filled the office. What you lack can be easily supplied. The speeches and the funds we can take care of. You are not rabid," he went on. "You could appeal to the conservative elements, who are tired of the industrial warfare. You are a man of fine appearance. You are tall, well built. If you are nominated, people will naturally turn as you pass and say, 'There goes the Labor candidate for mayor.' At the theater you will have a thousand people talking about you every night and advertising you, who scarcely give you a glance now. Think it over. I see a chance of making a big man of you."

Schmitz thought it over and a few days later consented.

"A fortune teller read my future and prophesied that within a year I should hold a high and mighty position in my native city," he laughed. "I'm not superstitious,—but there's no use bucking against a hunch like that! Especially under the circumstances, when the case looks so good anyhow."

Ruef wrote the platform of the new party, adroitly avoiding anything that reeked of radicalism, remaining "true to every principle of organized labor, yet conservative, pledging fair dealing toward capital as well." There were planks calling for better schoolhouses, for abolition of the poll tax, and for arbitration of industrial disputes; public ownership of public services also was espoused, although the city's charter already endorsed that in principle.

Ruef composed a five-minute speech for Schmitz to make at the nominating convention. Eugene memorized it, and Ruef coached him to let his rival for the nomination—a leader of the iron molders union—speak first. This man bored the crowd with a bumbling, windy address. Then Gene stepped forward and delivered what Ruef modestly described as "brilliant epigrams" with theatrical fire. The delegates nominated Schmitz by acclamation and hailed him as the eloquent voice of labor.

Eugene proved himself an able campaigner. Ruef wrote the speeches and Schmitz put them across.

"Ordinarily Schmitz lacked application," Ruef later recalled. "He was not fond of work and always preferred to amuse himself. But he had a power of assimilating ideas and a gift of memory, and he developed a marvelous faculty for joining thoughts and sentences from many speeches, prepared for him, into new ones of his own. He developed remarkable self-confidence. If he sang a song, he did so with the impression that there was an entire repertoire behind it. If he delivered one speech, it was as if he could deliver any kind at any time. Social attention was as nectar to him even in his first campaign."

Ruef was attorney for the liquor dealers association and rounded up their powerful support. His political headquarters was the Pup restaurant, on Stockton Street just off Market, where he dined nightly, usually ordering the excellent dollar table d'hôte. After the meal he would adjourn to a private room on the second floor to receive reports, map strategy, and distribute favors. Although the "wise money" was betting four to one against a Union Labor victory, Ruef laid out $16,000 of his own for Schmitz's campaign; and as the excitement mounted and it appeared that in a three-cornered race, running against a Democrat and a Republican, Schmitz might have an outside chance, some of the more influential union leaders swung to the forlorn cause and hoped for a miracle.

On election day in November the miracle was delivered, Schmitz receiving twenty-one thousand votes to seventeen thousand polled by the Republican candidate and twelve thousand by the Democrat. Although by a minority of those voting, San Francisco had elected the first union labor mayor in the history of the United States. A shock of mingled exultation and alarm raced through the nation and was registered as far away as in Japan and the money markets of London. Red riot and anarchy, it was predicted, would flow from this insane jettisoning of all civic responsibility; San Francisco, the world was reminded, was still a city of dubious surprises.

Schmitz's victory did not extend to the entire Union Labor ticket: in fact, besides the mayor, the party managed to elect only three members of the board of supervisors, the legislative branch of the city government, the other members of the board being holdovers from the Phelan regime, mostly men of ability and integrity. Nonetheless, the jubilant labor forces celebrated frenetically. The musicians union, whose president had routed the enemy on two fronts, ordered its members into the streets to head victory parades, and theater orchestras bolted before the final curtain to join in the blare.

In the early hours, when the result was certain, Ruef telephoned to Schmitz's home, a modestly comfortable, gingerbread-trimmed house on upper Fillmore Street, to express congratulations. Eugene was asleep. Later, in the cozy basement room which Schmitz had fitted up as a den, they shook hands and raised glasses of champagne.

"We pledged eternal fealty," Ruef recalled. "We talked of the uplift of the masses and of the elevation of labor."

Ruef's political ideal (he often discoursed about this) was Mark Hanna, the Ohio industrialist who went into politics with the avowed purpose of placing William McKinley in the White House. Hanna accomplished his objective, along the way electing himself to the United States Senate. The Senate was Ruef's personal ambition. Schmitz, he felt, might serve as his McKinley.

Two months before the San Francisco election, McKinley had been shot by a weak-minded anarchist and Theodore Roosevelt became President of the United States, the youngest in the nation's history. The reign of Teddy, the tide of imperial expansion, of struggle against entrenched corporate power, of war on "malefactors of great wealth," the era of the "Big Stick," had set in. New men, young men, were grasping the direction of public affairs; Ruef intended to be one of those young men.

Schmitz was to take office in January. Prompted by Ruef, the mayor-elect gave out that he was going away for a rest at the home of his wife's parents in Watsonville, a farming community south of San Francisco; instead, he and Ruef headed in a northwest direction and checked in under assumed names at an antiquated hotel in the Sierra foothill town of Sonoma. There, day after day and far into the night, Abe put his pupil through a politician's catechism. Clause by clause, paragraph by paragraph, Schmitz memorized the city charter, the basic law under which the municipality functioned, and then listened to an expository gloss which Ruef supplied out of his political experience and legal acumen. Strategy was mapped, appointments were discussed, nothing was overlooked that might contribute to a favorable debut, and before Christmas Schmitz was graduated *magna cum laude*.

Those weeks were idyllic for Abe. *He* had no aversion to work, and undistracted by routine affairs he indulged the wildest hopes.

"We were the only strangers in the little village," he recalled. "We had left our whereabouts unknown except to our immediate families. There, in undisturbed peace, we talked and planned night and day. I saw the Union Labor Party a spark in California which would kindle the entire nation and make a Labor President. I saw the Union Labor Party a throne for Schmitz, as mayor, as governor,—as President. Behind that throne I saw myself, its power, local, state,—national. Looming in the distance, I saw myself United States senator." The view from the shore of the Western Sea towards the populous and storied East was intoxicatingly bright.

Schmitz's homework paid off handsomely. Upon his return to the city, he favorably impressed even the most critical observers. Mayor Phelan warmly congratulated him and conceded that there had been merit in labor's revolt; Phelan termed the election "a splendid object lesson in popular government." But, in a private letter to his old friend John H. Wigmore, Franklin K. Lane predicted shrewdly that the new mayor would "surprise the moneyed people and anger the laboring people with his conservatism." And a newspaper reporter (who had voted for Schmitz's Democratic opponent) came away from an interview scoffing at the campaign talk about a "boycott by capital" if Schmitz moved into City Hall.

After the inaugural, the partners settled down to achieve the next step in their program. George B. Keane, Ruef's confidential law clerk, was installed as the Mayor's secretary and liaison man, and no move was made without careful consideration of its vote-getting value. Ruef worked tirelessly and contentedly: politics became almost his entire business, his law practice devolving more and more upon assistants.

In spite of their plans, Schmitz's first appointment was made against his wishes and with bad grace. The unions, mindful of their recent strike defeat, were eager to gain control of the police force, and they insisted that Harry W. Hutton, a lawyer who had represented the unions during the big walkout, be appointed to the police commission. Schmitz disliked Hutton, but political necessity dictated, and under strong pressure the Mayor gave him the preferment.

San Francisco at that time was governed under a charter which Mayor Phelan had been instrumental in obtaining, and which had eliminated many abuses and greatly strengthened the mayor's authority. Under this charter, the city's chief executive named the administrative boards, appointing the members and being empowered to remove them at will. The principal boards were the fire commission, the police commission, the board of public works, the parks commission, the board of health, and the board of education. Appointments were made in rotation, one member each year as an incumbent's term expired; thus a new mayor's control of these commissions which transacted the business of the city was sharply limited, two and three years being required to give him a majority of the three-man and four-man groups, and a mayor's term of office was for two years only.

The backstairs scheming by which Schmitz had been elected became clear to the public shortly after his inauguration. As a means of serving notice on the political fraternity of Ruef's influence with the new regime, an obscure weekly newspaper, at Abe's instigation, published a thank-you note composed by the Mayor, effusively acknowledging Ruef's services. The letter was similar to scores which Eugene scattered facilely and which carried no great significance; but this letter was important, because it officially and publicly recognized Ruef as the master boss of the Union Labor administration.

My dear Ruef [Eugene wrote]:

Now that the election is over and I am to be mayor of my native city, I wish to express to you, and through you to all your loyal friends who supported my cause, my profound appreciation of the generous, whole-souled, substantial, and effective support accorded me in the exciting campaign just closed. Viewed from your prominent position in the Republican Party, I know the seriousness of the step which you took when you voluntarily and unconditionally offered me your valuable aid, and I cannot in words properly give utterance to my deep feeling in this regard. I can only say that your action is worthy of yourself, and that no higher praise can be accorded you.

I have now for fifteen years enjoyed your acquaintance and friendship and your services as my attorney in many capacities, and I say without hesitation or flattery that I have yet to find a more honorable, a more loyal, a more able attorney, or a truer friend.

I feel that I owe a great deal of my success in this campaign to you and your friends, and I shall not permit myself at any time to forget it.

Though you have never asked or even suggested it, I shall, with the utmost confidence and with a sentiment of absolute sincerity, feel myself privileged at all times to consider you as my friendly counsellor and to call upon you whenever I may require assistance in the solution of any of the perplexing and complicated questions which must necessarily arise in the conduct of so vast and important an office.

I trust that you will not hesitate to say that I may do so. Again and again thanking you and your friends, I am,

Very sincerely yours,

EUGENE E. SCHMITZ

To a reader with half an eye, this amounted to a promissory note
on City Hall, and at the same time, it added to the boss's prestige in
Republican circles. Abe had intended it to have that effect. But unexpectedly, and unfortunately for the partnership, it caught the irate
eye of the most hated, most loved newspaper editor in the West—
rampageous, unpredictable, crusading Fremont Older of the San
Francisco *Evening Bulletin.*

"A letter of marque to prey upon the unwary public!" he exploded.
And chewing fiercely on his cigar (he chain-smoked Havanas), he
began to look into the situation. That there was corruption in the
making, Older was sure.

3 Discordancies

In seven years of headline hunting, Fremont Older had lifted the
Bulletin into a position that justified his masthead brag: "Largest Circulation of Any Afternoon Newspaper West of Chicago." The paper
was moribund when he was hired as managing editor, and he had
staved off bankruptcy by feeding the public a sumptuous diet of sen-
sationalism and lurid reporting,—murders, the hounding of amorous
clergymen and thwacking of rascals generally being the staples of the
robustious bill of fare.

A lath of a man, six feet two, lean and bristling with energy, sporting a handsome mustache and a balding head, Older was a mixture of
uproarious humor, careless daring, and milk-soft sentimentality. By
his own admission, he was able to do nothing except excessively.
With his brainy and beautiful wife, Cora Baggerly Older, he lived in
style at the Palace Hotel, spent every nickel he earned, enjoyed a
lively set of friends, went everywhere, knew everybody, and discovered
news in the least likely places.

Older's publisher and employer, R.A. Crothers, was his antithesis.
Born of a wealthy Canadian family, he had been educated at McGill
University in Montreal, acquiring a lifelong addiction to reading
ancient Greek poetry—in Greek. Gentlemanly and correct, he de-
tested the bathos and vulgarity of the journal which was his inherited
responsibility, and to condoling friends would lament: "I can't find a

thing in it that I can read,—but do you know, people seem to like it."

Although popular, the *Bulletin* was not the most puissant daily in San Francisco. More influential was William Randolph Hearst's *Examiner,* the morning newspaper which had launched him on his fabulous career as press magnate. During the 1901 transport strike, the *Examiner* alone had supported the unions, and in the mayoral campaign of that year, Schmitz, as labor's standard-bearer, received the *Examiner's* friendly endorsement, although Hearst was averse to Abe Ruef.

The publisher, then living in New York where he was embarking on that freebooting political career which he confidently expected would carry him to the White House, was noisily wooing the backing of labor and hard-pressed minority groups in his campaign for election to Congress. Seeing in the San Francisco Union Labor Party a possible instrument for his own aggrandizement, he invited Mayor Schmitz to come to New York and speak on his behalf. With Ruef's consent, Schmitz accepted, and in due time assured an enthusiastic rally in Madison Square Garden that labor in the West believed in Willie Hearst, a San Francisco man. Hearst was elected, and in gratitude continued to support Schmitz through the *Examiner.*

On a roundabout journey homeward, Schmitz was the object of curiosity and adulation as the first labor leader to occupy a high public office. Everywhere, he recruited friends. In Washington he invited President Roosevelt to dedicate the Admiral Dewey monument, commemorating the Battle of Manila Bay, in San Francisco the following May; in Chicago he was honored with a civic banquet; he appeared before the national convention of the American Federation of Labor in New Orleans.

The sequel to this foray was the arrival of President Roosevelt in San Francisco for the dedication ceremonies in May, 1903. Ruef realized that his violinist-protégé faced a stern test on this occasion of civic glorification. The town was determined not to be outdone in hospitality: the President was to be entertained at a Golden Banquet, —"on golden service, with golden wine, and golden oratory, at the golden Palace Hotel." The tables were laid with cloth of gold trailing bullion fringes and tassels (a touch Ruef considered pretentious), and the guests paid twenty dollars in gold apiece. San Francisco's prestige as the Star of the West was at stake, and in rich men's clubs there was moaning about the misfortune of having a union fiddler for official host.

Ruef was anxious. He wrote a short, graceful speech which Eugene memorized. But during the banquet, sitting among the diners, the boss overheard remarks betraying apprehension that the Mayor would mortify the high-toned assemblage by some workingman's *gaucherie* or crass vulgarism. To his relief, Schmitz, seated beside the President at the table of honor, appeared the most self-possessed man in the room. When Roosevelt turned the conversation to music, the Mayor replied with verve and authority; and at speech time, Eugene's resonant voice and well-turned phrases drew spontaneous applause; it was agreed that not even the President had spoken more aptly. Distinguished citizens, who had not deigned to notice the Mayor upon entering, crowded around him with heartfelt congratulations, and Ruef glowed. Schmitz, he sensed, had arrived; the pupil was an honor to his tutelage.

Perquisites had been falling pleasantly to the curly-haired boss. Although he held no official position, describing himself merely as counselor to the Mayor, Ruef found his services as an attorney in demand. He seldom made overtures: he did not need to. At City Hall, petitioners grew accustomed to hearing their handsome Mayor murmur negligently, should their business involve contracts or some remunerative transaction with the city, "Why don't you see Mr. Ruef? He knows more about such matters than I do. He's a lawyer, you know."

"Seeing Ruef" involved payment of a legal fee.

There were some who did not come by way of the Mayor's office. For example, Schmitz's election had hardly been certified before Ruef was waited upon by an emissary of the Pacific States Telephone & Telegraph Company, Theodore Vail Halsey. This courtly gentleman explained that he should like to engage Mr. Ruef's services as counsel for the company, which held the telephone monopoly in San Francisco. There would be no court work involved, Halsey elaborated suavely, but the directors desired to feel free to call upon him for advice on points of municipal law, a field in which he was understood to be proficient. They could pay a retainer of $250 a month, which Halsey would bring to Ruef's office in cash every month,—and no receipt would be necessary. By coincidence, Pacific States just then was under fire because of its inadequate service, and there was agitation to bring in a competitive system; in fact, several well-heeled rivals had been angling to obtain a franchise from the city for years. Ruef accepted this retainer (later the company voluntarily raised the sum to $500 a month), and if the remittance was a day late he did not scruple to telephone Halsey and add his complaint about the wretched service.

Another unsolicited windfall came from the United Railroads, the street-car combine that had just been created by Eastern capital under the management of a distinguished Southern aristocrat and lawyer, Patrick Calhoun. The United Railroads' general counsel, Tirey L. Ford, retained Ruef as a consulting attorney at a monthly fee of $500; the company had its own legal staff, Ford explained, but on points of municipal law the boss might be able to guide them. The retainer was paid by Ford personally in his office, and he *did* take a receipt. A measure of the ethical laxity of the time may be taken from the circumstance that for several months after he became the legal representative of the street-car corporation (a business which existed at the pleasure of the public authorities), Ford continued to hold office as Attorney General of California, and few people thought the worse of him for it. Ruef was charmed to be solicited by a man so eminent and widely esteemed.

Other retainers for vague legal services were proffered, and Abe took them. Gradually, the seeds of avarice which were in his makeup sprouted and bloomed, and it was reported that he prowled in quest of any fee, of any size, from sources reputable or disreputable, he cared little which.

Fremont Older, watching and testing the wind, sensed that something sinister was stirring, something shadowy and elusive, as he put it,—"scraps of talk, small bits of evidence, little intimations. I heard of bootblack stands, houses of prostitution, gambling joints that were being forced to pay small graft money. Nothing definite, merely hints here and there, a glimpse of something not quite clearly seen, an atmosphere that began to envelop the city." With the 1903 election approaching, Older endeavored to unite the Republicans and Democrats on a single candidate able to crush Schmitz's bid for a second term; but although both parties longed to end labor's rule at City Hall, rival jealousies supervened. Once more, three candidates for mayor took the field. (The Democrats' choice was Ruef's one-time reform friend, Franklin K. Lane.) But from the first it appeared that Schmitz would emerge the winner.

In the *Bulletin*, Older pilloried Ruef and Schmitz savagely, but the intensity of his attack and the sparsity of the evidence he produced against the pair annulled his efforts. A cartoon depicting the boss lording it in the Mayor's chair, surrounded by bags marked "Boodle" and puffing an oversize cigar, was an example: it fell flat because everybody knew that dapper, pliant Ruef did not wear loud clothes and never smoked cigars, in fact was continually giving away the dozens he was forced by social custom to accept in lieu of drinks during his rounds of the political bars. Ruef was nettled by Older's attacks and retaliated in various ways; but when the ballots were counted, Schmitz had won by a stepped-up margin. However, again Eugene was unable to carry his slate, only two Union Labor supervisors being elected with him.

On election night Fremont Older watched a mob of harlots, pimps, Barbary Coast bouncers, Tenderloin dandies, and hoodlums—"the push"—dance drunkenly past the *Bulletin* office, screaming vilification of the newspaper that had vilified the boss. This bacchanal Older interpreted as signifying that the forces of misrule, intoxicated by their victories, were swarming into the open, the lid was really off, and a harvest of graft was ripening.

4   "Municipal Whisky"— "Municipal Cigars"—"Municipal Crib"

Quotations on Abe Ruef's legal *expertise* advanced several points after this second triumph, and he made the new status clear in one important quarter by ceasing to give receipts for his monthly fee from the United Railroads. Tirey Ford bowed to his wishes, and the cash retainer continued to be paid from hand to hand, by Ford to Abe, without embarrassing records.

A far-reaching consequence of the 1903 election was that Mayor Schmitz gained control of the city commissions. The board of health he already dominated, and in January, 1904, at the start of his second term, he was able to appoint a third and deciding member to the remaining boards. Of these, the board of public works and the police commission were the most productive of results.

The public works board comprised three members, and their secretary was Herbert L. Schmitz, the Mayor's younger brother,—a smooth-shaven conniver whose most distinguishable traits were impudence and greed. Head of the board was Frank Maestretti, crafty political henchman of the boss. The public works board controlled all construction, issued building permits, paved and repaired the streets, and enforced the fire ordinances.

The four-member police commission ran the uniformed police force, elected the chief of police, determined promotions and demotions, and issued licenses to sell liquor. In choosing police commissioners after Hutton, Schmitz had dared to run counter to the recommendations of his union supporters, and in 1903, over labor protests, had named John A. Drinkhouse, a crony of Ruef. In 1904, the Mayor appointed Thomas Reagan, an active worker at election time and a former official of the street pavers union. In 1905, the sweep was made complete by the appointment of Dr. Joseph Poheim, a nightly companion of Ruef at the Pup restaurant.

Older attacked all these appointments as indications of intended graft. Getting down to cases, he exposed a lucrative traffic in liquor licenses: not only did the liquor dealers association employ Ruef as counsel, but the saloons also retained him directly at annual fees ranging from $50 to $1,000, depending upon the size of the business. If the retainer was not forthcoming, Older charged, the liquor license was suspended or revoked for some specious reason. Since licenses came up for review every three months, there was always an opportunity to exert pressure.

The *Bulletin* asserted that a list of license applications passed every week from the Mayor's office to the police commission, bearing notations after certain names, such as "Not yet," "This is my friend," "Let go," "Don't bother," "Don't press," and "O.K. Many Thanks." Schmitz was indignant at the allegation and roundly denied knowledge of any such irregularity; but later—much later—such a list was produced in court, and a grand jury unearthed hundreds of license applications bearing similar endorsements, often in Schmitz's handwriting.

Graft in street repairs, controlled by the public works board, by
now was notorious; but when the *Bulletin* sidetracked a bill for
$6,224.20 presented by F.M. Yorke & Company for repairs never
made, and which the Yorke company's equipment demonstrably was
incapable of making, Father Peter Yorke, brother of F.M. Yorke and
champion of the labor unions, instigated a boycott of the newspaper
by workingmen and church members.

Undeterred, Older published that Mayor Schmitz was secretly a
partner in the Dineen Building Company, and that applications for
building permits were stalled in the public works board until the applicants took their work to Dineen. The Mayor often recommended
the company as especially qualified by reason of long experience with
the city's fire laws. Dineen's charges were considerably higher than
those of competitors.

The *Bulletin* really got the town talking, however, when it exposed
what it labeled "municipal whisky," "municipal insurance," and "municipal cigars." The Hilbert Mercantile Company, wholesale dealers
in liquors and bar supplies, was disposing of an abnormal amount
of cheap whisky at high prices to saloons in the red-light district.
The *Bulletin* printed a facsimile of the firm's business card, which displayed "ABE RUEF, ATTORNEY" in bigger type than the name of the
company. The Hilbert brothers, Fred and Christian, both close friends
of Mayor Schmitz, were further padding their income, the *Bulletin*
said, by doubling all orders and taking notes instead of cash from the
saloonkeepers for the overplus. These notes they then discounted at
the banks.

"Municipal cigars" gave off their peculiar aroma after the appointment of Drinkhouse to the police commission. Drinkhouse held the
agency for a brand of Cuban cigars (the "Lopez" brand), and the
San Francisco cigar-makers union protested that saloons were being
compelled to stock foreign-made "Lopez" perfectos under threat of
losing their liquor licenses.

Mayor Schmitz was shocked. A protest by a labor union called
for investigation, and Eugene constituted himself a board of inquiry—
with Drinkhouse as expert adviser. The commissioner produced a list
of his customers, among them being three hundred sixty-five saloons,
of which three hundred thirty-nine had become customers since his
ensconcement on the police commission. At this clear proof that

Drinkhouse could not possibly be using intimidation, Schmitz smiled
in relief: were threats being employed, the Mayor pointed out, every
one of the city's thirty-five hundred or so licensed premises would be
stocking "Lopez" cigars! The union replied that most of the thirty-five
hundred licensed places were groceries or small bars that did not stock
any cigars, and a wholesaler handling a competitive brand submitted
records showing that his cigar sales declined from 87,350 a month at
the time Drinkhouse was appointed commissioner to 36,700,—a drop
of more than fifty thousand in six months. But the Mayor exonerated
his appointee and scolded the union members for letting themselves be
used as "the mistaken tools of the sworn enemies of an administration
which is sincerely your friend." The cigar makers wanted none of such
sincerity and retorted that Mayor Schmitz no longer stood for labor,
he stood for graft. Slowly the *Bulletin* was making headway.

"Municipal insurance" concerned Police Commissioner Reagan,
the street paver, who began to write insurance policies soon after he
assumed public office. The *Bulletin* published lists of brothels and
saloons which were suddenly insuring themselves against fire, flood,
or other dire calamity, and twitted that the fire they feared was not a
conflagration. Reagan heatedly denied there was any coercion. The
grand jury looked into the matter, but was stymied when several
saloonkeepers who had been loud in complaint testified, after thinking the matter over, that they had no grievance worth mentioning.

To silence the gadfly *Bulletin,* Ruef instigated a boycott of the
newspaper by liquor dealers and the police force, and engineered a
newsboys strike enforced by Barbary Coast toughs. Older and Crothers
were harassed by arrests for criminal libel and subjected to indignities
in the police lineup. Older enjoyed the farce, but Crothers shrank from
being herded with drunks and scabby vagabonds, and at last he ordered his rampaging editor to drop the profitless crusade. Then, on a
night in September, 1904, an incident occurred which forcibly
changed his mind. While crossing an alley behind the *Bulletin* plant,
Crothers was knocked unconscious by unidentified assailants and narrowly escaped being killed. There was no attempt at robbery, and the
publisher and Older both were convinced that the assault had been inspired by Ruef. A police investigator added insult to mayhem by telling an *Examiner* reporter that it was a case of "too many Scotch
highballs." This infuriated the battered, temperate Crothers, and he

authorized Older to keep up the fight until all such traducers were in jail or exile. He never wavered. When the policeman who had uttered the slanderous remark was swiftly promoted to sergeant, Older published that it was a reward from the boss.

The most repercussive of Older's remonstrances was the outcry he raised over the "municipal crib." That name stuck. The crib houses of San Francisco stood on the lowest rung of commercialized prostitution: they were whoring on the assembly line, specializing in rapid turnover at proletarian prices, and the diseases they dispensed were a gratuitous bonus. The dens had been a blight on the city, resented and deplored, for decades.

In 1904, three partners, headed by a former secretary of the fire commission whom Mayor Phelan had discharged for cause, purchased a tumble-down shack, used as an opium den, at 620 Jackson Street in Chinatown. The board of health condemned the building and the board of public works razed it,—at no expense to the new proprietors; and on the site was erected a two-story brick structure which professed to be—if the sign across the front could be believed—the Standard Lodging House. The Dineen Building Company handled the construction.

A building inspector, struck by interior arrangements that were only too obviously standard, reported that the building was intended for purposes of prostitution: a bar and restaurant occupied the ground floor, and the upper floor was partitioned into cubicles. Works commission secretary Herbert Schmitz reprimanded the inspector for a libidinous imagination, and pigeonholed the report.

The operation had been in full swing for six months when Older broke the story under the headline: GANG GIVEN BROTHEL CORNER! A hundred prostitutes, said the *Bulletin,* well, one could hardly say manned the house, but were mustered on the premises, working in eight-hour shifts, under the protection of City Hall, as was evidenced by the activity of the police in closing other brothels in the vicinity.

The outrageous charges of the *Bulletin* were investigated by the current grand jury,—the so-called Andrews grand jury, which, thanks to Older's alertness, was the first in many months not subservient to Ruef. Mayor Schmitz was interrogated, and repudiated the *Bulletin*'s vile assertion that Ruef and he were sharing in the profits of the crib.

The grand jurors then asked him why he had guaranteed the lease of a Mrs. Berlin, who was running a bawdy house at 554 Geary Street.

"Good God, gentlemen!" the Mayor exclaimed. "That lady is as pure a woman as any one of your wives! I guaranteed her lease simply because she was an old friend!" He did not explain why he had guaranteed a lease for the same woman, at a previous address, from which she had been evicted for conducting a *maison de joie,* as San Franciscans liked to call it.

A few days after the Mayor's denials, the grand jury foreman sent an investigator to 554 Geary Street, where he was offered all the services usually purveyed by a house of ill fame.

The grand jurors themselves visited 620 Jackson Street, found two city policemen posted at the door to regulate traffic in and out, and procured the arrest of nearly eighty working inmates. All were promptly released on bail arranged by a sharp-nosed attorney named Henry Ach, Abe Ruef's second in command in the 40th Assembly District. Ach served notice that the defendants one and all would demand separate trials, thus insuring that the Magistrates' Courts would be tangled in futilities for a long while.

Next, the man who ran a cigar and perfume counter in the self-styled lodging house secured from Superior Court Judge J.C.B. Hebbard, a Ruef protégé of frequent befuddlement, an injunction restraining the police from making further raids to the detriment of the perfume business. When the *Bulletin* criticised this action harshly, the presiding judge of the Superior Court, Judge James M. Seawell, at Hebbard's request, assumed jurisdiction himself; and becoming confused by the conflicting testimony, went to 620 Jackson Street one evening and stood across the way for an hour, counting more than six hundred men who passed through the doors. It was like a theater lobby at curtain time, he reported in court, and he voided Judge Hebbard's restraining order. Nevertheless, the "municipal crib" continued to flourish intermittently until 1907.

Both Schmitz and Ruef defended the propriety of the brothel (while disclaiming any personal connection) on the ground of civic utility. Prostitution existed before he took office, the Mayor reminded the press, adding that the consensus of responsible opinion was that the best way to mitigate the irremediable evil was by means of "segregation and humane regulation," which he preferred to leave to the police.

The plain fact was that the *Bulletin,* while its scandal-mongering diverted the volatile, light-hearted populace, was not inspiring any notable rallying round the guidon of righteousness. But Older kept trying.

5 "Turn the Rascals Out!"

San Franciscans were pleasure-loving, times were flush, and few citizens wanted a change. As for peculating politicians,—well, their peculations at least were tolerable. The other newspapers either ignored the *Bulletin's* campaign against crookedness in office, or belittled it. The *Examiner* continued to endorse Schmitz (thereby, taunted the *Bulletin,* earning the privilege of "resting its head on the very bosom of Abraham"), and the *Morning Call* dismissed the *Bulletin's* outbursts as "newspaper hysteria," while the *Chronicle,* the city's third morning newspaper, did not become bitterly censorious of Ruef until the boss threatened the ambition of its proprietor, Michel Harry De Young,—a man of French ancestry like Abe. De Young, a Republican, also wished to become a United States Senator.

In 1904, Ruef signalized his domination of the city's Republican forces by a gesture that politicians understood. He became a delegate to the Republican national convention in Chicago (the convention that was to nominate Theodore Roosevelt for a second term as President) and was escorted to the train by a parade of municipal office-holders and political small fry (Abe's "army of tax-eaters," snorted the *Bulletin*) carrying floral displays, among which stood out a huge "R" in red-white-and-blue roses; and the marchers made clear that "R" stood for "Ruef" and not for "Roosevelt."

In the August, 1904, primary elections, Ruef consolidated his grip on the city by making a clean sweep of both the Union Labor and Republican delegations to the next state and city nominating conventions. He also clamped a firm hold on most of San Francisco's representation in the State Legislature, and since United States Senators were elected then by the legislators, this edged him closer to his

ultimate goal. Alarmed by this surge of strength, the *Chronicle*
acrimoniously promoted a grand jury inquiry into vote-stealing, in
which Public Works Commissioner Maestretti and three "ballot-
stuffers" were indicted. Two of the men went to prison, sentenced by
Superior Court Judge William P. Lawlor, who thereby incurred Ruef's
enduring enmity. Maestretti was tried and acquitted, after Ruef had
advanced money for counsel fees. Later, when Frank was "getting
his" and Ruef dunned him for the loan, the commissioner laughed in
his face.

At length the *Chronicle's* ire against "malodorous officialdom"
broke into an editorial Philippic which aligned it firmly in opposition
to Ruef and Schmitz, without in any way approving Fremont Older.
Said the *Chronicle* bluntly:

> ... Grafting goes on in every department controlled by the Ruef-
> Schmitz administration. ... Grafting schemes and schemes to violate the
> election laws are as common at City Hall as is the transaction of official
> business.

This was mere prelude to the crescendo of denunciation which
the *Chronicle* directed at the Schmitz-Ruef coterie. Of more immediate
distress to the city administration, however, was the rebuff being given
to a municipal bond issue of $17,000,000 voted by the supervisors for
much needed public improvements,—schools, street grading, parks,
playgrounds, and similar projects. Although the city's financial rating
was high and it had no outstanding bonded indebtedness, nobody bid
on the bonds, and the pointed disinterest of the banks was embarrassing. The *Chronicle* trumpeted that bankers were shying away from the
"stench of graft enveloping City Hall"; political experts interpreted
the action as a covert move to discredit Schmitz and get him booted
out of office by an exasperated electorate, for it galled the "money
crowd" to see the mayor of the labor unions in power. Schmitz bragged
that he knew "a certain party" who would take up the whole issue,
but no bids came in.

At this juncture, Ruef paid a call upon a man with whom he had
had a personal encounter several years before, and that an unsatis-
factory one. This man was a leading member of the "money crowd,"—
banker, investor, and financial wizard Rudolph Spreckels.

The Spreckels clan was a source of piquant gossip in San Francisco. The family had been established in the state by Claus Spreckels, a crusty, obstinate, ruggedly individualistic German immigrant, who in middle life acquired an immense fortune as the sugar monopolist of the West. He owned refineries, cane plantations in Hawaii, steamships, and many subsidiary enterprises. Claus did not run with the pack of millionaires: he was secretive and rock-hard in business dealings, quite as willing to fleece a brother capitalist or fellow club member as to skin the public. Because of these unamiable traits, to which were joined bulldog tenacity and a disconcerting habit of winning, he was feared and respected but not loved, and naturally he had given rise to countless anecdotes.

Claus had four sons, and all of them inherited something of his character. In order of their ages, they were John D., the eldest, Adolph, Claus Augustus (Gus), and Rudolph. When he was a small boy, Rudolph amused his older brothers by stating his ambition: to be a millionaire. In the family mansion on Howard Street, he heard business discussed constantly—little else, in fact—and at seventeen, his father put him in charge of one of his riskiest operations, a sugar refinery Claus had built in Philadelphia in a death struggle with the Eastern sugar trust dominated by the Havemeyer interests. The latter had dared to encroach on Claus's territory; but instead of surrendering, the tough fighter invaded the Easterners' market in reprisal. Rudolph was sent East on his own, to sink or swim. In two years he whipped the trust, a truce was entered into, and the Easterners bought the refinery at a tremendous profit to old Claus.

Coming home, Rudolph found the family embroiled in an epical quarrel over the disposition of a sugar plantation in Hawaii. Claus wanted to sell the place, because it was showing a loss. John D. and Adolph sided with their father, but young Gus was arguing to get control of the property, maintaining that only inefficient management kept it from returning a profit. Rudolph sided with Gus. In a fit of rage, Claus disowned the two youths, and to prevent their launching out independently, blackballed their credit in every bank on the West Coast. Rudolph succeeded in raising capital privately, however, and with Gus purchased the Hawaii estate, developed it profitably, and then sold out and retired from further money-making. At twenty-six years old he was several times a millionaire in his own right.

With his lovely wife, Rudolph moved into a mansion on San Francisco's opulent Pacific Avenue, created a baronial country estate at suburban Burlingame, acquired a racing stable (Borghesi and San Alviso were stars that won under his colors: red, with brown sash and sleeves), and settled down to a life of leisure and social gaiety. Since the family uproar, his brothers John D. and Adolph had not spoken to him, although John D. lived two blocks away.

Against his father Rudolph had his revenge when they clashed in backing rival gas companies and Rudolph won. The old man warmed to him after this and they became reconciled; and for years Rudolph managed his father's affairs during the latter's absences from the city. "I was never beaten but once in my life," Claus would boast with a twinkle,—"and by my own boy, too!"

Such was the background of the man—a suave exemplar of fashion, leader of a lively social set, financier of brilliance and unchallenged uprightness, who made his own decisions and, like his father, did not run with the crowd—whom Ruef approached in the spring of 1904 in regard to the municipal bonds that were so ignominiously going begging. Abe had had a slight brush with Spreckels when the latter was reorganizing the San Francisco Gas & Electric Company. Introduced by a well-known broker and member of a prominent San Francisco family, Charles Sutro, the boss at that time had airily proposed that he be retained as the company's attorney. Rudolph had replied coolly that they were satisfied with their legal staff, and Ruef had bowed himself out; Spreckels remembered particularly that Abe had given himself quite a build-up as a lawyer.

The appearance of the boss at Spreckels' office on lower Market Street in 1904 puzzled the financier, who had no political interest whatever; indeed, at thirty-four he was almost proud that he had never voted. Ruef got down to brass tacks directly: that bond issue. The three-and-one-half percent yield certainly was attractive, and the city was solvent and growing prodigiously.

"Why don't you and a few of your friends get up a syndicate and bid on the issue?" Ruef asked. "If you do, I can guarantee that you won't have to bid above par—the city can't dispose of them at less than par—and I also can guarantee that your bid will be successful."

There was a pause while Spreckels silently studied this man, so different from himself. The capitalist was tall, floridly handsome, large-framed, reserved, and dignified, and he faced his visitor with the bold, unwavering blue-eyed stare of a Teuton aristocrat. Ruef was little, alert, nimble of movement, and quick-witted; his sharp features were crowned by carefully brushed, glossy black curls, and his dark eyes shifted evasively. While he waited for Spreckels to reply, he drummed on the porkpie hat on his knees that was in up-to-the-minute style; oddly, Spreckels and he patronized the same fashionable hatter.

When at last he spoke, Spreckels did not hide his amazement.

"I do not understand how anyone can make such an agreement. What do you propose to do? How can you carry out such a promise?" he asked.

"Why, that's a simple matter," the caller smirked faintly. "You know my connections with the labor unions. Just when the bids are about to come in, I'll arrange to tie up this town,—we'll have the biggest street-car-transportation strike the community has ever known. And then I should like to see any of your bankers, or your capitalist friends, bid on the bonds under those circumstances. Except you, of course, and the few in the know."

Spreckels' eyes changed color swiftly to a forbidding slate gray, a peculiarity when his anger was aroused. He recalled the bloodshed and violence brought on by the 1901 strike, still a bitter memory; the suffering and material losses and the poisoning of public trust; and he was horrified at the prospect of a deliberately precipitated repetition. His voice was cold when he aswered.

"Do you mean to say, Mr. Ruef, that for the purpose of making money you would bring about a strike that might even entail bloodshed? For the mere sake of making money?"

The little man flushed. "Oh, no, Mr. Spreckels!" He laughed lightly. "I was only joking."

And glibly turning the conversation, in a few moments he withdrew.

The shock of that brief, unsought interview jolted Rudolph Spreckels out of his self-centered complacency as merely a rich man. That his city, San Francisco—the place of his birth, where his home, his fortune, his affections, his pride as a man and citizen were rooted—should be at the mercy of such cynical manipulators of human lives, filled him with wrath. He had never thought much about the matter before: politics was not a gentleman's affair. But that sudden glimpse into the brutal reality behind the pretense of democratic processes was challenging. Something should be done to eliminate the atrocious outrage to himself as a San Franciscan, he found himself thinking; and since he was a practical man, dealing in the concrete and possible, little given to imagination or introspection, he looked around to see what positive action might be taken. Realizing that in the world of political maneuvering he was a tyro, he turned to his friend and fellow investor, James D. Phelan, a rich man who had explored the political thickets and knew his way through that maze. Phelan briefly sketched what was going on, and then introduced Spreckels to Fremont Older, who enthusiastically filled in the details.

It was about this time that the police commissioners fired the incumbent chief of police, a Phelan-regime holdover, and jumped a corporal, Jeremiah T. Dinan, over seven captains to become the new chief. The city buzzed that Jere owed this dizzy promotion to his friendship with Herbert Schmitz and to Mrs. Dinan's intimacy with Julia Schmitz, the Mayor's wife. The *Bulletin* scornfully said the outgoing chief had been made a scapegoat for the misdoings of his superiors, and dismissed Dinan as "a graduate of the stool-pigeon school of sleuthing."

The mayoral election of 1905 was approaching, and this time Schmitz's opposition united on a joint candidate,—John S. Partridge, a colorless lawyer whose principal merit seemed to be that neither the Democrats nor the Republicans knew anything against him. Weak as his appeal appeared to be, the experts rated him a "shoo-in" to beat Schmitz, since the Mayor had never polled a majority of the ballots, and the combined forces of the Republican and Democratic parties outnumbered Union Laborites two to one. Besides, the all-powerful influence of the Southern Pacific's political machine, astutely directed by the Railroad's chief counsel, William F. Herrin, had been set in motion to cut down the growing power of boss Abe Ruef. Herrin had taken alarm when Abe attempted to obtain Republican endorsement for Schmitz in the mayoral race, as a stepping stone to the governorship. The bid failed, but Ruef's ambition was laid bare.

The Schmitz-Partridge campaign was vitriolic; but San Francisco loved a brannigan and this was one. Partridge tried to concentrate on the scandal of the "municipal crib," plastering billboards with his pale pink slogan: WHEN I AM MAYOR THE RED LIGHT SHALL NO LONGER BE ABOVE THE FIRESIDE LAMP. But Schmitz countered that calumny and defamation were his opponents' only weapons, that they had been systematically calumniating him, aspersing his good name, for two years in the realization that only by persistent lying could they undermine the voter's confidence in his administration. There is a revival hymn, "Only Trust Him," the political equivalent of which the Mayor sang and sang in a dozen keys daily. "If you re-elect me to office," he vociferated, "I promise to give you two more years of an administration the like of which San Francisco has never seen before!"

Ruef, called upon for a *tour de force,* performed prodigies. He rented the biggest theater in town and addressed a capacity audience from eight o'clock until midnight,—and the audience stayed. At his own cost he had printed one hundred thousand copies of this marathon speech and laid a copy on every doorstep in San Francisco. He overlooked no trick which might help his cause and embarrass his opponents. At one point he distributed to all newsdealers rubber stamps reading "SCHMITZ is Our Choice for Mayor," with instructions to stamp the motto on every copy of the *Bulletin* they handled,—a device the *Bulletin* denounced on its front page in large type as "despicable."

The more the opposition harped on civic corruption, the more blithely Ruef ridiculed the canard that anybody was grafting. The Schmitz administration he extolled as "the cleanest and most moral of any in the United States.... as clear as the light of day, as pure as a mountain lake." Before a working-class audience he merrily began his speech with "Ladies and grafters...," and amid the laughter went on to allude to his own "culture and refinement."

"Three cheers for the North Beach hoodlum!" yelled a runner, and Abe acknowledged the tribute with a bow.

The newspaper phalanx was almost solid in grim determination to rid the city of Schmitz and drive out Abe, and the mountainous charges of vice, malfeasance, and rapacity which the *Bulletin* alone had trumpeted so long were marshaled systematically. WHAT IS THE EVIDENCE? inquired the *Morning Call* editorially, and summed up what most of the press was saying:

...Against the air-tight secrecy and the open use of every official obstruction, it is disclosed that Mr. Ruef is the actual administration. He is under every pile of municipal dirt. Poke where you please and he squeals. The grand jury felt of the situation and published what it felt. Immediately Mr. Ruef began to foam and yell at the grand jury. . . . The clergymen of the city... spoke their minds freely, and pleaded with their congregations to end the carnival of vice by voting for a change. Then Mr. Ruef hired a hall in which to make faces at the clergy. The newspapers... published what is known of the graft and crime.... Then Mr. Ruef grew red in the face, his choler rose and he poured himself upon the newspapers. When the administration is kicked, Mr. Ruef rubs Pond's extract on himself and says things. When criminals are sent to the penitentiary for stuffing the ballot box, Mr. Ruef indulges in sad reflections upon the miscarriage of justice. When a citizen denounces graft, Mr. Ruef says he is being personally abused. Stick pins in the board of works, and Mr. Ruef bleeds. Take a whack at the election commissioners, and a bruise turns blue on Mr. Ruef's reputation. Speak of the sinks of vice that pay a price for immunity, and Mr. Ruef advances to the footlights to declare that he does not use tobacco, that the taste of beer is a flavor unknown to his chaste palate, and that he goes home every night and stays there "till daylight does appear."

So, by circumstantial evidence it is proved that we have a government of Ruef, by Ruef, and for Ruef. Poor Mr. Schmitz is out nights getting a frog in his throat, pleading with the people to re-elect Mr. Ruef as Commissioner of Commissions and the Board of Boards, to run San Francisco, for a consideration.... [Schmitz] does not need vindication. He needs a rest.

The broadside delivered by the *Chronicle* was quite as devastating: TURN THE RASCALS OUT! it screamed, and verbally diagrammed the plight of the city and the real issue in the campaign:

...Schmitz hardly counts. What he is told to do he does. Ruef is by all odds the most dangerous boss this city has hitherto endured. . . . For four years it has been known that if one wanted anything which the administration was not compelled to grant, he must see Ruef. If you wish for a job for yourself or your friend, you must see Ruef. If you wish for a license for a grog-shop or a theater, you must see Ruef. If you desire to construct a building in defiance of the fire ordinances, you must see Ruef.... His baleful influence covers our city like a pall. Never since 1856 has there been so vile an administration.

These were words to inflame, for 1856 was the year of the Second Vigilance Committee, which hanged the gambler-politicians Cora and Casey. Thousands of San Franciscans as children had lived through those feverish days; there were survivors of the Committee still active in the community, revered relics of a legendary time.

To ride out so furious a storm seemed hopeless, and the outlook appeared bleak for the Union Laborites. Privately, Ruef admitted that the oracles were monotonously unfavorable. The *Bulletin,* in a long, candid analysis of both sides' voting strength, totted up the figures five different ways, and each time mathematically proved that Schmitz did not have a glimmer of a chance of survival. Although outwardly the boss never lost his dapper air of confidence, he was fighting desperately, not to extend his sway, but to preserve what he had.

His traditional antagonist, the *Bulletin,* was mounting a campaign less frenetic than those of previous elections, firing daily salvos of round shot tamped down with deadly facts, rather than relying on the scatter shot of surmises and gossip. In page-wide articles the slimy trail of Schmitz and Ruef was retraced soberly and with telling effect. But toward the wind-up, the cumulative effect of this calm assault was largely negated by Older's overzeal, when he fell into the absurdity of depicting Abe Ruef as a stupid man,—almost as stupid as "slow-witted, dull" Eugene. The basis of this curious contention, risible on its surface, was Older's inability to understand Abe's canny grasp of crowd mentality. Political bosses invariably had found it expedient to lurk in the shadows, the *Bulletin* argued solemnly, while their puppets strutted the stage apparently untrammeled; but Ruef was avid for the public's applause, he was his own most active stump speaker. Such abnormality the *Bulletin* could attribute only to colossal vanity; and a ponderous dissertation attempted to prove that Ruef was "a moral idiot," devoid of all comprehension of right and wrong.

"In the face of accusations and proofs...Ruef remains more than serene,—he is jaunty," declared Older's pre-Freudian analysis. "[Schmitz] is a rascal, a very avaricious, coarse, and determined one, so fond of money he is willing to undergo disgrace in order to procure it, but truth demands the admission that he is a better man than Ruef.... In the event of Schmitz's defeat, which seems certain, it is extremely likely that legal evidence will be forthcoming to prove in court what the last grand jury considered morally true. That happening, Schmitz will make the journey to San Quentin crushed, bowed, and in dejection, a picture of unnerved wretchedness.... But Ruef will take the stage for the prison smiling without and calm within, cursing his ill luck, no doubt, but a chipper, impudent, and swaggering moral idiot to the last."

Armed with irrefutable logic and infallible prevision, the fusionists staged their wind-up rally confidently on the evening of November 4th, three days before the balloting, in Mechanics Pavilion, a barnlike structure that housed cotillions and cattle shows with equal facility. Fifteen thousand perfervid partisans packed the flag-draped auditorium, speculating on what the featured speaker would say. That speaker had been publicized in advance as "the eloquent lawyer whose name is a terror to big and little grafters ... specially selected by President Roosevelt to break up the gang of timberland thieves in Oregon, which he has done, and in California, which he is to do."

When introduced to the crowd, this much-heralded fountain of eloquence proved to be a rather stumpy person, bristling with wiry energy and cheerful pugnacity, his face smooth-shaven, with pink cheeks, a firm mouth, and friendly, wary eyes blinking behind gold-rimmed spectacles. The obligatory frock coat and striped pants hung awkwardly upon him, but when his high-pitched, aggressive voice rang out, the throng stood up and cheered.

"There are more bunco-steerers and thieves in San Francisco than ever before in its history,—and every one of them is howling for Schmitz for mayor!" he shouted, and thousands roared agreement. "If Schmitz is re-elected and this graft continues, I will devote my best energies to sending Abe Ruef to the penitentiary! I personally know that Abraham Ruef is corrupt, and I say to you that whenever he wants me to prove it, I will! The issue is not between Schmitz and Partridge, but between Abraham Ruef and the decent, honest citizens of the city of San Francisco! I say to you, that if Schmitz is re-elected mayor for another two years, that the people of San Francisco will send for me in whatever part of the United States I am, and beg me to come back here and put Ruef in the penitentiary, where he belongs! I guarantee that if I take charge of a grand jury in this city, it will return indictments against Ruef for grafting inside of a week!"

This was fighting talk, uttered by Francis J. Heney, prosecutor extraordinary. It was profoundly to alter the lives of many men, not the least his own.

Optimism in the Partridge camp ran high. With the facts against Ruef and Schmitz so damning and so thoroughly aired, with the mathematical tide running indisputably in their favor, how could Partridge's partisans be other than confident? Eugene E. Schmitz's perennial red campaign buttons, it was chuckled, would become historical curiosities after November 7th. Fremont Older, exhausted by his labor, penned a column of gracious compliment to the fusion candidate and his managers upon their excellent conduct of the fight —"now that the campaign is practically at its close and the election of Partridge is conceded by all experienced judges of politican conditions." True, the "steam beer boys" were whooping it up in a monster parade on behalf of Schmitz, but Older and his associates were sanguine of victory. The day before the voting, a final clarion call was sounded by the *Bulletin* in tones of triumph, headed, REDEEM THE CITY TOMORROW.

Tomorrow is for San Francisco the day of atonement and redemption [the message ran]. Like the Prodigal, we have gone astray and for four years have fed upon husks and been the companions of swine. Tomorrow we return to decency and the fatted calf.... Tomorrow, no longer a Magdalen by the wayside, this city takes its place again in the march with the other cities of the land.

Election morning, the *Bulletin* headlined that BIG VOTE FAVORS PARTRIDGE. A novelty of the balloting was the use of voting machines; hence the outcome would be learned quickly. Although inexplicably the betting odds held at ten to eight in favor of Schmitz, the fusionists were not downcast. The *Chronicle,* anticipating a triumph, announced that the minute the result became certain, a star bomb would be shot aloft from the tower of its building at Kearny and Market streets, the crossroads of the city: white would proclaim Partridge the winner, and red—if, by remote chance, "to tell the city's shame"—would signalize two more years of Schmitz and "the unspeakable Ruef."

Fremont Older awaited the returns in his office. He did not have long to wait, and by seven o'clock he was stunned. Not only Schmitz, but the entire Union Labor ticket was snowballing across the city! In every district, residential or business, decent or disreputable, rich or poor, the trend was the same. Sick and uncomprehending, Older groped his way to the Palace Hotel, where he collapsed on his bed.

At 7:30, the result was beyond all doubt: Schmitz had rolled up forty thousand votes against Partridge's twenty-seven thousand, and all eighteen Union Labor supervisors, together with the party's candidates for city attorney, city treasurer, county clerk, district attorney—the whole slate without exception—had been swept into office by comparable margins.

The *Chronicle* fired its star bomb—red—and suffered the further humiliation of setting its own tower on fire.

Across the street in the Palace, Older was aroused by the shouts of bellboys ordering everybody out of the building; it was feared that the hotel would burn, too. With his wife he stumbled into the street, where, directly opposite, the *Chronicle* tower was blazing. Fire engines wheezed, horses whinnied, firemen darted through the murk carrying axes and hoses, and nervous policemen pushed back straining spectators. On diagonal corners the *Examiner* and *Call* buildings were being wetted down to save them from flying sparks.

In the midst of this inferno, down Kearny Street toward the intersection advanced a solid front of marchers, holding up in the glare the little boss, Ruef. This crowd, upon learning of the staggering victory, had rushed, not to Schmitz's headquarters, but to the law offices at Kearny and California streets, had seized the boss, and hoisted him to the shoulders of two prize fighters. Triumphantly they bore him down the street to where the *Chronicle* was going up in smoke. The paraders snake-danced up Market Street, veered off to smash the windows of the *Bulletin* routinely again, and melted into the Tenderloin to carouse through the night.

To Older's haggard imagination the scene was a romantic's conjuration of Hell,—leaping flames, prancing demons, cries, pandemonium. The danger to the Palace passed, and Cora Older led her husband back to their rooms, reeling like a drunken man. Let them burn the whole town down,—Abe Ruef owned San Francisco now!

PART TWO

"Folly is set in great dignity, and the rich in low place."

1 A Fighter of the Old West

When Francis J. Heney threw down the gauntlet to Abraham Ruef in Mechanics Pavilion on November 4, 1905, French restaurants were in his mind. Say "French restaurant" to a San Franciscan of a certain age, and if he goes back "before the fire" his eye probably will light up or mist with some rememberance of youth, or with unfading indignation. French restaurants, as the term was understood in San Francisco, were neither properly French nor merely restaurants. The cuisine was Gallic, but many of the cooks were Chinese, trained in the secrets of an earlier generation of Parisian chefs; and although they dispensed food and drink, the restaurants operated as a type— a very risky type—of assignation house, long sanctioned by custom.

Marchand's, the Poodle Dog (there was both an Old and a New), Delmonico's, Maison Riche, Tortoni's, the Bay State, the Pup,—the names were redolent of good living. The rich, the famous, the busy businessman and the banker out for a discreet lark patronized them: everybody who was anybody sooner or later might be encountered there, on one level or another.

On the ground floor in a public dining room was spread what was believed to be the best dollar dinner in the world,—or if not the best, among the best, and the others were in San Francisco. This dining room was perfectly respectable; a householder might dine there with his wife and daughter with propriety, and many did, for San Franciscans "ate out" frequently, a habit inherited from the early days when most of the population were transients and unmarried men, and cooks were few. Although only one-fifth the size of Chicago, San Francisco in 1900 had more public eating places.

The second floor of the French restaurants was given over to private dining rooms, still respectable, although seldom entered by respectable women.

But the third, fourth, and fifth floors were something else. There respectability expired; the dining rooms were in suites with bedrooms, and the atmosphere of discretion was as thick as the drapes. A *dîner à deux* with a magnum of wine (and a gentleman ordered only champagne),—the upper floors of the French restaurants were designed for just that. Delmonico's elevator was big enough to hold an automobile driven from the street, and the prices mounted with the altitude: the elevator man at the New Poodle Dog wore diamonds, owned real estate, and never spoke to anyone unless spoken to.

In January of 1905, these restaurants had encountered a novel reluctance on the part of the police commissioners to renew their liquor licenses, and without the right to sell champagne they were as good as dead. Fremont Older of the *Bulletin* learned about the impasse at Marchand's one day when he noticed the proprietor, Pierre Priet, sunk in dejection.

"Ah, Mr. Older," the old man lamented. "They are going to put me out in the street. After all these years building up this business!"

"You should see Ruef!" Older laughed.

Several days later the editor dropped into Marchand's for lunch and saw Pierre contentedly sipping black coffee and reading his *Chronicle* at peace with life. The innkeeper removed his spectacles and twinkled: "Your advice was fine, Mr. Older! When one is sick, one sends for the doctor. I send for Doctor Ruef. I am a well man again!"

Older made inquires, and that afternoon got out a special edition of the *Bulletin* charging that the French restaurants had paid Abe Ruef $10,000 for protection, and predicting that the obstacles to renewal of their licenses would shortly be surmounted. And Older dared Ruef to go before the police commission on behalf of the restaurants, in view of this revelation.

Ruef "saw" his critic; he appeared before the commissioners, argued his clients' cause, and proposed a set of rules which, he said, he believed the restaurants would agree to abide by; they were regulations similar to those governing hotels and lodging houses, requiring, for example, the keeping of a register of guests. The police commissioners listened and took his plea under advisement for two weeks.

Then, with a blare of publicity, Mayor Schmitz removed Commissioner Hutton for moral derelictions, publishing an open letter containing evidence gathered by the Commissioner's own police that he was living with a woman not his wife. Hutton, it was brought out later, had been voting against renewing the French restaurants' licenses.

Five days afterward, the remaining three commissioners met and voted, two to one, to approve the licenses. The restaurant owners were charmed, although they were puzzled by the fact that the rules submitted on their behalf by their attorney, Ruef, were precisely the regulations under which they had been operating for years.

Francis J. Heney knew something about this hocus-pocus, and this, among other matters, was in his mind when he declared that "I personally know that Abraham Ruef is corrupt."

Heney was a San Franciscan, not by birth but by upbringing. He had been born in Lima, in upstate New York, March 7, 1859; hence was five years older than Ruef. His parents were immigrants, his mother German, his father Irish,—the ancestral strains of Schmitz reversed. The Heneys moved to San Francisco when Frank was four years old and settled "South of the Slot,"—south of Market Street, that is, on the "wrong side" of the broad avenue that bisected the city economically, culturally, and geographically. "South of the Slot" was the district of workingmen and small factories, the district of teeming families, where hard-fisted men drank the locally favored steam beer and never saw champagne, and where a boy learned to use his fists almost as soon as he could toddle.

As a boy, Frank Heney fought in street gangs and singly. He aspired to attend high school, but his father put him to work in the family's furniture store. Frank enrolled in night school, and was so eager to learn, his teachers coached him to pass the tests for admission to the University of California. Again his father said no, and Frank went on a prolonged drinking spree in rebellion. Sobering up, he passed the examinations for a teacher's certificate, and for three years taught school, putting by money to pay his way through college. Finally, at twenty, he matriculated with the class of 1882. (Abraham Ruef, who had no money cares, would matriculate one year later, aged fourteen.)

But Heney was not fated to be college-bred. In his freshman year he horsewhipped a student who had written a slanderous article about him, and when the chap drew a pistol, offered to shoot it out then and there. For this breach of discipline (proposing to fight a duel on the campus, not for carrying firearms) the university expelled fire-breathing Frank. Offered a job teaching school in a mining town in Idaho, he took it to get away from the scene of his defeats.

Heney's height was the same as Ruef's, five feet, eight inches, and his best weight was one hundred twenty-six pounds; but his bantam size never kept him out of a scrap. In the mining-camp school he enforced authority with a length of stove wood, cowing a rebellious clique of scholars standing six feet and taller. When teaching palled, he turned to hard-rock mining, but about all he got in the mine shafts was chronic sciatica. Meanwhile, his ambition had turned to the law, and coming back to San Francisco, he worked his way through Hastings law school, completing the three-year course in two years and being admitted to the California bar in 1883. (That was the year Abe Ruef spent polishing his senior thesis on "Purity in Politics.")

Arizona seemed a good place to bake out sciatica, and Heney's brother, Ben, owned a ranch near Tucson. In the Eighties, Arizona was the prototype of all the dust-and-deviltry, gun-and-whisky-slinging heroics of the Wild West, and young Heney was as devil-may-care as the next fugitive from civilization. He quickly gained a name for hard drinking and straight shooting; then, looking for more excitement, he took over the management of brother Ben's trading post at Fort Apache. Geronimo was on the prowl. Frank learned Apache ("only about six hundred words in the lingo") and several times faced down whiskied-up braves swooping around the post on runty ponies, brandishing weapons and howling in an attempt to make the white man show fear. If he flinched, a general massacre probably would result, he had been warned, but Heney did not flinch.

A law office in Tucson seemed tepid after such employment, but Frank hung out his shingle,—and spent his time brawling in the saloons. One day he was thrashed by a man, an Easterner, whom he had bragged he would pin down, and hot for revenge, he went into training for a return match. He started by giving up whisky and cigars. In a short while he discovered that by channeling his vitality into business, he could build up an interesting and profitable law practice. So instead of fighting his Eastern opponent again, he publicly thanked him. Thereafter, although he took a drink with convivial companions, he stayed within the bounds of sobriety.

In 1891, the bully of Tucson was a Dr. J.C. Handy, and he did not like Frank Heney. Handy was a powerful, bearded man weighing more than two hundred pounds, and he was given to maniacal rages. He had long terrorized his wife, left her, and took up with one of the town trulls. He ordered his wife to get a divorce, but because there were five children, Mrs. Handy refused. This infuriated the mentally unstable doctor and he filed his own suit, threatening to run out of the territory any lawyer who accepted his wife's case; two attorneys speedily retired from the lists. Mrs. Handy appealed to Heney, who not only agreed to represent her, but chipped in every week to help feed her brood.

Handy spread word that he intended to kill Heney with Frank's own gun. Heney's hair-trigger temper was well known, and Handy boasted that he would goad him into drawing, then wrest the pistol away and kill him with it, later pleading self-defense. He imported two gunfighters to follow Heney about, muttering the sort of taunts no Western man was expected to overlook. But Heney kept his temper, and at the trial won the case for Mrs. Handy easily.

Dr. Handy went berserk. Grabbing Heney as the latter came out of his office, he slammed him against the building and started to throttle him. Impulsively, Heney reached for his pistol; then he recalled Handy's boast, and instead held out both hands, empty. The unexpected gesture nonplused the big man, who relaxed his grip. Heney wrenched free, ran into the street, turned and drew. Handy lunged for the gun; they wrestled, the doctor twice lifting his slight opponent off the ground, and during the scrimmage Heney fired. The bullet tore through Handy's intestines, but he kept wrestling until bystanders pulled him away; then he walked to his office, lay down, and spent a whole day dying.

The incident—the provocation, the struggle for the gun—had occurred before witnesses. Heney insisted on a thorough inquiry, and was not only exonerated, but assured that half of Tucson felt he should have clipped Handy long before.

Frank Heney later became Attorney General of Arizona and a Democratic political leader there. At the turn of the century he came back to San Francisco and won success as a tenacious and utterly fearless corporation lawyer. He had little polish; his speech, tangy of the range, often ruffled city opponents; but he was acknowledged to be adroit and always ready to back up his words,—a man who could not be bought, bullied, bluffed, or buffaloed. In 1904, President Roosevelt, casting about for a fighting prosecutor to break up a gang of timberland thieves who were filching millions of acres of government lands in the Pacific Northwest, selected Heney, and he became a special assistant to the United States Attorney General. To work with him, Roosevelt detached from the Secret Service its star detective, William J. Burns.

Against tremendous odds, against social ostracism and pressure from above and below, Heney in Oregon obtained more than one hundred indictments, convicted a United States Senator (John H. Mitchell, political boss of Oregon, who died while his conviction was on appeal), brought a Congressman to the bar of justice, and broke the United States District Attorney, who was pretending to prosecute but secretly was protecting the thieves. By 1905 Heney had gained a national reputation, and he was considering accepting the offer of a law partnership in New York City. But as a San Franciscan he was outraged at the plundering of his city by rapacious politicians. All this lay behind his fervid election-eve offer to put Abraham Ruef "in the penitentiary, where he belongs!"

2 A Trip to Washington

Ruef did not overlook this boldly publicized challenge. He immediately addressed an open letter to Heney, which read, in part:

In the published reports of your speech at Mechanics Pavilion last Saturday night you are represented as saying: "I say to you, moreover, that I personally know that Abraham Ruef is corrupt, and I say to you whenever he wants me to prove it in court, I will. . ."

In making the statement that you personally know that I am corrupt you lied. You cannot personally know that which does not exist.

In making the statement at a time and place which allowed no opportunity for a legal showing before the date of the election which you seek to influence, you showed the same courage which put a bullet into the body of Dr. J.C. Handy of Tucson, Ariz., in 1891, for whose killing you were indicted for murder, and upon trial were acquitted because you were the only witness to the deed.

You say whenever I want you to prove it in court you will do so. I want you to try to prove it, and at once. I demand that you begin at once . . . I give you here and now full consent and authority to proceed, and I go further and ask that you do so . . .

The truth about Tucson had been known to Ruef and others in San Francisco for years, but to the public the scandal was new and provided an exciting last-minute election titillation. Ruef's letter was published on election morning, together with a Ruef-inspired demand by the *Examiner* that Heney be required to answer to the grand jury for his statements. The current grand jury had succeeded the Andrews grand jury and was notoriously under the boss's control; one of his most servile creatures, loose-lipped, impudent Myrtile Cerf, was its secretary. Heney telephoned to the foreman that he would appear voluntarily, if the jurors would assemble early enough the next morning to permit him to catch the noon train for Washington, where he was awaited on official business.

The jury met at 8:00 A.M., and the District Attorney, Lewis F. Byington, demanded Heney's proof. Heney looked over the panel and replied that, first, he could not produce his proof on the instant, and, second, that he would not in any case, because he did not believe he was being examined in good faith or that the jury had any intention of indicting anybody. One of the jurors then put a hypothetical question: "Supposing that you could show that Ruef took $10,000 as a fee for protecting certain interests,—would that be a crime?"

Glancing contemptuously toward Byington, Heney snapped: "If I were before you, I could show you how to make a crime of it without any trouble!" Then he left and caught the train.

The *Examiner* printed a detailed account of the supposedly secret proceedings and sneered that Heney's bluff had been called.

Said Ruef: "This means Heney's exit from political life."

Fremont Older declared that the grand jury session had been arranged expressly for the purpose of peddling a lie through the *Examiner,* and he published rebuttal telegrams from prominent Arizonans, including a Supreme Court Justice and the Governor of the territory, confirming that Heney had been completely exonerated in the Handy affair.

Older gloomed through November after the 1905 election; San Francisco, he deduced, enjoyed being debauched, for Schmitz's strength had shown overwhelmingly in middle-class districts, not in the precincts where wage-earners predominated. Evidently Schmitz's perpetuation in office was desired by the so-called respectable element! Nothing, Older despaired, nothing short of the power of the United States government could stop Ruef now.

Quixotically, the editor decided to go to Washington and enlist the help of the President. He became obsessed with the idea, and although his wife thought he was daft, she agreed with Crothers that Fremont needed a rest, and a trip to Washington might be just the thing. Hoping he would not dream up some wilder scheme, they put him aboard the train; the journey was kept a secret among the three.

December found him in the capital. Yes, the White House would receive Mr. Older.

The President greeted the editor with teeth flashing a "dee-lighted" smile.

"How is your bassoon mayor?" he asked.

Older replied that the bassoon mayor, not content to fiddle while Rome burned, was cutting the hoses of the fire-fighters.

Roosevelt listened sympathetically; he had tilted against corruptionists in New York, and he understood the difficulties. But when Older asked that Francis J. Heney be released to clean up San Francisco, the President demurred. Heney was engaged in a most important task for the federal government, he replied, and should not be diverted. Perhaps later.... The editor was sent on his way with a bully handshake.

Unwilling to take no for an answer, Older called on Heney at the Willard Hotel. Heney said he would indeed be willing to undertake a cleanup, on certain conditions: first, he would need the President's consent; second, he must have William J. Burns as investigator, and Burns was a government employee; third, where was the money coming from? Investigation on a scale big enough to do any good would cost much more than the slender budget of the San Francisco District Attorney's office.

How much money would be required? Heney guessed $100,000 would be a minimum, and it would have to be posted in advance.

"I'll get it," said Older, oblivious of the fact that he himself lived from payday to payday.

Heney then called in Burns, but the detective was cool: he doubted that anything could be done, both because of the financial barrier and because there was no indication that the people who promoted and protected public corruption would be touched. These people, Burns emphasized, were not petty crooks, whom any city police force could round up; they were community leaders, men held in esteem, occupying positions of honor and power. Did Older and his crowd think of going after them?

Absolutely, responded Older; anybody guilty of wrongdoing.

The talk at the Willard was held on December 2nd, and the easily kindled editor hastened back to San Francisco, determined to raise the necessary funds. His main reliance lay in James D. Phelan and Rudolph Spreckels, two rich men who he knew were disturbed by the freebooting going on. He approached Phelan first, giving a full

account of the President's and Heney's feelings. Phelan heartily
favored an investigation, if Heney could be in charge. When Spreckels
was brought into the discussion, he forged beyond Older's objectives,
exclaiming:

"I'll go into this! I'll back it to the limit; but I want one understanding,—that our investigation must lead to William F. Herrin!
Herrin is the man who has corrupted our state. He is the man who
has broken down the morals of thousands of our young men, who has
corrupted our legislature and our courts, and corrupted supervisors
and coroners and sheriffs and judges! He is the bane of California! If
we go into this fight, we've got to stay till we get Herrin!"

This was reaching for "higher-ups" with a vengeance. But actually,
Spreckels was voicing the philosophy he had heard his father ex-
pound in the family circle times without number: none of the
Spreckels clan ever was a "Railroad man."

The three men proposed, in this first consultation, to organize a
secret committee of outstanding citizens to finance and direct the
crusade,—a sort of unarmed vigilance committee. Spreckels at once
set about enlisting his friends, confident that the campaign would
quickly fructify.

3 Roses in City Hall

Election victory had brought unforeseen problems to Abraham
Ruef. The campaign's vociferations had frazzled Mayor Schmitz's
voice to a croak, and desiring to rest up in an atmosphere of pronounced calm, he went to Los Angeles for two weeks. Ruef went
with him. The most exciting thing that happened to either of them
during their stay was the mayor's arrest for speeding on a downtown
street at fifteen miles an hour (the limit was twelve); Los Angeles
disapproved of fast living in any form.

When the two men returned north, Abe looked over the assort-
ment of absurdities which the electorate had dumped in his lap.

The new Union Labor supervisors were a gamy lot. Many of their
names had never before been exposed to the public, and the *Bulletin*
had greeted their nomination with a contemptuous editorial headed,

"Ruef's Collection of Clowns." The oddest jumble of political non-descripts ever gathered, Fremont Older had characterized them,—hungry for office, weak in judgment, and "so silly in their egotism that they would listen to the persuasive boss offering them a nomination," although nobody knew better than Ruef that they "could never be elected." In this respect, Older's information had been correct: Ruef had encountered the utmost difficulty in filling the Union Labor slate, numerous prospects having turned down the suggestion of a candidacy under his sponsorship with horror. In consequence, Ruef had strewn the nominations among political nonentities as a means of bestowing cheap and harmless compliments. One of the winners he had never laid eyes on, and about some of the others he knew almost as little. Indeed, coercion had been necessary to complete the ticket: the *Bulletin* published, and met with no denial, that the successful candidate for coroner, William J. Walsh, "a boy doctor employed at the Emergency Hospital," had accepted the nomination to a position he neither craved nor felt himself fitted to occupy, only under the threat of losing his job if he refused.

Topping this grab-bag roster was James L. Gallagher, a former city attorney, who had served a short while on the last board of supervisors through appointment by Mayor Schmitz to fill a vacancy. Big Jim liked to make a speech, and he did possess some slight knowledge of municipal affairs.

Three other incumbents had been elected by the Republicans in 1903 and this time had also accepted Union Labor endorsement. These were Charles Boxton, a dentist much publicized locally for his record of bravery in the Philippines fighting; W.W. Sanderson, a colorless wholesale grocery salesman whose father had been an undistinguished mayor in the nineties; and Louis Achille Rea, a prosperous painting contractor and leader among the Italian Swiss in North Beach.

At the instance of Gallagher and Schmitz, Ruef had assigned the other seats on the board to labor-union representatives as a matter of policy, although not one of these carried weight even in labor circles.

Typical was Thomas F. Lonergan, who had been president of the bakery wagon drivers union. A cheerful, bumbling, simple-minded immigrant, he drove a wagon for Folev's bakery, earning $15 a week.

Sam Davis owed his selection to his membership in Mayor Schmitz's union: Sam had beaten a drum for fifteen years in the Tivoli Theater orchestra.

John J. Furey was a blacksmith's helper who had saved enough money to buy a retail fur store on Powell Street; he still worked at his trade.

Edward I. Walsh operated a stitching machine in a shoe factory, and was active in his union.

Jennings J. Phillips was a pressman for the *Evening Post,* the newspaper Henry George had founded, now moribund and kept alive by a Railroad subsidy.

Ferdinand P. Nicholas was president of the carpenters district council and popular there, but unknown to the public generally.

Max Mamlock was a union electrician.

Daniel G. Coleman, dubbed "the boy orator," had been a tireless speaker at meetings of the retail clerks union; he had seized with avidity every opportunity to orate during the campaign.

James T. Kelly was known as "Gassy" because of his propensity to deliver opinions in a loud voice on every mentionable and unmentionable topic. By trade he was a piano polisher and a good union man.

Michael William Coffey was "a darlin' man" who had served as president of the hackman's union, and took vast pride in owning his own hack at the stand across from the Mint on Fifth Street in front of the drug store that kindly let him use their telephone.

With Patrick M. McGushin the *Bulletin* had sport, defining him, more or less accurately, as "a bartender who is also a poet; his verse and his whisky are well matched." The newspaper regretted that it was unable to offer its readers a sample of either.

To mollify the mercantile and employer interests, there were also three businessmen on the winning slate: George F. Duffey, a contracting plumber and part-owner of a plumbing supplies firm; Cornelius J. Harrigan, a "South of the Slot" grocer, who was popular among workingmen because of his open-handed extension of credit during the 1901 strike; and Andrew M. Wilson, sharp-trading partner in a moving and storage business. This completed the list of eighteen supervisors.

Wilson's name had been added at the last minute without his

knowledge or consent. George Keane had suggested him, although all Keane knew about the man was the little he had gathered when they occasionally ate lunch together in a restaurant near City Hall. Wilson had been incensed when told he had been honored without a by-your-leave, but was talked into letting his name stand, on condition that he should not be required to electioneer. He had ignored the whole campaign, and Ruef had never met him.

Some nominees for minor city jobs, swept into office by the landslide, had been chosen for reasons completely frivolous. For example, the Union Labor candidate for city administrator was picked because he looked like "Foxy Grandpa," a comic-strip character having a vogue just then. That ought to get him votes, Ruef snickered as he scribbled down the name, and it did.

When Abe looked over the appalling results of letting the people speak, his uppermost feeling was one of resigned contempt. But he quickly saw that these men, if left to their untutored impulses, would bring down his laboriously constructed political machine in a crash of scandal; already they were naïvely comparing notes on the likeliest sources of graft, accepting as axiomatic the saying that all supervisors grafted. Tom Lonergan more than facetiously had discussed with his bakery boss the chances of retiring, in two years, worth $100,000,—in the meantime drawing supervisor's pay of $100 a month, which was better than his driver's $15 a week. Mr. Foley scratched his ear and wondered.

To bring this ravenous pack under control was Ruef's first concern. Calling them to his office, he read the riot act and concluded with the promise: "Now, you sons of bitches, if any one of you takes a dollar I'll prosecute you myself!"

And he meant it, although not for the reason his sullen listeners imagined. Some of the elective hopefuls looked reproachful: wasn't he taking plenty? Ruef tried to make clear to them the difference between his accepting a lawyer's fee and their accepting a bribe,—a difference boiling down to a long stretch in prison. He held no office of public trust or emolument, and, therefore, in the legal sense could not be bribed. They could. The distinction was lost on most of the group, but their awe of the boss was salutary, and they promised to affect honesty.

But Ruef knew their greediness and that they must be given some form of *douceur* if they were to be held in line; and after considerable debate, he conveyed through Gallagher that he would split his "special" legal fees with them, fifty-fifty, their half to be divided equally among them, no favorites and no holdouts. Big Jim would be Ruef's spokesman, his "whipper-in," and would steer official policy. But the warning was sternly repeated: under no circumstances any petty, personal grafting.

Inauguration day was Monday, January 7th. On the evening preceding, Ruef inaugurated what was to become a regular Sunday evening caucus of the members of the board, to drill the awkward squad and insure that they would not disgrace him or betray his interests at their official, public meeting the next day. These caucuses were a unique political expedient, the product of Ruef's ingenuity and thoroughness. In strictest secrecy, questions of policy and pending legislation were discussed and agreement was reached on the disposition of votes. The rule was that each member must vote in public the same way he voted in caucus; there was to be no deviation, second-guessing, or spontaneous rebellion. George Keane, who had been shifted from the Mayor's office to the post of clerk of the board of supervisors, served as Ruef's watchdog, and kept minutes of the caucuses exactly like those of the official meetings. Mayor Schmitz, ex-officio president of the board, was present frequently, and joined in deciding on "program" (the current political slang for the party line) for the coming week.

Although he had no official standing, Ruef received a weekly notification of the caucus identical with those sent to the board members. This form read (in sample):

HON. A. RUEF, SAN FRANCISCO—Dear Sir: I respectfully beg leave to notify you that the Board of Supervisors will meet in caucus on Sunday evening, June 24th, at 8 o'clock P.M., at Hamilton Hall, Steiner Street, near Geary. Your attendance is respectfully requested. Yours truly,

GEORGE B. KEANE, CLERK.

No political boss ever devised a more efficient method of control. Every Sunday evening he passed his troops in review and could make his pleasure or displeasure felt directly, and his decisions were his own: he was trammeled by no board of overseers, no "sachems" or party directorate peering over his shoulder, whom he must placate. Being by nature *rusé,* preferring to gain his point by indirection and persuasion, he exercised his authority with tact and good nature; nevertheless, when the need arose he could be scathingly caustic, and his airy, biting sarcasms were more feared than his anger.

Drilled, scrubbed, and happy, the city fathers were ushered into office amid a proliferation of flowers such as City Hall had never experienced. Red roses in a horseshoe design was the most popular set-piece, although Ruef sent Schmitz an American flag in full bloom which delicately reflected the Mayor's dream of acquiring a national aureole in time.

During the induction ceremonies, Ruef sat beside Gallagher, and the Mayor made a speech. Alluding to the "most bitter and unjustifiable attacks on me," Eugene happily forecast that now, with a Union Labor board of supervisors to sustain him, "things will go more smoothly."

"Impossibilities are not expected of us," he perorated, "but, with the grave and complex responsibilities with which we are now invested, we must—we shall—give to the people of San Francisco the best municipal administration, the most economical, the most businesslike and most efficient in realization which the city shall ever have seen!"

"That," said Francis J. Heney, a few days later at a private luncheon in the University Club across town, "is just what we must expect to contend with."

Phelan, Spreckels, and Older were at the table. Heney had brought good news from Washington: provided funds were assured, the President consented to release him and Burns for a San Francisco cleanup. Spreckels reported that his monied friends were reluctant to become identified with the project, but said he would underwrite the cost himself. Phelan was ready to contribute time, money, and political insight. Older pledged the utmost co-operation of the *Bulletin.*

In that case, concluded Heney, as soon as he could tie up loose ends in the land-graft prosecutions, he would return to San Francisco and start work; meanwhile, Burns could begin taking preliminary soundings.

The four men parted, committed to the endeavor.

That luncheon meeting and its purpose were known to only eight human beings: the four participants, publisher Crothers of the *Bulletin,* Mrs. Fremont Older, William J. Burns, and the President of the United States.

Within twenty-four hours, Abe Ruef had been apprised of the talk and its probable objectives. The instrument of this swiftly relayed warning was a justice of the Supreme Court of California.

4 Honesty Untimely Rears Its Head

In later years there was a grimly humorous saying in San Francisco that on the night the Union Labor board of supervisors was elected, every burglar alarm in the city went off of its own accord. But this was not observed at the time.

During their first weeks in office, the new board enacted several pieces of legislation that gave grounds for cynicism, although the public generally was not perturbed. Then, in February, the board stirred suspicion when it fixed the gas rate for the ensuing year. Determining the charges for public utility services was one of the supervisors' duties at that time, and the Union Labor platform, on which all eighteen supervisors had been elected, called for 75-cent gas (75 cents per thousand feet). After considerable shadow-boxing and debate about technicalities of gas manufacture and corporate finance of which they were ludicrously ignorant (Ruef quipped that the only thing most of them understood about gas was that when you touched a match to it, it burned), the board voted a rate of 85 cents. Still, the price had formerly been one dollar, so the customers tried to be grateful for qualified mercy. The difference (nobody pointed out) meant an additional $600,000 in revenue for the gas company, or an extra six percent return on its $10,000,000 capitalization. The paying public of course was unaware that before the new rate was voted, Ruef had quietly been retained as an attorney for the gas company, and that, in fact, he had written the ordinance setting the rate.

The city's telephone arrangements next came under the supervisors' scrutiny in a manner to arouse mutterings. The inadequate service provided by the Pacific States Telephone & Telegraph Company had been an endemic irritant, and during February and March of 1906 a rival system—the Home Telephone Company, which held the patents for the dial telephone and was backed by Los Angeles capitalists —stepped up its hitherto ineffectual attempts to obtain a franchise to install a competitive system; it already held franchises in Oakland, across San Francisco Bay, in Los Angeles, and several Midwestern cities. Pacific States had fought this attempted invasion stubbornly, but Abram K. Detwiler, the Ohio financier promoting Home Telephone's operations, seemed hopeful of getting favorable action from the new supervisors.

Complicating this situation was the political sensitivity of the issue of public against private ownership of utilities. Among the vigorous advocates of public ownership were William Randolph Hearst and his *Examiner;* and when the supervisors passed to print (the first step in enactment of city legislation) an ordinance authorizing the sale to the highest bidder of a fifty-five-year franchise for a competitive telephone system, without having submitted the measure to public hearings, the *Examiner* growled that "there have been whispers of bribery."

The *Chronicle,* also citing "ugly rumors," was deviously minatory:

> We do not wish to believe that any sort of undue influence was used, but the supervisors must realize that they have made the mistake of acting as a bribed board of supervisors would have acted.

So flickered the subjunctives like lightning along the horizon.

In the sunlight of popularity and political acclaim, the character of Eugene Schmitz had changed, or perhaps unfolded, and he and his thrifty (some said parsimonious), strong-willed wife, Julia, had taken on the coloration of social climbers. One friend who had ingratiated himself with the Union Labor mayor was a millionaire promoter who moved in the highest society, William J. Dingee. (The name was pronounced "dingy.") Schmitz had met Dingee on the train during a trip East, and the promoter had gone out of his way to be helpful. Closely associated in business with Dingee was J. Downey Harvey, son by her first marriage of Mrs. Eleanor Martin, San Francisco dowager omnipotent, and Schmitz and his wife were frequent guests in Harvey's home. The Mayor purred under the flattery of prominent men and women; he beamed when complimented on his air of breeding and when he was assured that nothing about him suggested a trade-union man.

It was, therefore, with the feeling that they were entering a congenial sphere that Eugene and Julia moved from their Fillmore Street home to a fine new dwelling at Vallejo and Pierce Streets, a few blocks away. The comfortable old house with scrollwork ornaments stood (and stands) at the foot of the hill where Fillmore Street plunges toward the bay, overlooking a swamp where now is the district called the Marina. The sidewalk in that vertiginous block is laid in steps. The house number was 2849, and the place had been built with $5,000 realized from the sale of Julia Schmitz's family farm near Watsonville, it was said.

The new mansion represented a triumph in economics, in view of its reputed $30,000 cost and the Mayor's salary of $6,000. During four years in office, Schmitz had collected $24,000 in pay, meanwhile living well, very well; yet as the new home progressed, the bills were settled in cash. More than thriftiness seemed involved; and the conclusion on the part of the public was that Gene possessed some hidden source of wealth. But if hidden, where? No bank was known to be favored with a fat balance opposite the name "Schmitz, E.E." The gossiping city shook its collective head and clucked and moralized, while cynics grinned and intimated that their musical mayor fiddled golden tunes.

The town, of course, was aware that the Mayor enjoyed perquisites. One of these was the contingent fund, which came to $3,600 a year; it was intended to enable the city's chief magistrate to meet the numerous demands of charity and hospitality inseparable from his position. No account of the use of this appropriation was required, and Schmitz drew the full amount every month.

The new mayoral domicile was graced by furnishings which, it was divulged, had cost the owner not a penny. There was a $1,250 Persian rug, given by J. Downey Harvey. Dingee contributed a massive silver

inkstand for the library table, oil paintings, knickknacks, and a span
of blooded carriage horses. The mansion was built by the Dineen company, and applicants for building permits at City Hall often were
referred to that firm by the Mayor.

"A mighty fine construction company," he would beam. "They're
building my home, you know."

At first Ruef was amused by Eugene's social foible, but toleration
wore thin when, soon after the new supervisors took office, the Mayor
proposed that a valuable city permit be granted to an enterprise in
which Dingee and Harvey were profitably interested. This was the
Ocean Shore Railway, a line being run down the coast sixty miles to
Santa Cruz. Dingee was a stockholder and also stood to gain by the
enhancement of properties he owned around Santa Cruz. The Mayor
urged that the railroad be granted a permit for a terminal inside the
city limits, which would give it virtual street-car rights. Schmitz also
insisted that there be no question of money, inasmuch as he had given
his word to his friends. Ruef comprehended that there are bribes more
potent than cash, and he was annoyed that Schmitz should try to
undercut him. When a second instance occurred, the boss clamped
down. This was in connection with the Parkside Realty Company.

The Parkside firm had acquired a strip of sand dunes, five blocks
wide and twenty blocks long, in an undeveloped part of the city
south of Golden Gate Park. This tract they had assembled piecemeal,
buying through dummies, purchasing one parcel from Ruef; they
proposed to subdivide the tract into home sites for sale to lower-
income families. The principal stockholder in Parkside was William H.
Crocker, son of the Crocker of the Southern Pacific "Big Four" and
president of the Crocker-Woolworth Bank; in his gaudy baronial
manor atop Nob Hill, William H. Crocker stood at the apex of the
social-financial pyramid of San Francisco. The president of Parkside
was J.E. Green, also a gentleman of wealth and social eminence.

In order to attract buyers, the Parkside investors needed a means
of cheap transportation to their tract, and the nearest street-car line
was a mile away. The United Railroads was not interested in building
a spur that would bring them little new revenue, since it would be
used almost wholly by passengers riding on transfers, and the Parkside
directors reluctantly resigned themselves to the necessity of construct-
ing their own line. When they applied to the city for a franchise to do

this, Green told the supervisors frankly: "We are prepared to carry passengers free, if necessary, depending for our profit entirely on the increased value of our real estate. We would be willing to give $100,-000 if anyone would build this road for us, and I would pay $5,000 to any individual who would bring us such an offer to build."

"Well," remarked Ruef when he heard about this frank confession, "if the Parkside crowd has money to throw to the birds, they might as well consider me a bird."

But Schmitz was urging that the franchise be awarded gratis, pointing out that it would build up that part of the city and add to the tax rolls. Abe was irritated. The Parkside people stood to realize a profit of $2,000,000 to $3,000,000, and he was miffed that land he had sold for $6,000 should be subdivided to resell for $20,000 and he not in the deal. Also, the Parkside directors had approached the Mayor over his head, with the design, he suspected, of undermining his authority. He insisted that the franchise matter be deferred. Then, after he had made his arrangements with the Parkside directorate, it was brought to a vote and approved. To ease the knuckle rap to Schmitz, Abe said that henceforth he would cut Gene in for a slice of his "special" legal fees.

Not least among the wordly wise gentry who extended a hand to the socially aspiring Schmitzes was Frederick W. Henshaw, who in 1906 was completing twelve years on the State Supreme Court bench. Justice Henshaw was a crony of Dingee, and a strange dubiety hovered around his name. This could be traced to nothing in his recent judicial conduct—he had a brilliant mind and had written opinions that were highly respected in the profession—and the public was not to learn the basis of this aura of mistrust until years afterward. The fact was that Dingee and Henshaw shared knowledge that in 1901 Justice Henshaw accepted a $410,000 bribe to reverse his vote in the contest over the will of the Comstock mining king, James G. Fair; the $50,000,000 fortune had been left in trust, and Henshaw's action broke the will and turned over the millions directly to the heirs. Dingee had arranged and passed the bribe.

It was affable, scholarly Justice Henshaw who happened to be enjoying a cigarette in the University Club on the day Heney,

Spreckels, Phelan, and Older sealed their bargain. It was he who discreetly relayed the word to Ruef.

Abe was not much alarmed; he was perplexed by more proximate problems, among them his precocious supervisors.

The city fathers were proving a wellspring of copy for a delighted press. Tom Lonergan, for example, endeared himself with reporters permanently on the day he argued against adoption of a motion to adjourn on the grounds that they couldn't vote to adjourn because there was no quorum present. Then again, Supervisor Gallagher, president pro tem, explained patiently to hackman Coffey, one hilarious afternoon, that "the City Hall is not a public utility, although the public uses it." And "Gassy" Kelly, after favoring his fellow members with an oration upon the unreliability of lawyers, no two of whom, he said, ever agreed, wound up by declaring that he would accept a lawyer's opinion—if it coincided with his own.

To one of Ruef's legal fastidiousness, such *gaffes* were a torment. As a matter of precaution, he had forbidden these male Malaprops to haunt his office; he dealt with them through Gallagher. Rarely did they disobey this order; but once, Andy Wilson (a pushing fellow with a roving eye for the main chance, in Ruef's own estimate) flouted instructions and showed up at Kearny and California streets. He found a police court judge sunning himself in the outer office, and persuaded this worthy to take in word to the boss that Wilson wanted to see him. The supervisor was admitted and found Ruef in conference with the bordello lawyer who had bailed out the victims of the grand jury's raid on the "municipal crib," Henry Ach. Abe asked sharply what was the reason for Wilson's intrusion. The latter explained that the telephone company was offering him a free telephone; would it be all right to accept it?

By no means, responded Ruef; he had made it clear that he wanted no petty grafting. (On the witness stand later, Wilson was positive Ruef used the word "petty.")

But such minor irruptions in the flow of political operations were unimportant. A really consequential crisis arose when the Union Labor District Attorney, William L. Langdon, unaccountably began to enforce the law against slot machines. These "one-armed bandits"

had been banned in the city since the Phelan regime; they were prohibited by state law. But suddenly the Ruef-dominated police commissioners legalized them, being moved (the newspapers sarcastically
phrased it) by a lawyer's plea "on behalf of at least five hundred
suffering saloonkeepers and oppressed, downtrodden liquor dealers."
In a trice the devices pullulated in dives and bars of the Tenderloin
and Barbary Coast.

Ruef, always broad-minded, defended the latitudinarian police
commissioners in reply to a scandalized clergyman, saying, in part:

> My personal view is that this city, no city, can be put into a strait-
> jacket. Neither should it run wide open. We must look at these things
> in a sensible way. Men are not alike. I know nothing about the temptations
> of gambling, never played cards or played the races. Others are given to
> these things.... I can't see any difference, however, between the poker
> games at the Pacific-Union Club and the gambling in a saloon, or the
> playing of a slot machine.

Such rationalization was not acceptable to William L. Langdon.
He had been superintendent of schools when Ruef selected him for
nomination as District Attorney, in the wan hope that his popularity
among the teachers might draw a few votes. And Langdon had accepted under no delusion that he had a chance to win, merely hoping
that the publicity attendant upon the campaign might attract some
legal business. A tall, angular Westerner with a gift of humor, Langdon believed that laws were enacted to be enforced. In fact, just after
assuming office he had told Fremont Older, holding up a copy of the
Penal Code: "My job is to enforce all the laws in that book. I mean
to prosecute any man, whoever he may be, who breaks one of those
laws. Any man. No matter what happens. Do you understand me?"
Older was edified.

When the slot machines reappeared, clearly the Penal Code was
violated. Since it was self-evident that the chief of police would take
no punitive action against an infraction of the law which his superiors
had sanctioned, Langdon made his own raids. In one place, just
opened amid lavish surroundings, he arrested two hundred forty-one
gamblers and kept twenty-six patrol wagons clanging through the
night carting the prisoners to jail.

For the Tenderloin, this aberration from all precedent turned the world topsy-turvy. In any city, the lid was clamped down on illicit activities *before* an election, then lifted and thrown away the minute the ballots were tallied. But to be permitted to run wide open before election, and then be closed down almost the instant the new District Attorney was seated—this was like being murdered by one's best friend! It certainly was not what had been paid for. For the moment, consternation precluded wrath: grieving saloonkeepers turned their slot machines to the wall and strove to understand. Commiserated the *Chronicle*:

And after all the most liberal contributions! Behind their closed doors the idle gamblers are trying to figure out what "lay" this dreadful Langdon is really on, and by what trade he had been induced to ignore all the promises, expressed or implied, which those assumed to be able to speak for him dispensed so freely when votes were in demand. There is a feeling in criminal circles that somebody is guilty of obtaining money under false pretenses.

5   A Little Trolley Wire

The boss had committed a blunder: unwittingly, in District Attorney Langdon he had elected an honest man. He was reluctant to admit this; Langdon's maverick maneuver he rationalized as a grandstand play to impress the groundlings with the District Attorney's incorruptibility, an excellent impression to foster. Furthermore, a brisk rap on the knuckles now and then was salutary to remind "the push" that there was a god in Israel. So Langdon received no open reprimand, merely a suggestion to observe moderation in all things, even official rectitude. Other matters were more deeply engrossing Ruef's attention.

At about the time of the 1905 landslide, Ruef had encountered Patrick Calhoun, president of the United Railroads; they met in the office of Tirey L. Ford. The street-car company had increased Ruef's retainer to $1,000 a month (no receipts), and Ford was discussing the political outlook with the boss when Calhoun entered.

"This is Mr. Ruef," Ford introduced his caller, "one of our prominent attorneys and influential men, who is our good friend and can be of service to us."

"Everyone has heard of Mr. Ruef," Calhoun replied, graciously shaking hands. "I am glad to know him and hope to know him better."

Calhoun soon left; but he and Ruef got together several times after that and Abe was a dinner guest in the street-car magnate's home on Webster Street, where Thornwell Mullally, Calhoun's young assistant, also was living. The boss came to admire Calhoun's eloquent reticence: never did he intimate that he was aware of Ruef's employment by his company. Bosses and corporation officials operated in much the same discreet manner, was Ruef's approving thought; obviously Calhoun was a man one could deal with.

Patrick Calhoun was an aristocrat of the buccaneer breed,—ruthless, daring, and successful. A distinguished corporation lawyer and accomplished lobbyist, he never forgot that he was the grandson of John C. Calhoun, the Great Nullifier and champion of slavery in the Southern states before the Civil War. Patrick, youngest child of Andrew Pickens Calhoun, second wealthiest cotton planter in the ante-bellum South, was born on the ancestral plantation at Fort Hill, Pendleton District, South Carolina, March 21, 1856.

The war ruined the Calhouns, and Patrick was destitute and an orphan at the age of ten. Spurred by a prodigious thirst for knowledge and a fierce resolve to emulate his grandfather, the boy largely educated himself, read law, and was admitted to the Georgia bar at the age of nineteen. During the postwar consolidation of the South's patchwork railroads into the systems that became the Southern Railroad, Calhoun was employed as attorney and confidential agent by the prime promoter, J. Pierpont Morgan.

Characteristic of Calhoun's curious blending of ferocious calculation with lordly magnanimity was his participation as a principal in the last duel fought under the code in the South. His adversary was a member of the Georgia Legislature, where the railroad consolidation bill was teetering in the balance. Calhoun waited until his opponent fired and missed; then, although he was known to be a sure shot, he discharged his weapon into the air,—thereby saving the man's life and the railroad bill.

Calhoun was a big man, with a stern countenance, drooping mustaches, and bold, steel gray eyes that bored through an interlocutor. Exuding oppugnancy, he once was described by the San Francisco *Chronicle* as "exhibiting corporative arrogance in its most exasperating form"; but he possessed fascinating manners and patrician charm.

Through Morgan, Calhoun had been admitted to the inner circle of Wall Street, and on his own account carried out public utility mergers in several cities before buying up San Francisco's crazy quilt of antiquated street-car lines and combining them into the United Railroads, comprising a near-monopoly of public transportation in the fast-growing city.

The lines included cable cars, horse cars, and steam-powered trams. A few were electrified, drawing their motive power from overhead trolley wires. Calhoun moved to standardize the system with an eye to economy and more efficient service, and applied to the city for permission, through a new franchise, to install trolley wires universally. Opposition arose at once. Electric street-car lines were relatively new, and there was sharp disagreement over their merits and drawbacks. Property owners objected that overhead wires would depreciate values along the streets where they were strung, that they were unsightly and were a hazard to firemen.

It chanced that two of the largest property owners in San Francisco were James D. Phelan and Rudolph Spreckels, and they spearheaded the organized fight against Calhoun's trolley-wire scheme. Both men were devoted to their city, for reasons sentimental as well as financial, and both were determined that as it stood in the front rank of the world's great cities, San Francisco should have every amenity and service enjoyed by cities elsewhere. They advocated, instead of unsightly overhead wires, that the power lines for street cars be laid in underground conduits, a system that was proving successful in both Washington and New York. Underground slots were costly to build, and Calhoun balked; he had heavily watered the stock of his corporation and was averse to spending one dollar more than was necessary. The dispute dragged on with increasing acrimony during 1905, while Calhoun's application for a new franchise languished in an official pigeonhole.

The result of the 1905 election changed the situation. Tirey Ford

alerted Ruef that the company intended to push its request for a
trolley permit before the incoming supervisors; Ruef cautioned that
opposition might be expected, that the public had been worked up
about the issue and there was strong sentiment against the wires. At
the same time, Calhoun engaged in private talks with Phelan and
Spreckels in a final effort to overcome or circumvent their scruples.
During these conferences, Calhoun made several proposals which
were disguised bribes, in the form of concessions that would benefit
their real-estate holdings, and each time he was smilingly rebuffed.
Calhoun, on his part, became convinced, or convinced himself under
the stimulus of wishful thinking, that the real motives of these two
principal objectors were not public-spirited, as they claimed, but
mercenary: he believed they resented the intrusion of an outside
capitalist into their sphere.

The issue was still in suspense, and street-car service was dete-
riorating, during the early months of 1906. When it became clear that
Calhoun would agree to nothing less than stringing overhead wires
throughout the city, Phelan and Spreckels decided to convince the
public of the superiority of the conduit system by a practical demonstration. They would, they said, construct a street-car line, using the
underground slot, and operate it in rivalry with the United Railroads'
cars; then let the riders themselves decide which method they preferred. The demonstration was to be carried out at no cost to the
taxpayers; several financiers, including Rudolph Spreckels' father,
Claus Spreckels, joined in floating the venture as a public service, organizing the Municipal Street Railways of San Francisco, incorporated
with a capital of $14,000,000, of which they subscribed $4,500,000
and paid in $450,000. One unprecedented stipulation in the com-
pany's charter provided that the city might take over the line at any
time by purchasing it for the exact amount of money invested, plus
interest. This would be a giant step toward public ownership of all
utilities, and when Claus and Rudolph called at City Hall to apply for
a city franchise for the line, they were overwhelmed with an effusion
of gratitude by Mayor Schmitz. Their unselfish action, the Mayor
crowed, would place San Francisco "in the very forefront of the
world's most progressive cities," and he called upon all citizens to
thank these patriotic men.

But within a few days Schmitz's ardor cooled, and when the Spreckelses requested an appointment to discuss the franchise matter further, the Mayor was too busy to receive them.

Undeterred, the incorporators filed the company's papers with the Secretary of State in Sacramento on April 17, 1906.

On April 18th, at 5:12 a.m., San Francisco was shaken by a tremendous earthquake, innumerable fires broke out, and by April 21st the city had been all but obliterated.

6   The Fiddler and the Fire

Schmitz and Ruef did not meet during the terrible days while the city burned. The boss was fighting the flames in North Beach; for five days he did not change his smoke-grimed, water-soaked clothes. When again he encountered the Mayor, a change had come· over Eugene.

Early on April 18th the conflagration raged out of control. The water mains had been shattered by the earthquake, and office buildings, hotels, stores, warehouses, banks, hospitals, schools were devoured along a miles-long front. Thousands of dwellings went up in smoke; other buildings had been shaken off their foundations and collapsed, pavements were buckled, streets lay buried under bricks and tumbled cornices. Communication lines were severed, food supplies destroyed, and anarchy and pestilence threatened. Refugees, stunned and terrified, scrambled to dubious safety on the encircling hills.

Mayor Schmitz had hastened to his office. Gertrude Atherton, the San Francisco novelist, recalled that "on that terrible day everybody was either at a pitch above normal, or hopelessly demoralized." Schmitz, being an artist, was keyed up several notches higher than concert pitch, and through the frenzied days ahead he enacted superbly the role of tireless, inspiring leader.

The public services were in chaos, and at the suggestion of his friend, J. Downey Harvey, the Mayor created a committee of public safety, termed the Committee of Fifty, to serve as a governing junta in the emergency. The most prominent and ablest men in the city were recruited, including Phelan, Rudolph Spreckels, and Heney, just

returned from Washington. By proclamation, the Mayor warned that
looters would be shot on sight; he ordered the people to remain indoors between dusk and dawn; and to any plausible suggestion for
fighting the fires, he responded with a brisk, "Do it; I place you in
charge." The result was action, and above everything, Schmitz was
an actor.

Millionaires and schoolmen scurried to carry out the Mayor's
commands. Phelan transported dynamite in his high-backed, open
automobile to blast lanes in hope of checking the holocaust. Spreckels
commandeered food for distribution to the thousands of homeless survivors crowding the parks and open squares. Schmitz was caught up
in the stupendous drama, and from the ordeal emerged a hero by
popular acclaim, lionized as "the man of the hour." After the fires
had been subdued, he surveyed the blackened ruins spreading for
miles and proudly announced: "Political history for me will date from
April 18th."

The moment of glory was of brief duration. In a few weeks the
supporting players in the stellar cast dispersed to grapple with their
own overwhelming difficulties, the lurid backdrop was whisked aside,
and Schmitz's strutting heroics were out of place. But heady intoxica-
tion lingered, and Schmitz was deluded by the crisis into believing he
really was a great man. This added one more complication to Ruef's
many acute problems.

Abe's personal losses in the disaster were substantial, although
those of propertied men like Phelan and Spreckels were far greater,
Phelan losing more than a million dollars in the destruction of one
uninsured office building. When the Committee of Fifty was formed,
Ruef's name was not on the list; Schmitz added it as an afterthought.
But when this committee was replaced by a more permanent Committee of Forty on the Reconstruction of San Francisco, Ruef was placed
in a key spot,—in charge of subcommittees. At this evidence of the
boss's hand on the rebuilding program, Rudolph Spreckels resigned
in disgust. Heney's name was not on the second list at all.

From all over the world, assistance poured into the devastated
city. Los Angeles started a train northward, loaded with food and
medical equipment, within a few hours of receipt of word of the
disaster,—although rumors were bruited that all San Francisco had
slid into the sea. Other shipments followed rapidly,—blankets, cloth-

ing, tents, doctors, nurses, everything that could help a destitute people. Millions of dollars were subscribed in a few days to a relief fund placed in James D. Phelan's charge. President Roosevelt, mindful of keeping this huge cash sum out of the hands of Schmitz and his coterie, by proclamation urged donors everywhere to send their contributions not to the city government, but directly to the relief committee,—an international compliment to Phelan's incorruptibility.

The work of reclamation began while the ashes were still smoking. Streets blotted out by rubble thirty feet deep were cleared within two weeks; at the end of that fortnight the first street car rattled along Market Street, with Mayor Schmitz handling the controls and Patrick Calhoun and Abe Ruef waving from its flag-draped windows. The car was a symbol of hope, and people digging in the ruins cheered as it went by.

Calhoun had hurried back from the East to take personal charge of restoring imperatively needed transportation facilities and assist in the organization of relief. In the rush to get the cars moving, he had strung a temporary trolley wire along Market Street (the principal thoroughfare) and nobody objected. He also held out the prospect of putting hundreds of men to work immediately, if he were permitted to rebuild the lines using trolley wires throughout. In a letter to the board of supervisors, he suggested that the long-debated issue be referred to "the public" for a speedy decision; but the newspapers, which for several weeks had been unnaturally quiescent under the shock of the cataclysm, found out that by "the public" Calhoun meant the supervisors, the public's representatives. Howls of protest arose. Nevertheless, on May 14th, less than a month after the earthquake, the supervisors passed to print an ordinance permitting the United Railroads to convert its lines to the overhead trolley.

Whereupon all the watchdogs barked. The *Chronicle* snapped that Patrick Calhoun was up to no good, although he was "too well bred, or perhaps too cautious a man, to tell the public to be damned." The *Examiner* frothed in an outburst of journalistic invective seldom surpassed, of which the concluding words were:

...It looks very much as if Patrick Calhoun, Thornwell Mullally, and their pals of the United Railroads had sneaked up behind San Francisco as she lay wounded from the earthquake and conflagration. In the guise of helping her, they were caught picking her pocket. If the supervisors aid and abet them, the people will be warranted in setting up their effigies in lasting bronze, a group of everlasting infamy, with the inscription: "THESE MEN LOOTED SAN FRANCISCO AT THE TIME OF THE GREAT FIRE OF 1906."

The city fathers, smarting from the way they had been ignored while the Committee of Fifty was running the city, resented the *Examiner's* roasting, and on May 21st they assembled in the back room of McGushin's saloon (their permanent shelter, City Hall, lay in ruins) and voted final passage of the trolley permit, without exacting in return any compensation whatever for the community,—whose inhabitants at that moment were living on the charity of the world.

On May 24th, Mayor Schmitz signed the ordinance. The franchise was to run for twenty-five years.

That day, a person who chanced to pass the United States Mint on Fifth Street, a fortress-like structure that had withstood the fire and loomed forbiddingly amid an expanse of gray desolation, might have observed two well-dressed men come down the wide steps, each carrying a heavy, paper-wrapped parcel about one cubic foot square in size. They got into a waiting motorcar with these parcels and drove away. The men were Tirey L. Ford, chief counsel of the United Railroads, and William M. Abbott, his prim assistant. The packages contained money,—currency in bills of small denominations, $1, $2, and $5, which the two men had just received in exchange for gold.

Those bills were the first installment of a compensation to be paid to Abraham Ruef, Eugene Schmitz, and the supervisors, which eventually would total $200,000.

Extraordinary sights were commonplace those melodramatic days, and on April 23rd an even stranger spectacle had passed unnoticed. On that day, five days after the earthquake, with fires still flickering sporadically, a well-dressed man picked his way through the shattered, blackened heaps of fallen masonry around City Hall and affixed a paper to a heat-warped girder. This paper carried notification that at two o'clock that afternoon bids would be received by the supervisors for the sale of a franchise to erect a competitive telephone system in San Francisco. The statute required that all bids must be submitted at the "regular meeting place" of the board, and the sign informed the passer-by (if any there should be) that the "regular meeting place" of the supervisors had been transferred to an assembly room known as Mowry Hall, a building with a roof over it. The man who posted the sign was Robert N. Frick, an attorney employed by the Home Telephone Company.

At two o'clock the board of supervisors convened, and Frick opened the sale with a bid of $25,000. No other offers were forthcoming, and the franchise was knocked down to the lone applicant for that nominal sum.

That franchise had been written by Abraham Ruef, attorney.

A rival telephone syndicate, which also had been angling to obtain a foothold in San Francisco, later attested that had they imagined a sale would be held during the catastrophic prostration of the city, they would have been on hand, ready to bid as high as one million dollars for the same franchise.

That day, aboard a train bringing emergency relief supplies from Los Angeles, was a strongbox, bulging with a quarter of a million dollars in gold and greenbacks, with which (and the thanks of the Home Telephone Company) were to be compensated Abraham Ruef, Eugene Schmitz, and the supervisors.

But Heney, Spreckels, and Older also were at work. On May 25th, the day after Schmitz signed the trolley franchise, Al McKinley, a Burns detective, was assigned to shadow Ruef.

7   "The Shame of California"

All threads of normal life in San Francisco had been snapped by the April 18th calamity. Horror, suffering, dismay were everywhere. The population fell to 175,000 as hundreds of thousands of victims, bereft of homes, possessions, employment, cast adrift without food or shelter, terrified by after-shocks that jolted the ground under their feet, sought refuge in nearby communities or fled the ill-omened region altogether. Nevertheless, with a courage and resiliency that evoked the admiration of the world, the remaining survivors set about recreating their shattered metropolis.

While men and women struggled with the difficulties of maintaining bare existence, other projects were jettisoned; for several weeks, Older did not see either Heney or Spreckels. Then, early in May, he chanced to run into Heney on Van Ness Avenue, the wide boulevard at which the fire had been halted and which was being transformed into a shopping center. Older pulled Heney inside a tent pitched by the sidewalk. What about the graft inquiry? Heney replied that he was ready to go ahead; and a couple of days later they waited on Rudolph Spreckels in the wooden shack he had patched together on the site of the First National Bank, of which recently he had become president. The immaculate clubman was dressed in logger's boots and corduroys, the standard costume of businessmen entering the area of the ruins. Far from being too preoccupied with personal problems to embark on the graft investigation, Spreckels was impatient to get started. All around, he perceived a foul drift moving, a new crop of graft and extortion spawned amid the chaos.

The three men struck their final bargain that day. The terms of William J. Burn's employment were settled, and it was arranged that he should be brought to San Francisco at once. When Spreckels broached the question of Heney's fee, the lawyer, glancing through the open doorway at the appalling destruction, replied: "If you are willing to sacrifice your money, risk your reputation, your business, your friendships, maybe even your life—because I know the storm we are heading into—I'd be a pretty poor sort of citizen if I couldn't risk my time. This is my city. I will undertake the job and give all my energies to it, on one condition,—that I am never to receive one cent of compensation from you or anybody else. That will be my contribution toward making a better San Francisco."

That no-fee bargain was kept.

In mid-day, Burns arrived and set up headquarters in the Gladstone Apartments, a four-story brick block of flats already refurbished, at Polk and Eddy streets, not far from the burned-out City Hall. From there he deployed a staff of investigators unknown to the local underworld, spotting them as chauffeurs, housemaids, gardeners, secretaries, in homes, offices, churches, clubs,—wherever information might be gleaned. His spies penetrated everywhere: men and women of refinement were brought from the East and introduced by Phelan and Spreckels into their social set; even Supervisor Gallagher's civil-service chauffeur turned out to be on Burns's payroll. From the reports of these operatives, Burns patiently pieced together the picture of official maldoing. Almost everybody in town believed there was crookedness, but it was Burns's job to produce the evidence that would prove this crookedness in court. The assignment called for all the detective's intuitive skill, psychological flair, and perseverance. Spreckels paid the mounting bills without a murmur.

Politics paused for no convulsion of nature. Dazzled by the adulation he had received during the emotion-packed days of the conflagration, Mayor Schmitz was drifting into grandiose delusions: he believed he was a man of destiny, and he wanted to move into the governorship of the state in that autumn's election. To Ruef, the notion was chimerical. He had become convinced that Schmitz could never rise higher than mayor of San Francisco: the Republicans of the state would never accept him as long as he wore the Union Labor label, and to discard that would be political suicide.

But Schmitz was slippery. He had other advisers now, among them Frank Maestretti, the president of the board of public works, whose excessive zeal at the ballot box on Ruef's behalf once had landed him in court. Times were unsettling, old relationships were being abraded by the calamitous events, and Maestretti now was ambitious to supplant Ruef as city boss. He had formed for the furtherance of this intrigue a super-secret society called "The Sovereigns of America," equipped with ritual, regalia, and passwords, and dedicated loftily to "liberating San Francisco from boss rule." Into this cabal he had gathered a number of political malcontents.

Ruef heard about the clique and learned that it included one of his close confidants, Dr. Joseph Poheim, now president of the police commission. Poheim and Maestretti he marked for decapitation, but he moved stealthily. In July, Poheim got the axe, ostensibly for grafting personally on saloons (Poheim owned a firm selling bar glass-ware); against Maestretti, the boss did not risk moving yet.

Schmitz at the same time was conducting a purge of the police commission. He ousted Thomas Reagan, the street paver-insurance man, for knocking down graft privately and failing to "divvy." When the Mayor published that Reagan was blackmailing *maquereaux* (San Franciscans used the French word for pimps and brothelkeepers), Reagan struck back savagely in an open letter that ended: "I have not now, nor in the past, nor will I in the future, covet, take, or carry one dollar belonging to an unfortunate. I would never think of defrauding your honor."

In the August election of delegates to the Republican state convention, which would select the party's nominee for governor, Ruef captured the entire city representation, and by this coup gained the power to name the candidate. There were two aspirants in the running (Ruef excluded Schmitz from consideration and sometimes, for several days in a row, got Schmitz to agree): the incumbent governor, George C. Pardee, and Congressman James N. Gillett. Neither commanded a majority of the delegates; Ruef's votes would be the deciding factor.

Ruef believed Pardee had broken his word on a patronage pledge, and refused to support him. Gillett was the Railroad's candidate. Ruef, alert to exploit this situation for his own furtherance, announced as his dark-horse candidate a wealthy San Jose publisher, J. O. Hayes.

Herrin, the Railroad's political boss, acted immediately. In a conference in Ruef's home (just down Pierce Street from Schmitz's handsome residence), Herrin, Abe, and Schmitz worked out a deal whereby Ruef, once he became convinced that Hayes stood no real chance, would release his delegates to vote for Gillett. In his own mind, Ruef counted upon impressing Herrin with his strength and placing the Railroad under a lasting obligation by delaying this release until the last minute. Herrin's gratitude for the boss's promised co-operation was prompt and practical: he handed Abe some $14,000 in cash for "campaign expenses."

The convention met in a big tent in the seaside resort town of Santa Cruz during the first week in September. Herrin did not appear publicly, but his private railroad car was parked on a siding. There was the usual spate of party oratory and back-room huddles, and at the last moment Ruef threw his votes to Gillett, giving him the nomination on the first ballot.

This victory called for a celebration, and Major Frank McLaughlin, a big wheel in Republican affairs who lived in Santa Cruz, entertained Gillett and his supporters at dinner that evening. Thinking to preserve a souvenir of the happy occasion, the Major called in a photographer, who snapped the group in convivial pose. Seated in the center was the benign host, and at his right hand sat Abe Ruef; all the others were standing. Gillett rested one hand affectionately on the little boss's shoulder, and nearby stood the nominee for lieutenant governor, Warren R. Porter. Jovial Walter Parker, Herrin's deputy in Southern California, caressed a well-lined waistcoat, and at the right stood San Francisco's Superior Court Judge F.H. Kerrigan, who had served the Southern Pacific's interests famously in a certain decision and had just been rewarded by nomination for a seat on the Court of Appeals at a big boost in salary. Behind him hovered Congressman Joseph R. Knowland, while a shoal of Southern Pacific legal apologists and lobbyists smiled at the camera. Guarding the far right flank was Justice Frederick Henshaw, nominated for a second twelve-year term on the Supreme Court bench. Ruef, looking tiny amid so much political beef, beamed as proudly as,—well, Mr. Punch.

Among political blunders, that photograph, which was published in the San Francisco *Call,* probably never has been exceeded. A little more than a year later, Major McLaughlin would be dead, a ruined man, a suicide after shooting his daughter; the little boss would be under indictment; and the peccancies of others in the genial group would be exposed. Later still, that photograph was to stare down from billboards all over the state, underscored: THE SHAME OF CALIFORNIA!

But not yet. Politically, Ruef basked in halcyon weather during September, 1906. He was forty-two years old and at the peak of his power, and ahead he saw only success. By 1909, he estimated, he would be strong enough to claim the United States Senate seat which would fall vacant that year.

October was to be a month of hurricane.

8   Schmitz's Dream of Glory

Schmitz, turned down in his grab for the California governorship, had a new bee in his bonnet: he was sure he had become a world celebrity, and he proposed to capitalize on this renown, and gain political and social stature, by undertaking a grand tour of Europe. He imagined himself hobnobbing with prime ministers and dining with crowned heads, perhaps discussing with Kaiser Wilhelm in Berlin the reprehensible refusal of certain German insurance companies to honor their policies and settle fire claims; these were the companies who were invoking the earthquake-exemption clause, and many holders of their policies in San Francisco were incensed. Schmitz had no doubt that he and the Kaiser could patch up the difficulty, and along the way he might pick up some dandy ideas for rehabilitating San Francisco.

Ruef tried dissuasion from what he perceived was folly. The city was groping toward recovery slowly and the people needed aggressive leadership more than ever, he pointed out; but Schmitz had his own notions and other advisers. Prodded by Maestretti, the Mayor packed his trunks, while Julia rapturously jotted down reminders of purchases she must make in Paris. At the end of September, the Mayor announced to the public his imminent departure; but the public, for the most part, was too absorbed in its scramble to live to pay much attention to Gene's vagary.

"I am utterly worn out with the trying experiences and duties which have befallen me since the April calamity," Schmitz told the press. "I feel that I have earned a vacation."

Supervisor Gallagher, as president of the board, would be acting mayor during his absence, he added, and would enjoy complete freedom.

"He will have the authority to make any appointments to municipal offices in the event vacancies occur," the Mayor explained nonchalantly, and the phrase seemed to carry political overtones. "Whatever he does has my endorsement in advance."

Under heavy-lidded eyes, Frank Maestretti craftily construed this ambiguity. He had been warned that the Mayor was planning to make him walk the plank on charges of grafting, and that Eugene was leaving town so as to be out of sight and hearing of the distressful splash. But Frank felt secure: did he not have Schmitz's word of honor that his position would not be touched during the Mayor's absence?

"They don't dare accuse me of graft," Maestretti scoffed to inquisitive reporters. "They know I'll retaliate."

How about Ruef?

Maestretti was disdainful. "Ruef's an easy man to beat, if you know how."

On the evening of September 30th, Schmitz bade farewell to his supervisors at a banquet in a fashionable uptown restaurant. At the host's right hand sat Ruef, at his left, Gallagher. Reporters found the food delicious, the wines the finest and dryest, the cigars irreproachable.

Addressing his guests as "honored and dear friends," the Mayor praised them and himself for "wonderful, loyal service" during and since the fire. He was going abroad, he said, to study civic government in the great capitals of Europe, to probe problems of municipal ownership, and perhaps negotiate a settlement of the German insurance claims.

"I am leaving the office of the municipality in good hands," he went on. "Mr. Gallagher is a gentleman whose loyalty to the administration has been tested on the firing line. I have not asked him to do anything in particular; I have not attempted to outline a policy for him to pursue. I will leave it to him to decide on his own policy, which I know will be in line with the interests of the people."

He raised a delicately fluted glass.

"In conclusion, I want to say this: I am not a politician; I do not do things for political reasons. I do what I think is right and best and in the interests of my friends. My friends are my friends for personal reasons, and not for political ones,—not because they have power, but because they are dear to me!"

With a bow to the little boss, the toast was drunk. Abe lipped the champagne and declined a cigar; he was enjoying the festivities and contributing his quantum of wit.

Seconding the toast, Gallagher declared the supervisors were grieved by the Mayor's departure, but he felt that his colleagues might find solace in the thought that Ruef remained.

"I shall have the opportunity to carry out the policies of our Mayor," exclaimed the acting-mayor-to-be, "and I am thankful that I shall have the assistance and advice of his attorney, Abe Ruef, to guide me."

The toast was drunk again, and Abe smiled. Then everybody

laughed while Supervisor Pat McGushin spun out long-winded advice
on what the Mayor should see in the Old World. In Germany and
Austria, Pat predicted, the people, upon beholding handsome Gene,
would troop after him like a Pied Piper, all wanting to come to San
Francisco. But stay away from Russsia, that land of anarchists,—one
of those bomb-throwers would surely be misled by Schmitz's aristo-
cratic air into mistaking him for a grand duke! There were guffaws at
this, but Pat floridly protested that he knew what he was talking
about, because he never talked about things he wasn't familiar with.

Did that apply in respect to the red-light district? Ruef inquired
politely, amid more merriment.

Sam Davis, the erstwhile drummer, expounded his philosophy
concisely: "When I was elected supervisor, I was told by the Mayor
that all he wanted me to do was to do what was right, and I have always followed his advice." All this gabble about a split-up between
the Mayor and the boss, declared Sam, was untrue, as their very
presence there proved. "The people of San Francisco ought to be
grateful to Abe Ruef for all he has done for them!" he concluded, and
sat down to loud applause, in which Ruef joined courteously.

The boss then responded, eulogized the virtues of loyalty and
friendship, and exhorted the supervisors to emulate their Mayor as a
virtuous example.

"Gassy" Kelly was too full to be coherent, but Supervisor
Boxton, the dentist who popped champagne corks with the same
facility as teeth, and was at his waggish best after the fourth or fifth
pop, extolled the Mayor "and also our good friend and counselor,
Abe Ruef. There have been times," he drolly confessed, "when I was
tempted to stray from the right path. Such moments come to all of
us. But every time that happened, Abe Ruef was always at my side
to tell me what was right and what was wrong, and steer me in the
right direction. I call for three cheers for Abe Ruef!"

The cheers were given riotously, and Abe repeated urbanely:
"There is nothing in life more exalted than true friendship."

On the morning of October 1st, Schmitz set out. His entourage,
besides his wife, included Fred Hilbert of "municipal whisky" mal-

odor. The Hilbert company had gone smash when fire-ruined saloon-keepers were unable to meet their notes, but neither Fred nor his brother seemed noticeably crippled in pocket.

The public, of course, was unaware that the Mayor's tickets for the trip were a gift from the Santa Fe Railroad (a little matter of permits to build warehouses in the city—with Schmitz part-owner of the warehouses—had prompted this token of appreciation); they merely noted that Gene was traveling first class.

A numerous retinue of friends, well-wishers, and officeholders accompanied the party to the train. Chief of Police Jeremiah Dinan wore pearl gray gloves. There was Superior Judge Carroll Cook, a true Ruefian; his colleague, Judge Thomas F. Graham, a dandified gentleman with a silky, pointed beard and wistful eyes, whose abhorrence was dissension; and George Keane and Coroner W.J. Walsh; also, of course, Ruef. The little boss scarcely let go of Schmitz's hand until the train pulled out.

Four days thereafter, acting Mayor Gallagher ignominiously fired Frank Maestretti from the board of public works because of asserted "lamentable failure to clear the streets and sidewalks of the debris which has littered them for more than five months." This dereliction Gallagher stigmatized before the supervisors as inexcusable. He then called for a vote ratifying his order of dismissal. There was a rippling of "ayes." No showing of "noes" was requested.

From the rear of the hall, Abe Ruef was watching. After the act of expulsion had been approved, Gallagher sat in the presiding officer's chair looking blank. (He was to become known as "the statesman with the blank look.")

"Haven't you forgotten something?" called the boss.

"Oh, yes," Gallagher started, and promptly appointed Supervisor George Duffey the new president of the board of public works. Nobody was more astonished than Duffey.

Maestretti refused to believe in his dethronement. He telegraphed to Schmitz, who was relaxing in the royal suite of the Waldorf-Astoria Hotel in New York City, reminding him of the Mayor's word-of-honor. No reply came back.

"I don't believe he ever got the telegram," Maestretti protested.

Nevertheless, he stayed dethroned; and soon, according to rumor, he was supplying priceless information to William J. Burns.

9 "A Reign of Terror"

Behind the scenes, Heney was hard at work. As a point of readiest attack, he had chosen the French restaurants license scandal; this he believed would afford a court-tight case quickly, while Burns was exploring the labyrinth of official bribery. As a preliminary step, Heney formed a law partnership with Charles Cobb, a young attorney from San Jose, and John Joseph Dwyer, a lawyer-politician who had been prominent in the Democratic reforms of the Phelan era and now was working closely with Hearst; because of his political coloration, however, Dwyer's connection with the firm was not emphasized. One of Heney's purposes was to ensure that his associates in the graft investigation might have informed legal guidance, should he be temporarily out-of-town; Heney was moving with thoroughness.

Before any prosecution could be started, he required two things: an independent grand jury, free from Ruef's control, and official status, which could come only through the co-operation of District Attorney Langdon. Fremont Older undertook to obtain the first; Dwyer, the second.

The current grand jury was subservient to Ruef. Myrtile Cerf, its secretary, was a clerk in Ruef's law office, as well as being on the city payroll as an accountant at $300 a month. Cerf was an impudently sly young man, smooth-shaven, with moist lips and a liquorish grin, who wore a derby hat, high stand-up collar, and a diamond in his cravat. He bragged of loyalty to the boss, a loyalty that never flagged.

The process of forming a grand jury was this: each of the twelve judges of the Superior Court submitted twelve names; and from these, nineteen were drawn by lot to compose the panel. The District Attorney supervised the public drawing in the court of the presiding judge. Older had learned the trick by which Ruef managed to get amenable grand juries: the court clerk, a Ruef appointee, segregated the slips of paper bearing the names of men accessible to Ruef's influence into a loose bundle, which he dropped with the other slips into the teller box; then, at the drawing, his hand groping through the opening in the lid could feel the bundle and pull out enough of the desired names to ensure a majority of the members. Older had tested his discovery at the drawing of a previous grand jury by demanding that all the slips be emptied on a table (any citizen could do this) and the mass broken up and shuffled in plain view; the result was a jury (the one headed by Thomas P. Andrews) over which Ruef had no control, and which had exposed much rottenness in municipal affairs. It had been blocked, finally, by the withholding of funds.

Thomas P. Graham was the current presiding judge of the Superior Court (the office rotated annually), and to him Older appealed, explaining the drawing ruse. Graham, although he had a judicial conscience, was a pet of Ruef,—he had, in fact, been a member of the party accompanying Schmitz to the train; but he quailed at the prospect of incurring a *Bulletin* drubbing, and somewhat testily he consented to impanel a new grand jury. The prosecutors were elated.

Heney's second requisite—official status through the District Attorney's co-operation—proved only slightly harder to obtain. Langdon, who had been elected by Ruef's machine, was now reaching for higher political honors by running for governor of the state against the Republican-Railroad-Ruef nominee, Gillett. Langdon was the candidate of the Independence League, a political catchall thrown together by William Randolph Hearst, and Dwyer was California president of the League and Langdon's campaign manager. The two men met at the inland town of Fresno, and Dwyer transmitted the request that Heney be appointed an assistant district attorney of San Francisco, in charge of prosecuting grafters. Dwyer disclosed the financial support guaranteed by Spreckels, Burns's activity, and other developments to date.

Langdon hesitated. Such a step, especially during a political campaign, would place him in an invidious position: should the proposed prosecution fail, he would be shouldered with the blame; should it succeed, Heney would reap the credit. And a political, self-serving motive undoubtedly would be assigned. Also, there was the question of Hearst's attitude, which would determine that of the *Examiner;* Hearst's approval was a *sine qua non.* So Dwyer appealed to the publisher, and Hearst, deciding that Schmitz had become a political liability (Hearst never had swallowed Ruef), gave his consent to Heney's appointment.

There remained one more obstacle, for while Langdon liked Heney, he would have preferred to give such an assignment to a close friend, a lawyer who at forty was making a name in San Francisco

as a fearless, effective courtroom pleader,—Hiram W. Johnson. But
the intimation that Heney carried White House blessing tipped the
scales, and Langdon agreed to make the appointment whenever the
moment was deemed ripe. He did lay down one firm stipulation,—
namely, that he should be acknowledged the responsible head of the
graft prosecution and should be kept fully informed at all times. This
insistence on assuming responsibility called for moral courage; in
Heney's words afterward, Langdon was the bravest of them all.

Conditions in San Francisco, meanwhile, had worsened. The city
was splurging in a burst of spurious prosperity, as insurance companies
paid fire claims and put large sums of cash into circulation. Much of
this was spent foolishly. Hotels, restaurants, theaters mushroomed in
temporary buildings. Luxurious shops blossomed along Van Ness
Avenue, stocked as abundantly as before the holocaust; automobiles,
silks, and diamonds were in demand. The St. Francis Hotel, burned
out of its home on Powell Street, moved into a one-story wooden
bungalow (the Little St. Francis) erected in Union Square, across the
way. The clubs—the Bohemian, Union League, Lotus, Family,
Pacific-Union, Olympic, and the rest—moved into makeshift rooms
and continued to exert a stimulating influence on community life. But
impermanence underlay the bravado: many persons believed another
devastating earthquake was imminent, and splurged recklessly during
the little time they felt remained.

Graft pullulated to an extent inconceivable in settled times. In
October, the *Pacific Unitarian* reported gloomily that "everyone seems
to find in San Francisco's present condition an opportunity for immediate gain, and the ability to get anything is too strong to be
resisted." As a depressing corollary, the same magazine observed:
"Every student of current events knows how hot are the handles to all
social questions." The whole city was in a frenetic mood resembling
delayed traumatic shock. And suddenly the graft touched everybody.
"Let no dishonest dollar escape!" seemed to have become the slogan
of everybody remotely associated with public office, and racketeering
the business of many city departments. It was a time of municipal
depravity.

The municipality licensed twenty-seven kinds of business, including such diverse occupations as auctioneering, assaying, stockbroking, carpet-cleaning, and fortune-telling; it regulated bathhouses, livery stables, saloons, dairies, bowling alleys, debt collectors, insurance adjusters, dyers, billiard rooms, real-estate brokers, cycleries, railroad agents. Nearly six thousand persons were engaged directly in these activities, thousands more were connected indirectly, and the squeeze was put on them all,—all, that is, except some thirteen hundred who were exempted from paying any license fees at all. A. Ruef was attorney for these. He had nothing to sell, he would inform clients: "I have no goods to deliver, I am only your counsel." Nevertheless, the goods usually were delivered.

Not one theater in town complied with the fire ordinances, but after the owners had signed over a third of their capital stock to Ruef or his dummies, inspectors from the board of public works were unable to detect any violations. Recalcitrants who declined to be blackmailed found their theaters closed for legitimate reasons. Contractors, butchers, produce dealers were levied upon. The board of health imposed fantastic rules of cleanliness on milkmen, but after these made up a "lawyer's fund" and retained a Ruef-selected attorney, they were not incommoded.

The supervisors set up a commissary department, under no sanction from the charter, which purchased supplies for jails, hospitals, almshouses, and other public institutions. Among its purchases was $175,000 worth of printing within a few months,—a large portion of the cash collected from the city treasury for this item being kicked back to a Swiss named Robinson whose major occupation seemed to be hanging around Mowry Hall.

The City Commercial Company, a firm which had no address, no telephone, kept no books, and owned no inventory, billed the city for $10,000 worth of "sundries" every month.

James A. Snook & Co., 247 Davis Street, another commission house which carried no merchandise, placed no bounds on the variety of supplies it procured for the city,—fifty shovels for the board of public works, ten crates of olive oil for the county hospital, one hundred bottles of fine old brandy for the almshouse (Maestretti was boss of the almshouse district), tobacco, seedless raisins, frying chickens, flypaper, brushes, mats, gasoline, oakum, tableware, street-sweeping brooms, and collar buttons. Snook & Co. ran up a $100,000 credit balance in no time. Herbert L. Schmitz was reputed to be the "& Co." behind James A. Snook.

Housing, for living purposes or business, was almost unobtainable. For a while, Ruef rented the kitchen and bathroom of a flat on Pine Street for an office, and felt lucky to get that. Soon a two-story wooden building sprang up at the corner of Bush and Fillmore streets (although the fire laws forbade the erection of any wooden building more than one story high during the emergency), and he took over six sunny rooms on the upper floor for law offices; congenially, a bank and a French restaurant shared the floor below him.

Rents were exorbitant. The city fathers made no attempt to salvage damaged city buildings but carried on the municipality's business all over town,—in basements, garrets, bakeries, private dwellings, shacks, synagogues, pretentious clubs, and Salvation Army halls. Fire Commissioner Werden (whose beer the saloons were being forced to buy or lose their licenses) rented the basement of his home to the city for three times the value of the whole house. A friend of Ruef leased a dilapidated residence for $100 a month and sublet it to the city for $500. Another collected $7,200 a year rent for a building that could have been bought for $12,000. Mayor Schmitz established his office in three rooms of a private dwelling on the corner of Post and Franklin streets, for which the city forked up $250 a month, while the landlord lived on the premises. The city was paying $98,654 a year in rentals, while municipal property that might have been repaired and utilized remained untouched.

"Are we all gone clean daft?" cried the *Chronicle*. "What kind of a city is San Francisco?"

Travelers, some of them writers for nationally respected magazines, provided one answer to this despairing question, and it was not flattering. It was widely published how brothels were invading neighborhoods from which they had been excluded before. A fancy house opened on Webster Street just back of St. Stephen's Episcopal Church, and the girls passed out cards to men coming from vespers. Although the rector protested, the police perceived nothing amiss. Householders reported being awakened by screams and, through the unshaded windows of the nearby dwelling, beholding naked men and women in orgiastic exercises, but the policeman on the beat remained oblivious.

The real-estate pages of the newspapers carried photographs of a new "municipal crib" going up in Chinatown, this time at 614 Jackson Street; and another of equal dimensions and blatancy, and obviously officially sanctioned, being erected on nearby Commercial Street for Jerome Bassity, the so-called King of the Maquereaux, a porcine politician-pimp who flashed with diamonds, wearing them even on his toes in bed.

Police enforcement was deplorably lax when it existed at all, Chief Dinan espousing a policy of compromise with lawbreakers: he might advise the victim of a holdup to accept partial restitution and drop the charge, and sometimes would personally see that some of the loot was returned. Joe (Kid) Sullivan, lord of the pickpockets, was seen riding with Dinan daily in the Chief's official automobile, and Sullivan's old-time partner, Annie Piggot, who had been exiled from the city for years, operated without molestation. Sullivan lined up his squads and marched them off to designated districts where they plied their skills, and only the victims seemed perturbed by this disciplined disorder.

The bars had been closed during the crisis, and when they were allowed to reopen, everybody had to get a new license. Pat McGushin opened a flashy bar on Van Ness Avenue at Fulton Street, a choice location (San Francisco's Opera House stands about there now), although by agreement with the merchants, saloons had been debarred from Van Ness Avenue. Pat's was the sole exception.

Along Fillmore Street, penny arcades specializing in sexy peepshows were lighted all night long, and welfare workers frequently saw proprietors place footstools for little girls to stand on so they could peer through the slots of the machines.

And Ruef's hand dipped into everything.

The itching palm even reached into domestic arrangements, such as permission to cook in one's kitchen. After the disaster, householders were forbidden to light fires indoors until their chimneys had been inspected for earthquake damage, and for months cookstoves lined the curbs along residential streets. But after a while it became known that if one gave a man (not necessarily a city inspector) $5 or $10, one's chimney would be inspected and approved speedily; while the moralist who on principle refused to submit to petty extortion continued to cook under the sky.

As if these exacerbations were not enough, that autumn the United

Railroads carmen struck for higher pay. Calhoun made an offer, which was rejected; he then announced that he would run the cars with strikebreakers. In a union-labor town, this was a declaration of war, and the harassed public braced for violence; but at the last minute the disputants were persuaded to arbitrate. Francis J. Heney was named by the company as one member of the three-man arbitration board, the others being Father Peter G. Yorke for the men and California's Chief Justice William H. Beatty. Heney took the precaution of making his position crystal clear, stating: "I wish it to be thoroughly understood that I am acting in this matter purely as a judge. I am not an attorney for the United Railroads and I am not accepting a dollar from the United Railroads."

Patrick Calhoun left the issues in the arbiters' hands and departed for the East. The glimpse Heney gained at this time of the street car corporation's affairs was to influence his future course radically.

Then—while the citizens were bedeviled by grifts, grafts, and natural calamity—a new scourge struck them,—an unprecedented outburst of crime. Robberies, assaults, murders occurred daily. After dark, the desolate burned area was a lair of brigands, who crushed the skulls of the unwary with gas pipe. Newspaper headlines screamed:

DAYLIGHT HOLDUP!
A CRIMSON RECORD—9 MURDERS, 25 ROBBERIES,
    10 BURGLARIES!
THEFT REPORTS POURING IN!
WOMAN CHASED BLOCKS!
GOVERNOR OFFERS REWARD FOR TELLER'S MURDERERS!

The whole town armed. Hardware dealers sold an estimated twenty thousand pistols in one month, and women walked the streets clutching long hatpins. Merchants formed safety patrols for their own neighborhoods. Banks and offices bristled with weapons. Armed guards stood beside clerks in the post office. The St. Francis Hotel cautioned its guests not to venture after dark more than a block away, because beyond that distance the hotel could not provide protection. People ceased to go out at night at all. Theaters went vacant, lodge meetings and evening church services were deserted, social gatherings were abandoned.

The police seemed supine, no matter how sternly newspapers and pulpit orators voiced the popular sense of outrage, and bold-type incentives to violent action began to appear. DRIVE OUT THE SLUGGERS! PATIENCE IS EXHAUSTED! IT IS NOW TIME FOR THE PEOPLE TO ACT! was one such exhortation, and similar cries were echoed in reputable quarters. A proposal was advanced that one thousand determined men should make a house-to-house search for criminals and suspicious characters and dump them aboard ships in the bay, to be taken nobody cared where, but away. There were vigilante mutterings; and in an editorial printed three columns wide, the *Chronicle* gave expression to the thought that was in thousands of minds:

That this city has become a refuge for desperate criminals is evident. It is high time for us to protect ourselves. There is a reign of terror. The city is infested with people who do not work and are well supplied with money. Brutal robberies occur in broad daylight and in crowded streets. Villainous faces are everywhere in evidence. Neither man nor woman feels safe out of doors after dark. They hardly feel safe at their own firesides. There must be a change. In former years the people of this city have shown that they would not patiently stand still and be murdered, and their acts received the moral endorsement of mankind. We do not wish a repetition of those scenes, but we know that present conditions are not to be endured by any virile community.

This was the speech of vigilantism. Violence was in the air. The least alarmist citizens felt it, the scholarly president of the University of California, Dr. Benjamin Ide Wheeler, telling an audience, during a lecture on education in Los Angeles, that "if any more bad men come to San Francisco, it may be necessary to get rid of some of them by means of the scaffold!"

With exactions and abuses become unbearable, the times chaotic, and the authorities helpless or heedless, the citizens were further goaded by reports that Mayor Schmitz was spending money like a Nevada millionaire on his junket through Europe. People struggling to re-establish their lives on a safe footing demanded relief. But Heney, Spreckels, and Older were not ready to open hostilities yet; they needed more time to build their case.

Then a spark was struck in an unlikely quarter. A group of businessmen, none of them especially prominent but all of solid financial standing, circulated a call for a public mass meeting to be held in Union Square on Saturday, October 13th, at 3:00 P.M. There was nothing inflammatory in the name of the group—the Potrero Commercial and Manufacturers Association—but the objective set forth in their proclamation was aglow with the explosive incandescence which twice in the city's history had erupted in mob rage and summary hangings.

The purpose of the meeting, its sponsors announced, was to set up a COMMITTEE OF ONE HUNDRED TO INVESTIGATE AND PUNISH OFFICIAL OUTLAWRY.

PART THREE

"Be not over much wicked, neither be thou foolish: why shouldst thou die before thy time?"

1 Debonair and Smiling

Heney and Spreckels were invited to participate in the Union Square rally—Spreckels was offered the chairmanship—but both declined, fearing their own plans might be compromised; Spreckels also suspected that the movement was basically one of employers against labor.

Notification of the rally brought no pause in the carnival of crime, although the police commission did take cognizance of the public's restiveness by sternly ordering Chief Dinan to "restore confidence in his department" within thirty days. On October 10th, when the arrangements committee met, speaker after speaker denounced police laxity. Demanding that they "get at the root of the evil," the president of the draymen's association cried: "This is the wickedest and most dangerous city on the continent! There is nothing that will touch it, from Mexico to the North Pole! If we do anything, let's not do it in a babylike manner—let us be men! I recommend you, gentlemen, that you take off your gloves and deal with this matter as it deserves!"

Resolutions were drafted denouncing the "apathy and moral cowardice" of the citizens, and calling for stated reforms: "One-man boss rule to be destroyed... public funds honestly administered... corruption in public office punished... crime and corruption in our midst stamped out...." But objections were raised that such language was "revolutionary," and the wording was toned down, emerging as an innocuous call for action; significantly, the editing was done by the committee's lawyer, Samuel M. Shortridge, who was known to be not unfriendly to Abe Ruef.

Gallagher, the city's temporary mayor, viewed the forthcoming rally with no favor.

"There will no lynching in this city," he declared. "I sincerely hope that at the meeting in Union Square Saturday the leaders will have enough sense to do nothing that will injure the city. They will call it a 'committee of safety,' but other cities will call it a vigilance committee, and that will do irrecoverable harm to San Francisco. The plan is un-American."

On Saturday, the sponsors of the rally were appalled by the thousands of citizens who crushed around the makeshift building in which the committee naïvely had expected to hold their meeting. This structure, housing the emergency offices of the California Promotion Committee, was a mere wooden hut with a porch about ten feet square. The chairman of the sponsoring group, William A. Doble, a conservative businessman little known to the public, had no experience in controlling such an unruly assemblage. He was aghast when he saw a young man shinny up the flagpole outside the window, swing on the halliards, and yell: "It's all right, boys! These ropes are strong enough for Ruef!"

Hurriedly, Doble transferred the meeting out-of-doors, utilizing the porch as a rostrum; his hope was to get through the motions of orderly procedure rapidly and let the dangerous concourse disperse.

"There is no need for discussion of the subject before us," he began. "We all know what we are here for."

Whereupon he ordered read the resolution approving the forma-tion of a "Committee of 100." This Shortridge did, so perfunctorily and in such haste that few persons either heard or understood him. Doble immediately called for a vote, declared the resolution adopted, and adjourned the meeting.

This suited nobody, and bereft of a presiding officer, the crowd became boisterous. Mayor Gallagher squeezed to the front of the platform and called authoritatively: "I would suggest that you disperse to your respective homes!"

Hoots, catcalls, hisses greeted Big Jim, and one of the city's most influential rabbis, Dr. Jacob Nieto, cried back: "We are entitled in a civilized community to be guaranteed the safety of our lives and property! If our officials cannot do their duty, let them get out!"

"We want no vigilance committee, no committee of safety!" shouted a labor spokesman.

The crowd cheered and jeered. Actually, the square was packed with Ruef's claque—officeholders, Tenderloin bruisers, Barbary Coast pimps, political errand-men, "rockrollers" of "the push"—for the boss had planned to capture the meeting since its first announcement, and was watching from a window of the adjacent Little St. Francis Hotel.

Doble then retreated behind Shortridge; and the latter, a deaconesque debater and campaign orator, raised his arms and struck the pompously patriotic note: "Citizens! Do you love this city? Though it be in ruins, the hearts of her people are not downcast! Not a man here but would lay down his life to protect the men, women, and children of this city! I know that you believe in the principles of law and order. We are not here to make speeches, for it is not a time for the display of speech. Neither is it a time for going into details about our condition...."

He was interrupted by half-dozen voices shouting against each other, and citizens who had hoped for effective action to lighten their woes began to leave in disgust. Then the boss appeared on the steps, looking dapper and confident, surrounded by burly bodyguards. As he lifted his hand for silence, the crowd whistled and groaned.

"I come here at the invitation of those who have the good of this city at heart," the slight figure commenced. "I come here as a private citizen, as a man of respectable family, as a man of property interests."

"Oh!" "Ah!" yelled the crowd, while heelers whistled.

"As a man of large property interests," the boss continued nervily, "acquired before I had anything to do with politics, acquired by hand and brain long before political considerations entered my life."

The laughter this evoked he let run its course.

"I came not as a political boss—as you have seen me described in unreliable and untruthful newspapers—but as an individual, to assist by word and deed. The conditions here are not so much the result of municipal inefficiency as of the sad calamity, which has attracted the harpies of the world. I have come before you because I knew that I could get justice from an audience of respectable American citizens, while I could not from newspapers that are edited by ruffians worse than any who prowl the streets."

He raised his tone.

"None of the stories published about me from day to day have an iota of truth! I did not come here to say this, but I am urged to do so on account of the remarks that have fallen from the lips of men here. Give the policemen a chance to redeem conditions if they can, and if not, we will remove them."

"Who do you mean by 'we?' " yelled a voice.

"I have nothing to do officially with the city government," the boss replied smoothly. "When I say 'we,' I mean that any influence I may possibly have, by reason of any ability or any other qualification I may have, will be put at the disposal of these men."

The parallel of Marc Antony's funeral oration striking him, he parodied it, sarcastically calling his enemies "honorable men." A lawyer named Truman broke in hotly, and Ruef answered this "honorable critic" by alluding to Truman's former position as director of an insane asylum and suggesting that he had "absorbed some peculiar mental traits there."

"You are a natural-born liar!" yelled the infuriated lawyer, while the crowd, which by now was almost exclusively "the push," cheered delightedly.

An elderly woman demanded: "Mr. Ruef, do you know there are many poor men and women who are suffering? Please tell us how much wealth you possess."

Hand on heart, the boss replied: "I deny that I ever got a five-cent piece for any corrupt action in my life, privately or publicly."

Against the abuse of the newspapers he was helpless, he protested, because "no judge would dare to decide against a newspaper. However, if any of you think that arresting one of these newspapers will clear my skirts, I'll arrest one of them tomorrow—no, Monday. I am a victim of their dirty abuse."

"When will Schmitz be back?" shouted a heckler.

There was no reply, but the boss continued to exhort the throng to "give no credence to the lies you see in the newspapers about public officials."

Police Commissioner Hagerty, his face rubicund from the reflections of McGushin's mahogany bar, bawled for three cheers for the boss, and with these cheers the meeting broke up rowdily. Hagerty, Gallagher, and other friends swaggered off with Abe to Tait's restaurant for a celebration.

The honest citizenry was humiliated and disgusted. Heney and Spreckels were deeply alarmed, fearing that the rally organizers' ineptitude might sidetrack their project. With their support, Dwyer hurried off to talk with Langdon again. Then events moved rapidly.

The Union Square fiasco had occurred on Saturday, October 13th.

On the following Thursday, Presiding Judge Graham discharged the current grand jury and prepared to empanel a new one.

Two days later, on Saturday, District Attorney Langdon announced the launching of a searching inquiry into municipal corruption, and appointed Francis J. Heney deputy prosecutor in charge.

On the succeeding Wednesday, October 24th, Heney was sworn, his first official act being to supervise the drawing of a new grand jury. Eighteen names were taken from the box, with the drawing of the nineteenth and final name set over to Friday, October 26th.

But before that could take place and the jury could be constituted —on Thursday, October 25th—Abraham Ruef, acting through Mayor Gallagher and the board of supervisors, suspended Langdon and appointed himself District Attorney of San Francisco, for the purpose, he announced, of prosecuting a real inquiry into alleged municipal grafting, which would be conducted vigorously, without fear or favor or hope of gain.

2   Raising the Whirlwind

Ruef had carried out his nervy coup in the belief that he could head off the crisis, but his effrontery was too extreme for the public to overlook. During the previous two weeks the rumor had spread that the supervisors had been bribed to grant the United Railroads the overhead trolley franchise,—the figure commonly mentioned being $4,000 in cash supposedly handed to each supervisor. Reporters, digging to find whether there was any substance to this rumor, questioned Frank Maestretti, who, vindictively furious at having been booted off the gravy train, was understood to be providing Burns with information. With a roll of his eyes, Maestretti "guessed" that $4,000 figure was about right,—at least, from what he had heard; Maestretti was too crafty to defect openly.

One day Supervisor Wilson (who was running for election as State Railroad Commissioner with Ruef-Railroad backing) came to the boss's office in great agitation. Drawing back the window shade, he pointed to a man on the sidewalk haranguing Myrtile Cerf. The excited speaker was a pugnacious political lawyer named Herbert Choynski, who was at outs with Ruef, and he was declaring loudly that, yes, the supervisors had got $4,000 apiece for that franchise and Abe had knocked down $500,000 to $700,000 for himself. Cerf taunted him with inability to prove the statements, and Choynski bellowed: "No, I'm not able to present legal proof of these charges! If I could, Ruef would have been behind prison bars long ago! And you can go to hell!"

That rumor—$4,000 apiece—would not down. Ruef speculated upon possible squalls ahead, and planned to circumvent the storm.

On the morning of Thursday, October 25th, he started by making good his Union Square promise to "arrest one of these newspaper editors"; he filed suit for criminal libel against Crothers and Older of the *Bulletin* in connection with an article published in that newspaper; Ruef averred this was the first "definite case" he had found.

This article extended the range of the boss's alleged corruption into a new field, namely, the acquisition of an adequate water supply for the city. The *Bulletin* declared that before the earthquake and fire, and on numerous occasions since then, Ruef had conspired with

William S. Tevis, socially impeccable millionaire inheritor of a land barony in California, to dump on San Francisco a new water system supplied from Tevis-owned watersheds around Lake Tahoe in the Sierras. The Bay Cities Water Company was the name of the scheme, and the proposal was to sell the city water rights for $10,000,000, of which $3,000,000 would be profit to the promoters, with Abe getting one-third of this in return for steering the swindle through the city government. This, said the *Bulletin,* despite the fact that engineers reported the Bay Cities group had been willing to sell the same water rights a year previously for a mere $200,000.

For some time there had been on foot a movement to provide the city with abundant pure water by means of a municipally-owned system drawing its supply from the Tuolumne River at Hetch-Hetchy in the Yosemite. James D. Phelan had been a leading advocate of this plan. Three independent engineers were employed by the city to analyse the alternative proposals (Hetch-Hetchy or Bay Cities) and make recommendations in favor of one or the other. After some study they resigned without reporting,—and let it become known that they had quit rather than draw up the report Mayor Schmitz was demanding they write, endorsing the Bay Cities project.

This new exposé the *Bulletin* printed, and Ruef haled the publisher and editor into court, where they were released on the nominal $100 bail customary in such cases.

This matter the boss took care of Thursday forenoon. Then he tackled the more momentous decision of what to do about Langdon and Heney. More accurately, he went through the motions of tackling this conundrum, because he had already decided in his own mind to rid himself of Langdon completely. To this end, he had drawn up an order suspending the District Attorney from office, supported by elaborately detailed charges involving misfeasance, malfeasance, and nonfeasance. These allegations were grouped under twelve headings. It was alleged that Langdon had neglected his duties by willfully absenting himself from the city during the crime wave; that he had been remiss in providing the chief of police with legal guidance; that he had encouraged representatives of German insurance companies to defame the character of Mayor Schmitz; that he had prevented the city from obtaining an adequate water system; that he had turned a blind eye to the raising of large sums of money by unnamed persons for the purpose of slandering the Union Labor Party and its Mayor; and so on.

The real venom in this remarkable document, however, was directed at Heney, for Ruef sensed where the greater danger lay. Langdon's crowning offense, this bill of attainder set forth, was his appointment of "one Francis J. Heney, [who] in a public speech ... aspersed the character and good name of a prominent citizen of this community [Ruef], and stated that he knew him to be corrupt," which action had "brought said Heney into obloquy and contempt." Furthermore, "said Francis J. Heney had publicly assailed the judges of the Superior Court ... as corrupt and crooked, and had denounced all or nearly all of them as dishonest and corrupt." Heney's position as arbitrator in the United Railroads-carmen dispute at the time of his appointment, the bill went on, was prejudicial to the public interest. And Heney, in fact, had "long been possessed of a purpose to effect a personal revenge both against the subject of his false charges [Ruef] and against Eugene E. Schmitz, mayor of San Francisco."

This lengthy accusation, typed and in form, lay on Ruef's desk when Gallagher appeared at the boss's office in answer to a summons on Thursday afternoon. The supervisors were scheduled to meet at half past two o'clock that day, and Gallagher had left word for the members to hang around until he returned. Big Jim found with Ruef an attorney who frequently served as a confidential emissary of Herrin, the Southern Pacific's political manipulator, and by this sign comprehended that powerful forces were in motion.

Abe handed Gallagher the order suspending Langdon. Jim read it through carefully (for typographical errors, he later testified), and at a nod from the boss signed it. Then the matter of who should replace Langdon in the District Attorney's office was broached, and several names were canvassed. The consultation was still going on when Henry Ach walked in at about five o'clock; he was offered the job, but fervently declined. Then Abe broke the news, namely, that he had decided to appoint himself District Attorney. The fact was that he had surreptitiously filed his bond, his oath of office, and his certificate of appointment in the proper municipal bureaus earlier that day, enjoining absolute secrecy,—and the perfection of his power may be judged from the fact that the secret was kept.

At last, at 6:30 P.M., Gallagher showed up at Mowry Hall, where all but two of the supervisors were dismally waiting. With George Keane, they clustered around Jim in a whispering huddle; then the acting mayor took the chair and opened the meeting with routine matters, all the while looking preoccupied. In due course the clerk, Keane, called for "communications from executive officers," followed with, "From his honor, the Mayor," and read Gallagher's suspension of Langdon: the hoarse voice droning through the legal phraseology was the only sound in the hushed room.

Reporters on hand were stunned, and the supervisors looked solemn. Gallagher explained that Langdon was only suspended, not dismissed, and would have an opportunity to appear before the board in his defense one week from that day.

It was Supervisor Sanderson who moved that the Mayor's order be accepted. Wilson seconded, and the chair called for "ayes." There was a ripple of response. Gallagher called for "noes." Dead silence.

Before proceeding to other business, the mayor pro tem interjected briskly: "I have today appointed Mr. A. Ruef District Attorney for the city and county of San Francisco in the place of William L. Langdon, suspended. Mr. Ruef has accepted the appointment."

At that, even the supervisors looked dumfounded; but in a moment expressions of sly satisfaction, mingled with unfeigned alarm, spread over their countenances, for not all of those present possessed the unlimited audacity of their boss. The board speedily adjourned until Monday.

Reporters pounced on the members as they sidled away, but elicited little enlightening comment. Gallagher was intercepted oozing through a side door.

"Didn't Mr. Ruef show some delicacy about accepting the appointment," Big Jim was asked, "when he is supposed to be the chief one against whom the evidence said to be in the District Attorney's office is directed?"

"No," he replied. "I asked Mr. Ruef to take the place. That's all there is to it."

If Gallagher was unperturbed, Supervisor Wilson was not; he hurried out to Bush and Fillmore streets in utmost agitation. His chances of being elected railroad commissioner (a position, it used to be remarked, affording "infinite scope" to an enterprising man)

were being irretrievably jeopardized, he complained; Ruef's action
would be interpreted everywhere as a confession of guilt.

Abe reassured him, saying he took too dark a view.

"You'll feel better after you have something to eat," he advised
sensibly.

Just then Marshall B. Woodworth, a former United States
prosecutor, arrived in response to a summons. Ruef turned to his
secretary and in a tone of curt finality dictated the following note:

Mr. Francis J. Heney: You are hereby removed from the position of
assistant district attorney of the city and county of San Francisco.
(Dated) October 25, 1906.   (Signed) A. Ruef
                                              Acting District Attorney

This letter he gave to his office boy, Charlie Haggerty, with instructions to find Heney and hand it to him personally at once. Then
he appointed Woodworth Heney's successor. This primary official
business disposed of, he set out blithely with Wilson for the popular
Tait's restaurant, re-established since the fire in a mansion on Van
Ness Avenue at Eddy Street.

When the boss drew up in his bright green roadster (nicknamed
the "Green Lizard"), excited reporters crowded around, and he
sketched a statement of policy, ending with this confident prediction:
"I will take possession of the office tomorrow morning, and the first
case I will prosecute as district attorney will be that which I brought
against the proprietor of the *Bulletin* for criminal libel."

He did not deign to name Fremont Older.

3   An Error in Tactics

The public dining room was crowded. Ruef's entrance caused a
flurry, but although a few acquaintances held back, many others
pushed forward to shake the boss's hand. Ruef took his usual table
and ordered the dinner with frogs legs, a dish of which he was fond.
Wilson perked up after the champagne arrived, and soon Henry Ach
joined them. Ruef was in high humor, telling inquirers that he had

"certainly turned the tables" on Langdon and Heney. There was a tense moment when Gillett—the Republican candidate for governor, who owed his nomination to Herrin's corrupt bargain with Ruef—came into the restaurant, saw the boss, and without a word passed along to an upstairs dining room; the election was only a few days away. One leading politician, however, George Knight, who was in the Gillett party, drifted over and shook hands with the beaming Abe.

"I'm the new District Attorney," Ruef chirped, and Knight replied with congratulations that sounded a trifle reserved, but he chatted for a few minutes in a friendly way. Reporters kept intruding, and over the meal Abe expounded his principles and position. This graft investigation, he said, he was convinced was simply a political dodge, designed to influence the election.

"If Mr. Heney and his friends had evidence of graft six months ago," he said with bland sarcasm, "there was nothing to prevent them from producing it then and filing complaints. It is extremely significant that they wait until the eve of the election and then commence the newspaper campaign, although the avenues of the courts have been open to them and are open now. But these gentlemen who have been doing so much talking overplayed their hand.

"I have accepted this office," he went on, "the first political position I ever held in my life, because I believe it to be my duty to an end this constant defamation, and to stop publication of matter detrimental to the city's growth and material interests. I will not stifle the investigation. I intend to have the fullest investigation, and not stop with mere newspaper talk. Certain publications have done more to injure this city in the eyes of prospective investors than even the fire and earthquake."

Yes, he would subpoena Heney, Burns, Spreckels, Phelan, Older, Crothers, all of them, and compel them to produce their evidence before the grand jury.

"Not a single fact will be suppressed," he promised, signaling the waiter to replenish his companions' glasses.

Against Heney, he showed concentrated animus, explaining that he had already dismissed him "because I do not believe that his moral standing is equal to the position. I do not think that a man who has accused practically every judge of the Supreme Court, including the presiding judge who is empaneling the grand jury, of being a crook and corrupt, is the kind of person to appear before the Superior judges in the work of the District Attorney's office. I have denounced Mr. Heney before as a murderer. I shall not at present say anything about the evidence brought to me regarding his relations with school girls, or his improper attempts to fix juries and influence public officials. Mr. Heney is a very erratic man since he took the Keeley cure, and not always responsible for his acts or utterances."

The Keeley cure was a treatment for chronic alcoholism then in vogue.

Charlie Haggerty returned from his mission of notification, and the boss inquired whether he had delivered the letter to Heney personally. Charlie nodded. What did Heney say? Haggerty looked embarrassed, then blurted: "He said he didn't recognize any authority of yours, and you could go to hell."

Ruef waved aside the retort, and when Henry Ach surmised that it might be a good idea to take possession of the District Attorney's office that night, Abe demurred.

"In the morning," he said, beckoning the waiter again.

There was little sleep in San Francisco that night. Already four members of Langdon's staff had descended on the District Attorney's office—two assistant prosecutors, the chief clerk, Al McCabe, and an employee in the bond clerk's office—and had broken open locks and were ransacking desks and files for every paper and letter that might be of help to Ruef. These papers two of the men carried off to a place of security, while the other two bolted the door, nailed fast the windows, and prepared to hold the fort until morning.

Heney received word of Ruef's usurpation at the Bohemian Club, where he was dining with friends. He went immediately to prosecution headquarters, which were in a decayed Victorian dwelling at 1109 Franklin Street, between Geary and O'Farrell, across an alley from the First Unitarian Church, an institution famous in the city. Because the old house was painted dark red, it was popularly christened the Red House, although Heney's enemies sneeringly referred to it as a "house of prosecution."

Heney rapidly assembled Burns and his law partners, Cobb and Dwyer, and called in Hiram Johnson as consultant. A telegram was dispatched to Langdon, who that evening was making a political speech in Woodland, a town twenty miles northwest of Sacramento. Working through the early hours, the group at the Red House drew up an application for a writ of injunction to restrain Ruef from acting as District Attorney, based on the contention that the District Attorney, a county and not a municipal official, represented the people of the entire state and was not amenable to removal by a city executive. At 5 A.M., they awakened Judge James M. Seawell, who signed a temporary restraining order. At 8 o'clock, Presiding Judge Graham assigned the hearing on the order to Seawell's court; and by the time Langdon reached the city, after having ridden a freight train from Woodland to Sacramento to catch the express southbound from Oregon, a policeman and two deputy sheriffs were on guard outside the District Attorney's office and the injunction had been served on Ruef, in bed.

Meanwhile, Fremont Older had received the news by telephone from Rudolph Spreckels; the latter called from his estate at Burlingame, south of San Francisco, to Older in San Rafael, a town about twelve miles north of the Golden Gate, where the Olders had been living since they had been burned out of the Palace Hotel. Older was incredulous, but Spreckels assured him the news was true, and Older spent the rest of the night studying what could be done to offset this unbelievable development.

His competitors, the morning papers, were spreading the full story of the supervisors' ousting of Langdon, coupled with scorching editorial condemnation. Shrieked the *Examiner:*

. . . The last stand of criminals hunted and driven to bay! They will stop at nothing! Langdon and Heney have driven the bribe-seekers and the bribe-takers to a condition of political madness!

The *Call* termed Ruef "district attorney by usurpation, a prosecuting officer to save himself from prosecution," and printed his picture on the front page with the caption: THIS MAN'S HAND GRIPS THE THROAT OF SAN FRANCISCO!

Not to be outdone, the *Chronicle* denounced "an arrogant band of boodlers," saying

... They boldly seek to overturn the law and to block trials that would send them to jail. . . . . As long as they felt safe from prosecution, they jauntily declared they would like to see the accusations fully justified, but the instant they began to realize the possibility of being sent to San Quentin, they turned tail and resorted to a trick which every man with gumption enough to form a judgment in such matters will recognize as a confession of guilt. If Heney is sidetracked, some other method will be resorted to by decent people to get at the scoundrels who have virtually admitted their guilt.

Beside these excoriations the newspapers printed the fighting defiance issued by Heney, who underscored the meaning of this challenge to the law.

The course of acting Mayor Gallagher and the board of supervisors is not only illegal [Heney wrote], but so revolutionary that it may well be doubted whether these unconvicted felons have not gone suddenly insane. History furnishes no parallel to their desperate audacity. Does any reasonable man doubt that this is a complete confession of guilt? We are now facing a graver crisis than we were on the morning of the 18th of April last, with all its horrors. . . . With the fullest sense of the responsibility resting upon me, I name among corrupt and criminal officials Mayor Schmitz, acting Mayor Gallagher, and each and every one of the eighteen members of the board of supervisors, and their boss, Abraham Ruef. I have the evidence to prove these allegations.

All over the city, outbursts like these were being read when the *Bulletin* followed with a call to arms. Older, who had caught that morning's first ferry into the city, got out a special edition embodying (in what for the *Bulletin* was strikingly restrained type) a front-page suggestion that all good citizens gather at Temple Sherith Israel at two o'clock that afternoon, when the nineteenth grand juror was to be chosen, to "uphold Judge Graham's hands in giving us justice." The editorial page of the *Bulletin* was bordered in black, while the indignant phrases glowed phosphorescently:

Nothing in the history of anarchy parallels in cool, deliberate usurpation of authority this latest exhibition of lawlessness in San Francisco. Government is seized to overthrow government, and used as a fort for thieves to batter down the forces of citizenship. The criminals, accused of

felony, have shown their hypocrisy by committing an act of anarchy
which, while it might be tolerated for the time being in San Francisco,
would result in the execution of these men in any government of Europe.

A hundred newsboys ran through the streets giving away twenty
thousand copies of this inflammatory summons; men snatched the
papers from the boys' hands and stared at the word "execution"...

By noon, a throng of angry citizens had assembled at Temple
Israel. Some had ropes in their pockets.

4 "Black Friday"

Impressive, domed, brownstone Temple Sherith Israel was the
largest and handsomest of the city's synagogues left unravaged by the
fire. It had been taken over by the city for emergency housing of
several departments of the Superior Court, on Saturdays and holy
days reverting to religious uses. Still standing and handsome, the building fronts on California Street, its stone steps leading up to wide
portals; on the Webster Street side, the left-hand side as one faces the
main entrance, a smaller door and windows denote the temple
offices, about forty feet back.

The crowd converging at that corner on October 26, 1906, knew
nothing about Judge Seawell's order restraining Ruef; that had happened too late for the morning papers to report. They only knew
that the raffish boss had seized the district attorneyship, and they were
determined to prevent a rape of justice. By one o'clock, several thousand citizens blocked the street, halting traffic; and inside the building
the corridors were so jammed that movement was impossible.

Chief Dinan ordered twenty-five uniformed policemen to the
scene, and every available detective was under instructions to wear
his badge conspicuously. Sheriff Thomas F. O'Neil, a staunch Ruef
man, marshaled all his deputies, calling them in from branch offices
and the county jail, and every city policeman on leave who could be
reached by telephone was hastened back into service.

The crowd—which consisted heavily of doctors, lawyers, educators, merchants, clergymen, leaders in social and professional life—

had not assembled to fight the police. But its temper was riotous. Dinan drove up and commanded that the corridors be cleared, whereupon burly bluecoats hustled and pummeled decent taxpayers into the street, while permitting known hoodlums to remain. Anyone who resisted was cuffed and kneed and slugged.

The crowd pressed stubbornly against the policemen shoving to clear the pavement outside. Rudolph Spreckels was among those ejected, but, white with anger, fought his way back in.

Heney and Langdon arrived and were cheered, the crowd opening a path for them to pass. But Judge Graham, tense and pale, the crowd greeted silently, staring at him as he went inside. Fate had been inconsiderate in alloting a pivotal role in the turbulent drama to this sentimental, seemingly ineffectual judge, who was best known for his soft-hearted and often successful efforts to reconcile married couples bent on divorce. There was also a practical consideration which nobody lost sight of—Judge Graham was up for re-election a few days hence.

Then Ruef drove up in the "Green Lizard," convoyed by a swarm of hangers-on. Two city detectives flanked him, assigned by Dinan that morning. Henry Ach fluttered close by, with Myrtile Cerf, P.H. McCarthy, Police Commissioner Hagerty, and a former prize fighter whose pistol pocket bulged. The crowd booed, then fell ominously silent as the boss stepped down from the car; he paled, but bore himself erect as he entered the building under thousands of hostile eyes.

The room Judge Graham had been using was too small to hold the spectators pushing in, and Judge Frank Dunne hastily adjourned a trial and lent the use of his slightly larger quarters. Langdon and Heney, misdirected by chance or purposely, were forced to elbow their way through the corridors calling for information, jostled and shoved by deputies and bailiffs. The entrance to Dunne's room was guarded by Sheriff O'Neil and the secretary of the police commission, who indicated with a nod or a gesture each person to be admitted, the bailiffs obeying without question. A fat "push" bailiff tried to bar Fremont Older, but the editor was six feet two inches of push himself, and the bailiff yielded. Among hundreds of well-known citizens who were manhandled was Dr. Shadworth S. Beasley, professor of anatomy at

Cooper Medical College; it took six policemen to wrestle him outside to the sidewalk where he shouted that "Ruef ought to be killed!"

In the courtroom, Abe was his chipper self. To indicate that he bore Langdon no grudge, he smilingly shook hands with the District Attorney.

"*De mortuis nil nisi bonum,*" he quipped, implying that Langdon already was politically dead.

At 2:40, Judge Graham took his seat. Observing the proceedings was the State's Attorney General, Ulysses S. Webb, and his presence caused much speculation, for no one knew who or what had prompted him to appear. Under California law, the Attorney General has the power to take a criminal action out of the hands of a District Attorney and prosecute it himself.

Then, with Langdon and Heney standing on one side of the teller box and Ruef standing on the other, the nineteenth grand juror was drawn—Morris A. Levingston, a liquor dealer.

Immediately, Heney moved to examine the grand jurors before they were sworn, in order to discover possible bias, prejudice, or ineligibility. He pointed out that a subsequent showing by a defendant that a juror was prejudiced against him might be grounds for impugning the legality of the grand jury and invalidating indictments.

"I now announce to the court," he said firmly, "that I intend as Assistant District Attorney to present charges of felony and misdemeanor against Abraham Ruef, and I desire to examine the members of this panel to determine if any member entertains bias or prejudice against Abraham Ruef. It would be a farce, it would be adding to the comedy of errors enacted last night, if we have a grand jury which is biased or prejudiced."

Ruef, "as an officer of the court," started to address the Judge, but Heney objected that since he was neither District Attorney nor Acting District Attorney, he should not intrude.

"I speak as a member of the bar," the boss countered, and Judge Graham permitted him to continue on that footing.

No legal sanction existed for the procedure Heney proposed, Ruef contended; in fact, such action itself might invalidate the grand jury.

"This gentleman," he observed, and then sarcastically retrieved the slip. "I wish to withdraw the word 'gentleman' as applied to him; it was uttered without thinking. This is an evident attempt to render this grand jury invalid. This person, who has launched his abuse in kept newspapers, would make the grand jury illegal so that nothing would come of any indictments. The propositions made by this person are in line with his general conduct of obtaining newspaper notoriety by making statements which will not be borne out by the events. The person whom he has named as fated for an investigation here and now defies him to produce any evidence of any offense, morally or legally, and defies him to produce any evidence in open court, instead of going before a tutored grand jury to get an indictment. As a private citizen of this community, I protest against the paid hireling of private interests, with a fund of $100,000 at his back, packing juries for the purpose of prosecuting public officials."

Outside the temple the crowd milled and shouted, uninformed as to what was happening. On the Webster Street side was a strip of grass between the sidewalk and the building, and here clustered a score of influential men, glaring through the window at the white-faced Judge. The thought flashed through Older's mind that the line looked "like a first night at the opera," so many prominent faces were in it, and Heney later avowed that "that crowd put the fear of God into that judge."

Attorney General Webb gave his opinion that he knew of no law providing for the examination Heney proposed, but neither did he know of any statute forbidding it, and he suggested that Graham delay empaneling the grand jury until the point was settled. Two attorneys representing the Bar Association seconded this suggestion, and the grand jurors were dismissed while the lawyers argued.

Heney cited precedents to support his demand to examine the jurors before they were sworn.

"Suppose the foreman of the grand jury is biased or prejudiced," he said. "Does it require any argument that now is the time to make this examination, instead of waiting until we have presented our evidence to the jury? Shall we first give those whom we accuse time to bribe witnesses or get them out of the country? Shall we let the defendant come in and quash the indictment, if there has been any bias or prejudice, and thus protect himself against prosecution?"

As counselor for Ruef, Henry Ach suggested that the best solution

might be for Heney, Webb, and himself jointly to submit to the State
Supreme Court the question of whether Langdon or Ruef was the
District Attorney. Heney replied that it was his policy as prosecutor
"to have no conferences, treaties, or alliances with persons charged
with crime, or with their attorneys."

Turning to the bench, he cried passionately: "After the miserable
fiasco of last night, what more important duty for this court to perform than immediately to say that the law is more powerful than
any man or set of men in San Francisco? It is said that we do not know
all the matters which will come before the grand jury." His voice
swelled to a roar. "What has that got to do with it? We do know what
will be put before the grand jury the first hour it meets—and that
relates to Abraham Ruef!"

The packed courtroom, despite the glowering heelers, broke into
frenzied applause, and the shout was taken up by the crowd outside.
Judge Graham hastily adjourned court until Monday.

Heney and Langdon emerged from the building to a bedlam of
triumph. Speeches were demanded, but Heney shook his head. Standing behind him on the synagogue steps, Spreckels urged him to say
something; finally the cocky little prosecutor called out, with a grin:
"In the future I will make my speeches in court, gentlemen!"

Some of the mob pelted after Langdon's departing automobile,
but a dense mass remained around the Webster Street door, waiting
for Ruef. At last the boss appeared, looking pale and fatigued. Although he was preceded by Chief Dinan and the two detective bodyguards, the throng surged forward, and were fought back by the
police, using clubs and pistol butts. Slowly the detectives inched the
frightened boss along Webster Street toward California, where his
car was parked. As Ruef passed, Dr. Beasley lunged and shrieked,
"Hang him from the lamppost!" Dinan and the detectives sprang on
the Doctor and dragged him, struggling, up the street. A group of
Cooper medical students tried to rescue him, but they were clubbed
back, and Beasley was hauled to jail and thrown into the drunk tank.
His students bailed him out that evening.

Tenderloin bruisers wearing brass knuckles closed in behind Ruef
and held off the crowd. "Rockrollers" gripped revolvers visible

in their pockets and threatened to shoot. Standing on an automobile
a block away, Cora Older saw Ruef go down, and a man near her
cried, "They've lynched him!" She turned away, sickened.

But by push and pull the policemen succeeded in reaching the
"Green Lizard" and hoisted Abe aboard, while a cordon of rounders
yelled "Speech!" Ruef was too shaken to muster more than a pallid
smile; he sat quivering with fright until the car started with a jerk
and moved swiftly down California Street, outdistancing a hundred
men sprinting behind it.

California was aroused as it had not been since '56.

Chairman Doble of the abortive Committee of 100 declared: "I
regard the spectacle of Abe Ruef attempting to act as his own prosecutor one of the most shameful that the people of any city have ever
been called upon to behold."

Archbishop Montgomery, Roman Catholic prelate, shook his head
in sorrow: "We are making a rather ugly confession of our civic sins.
We are losing the respect of those who came to our aid so generously
in our hour of need."

Raphael Weill, merchant, clubman, and *bon vivant,* a surviving
member of the Vigilance Committee of 1856, spoke with the fervor
of his youth: "This is not a time for words, it is a time for action!
If necessary, we will jump the law to attain justice! If Abe Ruef and
his gang intend to seize the whole machinery of the law, and ad-
minister the law as they please, the honest men of San Francisco
must turn them out. It is no time for compromise, no time for parley.
Everything, if necessary, must be sacrificed to redeem the city from
this accursed deal. Turn the gang out!"

Newspapers vied in denouncing the spectacle of "Ruef heelers
with their hands on their pistols threatening to shoot down citizens
of the city of San Francisco who would dare to approach too near the
sacred person of their Tenderloin idol." Politicians scurried for cover.
In Fresno, candidate Gillett hastened to put himself on record: "I
am utterly opposed to the methods of Ruef and Gallagher. Let the
guilty be punished." Back-country journals supporting Gillett broke
into a rash of "explanations," telling the "truth" about that Santa
Cruz photograph with Gillett's hand resting so fraternally on Ruef's

shoulder: it signified nothing politically, the explanations read, it was simply a gesture among friends. And the Los Angeles *Times,* partial to the Republican candidate, analyzed the convention vote that had nominated Gillett for governor and mathematically "proved" that Gillett would have won the nomination without the aid of a single vote from Ruef. "God help San Francisco, and God deliver the rest of us!" piously intoned the *Times.*

By evening, Ruef had regained his aplomb and was assuring reporters that when he left the Temple he had heard some cheering, but no hooting.

"I understand that Langdon telephoned to the medical boys to come over, and some from Hastings [law school] may have made some little disturbance. You know what college boys are."

He still was District Attorney, he insisted, Judge Seawell merely having enjoined him from exercising the office, and the injunction would of course be resisted in the hearing. However, he said he had decided not to prosecute the graft investigation himself; the public, in its present frame of mind, would not have confidence in it if he were in charge. Instead, his intention was to ask the twelve Superior Court judges to name an outstanding man to act as special prosecutor.

"I didn't assume the office, as Heney did, to gratify a personal, vindictive revenge," he sneered. "Before I get through with Mr. Heney, the people of this city will know more about him than they do now." His tone grew waspish with hatred. "I'll have him where he will wish he didn't start this!"

But the smile soon returned. He was toying with a telegram, which upon request he read aloud:

A. RUEF, SAN FRANCISCO: I HAVE JUST LEARNED OF THAT VILE, DAMNABLE, AND CROOKED MOVE OF YOURS. IF YOU GET HOLD OF THE GRAND JURY, SUBPOENA ME AND I WILL TESTIFY. T.P. ANDREWS

"That," said Ruef, "is from the foreman of the grand jury who put in months and spent thousands of dollars trying to trap me and gave it up as a bad job. I sent him this reply":

T.P. ANDREWS, SAN MATEO: NO CONTEMPTIBLE CUR LIKE
YOU COULD GIVE ANY EVIDENCE THAT ANY HONEST OR
SELF-RESPECTING MAN WOULD BELIEVE.

In San Francisco, that day was long remembered as "Black
Friday."

And in London, Mayor Schmitz read cabled accounts of the
turbulent events and went white. William J. Burns knew about
that pallor at once, for unknown to the Mayor, Burns's son was
shadowing Eugene every step of the journey.

5   Skirmishes and Avowals

On Monday, forty uniformed police under two captains cleared
the halls of Temple Israel before the arrival of Judge Graham to
hand down his decision on examining the grand jurors. Again, respectable citizens were hustled out, while thugs remained; even
attorneys having business in other courts were roughed up by deputies.
The sidewalk crowd was kept small by mounted officers; and to the
courtroom itself, only the principals and press observers were admitted.

Using precise language, Judge Graham ruled that the District
Attorney was entitled to examine prospective grand jurors, and that
Langdon, as District Attorney *de facto,* therefore might conduct the
examination either directly or through his assistants.

Ruef had shown up with additional counsel: besides Ach, Samuel
M. Shortridge and Marshall Woodworth, Heney's putative successor.
Shortridge requested the court's permission to present further arguments against the legality of the examination, and when Heney objected to this intrusion by counsel representing Ruef, Shortridge
posited unctuously that he was there as *amicus curiae,* discharging a
duty to make sure that the proceedings were without flaw. A "very
curious friend of the court," Heney could not help grinning, and
Judge Graham allowed Shortridge to make his argument. With
preternatural solemnity, the lawyer thereupon cited so many authorities the Judge was obliged to recess in order to read them all. Then
he affirmed his ruling, begging Shortridge to bother with no more

citations, and the examination of the jurors by Heney and Ruef's representatives began. The prosecution had won this round.

When the crowd outside heard that Graham had recognized Langdon, men danced for joy and slapped each other on the back like children. Heney and Langdon were received with cheers, and Heney radiantly announced: "We have won a sweeping victory. The people of San Francisco should honor Judge Graham for the stand he has taken."

Groans and hisses sped the departing Ruef, who ignored the demonstrators while press photographers snapped a picture of him and his friends in his automobile.

That day, Attorney General Webb made known that he would not intervene unless Heney should be disqualified, in which event he would appoint Heney to his own staff to continue the prosecution of grafters. Everybody, of course, was keeping a weather eye on the election a few days hence.

The boss had been disappointed by Judge Graham's prompt ruling; he had expected the Judge to hold off until after the election. Now Abe set about organizing popular support. In spite of his record, Ruef retained a certain amount of popularity; San Franciscans were volatile, easily distracted, individually self-centered to an unusual degree; it was a city of individualists. While they held their community in genuine affection, like other affectionate offspring they could be careless of her interests. Ruef long had cultivated the influential element by the astute use of favors; he found it flattering to be solicited by big men, and especially since the fire he had been helpful to many a hard-pressed businessman.

This surface popularity had misled him into believing he could bluff or jolly the people into accepting him as District Attorney, and the hatred evinced on "Black Friday" had shocked his self-esteem. To restore the façade of popular acclaim, on the evening before Judge Graham ruled, the boss appeared at a labor rally and listened approvingly while union bosses vilified Langdon, Heney, and the newspapers, praising Ruef and Schmitz.

The next Wednesday he spoke at an anti-prosecution rally at Dreamland Rink, where resolutions were voted to form a permanent

Municipal League "along the lines of New York's Tammany Hall";
its avowed purpose being to "repel libels and abuses and to wipe out
and destroy the influence of the press of San Francisco and make it
possible for citizens to live without their private lives being assailed
and laid open." Ruef promised to sign up twenty-five thousand members, fifty thousand if necessary.

"Some people do not know that the statements of these lying
newspapers are false," he said earnestly. "It is our duty to organize a
missionary league to go to these people and convert them."

On Saturday, the boss spoke for an hour and a quarter at still
another meeting, at which Supervisor Coleman presided, and reporters
came away with the feeling that Heney had been saved from more
devastating abuse "only by the limitations of the English language."

"Do you think it a brave and politic thing," asked Ruef in accents
of martyrdom, "for one little man to stand here and speak the truth
in the face of the four combined newspapers of this city?"

Abe's foes, however, were equally vocal. Organized labor did not
follow its bellwethers unanimously, the bricklayers, sheet metal
workers, sailors, plumbers, hoisting engineers, and electrical workers
voting confidence in the graft prosecution. At Stanford University,
Phelan was cheered resoundingly when he predicted the return of
vigilantes if the grafters were not driven out quickly. At an election
rally in Oakland, Ruef's name was hissed. And Heney reiterated
tirelessly that nothing would deter him from hunting down municipal
corruptionists— "the high as well as the low, and especially the high."

"It is far more dangerous to the community to give a bribe than to
take one," he told students at the University of California, "because
a poor man often is tempted by his necessities, while a bribe-giver is
criminally vicious."

When he observed that certain supervisors, who a short while
before had been working for $15 and $20 a week, were buying real
estate and riding in automobiles (motorcars being then a perquisite of
the rich), the city fathers protested that they had made their money
long previously, and had never infringed a frangible law or done
aught to deserve such horrid, nasty innuendoes. Their warblings cas-
caded in octaves of shivering denials.

But the discordancy of these disavowals with the hang-dog airs of
some of the prime suspects was not lost upon press or public. As one

newspaper observed, the supervisors seemed to be attributing to themselves "the utmost equanimity, while displaying the most apprehensive
disquietude.... Gallagher, in great perturbation, avers that he views
the approaching storm with the calm that belongs only to the man
whose chaste rectitude leaves him nothing to fear. Chief Dinan says his
conscience is clear. Boxton, Rea, Kelly, Nicholas, all take the stand
of injured innocence."

The denials of wrongdoing were certainly categorical.

"Heney is an unconscionable, unqualified, and scoundrelly liar,"
declared grocer Harrigan. Sam Davis was hurt: "It is hard to have
insinuations cast at you." And Coffey, the hack driver, stated that
investigation of his official actions would give him supreme pleasure.

Supervisor Sanderson, one of the few members of the board who
sometimes voted "no" and seldom attended the Sunday caucuses,
merely shrugged. Andy Wilson, taken up with his election prospects,
sneered that it looked like a trick to win votes, and added: "I never
took a dishonest dollar in my life."

"These charges are entirely false; there has never been any grafting
going on," was the rejoinder of George Duffey, the new president of
the board of public works, and round-faced Max Mamlock offered his
entire life as an open book wherein one might read the truth of his
assertion that "I never received a dollar wrongfully or did anything
that I am ashamed of. I do not think it worth my while to think about
this investigation."

Shoemaker Walsh's reaction: "I can hold up my head." But game-
cock Tom Lonergan was all for pursuing the matter to a knockdown
finish. "Let's get to the bottom of this thing!" he cried to the boys in
McGushin's saloon. "These cracks about graft have been made right
along; they ought to be proved or unproved!" Pat agreed across the
bar: "The more they investigate, the better I like it."

"Gassy" Kelly wanted to place himself on record: "I never accepted money or other consideration for any vote of mine." And
Supervisor Phillips shouted at a prying reporter: "Heney's charges
are simply outrageous! I don't know of a single dollar of graft that
has found its way into the pocket of a supervisor!"

Big Jim Gallagher was genial in his disclaimers of turpitude.
When a rumor circulated that Ruef was contemplating skipping out
clandestinely for Honduras, the acting mayor was asked whether he

had his bags packed, too. He responded with a jovial laugh: "I like San Francisco to her last ruin too well to leave! I have nothing to hide in this investigation. If there is graft in this administration, it is high time it was exposed, and I for one am glad this matter came up."

These declarations of official righteousness were embalmed in an affidavit which the supervisors filed in the hearing held by Judge Seawell to determine whether he should make his restraining order against Ruef permanent. This affidavit was signed by sixteen supervisors, and a similar attestation was submitted on behalf of Ruef. One tongue-in-cheek reporter described these documents as setting forth that the signers, "individually and collectively, are truly good in their own eyes and have been all their lives; and they want this thoroughly understood, because they repeat their assertions in four or five different ways."

"This affiant has never committed a felony of any kind or character, and has never been a party thereto," the affidavit stated, and went on to brand "all charges, assertions, and innuendoes" to the contrary "absolutely untrue and false."

Nevertheless, Judge Seawell ruled that the city charter gave the Mayor no authority to remove the District Attorney, and he made his injunction against Ruef's assuming that office permanent. In time he added another order, forbidding the board of supervisors from attempting to interfere with Langdon.

The prosecution had won another vital round.

Meanwhile, Heney continued to lay bare the boss's craftiness. Ruef had compelled the supervisors to sign the "purity affidavit," said Heney, in order to hold over them the threat of perjury indictments, should they be tempted to turn honest and tell the truth; but the trick would not work, because of legal technicalities. Heney stressed that Abe was fighting for time until the election, hoping to strengthen his hold on the courts.

The closing stages of the political campaign, in fact, were thoroughly imbrued with the graft issue, the fiercest contest centering around Ruef's attempt to elect two more Superior Court judges— Charles T. Conlan and Edmund P. Mogan—both notorious tools of the boss. Heney pointed out the far-reaching danger. Under the pre-

"HE'S MINE."

This cartoon by Tad (T.A. Dorgan, who was to become one of the most famous newspaper cartoonist of his day) was originally run in the San Francisco *Evening Bulletin* during the 1903 mayoral campaign, and was republished in the 1905 campaign with a new caption, "He's Mine." A winking Abe Ruef holds the key to the cage, which is shaped like the dome of the old San Francisco City Hall; the captured bird is Schmitz.

Eugene Edwards Schmitz–the "Handsome Gene" of an early campaign photo–who, as president of the musician's union, showed the bearing and poise that made Ruef tap him for election to City Hall.

Ruef, shortly after his arrest, arriving at Temple Sherith Israel for a trial session in a former classroom in the Temple School. Abe is dapper and confident as he greets well-wishers with a bright smile.

Prosecutor Francis J. Heney and William Burns *(above, right)* in court in 1908.

James D. Phelan *(below, left),* one of the spearheads of the graft prosecution, photographed *circa* 1908.

Rudolph Spreckels *(below, right)* in 1906. He was the man who guaranteed —and paid—the prosecution's expenses.

Fremont Older, as he looked around 1908. Older was the crusading editor of the *Bulletin,* the paper with the "Largest Circulation of Any Afternoon Newspaper West of Chicago."

Hiram W. Johnson *(left),* specially retained by the State, and District Attorney William L. Langdon arrive for trial preliminaries on behalf of the prosecution.

"OUR MAYOR."

Older was the first of the town's newspapermen to fight the rising graft at City Hall. This cartoon, which he believed would be devastating, failed to arouse his readers,—one reason being that it showed the boss smoking a fat cigar and sporting loud checks, while everybody in San Francisco knew that abstemious little Abe never smoked, and dressed very conservatively.

Ruef speaking at the Committee of One Hundred meeting in Union Square on October 13, 1906. The rally was called to take action against Ruef, but Abe captured it.

On to Washington (1907), where Mayor Schmitz *(center)* and members of the board of education arrived to receive a dressing down from President Theodore Roosevelt for San Francisco's segregation of Japanese children in one school for "Orientals": *(from left)* Alfred Roncovieri, board member; Thomas F. Boyle, Schmitz protégé and member of the board; Schmitz; Representative Julius Kahn, San Francisco Congressman who was trying to smooth over a sticky situation; S. F. Walsh, board member.

The convivial photo taken during the Santa Cruz Republican convention of September, 1906. Later designated "The Shame of California," the celebrators are *(seated)* Ruef and Major Frank McLaughlin, host; *(standing, left to right)* Justice Frederick Henshaw; Rudolph Herold, Southern Pacific lobbyist; J. W. McKinley, head of Southern Pacific's law department in Los Angeles; George S. Hatton, Southern Pacific lobbyist; James N. Gillett, nominee for governor; Walter F. Parker, Southern California political boss; Warren R. Porter, nominee for lieutenant-governor; Judge F. H. Kerrigan, appeals court nominee; Congressman Joseph R. Knowland.

The jury that convicted Mayor Schmitz, seated in the jury box at the Bush Street Temple where his trial was held.

Above: Patrick Calhoun, president of United Railroads, and his wife, arriving for his trial with a carful of lawyers. Looking back from the front seat is Thornwell Mullally, Calhoun's assistant, who was indicted with him for bribery.

Below, left: William M. Abbott, Ford's assistant on the United Railroads legal staff, shown as he looked in 1907. Abbott had carried part of the trolley bribe money from the United States Mint, for which he was indicted with Ford and Calhoun, though never tried.

Below, right: Louis Glass, Pacific States Telephone Company executive, convicted in 1907 of bribing the supervisors. This picture was taken at the time of his trial. Glass was confined in the county jail at Ingleside, but was later freed by Judge Lawlor.

Tirey L. Ford, chief counsel of the United Railroads, arriving for his first trial. Ruef was sent to prison for taking $200,000 from Ford to bribe the supervisors, but Ford was acquitted on the same charge. While Ruef sweated out his sentence in prison, Ford continued to live in a handsome residence in the most fashionable section of the city. Ford was also a member of the board of prison directors while Abe was a prisoner in San Quentin.

Samuel Shortridge, the ever-ready orator, as he looked in 1906. He was Abe Ruef's attorney, and afterward a United States Senator.

Abe's "prison" room was the one with the bay window on the first floor. In the basement was Schmitz's den, where he had a row with Police Commissioner Reagan at the time of the French restaurants gouge.

Abe and Elisor Biggy in the "parlor prison" at 2849 Fillmore. Abe, sitting next to the bed, reads a light novel. The serious-minded Biggy slept on a cot in the same room. The bedroom had been Schmitz's, with the plush-lined "boodle box" under his bed.

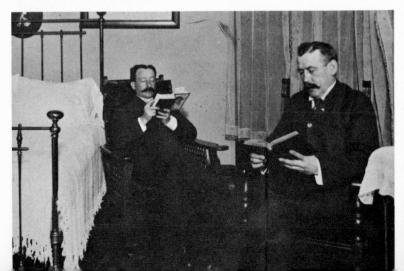

Judge Frank H. Dunne, who heard Ruef's guilty plea in the French restaurants case and who sentenced Schmitz.

Judge William P. Lawlor, who tried Abe Ruef twice—and sentenced him.

RUNNING FOR MAYOR

Above, left: Schmitz conferring with a lawyer during his trial before Superior Court Judge Dunne. It was not until after he had been sentenced to five years in prison that Schmitz was replaced as Mayor of San Francisco.

Above, right: A 1907 election campaign cartoon from the San Francisco *Chronicle.* Drawn by Bud Fisher, Schmitz is shown carrying "Mac" (really "Pin Head" McCarthy), the nominee of the Union Labor Party, hand-picked by Schmitz.

Below: Ruef enters the paddy wagon for his transfer to the county jail in 1908, where he was placed for his own safety, away from the outraged citizens of San Francisco.

Schmitz in the twenties—after he had shaved off his famous beard and mustache,—and dropped from public recognition. Even on the street he was seldom noticed. He tried to start a boom for himself for governor, but found no backing; then he wanted to run for mayor. But without his beard, he was dead politically, though he never discarded another political trademark, his black wideawake hat, a heritage from his days as a fiddler.

Abe Ruef penning his memoirs for the San Francisco *Bulletin* in 1912, when
Fremont Older led a campaign to get him paroled. Aged, balding, and
visibly affected by his imprisonment and disgrace, Abe posed for the paper,
which used the picture to illustrate the series in which Abe promised to tell
all, spare no one,—but didn't.

vailing system, the office of presiding judge of the Superior Court
rotated among the twelve members of that bench; and should Conlan
and Mogan be elected, in time each would become presiding judge,
and in that capacity would control the assignment of cases for trial and
also empanel grand juries. The threat was so grave that the San Francisco Bar Association mailed postcards to every voter on the registra-
tion lists, explaining how, on the new voting machines, they could cut
out Conlan and Mogan and still cast votes for other candidates; the
voting machine confusion was compounded by a trick which had
placed the names of the two disputed nominees on all three party
tickets,—Republican, Democratic, and Union Labor.

Incumbent judges seeking re-election were J. V. Coffey, Thomas
F. Graham, John A. Hosmer, and William P. Lawlor, the judge who
had dared to send two of Ruef's ballot box stuffers to prison. Against
Lawlor, the boss massed all his strength. In addition, Superior Judge
Carroll Cook was seeking a place on the appellate bench, an effrontery
so shocking to a Catholic priest whose parish abutted the Barbary
Coast that he denounced the jurist from the pulpit as having for years
"prostituted his official powers to the protection of the proprietors,
patrons, and inmates of loathsome brothels." Cook was hand in glove
with Ruef.

On November 6th the city voted, and the results brought little
comfort to the beleaguered boss. Lawlor was re-elected, Graham also.
Carroll Cook was defeated for the Court of Appeals, Conlan was
snowed under, and Mogan just squeaked past the wire, unseating
Judge Hosmer. But Ruef did elect all except five of San Francisco's
representation in the State Legislature, and George Keane, clerk of
the board of supervisors, was elected to the State Senate. Andy Wilson,
with a boost from the Railroad, made the grade to the State Railroad
Commission. Gillett was elected Governor.

Despite his rebuffs at home, Ruef held a strong hand at Sacramento, the capital, which might be played advantageously later.

Three days after the election, the new grand jurors were sworn
and elected Bartley P. Oliver their foreman. After considerable
search, a meeting place was found for them in a converted dwelling
on the corner of Geary and Gough streets, just around the corner
from Heney's offices in the Red House; the grand jury shared the
building with the temporarily displaced Native Sons of the Golden

West and Phelan's disaster relief committee. Heney, his eyes glinting with the joy of battle, began marshaling his evidence.

"All we ask the public at this time," he said, "is to be patient. We will put Ruef and his grafting allies where they belong."

6 "A Day to Be Remembered"

The Schmitz administration forces remained arrogant in spite of some supervisors' inward quakings and the grand jury's activity. The Sunday night caucuses were surrounded with greater secretiveness; shifted from the Mayor's office to Hamilton Hall, they were held behind guarded, locked doors, with every approach sealed off. The supervisors repeatedly denied that the graft investigation was discussed; all they talked about in the hush-hush sessions, they averred, was building more schoolhouses and the new hospital and other delightful civic projects.

Word did seep through the double-barred doors that a fresh legal assault on Heney was projected: the supervisors would try to oust him for supposedly taking private pay while acting as Assistant District Attorney, the Spreckels guarantee fund being termed a contravention of the charter. This attack failed to materialize, but Heney set the record straight in the most candid way.

"I have not received one cent for my services in this investigation and I do not want or expect to receive any money," he said. "Men like Ruef may not be able to understand my motive in entering this work. I felt, as a citizen of San Francisco, that someone should go at the disgraceful conditions here in a systematic manner and bring about a change. I am not, never have been, anxious to be rich. I am quite well fixed, have a good income, and am content. I am not looking for money. Neither do I want political position. If I were after money, I could make at least four times my highest income in any year by going to New York. I didn't go because I am resolved to live and die in California. I have lived here most of my life, and when I can strike a blow for San Francisco, I am going to strike it. I feel perfectly independent—and if I think I ought to say or do something, I should like to see anyone who can stop me."

He did not add, nor did the public learn until much later, that he was not touching the salary to which he was entitled as an Assistant District Attorney. Langdon's staff was small, the number of his assistants limited by law, and in order to create a vacancy which Heney could fill, one of the deputy prosecutors, Robert Duke, generously resigned; but at Heney's instance, the $300 a month salary carried by the post continued to be paid to Duke.

Heney now reckoned that a year would be required to clean up the situation, and he was prepared to give that much time to it. About his next move he refused to talk.

"The public must use common sense and wait," he snapped. "Why should I come out and disclose my evidence, and allow Ruef to spirit away witnesses, or have them rapped over the head some night? Ruef has harped on the fact that although the Andrews grand jury tried its best to secure an indictment, none was ever brought. I state emphatically that I know not only indictments, but convictions, could have been brought in several cases from the evidence produced, if Byington [the former District Attorney] had not been afraid." Then he grinned sarcastically. "With the detective bureau, the sheriff's office, and at least a majority of the police force behind him, Ruef hasn't a thing to fear—except honest evidence."

The talk in the streets was that Abe Ruef was too smart to get caught. But Heney was confident.

"I realize that my reputation is at stake," he conceded cheerfully. "I appreciated when I went into this that if I failed, I would be a dead one. A defeat for me would be complete. I am not giving out any false alarms."

B.P. Oliver, the grand jury foreman, a plain-spoken, quiet real-estate broker, also gave assurance that he meant business.

"I am a citizen of San Francisco," he said. "It is my birthplace, and I have lived here all my life, fifty-two years. Her best interests are of the first importance in my eyes, and I shall not shirk any duty that is in her welfare. Until our work is finished, I shall devote my entire time to it. My business will have to do without me."

He did not disclose that personally he was inclined to doubt the substantiality of many of the charges aimed at Ruef and Schmitz; much of the furor was newspaper exaggeration, he believed. He wanted to be shown.

On November 14th, the grand jurors assembled at ten o'clock in the morning. They remained in session until seven o'clock that evening, pausing only for lunch. All that day Burns herded to Gough and Geary streets a parade of surly, resentful, frightened witnesses; they stood on the stairways and in the halls of the old house, truculent and snarling, awaiting their turns to be questioned. Among them were noticed the proprietors of several French restaurants,—Antonio B. Blanco of the New Poodle Dog; N. Max Adler of the Bay State; Joseph Malfanti of Delmonico's; Jean Loupy of Ruef's favorite Pup, now a dreary heap of rubble; Edward Marchand of Marchand's; and Stanislaus Constantini of Tortoni's. They looked anxious and depressed.

Five former police commissioners also passed into the grand jury's room,—Howell, Hutton, Reagan, Drinkhouse, and Poheim. Howell had been a Phelan holdover for three years under Schmitz. Hutton was the commissioner fired for turpitude, to end the French restaurants license deadlock. Reagan, Drinkhouse, Poheim all had got the boot and were inimical to the boss and Schmitz, Reagan having stated to anyone who would listen: "I know Schmitz is a grafter, and I am going to help put him in San Quentin."

About the testimony, utmost secrecy was maintained. Hutton alone revealed that he had told the grand jurors about the list of saloon applications the police commission received regularly from Schmitz's office, with the names of those who were to get licenses checked, the others to be kept dangling until they saw "the right party."

On November 15th the grand jury voted indictments,—five jointly against Abraham Ruef and Eugene E. Schmitz for extorting money from the city's fancy assignation houses. It was charged specifically that they had extorted $1,000 and $1,175 from Blanco of the New Poodle Dog, the same sums from Malfanti of Delmonico's, and $1,000 from Pierre Priet (deceased) of Marchand's. Superior Judge Frank J. Murasky, acting as presiding judge during the absence on vacation of Judge Graham, set bond of $10,000 on each count, a total of $50,000 for each defendant.

It was just one year since Heney had denounced Abe Ruef in Mechanics Pavilion. The hall had vanished in the holocaust, but Heney was redeeming his pledge.

What evidence had impelled the grand jury to its action? Although the prosecution refused to show its hand, the public quickly learned in outline the behind-the-scenes events.

As early as March, 1904, Police Commissioner Hutton had embarked on a personal campaign to close the French restaurants. His motives were obscure. He termed the places immoral and a discredit to the city, and he tried to persuade his three fellow commissioners to refuse further renewals of the restaurant liquor licenses. In this he failed, although he did bring about a police commission inquiry into the restaurants, which attracted much salacious publicity.

At about the same time, Mayor Schmitz called Commissioner Tom Reagan to City Hall and discussed the restaurants, saying they ought to be closed, they were all bad. What about the Pup, asked honest pavior Reagan; the boss ate there nightly. The Pup was bad, too, the Mayor answered, although not as bad as the others. Schmitz urged Reagan to investigate for himself, and Tom visited the New Poodle Dog officially. He had never been in a French restaurant before. He arrived at dinnertime, was shown over the house most politely, and found everything orderly. He so reported to Schmitz, who suggested that he had gone there at the wrong hour; he should try, say, at midnight, and he earnestly counseled Reagan to support Hutton in disapproving the license extensions: two votes would be enough to settle the matter. Reagan yielded to the Mayor's persuasion.

Then Tortoni's became embroiled in a dispute with the cooks and waiters union, and in revenge the union sent two stool pigeons with prostitutes to the place, where they were conveniently discovered cavorting in a private room when the police broke in. Under pressure from the union, the commissioners revoked Tortoni's license, forcing the place to close.

The other restaurant owners took alarm, and alarm became panic when hearings on their renewal applications were postponed again and again and their lawyers were not permitted even to plead in their behalf. Early in January, 1905, the attorney for Max Adler of the Bay State warned that it looked like life or death for Adler's business; "the only man who can help you is Mr. Ruef." The restaurant men had sunk much money in their places—Blanco had put $200,000 into the New Poodle Dog, and Malfanti and his partners $400,000 into Delmonico's—and Adler decided to call on Loupy for advice.

The Pup was just across Stockton Street from the Bay State, and Adler had seen Abe Ruef and his hangers-on congregating there nightly.

After Adler's call, Loupy telephoned to Ruef, and the boss consented to become attorney for the restaurants for an annual fee of $7,000, this to be for two years, payable in cash, in advance. Negotiations scaled this down to $5,000 a year. The anxious proprietors made up a purse among them and delegated Pierre Priet to transmit it to the boss. Priet, suspecting that Loupy might be cutting himself in for a commission, took the money for the first year directly to Ruef's office. There, on January 6, 1905, Priet signed a two-year contract which Ruef had drawn up in the name of the French Restaurant Keepers Association of San Francisco; although he signed as president, Priet had never heard of the organization, nor had anybody else.

It was January 7th when Fremont Older found Pierre blissfully relieved of his worries, and that afternoon the final edition of the *Bulletin* carried the accusation that Ruef had bled the restaurants for a "lawyer's fee" of $10,000, and challenged the boss to appear on their behalf before the police commissioners. Ruef took the dare, and on January 18th obtained a two-week stay of final action.

At this point, Mayor Schmitz began singing a different tune to Tom Reagan, urging him to reverse himself and vote to renew the restaurants' licenses. Reagan refused to stultify himself in this manner, and Schmitz called him around to his home and fired a battery of arguments—politics, personal friendship, loyalty to the administration. He blustered and banged the table, passed out whisky and cigars, shouted about "ingratitude"; but Reagan remained obdurate: he wouldn't make himself look foolish by switching his vote in a hurry, he said. Commissioners Drinkhouse and Poheim joined the conference; they were willing to vote for the licenses; but not Tom, and his vote with Hutton's blocked favorable action. Finally Schmitz exclaimed, "Then I'll throw Hutton out!"

A few days later Hutton was dismissed with savage fanfare, the Mayor's notification citing names, addresses, and times in regard to Hutton's alleged consorting with immoral women and also the name of the unmarried woman with whom Hutton was living.

(That letter perished in the great fire, to the cleansing of the official archives of San Francisco.)

On January 28th the commission reconvened, and after Ruef

trotted out his dusted-off set of regulations, the three commissioners (the vacancy left by Hutton had not been filled) voted, two to one, to restore the licenses; Reagan was the stubborn dissenter.

That, in essence, was the evidence upon which the grand jury indicted Ruef and Schmitz for extortion. It had not been procured easily: witnesses were unfriendly, records disappeared, lawyers refused to talk, Adler and Loupy denied they had paid Ruef anything. Adler was indicted for perjury; Loupy, on Ruef's advice, requested and received permission to correct his testimony, and then confessed that, in return for his exertions in the license crisis, he had been let off with a payment to the boss of only $300. The entire "fee," it was said, Ruef had divided with Mayor Schmitz.

Ruef accepted his indictment with outward equanimity. He made no secret of having taken a fee from the French restaurant owners, but stressed that he had accepted it only after the *Bulletin* dared him to.

"The whole thing is absurd," he said. "I was simply acting in the relation of an attorney to a client. I took a fee for rendering legal services, according to the terms of a written contract with the French Restaurant Keepers Association, a copy of which I have in my possession. If it is extortion for an attorney to accept a fee from his client, we all might as well go out of business. I accepted the employment because of the flaunting challenge of a hostile and disreputable newspaper. I have often said that I never committed a dishonest or unlawful act. I repeat that. All I ask now is an immediate trial."

The manner of the boss's arrest was a subject of widespread curiosity. Sheriff O'Neil, whose duty it would be to carry out the ticklish assignment, stalled all day, telephoning to the "law offices" at intervals for instructions. Ruef spent most of the afternoon on the telephone, now and then coming into the crowded outer office where cronies were debating the prospects; peering around, he would inquire jocosely, "Isn't O'Neil here yet?" Supervisor Coleman pleaded with the boss to do something to stop "malfeasance of office" on the part of the District Attorney, and Abe smiled. In a corner a former judge, Treadwell by name, was assuring Gallagher that "you can't find twelve men in the city who will find him guilty," while Patrick Henry ("Pin

Head") McCarthy twirled his mustaches and scoffed at the "flimsy charge."

Toward evening, Ruef hurried off in the "Green Lizard," still protected by his police bodyguards, and half an hour later returned with bail bonds sticking out of a pocket. Another telephone conversation and he was ready to surrender. Again he called for his automobile; then, counting noses, cried grandly, "Let's do it in style!" and ordered two automobiles. And away they tooled, he with his bondsmen, while Gallagher and his pals followed in the second machine.

At eight o'clock the cars pulled up in front of the home of Judge Murasky. Sheriff O'Neil was waiting on the porch. The party went inside, bail was posted, and a few minutes later Ruef and the bondsmen drove away, all smiles. There was an embarrassing anticlimax when Gallagher's machine refused to start and the acting mayor was reduced to riding a street car back to Fillmore and Bush.

Heney's delivery on his promises thrilled San Francisco: public hope was rekindled, and the newspapers outdid themselves in congratulations.

Crowed the *Chronicle:* "Every decent man in San Francisco breathes freer today!" And the *Examiner* shot off a veritable Roman candle of triumph, ending with this rhetorical star burst:

... The light breaks, the reign of political terror seems at an end! Thursday, November 15, 1906, is a day to be remembered! It is a day of heroic events to be told to children and grandchildren! It is the day of the declaration of independence of California's great metropolis!

Heartened by these encomiums, the grand jury plowed grimly ahead, to the indignation of some, including Myrtile Cerf. He emerged from the jury room red-faced and sputtering: "It's got so a man can't earn an honest living in this city without having the grand jury after him! The way they are treating Ruef is an outrage!"

Supervisor Nicholas next was indicted, together with one Peter Duffy, a former elevator operator in City Hall, for taking a kickback on furniture purchases for the city; Duffy was accused of being the steerer for a furniture dealer, and Nicholas of accepting a "com-mission" of $26.10 on a $261 order for desks. The sums involved were trivial, but the public eagerly accepted the indictments as earnest of weightier ones to come.

Said Nicholas: "I consider myself honored by being the first man indicted after Ruef and Schmitz. I never took a dishonest dollar in my life."

Ruef said the case smelled of frame-up.

"Absurd on the face of it," he commented. "I don't believe any of the supervisors have taken graft; certainly I always advised them against doing anything of the sort. City officials, it is true, have told me of corporation agents coming to them and offering bribes, and I have myself given money to officials two or three times when they had been approached by persons offering bribes and they were in financial straits. I have done this as a friend, and advised them against accepting any favors which might put them in the power of cor-porations or agents who might later induce them to go in deeper."

He mentioned specifically having advanced money to Sam Davis to pay the building contractors when Davis blossomed out as a theater-owner; he seemed annoyed that Davis had not reimbursed him.

Davis had no comment to make on this revelation by the boss of avuncular generosity. And the other supervisors were stunned,—so stunned they were unable to find their tongues for several minutes.

"Abe Ruef never gave me a cent!" gasped Max Mamlock.

"I've never been in financial straits since I've been on the board of supervisors," Furey asserted, while Coffey cracked his whip and cried: "I never took a dollar and I'm ready to fight any man who says I did!"

Ruef commented that they were nervous and jumpy, naturally, with all the loose allegations flying about. "It's like being locked in a room with a wild tiger or a maniac, unarmed and unprotected," he sighed, and mused aloud: "If Francis J. Heney wants evidence as to bribe-givers, let him call on me."

Would he desert Schmitz? Not at all. "Now that Schmitz is in trouble, I don't intend to be less of a friend to him than I have been in the past. I will stick with him until the end,—that is, until we are vindicated."

For once he looked a reporter square in the eye.

7 Sordid Homecoming

The day before the indictments were voted, Mayor Schmitz had
sailed for home, and on November 22nd his ship, the Hamburg-
American liner *Patricia,* was sighted off Nantucket.

A few days earlier, Supreme Court Justice Henshaw had paid a
surprise call on Heney to inquire, in a friendly way, how the prosecution intended to handle the Mayor's arrest,—in New York, or wait
until he returned to California. The Mayor's friends, Henshaw explained, especially millionaire Dingee, wanted to arrange bail. Henshaw gathered that the Mayor would not be apprehended until he
re-entered the state.

Sheriff O'Neil frankly announced he would wait. "The Mayor,"
he replied, "is not a fugitive from justice; he is returning to justice."

Superior Court Judge Frank Dunne, to whose Department 6
Presiding Judge Murasky had assigned the Schmitz-Ruef trials, made
no move to expedite the arrest. "I see no reason why any difference
should be made in a case involving Mayor Schmitz or Mr. Ruef to
distinguish it from an ordinary trial," he said quietly. Judge Dunne
was a mild-mannered man, rather young for his position, but capable
of maintaining firm control of his court. He possessed sad eyes and a
patient air, and he disliked oratory.

As Schmitz's ship neared New York, the prurient-minded were
regaled by some particularly noisome revelations erupting in headlines.
These were disclosures made to the grand jury by a disillusioned
brothelkeeper, one Alfred Andrieu.

With a couple of partners, Andrieu recently had opened a crib-
house at 712 Pacific Street, a block away from the reactivated although
not rejuvenated "municipal crib" at 614 Jackson. Because he was
paying $440 a week for police protection (he submitted the cashier's
books to prove this), Andrieu had felt secure; but after three weeks of
profitable operation, the police closed him down (on a busy Sunday
night, too), because, they candidly conceded, he was cutting into
the revenues of the nearby "official" enterprise.

Andrieu named among the owners of the "municipal crib" Herbert
Schmitz, Henry Ach, and Billy Finnegan, a Barbary Coast dive-keeper
and Ruef henchman. Andrieu himself had once given the boss a

$600 tie pin, an "R" set in diamonds, which Abe wore complacently.

Burns brought in Chief of Police Dinan to tell the jurors why he had closed the Andrieu place and let the crib a block away stay open. Dinan became entangled in extenuations, maintaining that he would have closed Andrieu's place sooner, only he didn't know it was operating until a priest told him. The priest in question retorted that the Police Chief was lying, and one of Dinan's own captains testified that he had reported the Andrieu joint to the Chief the day it opened, and that Dinan was aware it was one of the lowest dives in the city.

Ach at once protested that he had no interest in the "municipal crib," although it was true that he had appeared as attorney for a number of persons seized there in a raid.

Then Burns produced the former manager of the "municipal crib," who gave a fascinating run-down on its finances and organization. This witness was brawny, beery Paul Heudried, who had managed the house from just after its opening in 1904 until the fire. The building had cost $10,000, and $45,000 was invested in the saloon and fixtures, he testified. The building application was filed in the name of B. Becaas, of 1860 McAllister Street, name and address fictitious. The application for a saloon license was in the name of Arthur Morfitt, a bartender working for Billy Finnegan. On the assessment rolls the property stood in the name of Delia L. Walsh, a person non-existent, but among the real owners Heudried included Herbert Schmitz, Finnegan, and a mysterious "Joseph Alexander," a man whom nobody ever saw and whom he had once heard described as "a sheepherder on the Mexican border." "Alexander," Heudried never doubted, was Abraham Ruef.

One hundred seventeen women, the witness went on, paid $30 a week for their cubicles, while sixteen more paid $20 a week for less desirable niches. Since the receipts from the bar paid all expenses, the upstairs take was practically pure profit. No books were kept. Heudried collected from the women every day as they left, putting the money in a cloth sack, which was picked up by one of the partners and taken to the bank. Herbert Schmitz, he swore, got approximately one-fourth of the profits,—$990 a week, or $51,480 a year. Herbert often was at the crib checking up, said Heudried, and on the premises it was taken for granted that Herbert represented his brother, the Mayor.

The grand jury called in Billy Finnegan, and he, too, said that "Jo-seph Alexander," the sheepherder, was Abe Ruef. He left the jury room crushed and frightened, and the next day both he and Andrieu received death threats. Finnegan and a number of other dive denizens promptly skipped out of town; Andrieu stayed and was arrested on a charge of inducting a woman into a life of shame. Reporters were unable to find either the woman or the two addresses she had given, and Andrieu was quickly released on bail. He hurried to confer with Heney and Burns, and shortly the grand jury indicted Dinan and Ruef for perjury and conspiracy in connection with the three-week protection of Andrieu's house.

A public howl went up for the Police Chief to resign; but the City Attorney obliged with a legal opinion that Dinan could not be removed on unproved suspicion. Heney said Dinan would be tried like anybody else, chief or no chief. And at least the grand jurors, after inspecting the "municipal crib" themselves, did get the place closed for a while.

Amid these sordid developments, Herbert Schmitz disappeared, and nobody was much surprised when he and George Keane material-ized on the dock at Hoboken to welcome the wandering Eugene.

The Mayor learned of his indictment from newspapers brought aboard the *Patricia* by a doctor at Quarantine in lower New York Bay. Reporters coming down the bay on a revenue cutter an hour later found him with tear-brimming eyes, face drawn and deeply furrowed. Julia Schmitz wept copiously.

In a stateroom interview, the Mayor laid his predicament to political jealousy.

"As I look at the matter, it is simply a political trick to discredit me with my people. By 'my people' I mean the people of San Francisco. Advantage was taken of my absence by enemies who were jealous of the prestige I had built up during my three administrations."

"Did you apprehend an indictment?"

"No, I did not expect it. It is a great shock to me. But when I learned there was trouble in San Francisco, I cut short my stay in Europe to return and face the charges, which are false—absolutely without foundation. I court the deepest inquiry; I want to clear my name of the stain that has been put upon it."

Graft in San Francisco? The Mayor laughed sourly.

"I fought graft. I found no graft in San Francisco. This action is simply a political move. District Attorney Langdon and his supporters are afraid of me. Even my enemies give me credit for doing my duty during the fire and in the hard times afterward. It's jealousy, pure political jealousy—maybe fear."

French restaurants had been around a long time, he explained; they were one of the gay adjuncts of a gay city and did no great harm; they needed no defense by him. But when he was pressed about the "municipal crib" disclosures, he spoke feelingly, and his composure broke: "No one ever held stock of that kind for me, with or without my sanction. I am not my brother's keeper, but I will say that I am very close to my brother, and I cannot believe the story. I tried to close that place, you know, but the courts gave an injunction to the man who owned the restaurant in the front of the place, and we couldn't get around that."

No, he had not been in communication with Ruef, and he could not credit Ruef's guilt.

"Ruef is my friend. When I have a friend, I do not throw him down because another man says he is dishonest. The minute I find out that Ruef is not a man of integrity and unimpeachable honesty, I will cut loose from him. But we stand indicted together and we will fight it out together. And we will win, because we are innocent."

At the dock, with Herbert Schmitz and Keane, was the Hoboken chief of police,—on hand not to arrest the Mayor, but to see that he was not spirited out of the state illegally. As Schmitz walked down the gangplank, friends rushed to shake his hand, threw their arms around him, patted him on the back, urged him to be brave. Women hugged and kissed Mrs. Schmitz. Unnoticed in the crowd stood Burns's son and another detective, watching every detail.

No California officers appearing, the Mayor and his party were whisked to Manhattan and the austerities of the Waldorf-Astoria.

The next morning, Schmitz started for home. At Omaha he repeated his faith in Ruef's innocence, dismissing every accusation with "all politics, just politics."

In San Francisco, the supervisors came away from a secret caucus reticent and sullen: Ruef and P.H. McCarthy were circulating word ` that everybody must be on hand to give the returning Mayor a gigantic welcome home at Dreamland Rink, and city payrollers were being tapped up to $25 apiece to pay the expense.

At the first train stop inside the California line, the Sierra town of Truckee, Schmitz was arrested, on November 28th. Three men boarded the train—Ruef, Cerf, and Deputy Sheriff Harry Knox. Quietly, with every possible consideration, Knox made the arrest in the privacy of a Pullman compartment. Julia Schmitz, who had thought Knox was there as a friend, burst into sobs, crying, "Oh, you can't do that!"

The Mayor felt his arrest keenly, and shut himself in the compartment with Ruef, refusing to meet reporters. At Sacramento, however, a cheering crowd of sympathizers on the platform made so much commotion that Schmitz relented and spoke briefly.

"Boys," he cried, "it does my heart good at such a time and under such circumstances to receive such a reception. It shows that I have many friends in California." Repeating that he was innocent, he said he was eager to face trial. But when a reporter asked about Ruef, a shade crossed the Mayor's face and he replied: "That is a different matter. I have nothing to say for Mr. Ruef. I can only speak for myself."

Ruef, for a change, declined to extemporize. "Not a word," he told the press, "but it's all right, it's O.K."

The train, running behind schedule, did not reach the Oakland terminal until 11:45 P.M. There, Chief Dinan was waiting with a delegation, which included a number of supervisors, to escort the Mayor across the bay.

At Dreamland Rink more than five thousand Ruefites had been waiting for hours, cheering speaker after speaker who denounced the graft investigation and called for the closing of ranks in this hour of peril. Father Yorke impassionedly urged all to stand firmly behind Schmitz, or see labor unions destroyed. He was frantically applauded.

There was superadded delay when the Mayor's auto broke down, and he did not enter Dreamland until nearly 1:00 A.M. The throng gave him a standing ovation, and he responded succinctly, blaming

the newspapers for his predicament and announcing that he had returned in fighting trim to trounce the maligners.

In the early hours of the morning, still in custody of Deputy
Knox, he crossed his own threshold at last. It was Thanksgiving Day.

8 The Man "Higher-Up"

As the graft investigation gathered headway, the prosecutors came
to realize that the trail would lead to Patrick Calhoun; other men of
wealth and position would be involved, but Calhoun would prove to
be the principal quarry and the most difficult to snare.

In September, 1906, just after Heney had become arbitrator in the
United Railroads-carmen's dispute, he had picked up indications that
the street-car company was deeply involved in municipal corruption.
The gossip about a payoff for the overhead trolley franchise was
persistent—$4,000 to each supervisor, said the rumor—and Ruef
himself had become alarmed by the stories reaching him about reck-
less spending on the part of supervisors who only recently had been
poor men. "Gassy" Kelly was said to have developed a breakfast fondness for fried eggs and champagne, and Lonergan was shouting
"Drinks for the crowd!" in bars along Fillmore Street, throwing
around as much as $50 a day in this way.

Ruef ordered the supervisors to get honest jobs which would
account for their sudden affluence, and some of them did.

When Heney was appointed Assistant District Attorney and resigned from the arbitration board, he had been asked by Calhoun to
sign a statement absolving the United Railroads of any suspicion of
grafting, and he had refused; this strengthened his suspicion that the
talk about bribes was substantially grounded. But he realized that
proof would be hard to obtain, and that Calhoun, powerful and ruthless, would do everything possible to prevent production of any proof.

Spreckels was elated by the trend. When he first undertook to
bankroll the investigation, he did not have Calhoun or any other corporation man specifically in mind: his eye was fixed on the politicians
at City Hall. But when the signs began to point toward Calhoun and
other big-business directors, he felt that progress was being made, for

behind Calhoun stood William F. Herrin, Spreckels' longtime *bête noire,* and behind Herrin loomed the owner of the Southern Pacific Railroad, E.H. Harriman, the Wall Street financier. Such men Spreckels believed to be the real corruptionists, the real subverters of democratic government.

Two weeks before Ruef and Schmitz were indicted, the newspapers for the first time alluded to the withdrawal of large sums of money from the United States Mint by United Railroads officials during the previous spring, and alleged that this money had been passed along to the supervisors as a bribe. The granting of the overhead trolley system without compensation—a gift to the street-car company worth several million dollars—rankled with the taxpayers, who still were receiving woefully inadequate transportation service. (Gertrude Atherton, only a little while after this, wrote that to travel by street car from the corner of Van Ness Avenue and Market Street to the Ferry Building, a distance of two miles along the city's widest thoroughfare, took one hour.) One detail of the newspaper accounts struck the public with particular force: the money in question had been withdrawn in currency, not in gold coin. San Francisco was a hard-money town; paper money was disliked and distrusted, and few bills of small denominations were circulated; indeed, many workingmen's households hardly saw paper money the year round.

The newspaper stories led Tirey L. Ford, the United Railroads general counsel, to issue a denial.

"This Mint story is like a great many others that are floating around," he said, "interesting but not important. The United Railroads made use of the Mint precisely as did others. You can rest assured that whatever monies this company deposited or withdrew from the Mint were used in the legitimate conduct of the company's business and not otherwise. As to the stories of graft that are floating around, I can only say that there is absolutely nothing in them so far as this company is concerned. What has been done by the United Railroads has been done openly and aboveboard and along clean and legitimate lines."

Tirey Ford, as a former Attorney General of California, was a man whose word might be expected to carry weight. But a week after Ruef and Schmitz were indicted, the newspapers headlined: BIG TROLLEY GRAFT TO BE PROBED. To this Calhoun, then in New York, replied in a long statement telegraphed to Thornwell Mullally as his representative in San Francisco. This blistering exculpation concluded: "The United Railroads of San Francisco never paid or authorized anyone to pay on its behalf a single dollar to the Mayor, supervisors, or any public official of the city of San Francisco or the state of California. I desire this statement to be broad and emphatic."

Burns noted that Calhoun used the words "any public official," but said nothing about possible payments to a person not a public official, for the purpose of official corruption.

Heney was confident and contented. The day after the grand jury returned true bills against the Mayor and the boss, the prosecutor married Mrs. Rebecca McMullen Belvin, member of a family long established in the San Francisco area. The quiet wedding was in the home of the bride's sister in fashionable Piedmont, on the Oakland side of the bay, with a Congregational minister officiating. Heney was too busy to take time out for a honeymoon, and the couple moved at once into a home at 1532 Green Street, on the edge of the burned district. Heney was forty-seven years old.

Spreckels, Phelan, Heney, Burns—all were enjoying social popularity. Spreckels and Phelan were members of the Pacific-Union Club (the first gentleman's club in the West), and as guest of one or the other, Heney lunched there almost daily. Bankers, financiers, prominent businessmen would drop past their table, and politely inquiring about their progress, would urge them to clean out those thieves at City Hall.

Time out of mind Spreckels had heard these clubmen complain sourly about being "held up" by greedy politicians; but when he solicited their help in putting a stop to the "holdups," he met with evasion or curt refusal. Close friends disclaimed possessing personal knowledge of bribery, saying they were just repeating common gossip, they had no proof. Others protested they could not afford to get involved in anything that might "hurt business,"—especially at that moment, when the city's recovery was just getting into stride. Acquaintances told Spreckels that he would be well advised to let the crusade drop, now that Schmitz and Ruef had been bagged.

Heney, who had been through the same experience in Oregon (cheered on by the "best people" until he indicted some of them), smiled sardonically and wondered when the tune would change here.

He foresaw the storm they were heading into. Although, like Spreckels, he was certain that some of the men in that dining room had bribed or connived at bribing public servants, grumbling all the while that they were being "held up," not one of his genial well-wishers would consent to face the grand jury.

Burns tried his hand with an appeal to any person who knew the facts about municipal wrongdoing to come forward without fear of being prosecuted or implicated. "No man who has been held up by the brigands that have had this city by the throat need hesitate to tell the truth concerning them," the detective said. "We are after the 'big fish' only, the men who compelled the payment of graft money. We don't propose to harm any person who, under compulsion, made payment of such money."

But in fine clubs and at dinner parties, nobody could imagine whom Burns might have in mind.

Under these conditions, many observers were less than sanguine that speedy justice could be dealt to handsome Gene and slippery Abe. Ruef's resources as a pettifogger were known, and the *Chronicle* was openly predicting that "if Ruef doesn't run away, we shall see the greatest struggle with technicalities that has ever disgraced our courts."

This gloomy prediction seemed bolstered by a news item that appeared about then, an account of the lawsuit brought by an attorney against a recalcitrant client; the attorney wanted a $2,500 fee which the client would not pay, and as plaintiff he told the court just why he believed he was entitled to the sum. His client, a cigar wholesaler named Haynemann, had sued a group of retailers for putting another brand of cigars in Haynemann boxes. He won a judgment, but one of the retailers, named Cahen, in turn sued Haynemann for $25,000 damages.

The attorney said he had advised Haynemann that his best course would be to keep Cahen's suit in suspense until the statute of limitations had run against the twenty other retailers, who would rush in with their own claims if Cahen won.

"Haynemann told me to use my ingenuity and get all the delay I could," the lawyer told the court. "I began by filing a demurrer. Then I moved to strike out certain portions of Cahen's complaint. I appeared in court eight times to ask postponements, and succeeded in getting them. Then the motion and demurer were argued before Judge Kerrigan, who denied my motion and overruled my demurrer. I got as much time as possible in which to make an answer, and I also got time to file a bill of exceptions to the Supreme Court. Then I suggested that we take the deposition of Cahen. This took three days, and I then discovered that most of his business was done through a nickel-in-the-slot machine, within the prohibition of the law. I suggested that we might make this additional defense and claim that Cahen wasn't entitled to judgment because he was doing an immoral business."

The attorney had been reluctant to take this line, he told his client, because it would "ruin what little credit I had with the saloon men" and would "reflect on the supervisors" who had approved the licensing of slot machines; it would seem to accuse the city fathers of acting illegally. But Haynemann instructed him to go ahead.

"Then I devoted a week to studying the law of the case, after getting all the time from the court I could. The other attorneys moved to strike out the machine defense, and we finally argued it before Judge Troutt. I obtained four weeks in which to file a brief. I was overruled so far as the machine defense was concerned, but the case is still undecided, and the statute of limitations has run against every one of Cahen's co-defendants, although it was begun in 1893."

The name of the lawyer vaunting these accomplishments was Henry Ach, chief counsel for Abe Ruef.

9   A Circus in Court

On Monday, December 3rd, the boss and the Mayor appeared in Judge Dunne's court for arraignment as accused felons. Ruef was represented by Ach and Samuel Shortridge, while appearing for the Mayor was Frank C. Drew—of the prosperous law firm of Campbell, Metson & Drew—and John J. Barrett, an assistant city attorney. The case had been called for November 21st, but had been continued until Schmitz could be present, inasmuch as the defendants were indicted jointly.

The public wondered whether Abe and his protégé had come to a parting. Dingee and other wealthy friends had gone bail for Schmitz, and rumor said they were urging him to drop Ruef, who appeared to be in deeper trouble. More significantly, a report gained credence that Dingee, Calhoun, and E. H. Harriman of the Southern Pacific were advising Schmitz to go it alone; in which case they would use all their influence to extricate him from his difficulties, and if successful would run him for Governor of California four years hence on the Republican ticket. This was a tempting bait, if the rumor was true; and it definitely was true that Schmitz had been entertained recently by Calhoun at the latter's home in New York City, and that Calhoun and Harriman had mutual interests.

Amid these rumblings about an actual or impending split between the indicted men, the proceedings at Temple Sherith Israel got under way. Ruef arrived without his two city bodyguards,—Heney had finally pried them loose. The strain seemed to be telling on the boss; in repose, his face was haggard, but his spirit was blithe. Schmitz arrived, pompous as a drum major in mufti, and paused theatrically in the doorway of the courtroom, sweeping off his black, broad-brimmed wide-awake hat (a political trademark) and running one hand through his raven black hair. His glance and bow toward Ruef were frigid. Neither man smiled. Later, while their attorneys were arguing for a delay, they leaned across the counsel table and conversed in whispers, but with no indication of cordiality. Judge Dunne allowed the defense a three-day continuance.

Meanwhile, in Judge Lawlor's courtroom upstairs, the case of Supervisor Nicholas and the elevator man, Duffy, was called. Their attorneys—Charles A. Fairall and Frank J. Murphy, both experienced on the shady side of the law—opened an attack on the indictments, alleging bias on the part of the grand jurors. They demanded the right to question the grand jurors, and for two days the unfortunate members of that panel were heckled on the witness stand. The best this fishing expedition could bring out was of no help to the defense; indeed, foreman Oliver stated under oath that "the testimony I have heard in the grand jury room has filled me with horror and disgust."

On December 6th Judge Dunne glanced at his calendar and called: "Number 303, Eugene E. Schmitz and Abraham Ruef, for arraignment."

Schmitz arose and the court clerk began to read the indictment. Ruef insolently remained seated.

"I'd like to know what is going on here!" broke in Heney. "Is the defendant Schmitz being arraigned alone, or is the co-defendant Ruef being arraigned with him? Nobody can hear a word the clerk is saying, and the defendant Ruef is not standing."

"Both men are being arraigned and Mr. Ruef doesn't have to stand up unless he wants to," sneered Ach, while Schmitz, hands in pockets, grinned.

The clerk started again. When he finished, Schmitz's attorney, Drew, asked for a continuance to plead. The request was denied.

The clerk then passed to the reading of indictment 304. Said Ach to Schmitz, "Keep your seat."

Heney again complained to the bench: "If this proceeding were to be conducted like any criminal case, and if the defendants would stand, we might know what is going on."

"I have ordered the clerk to proceed as in an ordinary case," replied Judge Dunne softly. "I think the sooner everybody understands that the defendants are in this court on exactly the same footing as if their names were John Doe and Harry Roe, the less friction there will be."

Ruef and Schmitz then arose and remained standing while the clerk read indictments 304, 305, 306, and 307, his voice growing fainter each time. But Ruef continued to express contempt by half-turning his back and chatting in a low voice with nearby friends. The Mayor scowled into vacancy.

The defense lawyers then asked, one after another, for time to prepare their answers. Patiently, the Judge reminded them that one delay had been granted for this purpose, and if there had been any misunderstanding, it was the fault of counsel.

"I object to that last statement!" shouted Barrett. "We deem it misconduct and prejudicial."

"I have already heard you three times on this point," Dunne rejoined wearily, "and as I have listened to considerable oratory in the course of my experience, I feel disposed now to proceed with the case."

"And I have listened to considerable oratory from you!" snarled Barrett, whose chief purpose seemed to be to goad the Judge.

Dunne ignored the provocation, but since the law allows a defendant twenty-fours hours to answer an indictment, he postponed the entering pleas for four days, until the following Monday. But again he cautioned: "By that time I should like it understood that the defendants are then to answer."

"Oh, we'll answer, or do something," Ach responded, and left the room laughing.

That afternoon, Ach subpoenaed the grand jurors for another examination for possible bias. Over the weekend, Mayor Schmitz appointed Barrett a fire commissioner.

Before Monday Ach had also subpoenaed every witness who appeared before the grand jury, on the contention that the witnesses had been bullied and coerced. Heney retorted that the defense wished to question the witnesses in order to discover what evidence the State held. In any event, the move promised to tie up the proceedings for weeks, and, for all practical purposes, place everybody on trial except the two defendants. This strategy was credited to the astuteness of Shortridge, and was welcomed enthusiastically by Ruef's political coterie.

On Monday Ach moved to set aside the indictments on nineteen grounds, and for good measure moved to erase from the record entirely indictments 303 and 304,—because, he said, the charges in them were the same as those in 305 and 307.

Next, Ach took up "a very important matter," the qualifications of one grand juror, Wallace Wise, who, it transpired, had served as a petty juror within the preceding twelve months. This, Ach maintained, disqualified him under the statute and hence invalidated the indictments he had voted on. Argument on this point raged all day, with Langdon, Heney, and Hiram Johnson speaking for the State, and the defense talking in relays.

Schmitz sat through the welter of words in apparent funk, his face drawn and pasty white. When Ruef greeted him with well-barbered smile, Eugene responded indifferently. A new attorney on the Mayor's behalf was Joseph C. Campbell, law partner of Drew and a noted corporation lawyer who seldom appeared in a criminal court; rumor

buzzed that he had been retained by some of the corporations who
were interested in saving Schmitz's hide.

The purpose of these delaying tactics set in motion by men who
had been demanding speedy trial was exposed by Heney in a parable:
"Recently there was an attorney who sued his client for a large fee
for having so delayed his trial that the statute of limitations ran against
it. It was for thus defeating justice that he sought his fee. I can draw
but one conclusion, which is that the defense is pursuing the same
tactics in this case."

Ach took exception to this "personal attack," but Heney went on:
"The people of San Francisco are entitled to know whether their
chief executive is guilty or innocent. Then let him go to trial and
establish that he is innocent, instead of quibbling here about legal
technicalities."

Barrett deplored the spectacle of "the chief executive of the city
[being] dragged up and down in the gutters."

Shouted Heney: "Then why don't you go to trial at once?"

Judge Dunne wondered whether there were not "some other way
to clear their reputations than by setting aside a regularly found
indictment."

Lawyer Murphy, coming downtairs from Judge Lawlor's courtroom, where he had been raising legal hurdles against the trial of
Nicholas and Duffy, made his own extended argument to quash the
indictment on behalf of Ruef. The grand jurors were kept sitting in
court all that day, and the next day, and the day after that, while
debate surged around the qualifications of juror Wise. A week was
consumed. Heney insisted that he would have the trials under way by
Christmas, but the impression grew stronger that Abe and Gene would
wriggle free yet.

Then Heney informed the court that Judge Lawlor had looked up
the case in which Wise served as a petty juror and it had been disposed
of more than one year previously, hence lay outside the scope of the
statute. Ach subpoenaed Judge Lawlor and questioned him on the
stand, and then argued that the case had not been finally disposed
of when it left Judge Lawlor's courts,—not, in fact, until it completed
the whole gamut of appeals through the higher courts. This called for
more learned argument and expenditure of more time.

And in the Nicholas-Duffy case, the arguments against the competence of grand juror Wise were repeated all over again *ad nauseam*. And when Max Adler, proprietor of the Bay State restaurant, appeared in Judge Lawlor's court for arraignment on his perjury indictment, Ach brought in the grand jurors for still a third going-over as to their possible bias against Adler.

The public reeled through ten days, trying to follow the bickering and hairsplitting of counsel; then Judge Dunne denied the motions to strike the indictments on the ground of juror Wise's asserted incompetence.

Lawlor was as expeditious as possible with Nicholas and Duffy; he refused to quash the indictments, then endured six days of argument while Murphy strove to sustain a demurrer, and finally, four days before Christmas, set trial date for the pair on January 21st.

Another round for the prosecution, but the resources of the defense had barely been tapped.

Chief of Police Dinan had surrendered on his joint indictment with Ruef, and his attorney turned out to be Lewis F. Byington, the former District Attorney. Byington obtained delays from Judge Dunne on entering his client's plea. The Chief was apparently not worried by the popular demand that he get out and spare the city the odium of having its ranking law enforcement officer under indictment as a lawbreaker.

In Dunne's court, grand jurors and other witnesses were mangled, piecemeal and collectively, by the roaring lions of the defense in an interminable attempt to adduce prejudice. Judge Dunne grew wearier and wearier, his expression sadder and sadder. Langdon was called to submit to questioning. Dwyer was called, and was forced to divulge that he had encountered grand jury foreman Oliver twice since the empaneling of the jury and each time they had discussed the weather. Burns was quizzed about the $100,000 guarantee fund. Former Police Commissioner Hutton was grilled, and so were Older and Crothers. Newspaper reporters were called in an effort to show collusion between the prosecution and the press. Barrett took turns with Ach in badgering witnesses and baiting the Judge; it was all to no avail.

When Rudolph Spreckels was called, a thrill ran through the courtroom.

Demanded Ach: "Did you, last February or at any other time, guarantee $100,000 to secure the downfall of Abraham Ruef or Eugene E. Schmitz?"

"I did not," came the reply. "I do not seek the downfall of Eugene E. Schmitz or any other person in this room. I guaranteed $100,000 to meet the expenses of prosecuting those who are guilty of crimes that have greatly damaged San Francisco. My object was [here Barrett noisily objected but was overruled] to ascertain the truth or falsity of certain information I had received from Ruef himself. At a conference I had with him, he told me he was in a position to do certain things . . ."

And Spreckels then revealed his colloquy with Ruef in 1904, in his office at 421 Market Street, when Ruef proposed to rig the bidding on municipal bonds by tying up the city in a transport strike.

As Spreckels related the episode, Ruef stiffened and listened intently. Whispering excitedly to Ach, he directed the questioning until it was brought out that the statute of limitations had run out in regard to the incident. Once this was in the record, Ruef relaxed.

Ach asked whether Spreckels had guaranteed the $100,000 because he had been denied a street-car franchise, and the banker replied firmly: "No, I determined to furnish the money over one year ago, and I propose to go on until the city is purged of grafters."

Ach then tried to learn the names of other contributors to the fund; all he found out was that while none of the grand jurors maintained an account at Spreckels' First National Bank, Abraham Ruef had a sizable balance there.

Off on another tack, the defense called witnesses who with remarkable glibness testified to hearing one of the grand jurors, Jeremiah Deasy, express prejudicial dislike of both the defendants. Joseph Bachman, a tailor who said he pressed Ruef's suits twice a week and Mayor Schmitz's once, and M. Sena, a self-styled "general merchandise broker" who dealt in "jewelry, old rags, diamonds, antiques, old bottles, and mostly junk," both swore that just before the 1905 election Deasy told them that Schmitz and Ruef ought to be in jail. Bachman recalled that Deasy swore outrageously,—which struck everybody as odd, because the venerable old man was a well-known

church leader (a later generation would call him a "dedicated" layman) and nobody could imagine him cursing fluently or otherwise.

Next, the technicalities causing all the delay (Schmitz and Ruef
both protesting still that all they wanted was swift trial and vindication) were sharpened exceedingly fine, and a trap was set to trip the
even-tempered Judge Dunne.

First, Ach moved to strike one indictment, number 305, and the
motion was denied. Then Ach averred that he had found new grounds
for the motion, and with cool effrontery repeated practically the same
grounds of challenge he had set up previously,—bias, prejudice, misconduct by the grand jury. After much time had been wasted on this
futility, the motion was denied again.

Then Campbell, on behalf of Schmitz, moved to set aside indictment 305 on virtually identical grounds. He argued his motion at
length. Judge Dunne said he would rule on Campbell's motion "when
the evidence is in."

This did not suit the defense's purposes at all; what they were
trying to get was an immediate ruling on indictment 305; then they
would repeat the process of challenge and delay in respect to each of
the other four indictments, one by one, counsel for each defendant
arguing separately at prodigous length. In this way, they might manage to keep talking until Christmas two years hence.

Campbell then announced that Schmitz desired a separate trial.
The prosecution was startled.

"That is my client's present desire," Campbell assured the court
in his most entrancing tones. "If your honor will decide the motion at
once, we will file a demurrer and plead tomorrow morning."

The Judge placidly repeated that he would rule "when the evidence is in."

Heney spotted the reason for this surprise maneuver: should
Dunne rule at once and grant Schmitz a separate trial, he would open
the door for Schmitz's defense to play the same obstructionist game
for him that was already being worked jointly for him and Ruef; the
practical result would be to block further grand jury action and
delay Ruef's trial indefinitely, because the prosecution could not
manage two major trials and the grand jury work simultaneously.

Campbell tried again and again to induce Judge Dunne to rule. Barrett spoke at length, demanding "justice" for his client.

"Sad, very sad," said Judge Dunne. "The motion stands submitted."

Two days later Campbell, without warning, backtracked and requested permission to withdraw his motion to dismiss indictment 305, inasmuch as the court refused to rule.

"I do not refuse to decide the motion," Judge Dunne countered, fully alert. "It is taken under submission." And realizing that part of the game was to exasperate him to the point of rashness, he rebuked Schmitz's counsel: "Mr. Campbell, you cannot blow hot at one time and blow cold at another in this court. You come here and move to set aside one indictment and leave the others in suspension. You come here one day with one motion and are back again the next day with a counter motion. I will rule on all your motions at once when the evidence in this proceeding, and in which your client is a co-defendant, is in." And with a finality that disclosed his awareness of the trap, the Judge concluded: "The motion as to all five indictments will be decided by me at one time. I do not propose to go through this proceeding five times over."

Soon it was Christmas, and Heney's prediction of having the trials rolling went smash. When court recessed over the holiday, Ach was saying that he had "three or four witnesses to call,"—and then he would turn his attention once more to the grand jurors.

Upon resumption the day after Christmas, William H. Metson— the third member of the firm of Campbell, Metson & Drew—appeared for Schmitz, and spoke earnestly of his client's desire for a speedy, separate trial.

For Metson's benefit, Judge Dunne repeated that he would decide the motions in respect to all five indictments "when the evidence is in." Judge Dunne was becoming a nuisance.

Attorney Barrett then offered to make any terms with the District Attorney in return for a speedy trial for Schmitz, and Hiram Johnson took him up.

"All right, have your co-defendant [Ruef] withdraw his motions in this proceeding and we will go to trial of your client tomorrow morning," he challenged. "This talk is all a bluff, a deception, a fraud, and a snare."

Metson stammered that they had no control over Ruef, that Schmitz and Ruef had separated their interests; and Dunne ended the farce by ordering Ach to proceed with examination of the grand jurors.

Juror Greenbaum was nagged and harried for two days. Ach wanted to know whether he read any newspapers; if so, which ones; and had he read an article headed: "Supervisor Lonergan and His Dizzy Blonde"? Juror Greenbaum had not read the article, so Ach read it to him, incidentally getting it into the record. Ach read columns of newspaper clippings. Judge Dunne held his temper and paid out rope.

Smarting under Dunne's invulnerability, Schmitz's lawyers asked presiding Judge Graham to assign Schmitz's case to some other department, inasmuch as Judge Dunne refused to grant a speedy trial. They averred that "the inability of the defendant properly to attend to the duties of his office, by reason of the delay in setting affiant's cause for trial, is injuring the reputation, business interests, and future of San Francisco."

"We are asking an immediate trial before any judge," Barrett urged. "The Mayor has been dancing attendance on the District Attorney in an effort to remove the stigma of disgrace from his name."

Retorted Hiram Johnson: "He doesn't desire a speedy, immediate, or any trial! He desires to bunco this court!"

Rule 4 of the Superior Court, Johnson pointed out, provided that a transfer could not take place without the consent of the judge before whom the case was pending.

Dunne, meanwhile, halted activities in his own court and spoke feelingly: "I am not unfamiliar with the tactics invariably followed by defendants who appeal to Judge Graham, a man of large sympathies. Judge Graham has seen fit in the past to interfere with the orderly conduct of business before this court. I want it distinctly understood that if the case of Schmitz is taken up by Judge Graham, both cases will have to go before him."

Out of court, Schmitz was telling friends that it was "program" for Judge Graham to transfer his case "to Judge Hunt or Judge Troutt or some Railroad judge." On being informed of this, Graham expressed astonishment, and said that he would not order a transfer without Judge Dunne's written consent. When Barrett urged him to ask Judge Dunne himself, Graham replied with pique: "Judge Dunne has intimated that I am a man of large sympathies and generous impulses. I am afraid if I were to meet Judge Dunne, I would not find a sympathetic chord in his body."

He washed his hands of the affair.

Commented Judge Dunne: "Rule 4 of the Superior Court is emphatic, and it does not require profound insight of the law to interpret it. Judge Graham has stated he 'thought' he would not find any sympathy from me. He could have said he 'would' not." Then, his underjaw jutting, he went on with grim sincerity: "I did not ask these cases to be assigned to my court, but now that they are under my jurisdiction, I shall perform my duty as a jurist. I shall do right."

When Judge Graham refused to intervene, Schmitz bowed his head in dejection, but Ruef's smile was no less bright. Judge Dunne must be circumvented some other way, and Abe was confident he could do it.

Already the scheme was under way in the State Legislature at Sacramento. It was a race against time.

10   Desperate Expedients

Judge Graham delivered his dictum on the last day of his turn as presiding judge, the last day of 1906. And in Sacramento, on that day, the state Capitol was awakening from its periodic somnolence under the influx of Senators and Assemblymen from the cow counties and inland cities, from the citrus-grove communities of the arid south and the fire-scarred metropolis by the bay.

The 1907 Legislature has been termed the most corrupt in the history of California. While this may be a not irreversible judgment, certainly it was the 1907 Legislature of which a politician, Mayor Glasscock of Oakland, said: "In that Legislature you couldn't pass the Lord's Prayer without money."

Conversely, with money (and the Railroad's assistance) you might reasonably hope to pass the devil's own program.

Ruef held a strong hand in the Legislature, controlling a solid block of votes in both the Senate and the Assembly. George Keane, who served him faithfully, was a Senator. But his chief ally was the Railroad. Ruef had always co-operated with Herrin's machine in state matters: his standing instructions to the Union Labor legislators he elected from San Francisco were to vote the labor side on all bills affecting labor, and on all other measures to follow the Railroad's lead. Herrin was appreciative, and Herrin was master of the 1907 Legislature.

The session was opened with prayer; then the members got down to brass tacks. Hundreds of ne'er-do-wells were grafted upon the Capitol payroll overnight. The Assembly in a rush hired eighty-five doorkeepers to watch three doors, and stenographers who could neither read nor write. Senators appointed well-known fancy ladies their clerks and gave them the privilege of the Senate floor. The hoggishness displayed by the people's representatives was so egregious that outgoing Governor Pardee exclaimed they had lost all moral sense, and newly elected Governor Gillett sternly condemned it.

But this wallowing in the trough of tax money was merely pre-liminary to consideration of some really radical measures that had been in preparation. Among these was a series of amendments to the Penal Code, drawn up by the attorney Fairall, the purport of which was only too obvious. One would prohibit bookkeepers and account-ants from testifying against their employers. Another would enjoin newspapers from commenting on a criminal case from the time of empaneling the grand jury to the rendering of the trial verdict. A third would confer upon the defendant in a criminal action the right to displace the judge by simply filing an affidavit of his belief that he could not receive a fair trial; the case then would mandatorily be transferred to another court, and might be retransferred upon the defendant's further affidavit or affidavits, until an acceptable judge was found. This measure, which was Ruef's principal hope, was known as the "change of venue bill," and it was written to become effective sixty days after enactment.

On January 15th, Grove L. Johnson, chairman of the Assembly judiciary committee (and father of Hiram Johnson, a prosecutor of Abraham Ruef), introduced this bill under the innocuous title: "An Amendment to Sec. 170 of the Penal Code." Grove Johnson, white-bearded patriarch of the Assembly and a Railroad wheelhorse, had quarreled with his son and bore Hiram deep-seated enmity.

On the San Francisco front, Ach and his associates continued to ballyrag grand jurors in Judge Dunne's court in quest of bias. Their success was nil. Foreman Oliver even blurted that the evidence he had heard was "absolutely appalling; it would take at least ten years to deal with it properly."

"Do you think Mayor Schmitz went to Europe on his salary?"

"No, sir," was the firm response.

Repeatedly Judge Dunne rebuked the attorneys for insolent and insulting questions. One juror was badgered for six hours, until Dunne compelled a termination. Fairall, now attorney of record for Schmitz, threatened to slap Heney's face, then thought better of it. The Judge told Shortridge to stop his derogatory questioning and sit down, and lectured Henry Ach: "When I tell you to stop talking, Mr. Ach, I want you to stop. You are putting words into the mouth of this witness. You must moderate your tone and stop yelling and shouting questions at the witness that tend to confuse him."

Thereupon Ach called himself as a witness and answered his own questions.

Schmitz then tried a new dodge to escape from the obnoxious Dunne. Surrendering to the sheriff on indictment 303, he applied to the State Supreme Court for a writ of habeas corpus and a writ of prohibition, based on the same points that had been advanced in Dunne's court against the indictment. The Supreme Court justices, to the Mayor's chagrin, deferred decision.

As the hearings dragged along, Schmitz developed the jitters. He was frightened and bewildered by the courtroom wrangles, and on the pretext of attending to official business, he absented himself until Judge Dunne sent bailiffs to bring him back from the littered mayoral desk. Schmitz was convinced that eventually the strategy of delay would fail and that he would have to go to trial,—before the implacable, odious Dunne.

Then a diversion offered which the Mayor grasped as heaven sent.

It was provided by the agitation in San Francisco just then over the segregation of Japanese pupils in the city's schools. The root of the misunderstanding struck deep into early California history. Chinese coolie labor had been imported under contract when the state's railroads were built, and these immigrants' depressed standards of living, coupled with their willingness to toil long hours at meager wages, incited the hostility of competitive American labor. The unions hated the Chinese, and harsh discriminatory laws had been on the statute books for years.

One of these laws empowered local school authorities to exclude "all children of filthy and vicious habits, or children suffering from contagious or infectious diseases," and to establish separate schools "for Indian children and for children of Mongolian or Chinese descent." Where such separate schools were established, Indian, Chinese, or Mongolian children must not be admitted into any other. This was racial segregation comparable to that enforced against Negroes in the Southern states, a practice which at that time was viewed generally with complacency or even positive approval.

San Francisco's schools had almost all been destroyed in the disaster; during the rebuilding, the board of education set apart one school for "Orientals," assigning to it Chinese, Korean, and the few Japanese pupils in the city. Whereupon the Japanese parents protested fiercely; a proud people who despised Chinese and Koreans, they maintained that they were neither Indian, Chinese, nor Mongolian, nor were they "Orientals." Pointing to the president of the board of education, Aaron Altmann (Abe Ruef's brother-in-law), the Japanese consul demanded: "If we are Orientals, what is Mr. Altmann's own race?"

The honor of Japan was touched, and Viscount Aoki, the Japanese Ambassador, protested that treaty rights had been violated. The argument grew so heated that jingoists on both sides began screaming for war. In Tokyo, Mayor Schmitz's photograph was flaunted as a true portrait of the devil, until the authorities, fearing riots, forbade such exhibits; while at the White House, sufficient alarm was felt for President Roosevelt to confer with Admiral Dewey on fleet placements.

At first surprised, then annoyed, and finally angered, San Franciscans took refuge in the state law and refused to budge, although

Roosevelt brought pressure to bear in an attempt to force the city to modify its policy. At a critical moment, a San Francisco Congressman, Julius Kahn, telegraphed to the San Francisco board of education (by whose authority no one ever found out) that "at the request of the President and Secretary of State, we ask you to come here immediately for a conference." Schmitz promptly included himself in this invitation and announced that he was going to the nation's capital to settle the international crisis.

Ruef was disgusted. He urged the Mayor not to go, it was running away from a fight; but Eugene's sycophants persuaded him that he would return covered with glory and laureled with fame.

Ruef was in the farewell delegation when the train pulled out with Schmitz aboard. Observing that the Mayor was absenting himself from the city without the permission of the board of supervisors, the boss let loose his sarcasms: "In his ardor to immolate himself on the altar of his country, Schmitz has given the board of supervisors the right to forfeit his office at any time. Of course, it is a great and glorious thing to save the country, when it needs saving. I think I shall ask the supervisors to authorize a $10,000,000 bond issue to fortify San Francisco against an attack by the Japanese."

On the way back from the terminal he quipped: "The country was saved the minute Eugene got aboard that train."

Mayor Schmitz departed on February 3rd, and patient Judge Dunne held in abeyance the proceedings as far as they touched the absent defendant until his promised swift return.

Dunne already had disconcerted the vociferating defense by serving notice that he was not fooled by their specious gambols, that he would not be taken by ambush, and that, in three words, enough was enough. On January 22nd, with examination of grand jurors no nearer a termination than ever, Dunne interrupted the courtly eloquence which Joseph Campbell, as Schmitz's chief counsel, was pouring out in support of his client's claim to a speedy trial, and proposed a method whereby this might be brought about. If Campbell would at once submit all his motions to quash all the indictments, and also his demurrer (for Dunne was aware that this time-consumer would materialize inevitably), then, the Judge informed the startled lawyer, should the motions be denied by the court, the Mayor could go to trial the next day.

This open-and-shut proposal took Campbell aback. He hesitated.

"I thought you wanted a speedy trial," the Judge prompted.

Campbell begged time to consult his client, and after a whispered conversation, realizing that his bluff had been called, he submitted motions to dismiss all five indictments.

"All of your motions are submitted?" Dunne made certain.

"They are, your honor."

"They are denied."

"They are denied?"

"They are denied."

Campbell took exception and pleaded for time to prepare his demurrer. Judge Dunne granted him one day.

Then turning to Ach, the Judge ordered him to cease his examination of the grand jurors and submit his motions to dismiss the indictments as against Ruef. Ach tried to argue, but Dunne said he had heard the evidence. Shortridge then attempted to argue the motions, and was rebuffed. Whereupon, in a surly tone, Ach submitted motions to dismiss, and heard them denied. Ach, too, was told to have his demurrer ready in the morning.

That same day in Sacramento, the Legislature, entrusted with the conduct of the state's weighty affairs, received bills making tipping a misdemeanor and prohibiting cigarette smoking; the Senate and Assembly voted to bar snooping representatives of the San Francisco *Bulletin* from the Capitol building; and both houses overwhelmingly passed resolutions censuring "the vicious, libellous press of San Francisco."

The weather turned atrocious; and with it, tempers. Snow fell on the Berkeley hills for the first time in twelve years, the temperature dropping to twenty-six above zero. Almost continuous rains played havoc with the booming automobile trade and disrupted social life. (At the same time, Los Angeles was experiencing a blizzard.) The popular feeling against Schmitz and Ruef and the assorted boodlers soured into a mood of sullen exasperation.

Heney felt the public discontent: rumors were being circulated that he would soon retire to Oregon, allowing the San Francisco investigation to wither away; Burns was reported about to be recalled to Washington.

To combat this skepticism among the people, whose support he vitally needed, Heney resigned his connection with the United States Attorney General and announced: "I intend to stay in San Francisco until I see every one of the grafters wearing stripes." But he warned that as long as the grand jurors were immobilized in court by the graft defense, the public need expect no further indictments.

Burns, for his part, indicated *he* was not leaving San Francisco by bringing his family from the East and registering as a San Francisco voter.

Heney learned that Ruef was attempting to undermine him in another quarter, in Arizona; agents of the boss were searching old records there and interviewing witnesses in an effort to get Heney indicted for the murder of Dr. Handy. An indictment, even if it should not stand up in trial, would remove Heney from San Francisco for months, because murder is a non-bailable charge.

Meanwhile, argument on the demurrers filed by Ruef's and Schmitz's counsel engaged the attention of Judge Dunne, and a novel line of reasoning was expounded which led straight to the Humpty Dumpty conclusion that even assuming the acts set forth in the indictment had been committed by the defendants, they did not breach the law, and therefore the Mayor and the boss were being prosecuted with malicious illegality. The public, in effect, was bidden to hold on to their hats while the lawyers took them for a ride on their *ad hoc* merry-go-round.

The crux of their contention lay in the wording of the statute defining extortion: it was, the law read, the obtaining of money by threat "to do an unlawful injury to . . . the property of the person threatened."

Ach and Shortridge set forth that a license to sell alcoholic liquors was not property, but a mere certificate of permission; hence, a threat to deprive a peron of such a certificate was not a threat against his property, and so, by the clear wording of the statute, could not be unlawful. It might be a threat to inflict injury, yes, but not an *unlawful* injury, the pleaders pleaded, and they read the law over and over with sinister inflexions. Did a citizen lose his rights by being elected to public office? Barrett asked. "Any person can oppose the granting of a liquor license, and a threat to prevent a man from getting a license is not a crime," he said. However the defendants' supposed actions might be viewed morally or socially, he insisted, they had merely done what they had a lawful right to do.

Dizzy after this spin, the public echoed Heney's cry of outraged despair: "What! You mean to tell me that if those facts exist they do not mean extortion? I say then, 'God save San Francisco from something worse than fire and earthquakes!'"

Ach put the case in terms any layman could comprehend by choosing for illustration a landmark of the town, the Claus Spreckels mansion on Van Ness Avenue at Clay.

"Suppose," he said, "I owned a lot adjoining the Spreckels mansion before the fire. That property is worth half-a-million dollars or more. Suppose I should go to Mr. Spreckels and say to him, 'If you don't give me $5,000, I will build a livery stable next to your residence that will damage your property at least $50,000. He gives me the $5,000,—but a little later, without further communication with him, I erect a livery stable, and when he complains, I say to him, 'If you will give me $10,000 I will tear down the stable, but if you don't, I will leave it, to the great damage of your property.' There would be no crime in either of my acts in that connection, because I had a legal right to erect that stable and also had a legal right to take money for either not building it or tearing it down."

Ruef watched his attorney expound this legal teaser with an air of complacency. Judge Dunne listened to the strained paradoxes for two days, then called a recess to collect his wits. Two weeks later, on February 15th, he overruled the demurrer, giving his considered opinion that despite the brilliant casuistry of the defense, extortion is a crime.

He then arraigned Ruef on the five indictments and compelled him at long last to plead. One hundred and ten days after his indictment, Abraham Ruef answered to each count, in a voice firm and clearly audible, without tremor, "Not guilty." Dunne set his trial for Tuesday, March 5th.

Then four of the five indictments against Schmitz were called (the fifth was still, at that point, pending an appeal to the State Supreme Court), and attorney Drew stated that his client was "away on public business."

"Do you expect us to sit here and wait for him, the man who wanted a speedy trial?" inquired Judge Dunne sadly. "Or shall we issue a subpoena?"

In furtherance of world tranquillity, Dunne allowed Schmitz one more week to appear and plead.

While Ruef was registering his innocence in Dunne's court, in the Assembly at Sacramento, Grove Johnson was leading the debate on the change of venue bill, ridiculing the imputation that the measure was designed to bail out San Francisco's boodlers.

"If they go from Judge Dunne to Judge Lawlor," he asked, "would that not be jumping from the frying pan into the fire? Is Dunne the only honest judge in San Francisco?"

The Assembly passed the bill. Approval by the Senate yet was needed, but George Keane was there.

The lights burned late in Shortridge's office during the next week; Ach bustled in and out, officious and evasive, and the newspapers reported that behind the scenes eminent legal strategists were contributing their counsels; yet few observers doubted that the brain coordinating and regulating every decision was that of the wily Ruef. He had regained much of his bounce, and his sarcastic wit was always at the service of a hard-pressed reporter. For example, when asked how he might feel about being shunted aside to give Schmitz a quick trial—would that be all right with him?—he chuckled gravely: "Oh, perfectly! I might plead guilty just to accommodate him, or I might commit suicide, although he hasn't quite asked me to do that yet." No, he had not heard from the Mayor in Washington. "But I rejoice that the country is saved."

It was a fact: there was no war. Conflicting reports trickled back about Schmitz's reception in the capital, some sources saying that President Roosevelt had snubbed the "bassoon mayor" in two White House conferences with members of the board of education, during which he laid down the law to them with "Big Stick" bluntness. A compromise had been patched up whereby the city's schools would be opened to all Japanese pupils except a few of near-adult age, who were seeking to enroll in primary grades, owing to their total lack of previous education and recent arrival in the United States. The compromise was a setback for the San Franciscans, and for Schmitz's delusive hopes, an inglorious collapse. He dallied on the trip home, telling wayside reporters that he probably would run for mayor again.

While Schmitz dallied, the Sacramento solons were diligently at work. The Senate judiciary committee reported the change of venue bill favorably, with an amendment attached in committee by Keane,— making it effective immediately upon passage, eliminating the sixty-day wait.

11 Thimblerig

Ruef's "Green Lizard" was very much on the go those days, and the boss was still smiling. Selection of a jury to try him was to start on Tuesday, March 5th, a few days after the Assembly's passage of the change of venue bill.

But on Monday, March 4th, the case of the People against Abraham Ruef was thimblerigged, with three courts serving as the shuffled cups, Abe as the bouncing ball, and justice, blind justice, was bilked again.

Senate approval of the change of venue bill was expected momentarily—George Keane was lobbying earnestly—and with its passage, Abe would be enabled to slip the trammels of Judge Dunne's invidious restrictions and submit his difficulties to some other judge, who would know how to construe the law when it was clarified for him by those shifty counselors, Henry Ach and Samuel M. Shortridge. Ruef needed time, a few days only, in order to let the Senate act. The maneuver he adopted took the graft prosecutors utterly by surprise.

On Monday morning, Ruef's bondsmen, the Aetna Indemnity Company, suddenly surrendered him to the sheriff's custody and vacated the $50,000 bond posted for his appearance in Dunne's court the next day.

Through counsel, Ruef then applied to Superior Court Judge J.C.B. Hebbard for a writ of *habeas corpus*. A battery of lawyers was marshaled to sustain the application—Ach, Shortridge, Fairall, and

Murphy—while Heney, Johnson, and Langdon came on the run to oppose the audacious move.

Judge Hebbard was tardy in assuming his seat. At once he called: "In the matter of Abraham Ruef on *habeas corpus*."

Henry Ach arose and presented the application, based on the familiar contention that the participation of grand juror Wise had invalidated the indictments, hence Ruef was being held in violation of the Fifth and Fourteenth Amendments to the Constitution of the United States; this, said Ach, furnished grounds for an appeal to the federal courts. Sitting confidently at the counsel table, Abe coached his attorneys in whispers.

Ach began an extended argument against the "pretended" grand jury, but Judge Hebbard cut him short: "Stop that verbiage. Proceed with the case."

Hiram Johnson protested that the issues had all been argued in Judge Dunne's court.

"Has the federal question been presented?" Hebbard asked impatiently.

"It has," said Johnson.

"It has not," said Ach.

"Show it to me," said the Judge.

Then Hebbard embarked on a tangled dissertation, winding up hopelessly adrift. And he refused to let Johnson produce the record of the hearings in Judge Dunne's department.

At this, Johnson made as if to walk out of the proceedings. "It would be a farce to sit here and present matters that a co-ordinate branch of this court has already passed upon, and we refuse to be a party to such a farce," he declared.

"Is that a threat?" leered the Judge.

"No threat at all. I simply say that a co-ordinate court has passed upon these questions, and it would be a farce for you, sitting on the bench, and for me, standing here, to again present the same questions. Your honor represents the judiciary and I the People, and I don't propose to be a party to such a farce."

"So be it," replied Hebbard with unction. "I am not hedged about by other judges. All I want is the facts, and then I'll give the law."

"All I want is an opportunity to present our record of the facts," responded Johnson, "and then your honor can decide."

"Indeed I will."

A recess was taken until 2:00 P.M. to permit the prosecution to produce the record. Judge Hebbard retired with uncertain step to his chambers.

To everybody in the courtroom it was plain that the Judge was drunk. Nevertheless, upon their reassembling, Johnson offered to prove from the record that in a four-day argument before Judge Dunne the federal question had formed an important part. Ach protested that the previous argument settled nothing, while Johnson submitted that Hebbard's sense of justice would not permit him to interfere with the proceedings of another branch of the court.

Hebbard had been mellowed by his sojourn in chambers.

"Excuse me," he said dreamily; "I differ with my colleagues in many matters of the law. I differ with my colleagues frequently. I will hear the facts."

Ach continued to harp upon the disability of juror Wise, until Johnson broke in that before such a travesty he believed the People's representatives should withdraw.

Judge Hebbard waved airily and said that withdrawal by the District Attorney would not prevent the court from dispensing even-handed justice.

"That is right, sir," answered Johnson, "and I hope it will not. But we decline to participate in any proceedings that we do not consider in conformity with the dignity of the court."

"The State of California can withdraw any time it pleases," repeated Hebbard with a glassy eye, "but it will not prevent the court from proceeding in accordance with what it deems its judicial duty."

"Again we protest," responded Johnson, gathering up his records, "on behalf of the District Attorney of this city and county and in the name of the People of California. We do not believe in this; we will not participate in it; and we take our leave of this court. We will not participate in any proceeding which does not, according to our own ideas, comport with the dignity of justice, the dignity of this court, or our own dignity."

And Langdon, Heney, and Johnson walked out of the room.

Judge Hebbard focused a wavering eye on his clerk.

"Send for the Attorney General that the State of California may be represented," he instructed, and retired to his chambers a second time, while Ruef whispered to his counsel smugly.

Half an hour later, Hebbard reappeared and said that Attorney General Webb was out of the city and his assistants did not feel free to participate without orders from him. In a melancholy vein he added: "I am very sorry the prosecution saw fit to treat this court so cavalierly as they have done. I do not know how to regard it. There is an imputation against this court. I do not think it is warranted." He nodded to Ach. "I understand that your desire is to take it to a court of last resort?"

Up to that point nothing had been said to indicate that such was the defense's purpose.

"Yes, your honor," Ach replied, "that is our intention."

Judge Hebbard thereupon denied the writ, but allowed an appeal to be taken to the United States Supreme Court, making this a basis for setting new bail of $50,000. The Aetna Indemnity Company posted the still-intact bond, and Ruef walked out of the courtroom looking content.

Within thirty minutes, his counsel had filed the appeal with the clerk of the federal circuit court in San Francisco, and an appearance before the Supreme Court in Washington was set for May 2nd.

The gulled bystanders—the public—were furious and helpless. Even Heney was crestfallen. He denounced the pretense of federal jurisdiction as "an absurdity so profound it would startle the brain of an idiot."

"We left the courtroom of Judge Hebbard," he stated, "because we came to the conclusion that there had been a complete understanding between Ruef's attorneys and the court regarding the action to be taken, and that the matter had all been decided upon in advance. In addition to this, Judge Hebbard was very much under the influence of liquor and in no condition to hear arguments. This is not an unusual condition with Judge Hebbard, for he has been a disgrace to the Superior bench of this city for the last three years, and this is a fact that is known to a majority of the members of the bar. It is his habitual practice to go on long debauches, during which he commits all sorts of breaks. It is time for the Bar Association to wake up and take some action before the courts come into utter disrepute, not only with the members of the legal profession but with the city generally. Hebbard originally had a brilliant mind, but the continuous and excessive use of liquor has nearly destroyed it."

That day in Sacramento the Senate passed by acclamation Keane's amendment to the change of venue bill, making it effective immediately. Speedy final passage of the bill was in prospect. Moaned the press, "graft never sleeps at the switch," and the *Chronicle* lamented that "the people of California, and especially of San Francisco, have sunk to such a condition of impotency as would secure the pity of the inhabitants of the most politically degraded country in the world."

Tuesday morning, before Judge Dunne, the court clerk called the name "Abraham Ruef" three times, but there was no response. Ruef's attorney, Shortridge, was on hand with other members of the boss's entourage, but none of them knew where Abe might be, they said.

"I have not seen my client since yesterday," Shortridge blandly informed the court, "but I am told that he is attending to his private affairs. I don't think he has gone out of the city, but I don't know where he is."

Henry Ach was evasive.

Dunne ruled Shortridge was a counsel without a client and Ruef a fugitive from justice. He ordered his bail forfeited.

This drew from Shortridge the objection that the case was before the federal courts, with a hint that Dunne might be embarrassed to find himself in contempt of the United States Supreme Court.

"Not embarrassed at all," replied Judge Dunne. "I would have you understand, Mr. Shortridge, that I am proceeding as though nothing happened yesterday."

He signed a bench warrant for Ruef's arrest and handed it to Sheriff O'Neil to serve.

Shortridge and Ach immediately petitioned the State Court of Appeals for a writ of prohibition to stay Judge Dunne from proceeding against Ruef, inasmuch as the indictments were invalid and the question lay before the federal court. Twenty-four hours later, the Appellate Court unanimously denied the petition without comment, thereby indicating that they deemed it to be without merit.

Within two hours, Ruef's legal deputies appealed this decision to the State Supreme Court, but they were beginning to look bedraggled. Judge Dunne awaited the event tranquilly. Ruef was in hiding; Judge Hebbard had been carried to a hospital, a delirious wreck; while in Sacramento, attorney Joseph C. Campbell, Schmitz's counsel, had appeared to lobby *against* the change of venue bill; Campbell, it was rumored, had withdrawn from the mayor's case! And the Legislature's adjournment day was not far off.

Across the nation, Ruef's exploitation of a drunken judge evoked outcries of revulsion. "Abe Ruef—still a lawyer in good standing—is exhibit A in the case of the People against the Legal Profession!" exploded *Collier's* magazine, and the publicly prodded San Francisco Bar Association called an emergency meeting for that Friday evening to consider the shocking travesty.

Hebbard had been a Superior Court judge eighteen years, owing his periodic re-election to the complaisance of Ruef and previous city bosses. A Superior Court judgeship at that time seldom held men of first-rate ability long: the salary was mediocre (only a few weeks before these occurrences the Legislature had raised it from $4,000 a year to $6,000 in San Francisco, and less in other counties) and the prestige was slight. Hebbard's deterioration through progressive alcoholism had been exhibited in many ways. In a volume of his musings in prose and verse (*A Deck of Cards and a Joker, Shuffled and Dealt by J.C.B. Hebbard, Sometimes Called "Jack" Hebbard.*) appeared a poem entitled, "The Clock":

> *Did you ever listen to the clock?*
> *Did you ever hear it talk?*
> *Did you ever in the night*
> *when you were not quite right,*
> *Hear it say as it ticked—*
> *"You drink*
> *I think*
> *You drink*
> *I think..."*

> *And when you couldn't sleep,*
> *And you wanted much to weep—*
> *Did you ever hear the clock,*
> *With its melancholy talk—*
> *"Too bad, too bad,*
> *I'm sorry you are sad."*
> *Did you ever hear the clock tick that way?*

Another rhyme expressed clearly enough his feelings toward his position. This was entitled "The Judge," and began:

> *Were you ever once a judge?*
> *Well, it's funny—it's a fudge...*

and concluded:

> *Ah! The shysters at the bar,*
> *Who know not moon from star,*
> *Are thick!*
> *Makes me sick*
> *In 'Frisco!*

If this were not sufficiently explicit, the previous January Hebbard had addressed a round-robin letter to the newspapers containing his opinion of himself and his colleagues, as follows:

This court has been criticized by the press, the public, and the leading lawyers of the bar as incompetent. My opinion is that it is not only incompetent but incorrigible, and ought to be impossible. We prolong the trial of cases beyond all reason. We delay decisions, or make them *pro forma,* for convenience, until the lawyers are tired. We fear public opinion, and we have not enough bowels to stand against it and decide cases according to the law and the Constitution. Personally I am in favor of a universal impeachment by the Legislature of the entire bench of San Francisco.

Such was the mentally tormented man whom Ruef utilized in his game of legal shuffleboard. The morning after his fantastic performance in court, Hebbard tried to shoot a reporter, was knocked down by a stranger in a brawl, was evicted from his hotel, and was forcibly carried, raving maudlinly, to a hospital where he was calmed with sedatives and guarded against all intrusion. Doctors said his breakdown was complete.

On Friday evening, at the Bar Association meeting, Heney formally repeated his accusation saying: "The charges reported by the press as having been made by me regarding Judge Hebbard I reiterate. But ten times more disgraceful and culpable than Judge Hebbard have been the actions of attorneys Ach, Shortridge, and Fairall in making a tool of an incompetent judge to further the ends of their client."

A hundred attorneys crowded the rooms, and speeches were made against Hebbard in tones of indignation and sorrow. Ach, seated three feet from Heney, warmly defended himself and his associates: Judge Hebbard, he said, was as sober as any person there present, including Heney,—"if he is sober." Several members supported Ach, and a committee was appointed to investigate and report. Ach moved that Judge Dunne also be investigated, but the motion was howled down.

12   Trocadero Rendezvous

Abraham Ruef, beneficiary of a bleary legal sleight of hand, walked out of Judge Hebbard's courtroom and assumed invisibility. All day Tuesday Sheriff O'Neil successfully avoided finding him. When a Burns detective telephoned that the boss had just gone into the restaurant in his office building at Fillmore and Bush, Burns himself took O'Neil there and helped conduct the search. They pried into closets, washrooms, the cold-storage room, the kitchen, coal bins, under tables, and peeped into empty barrels,—no Abe was found. They looked into the bank next door, then upstairs in Abe's quarters. O'Neil even offered to break open the locked door of the boss's private office, but Burns said no thanks. "If you're willing to look for him there," he chuckled, "it's a sure thing he isn't inside."

(Later Burns learned that the boss had been in the building all during the search, stepping back and forth through a door connecting the restaurant and the bank as the hunt shifted, and after the Sheriff departed, finishing his luncheon in good humor.)

Convinced that O'Neil had no intention of making an arrest, Judge Dunne handed the warrant to the next court official in line, Coroner Walsh. The coroner was no more successful than Sheriff O'Neil. He hunted all day Wednesday, and at 2:00 P.M. Thursday informed Judge Dunne that after due and diligent search, he had been utterly unable to find the defendant Ruef.

"Take the stand," snapped Dunne.

Heney then forced the Coroner to describe under oath the efforts he had made to carry out the order of the court.

"Well, I spoke to people on the street and asked if they had seen Ruef," replied Walsh.

"Did you go to Henry Ach and ask him if he knew where Ruef was?"

"No."

"Did you ask Ruef's father and sister when they last saw or communicated with him?"

"I did not."

"Did you search the Ruef home?"

"No."

"Did you attempt to see Samuel Shortridge, Charles Fairall, or Frank Murphy and get information from them?"

"I did not."

Shortridge sauntered in, resplendent in a new fawn-colored top-coat, green scarf, and red gloves with white stitching along the backs, smiling his oily smile; there was always something of the stage prelate about Slick Sam. He listened with a detached air while Judge Dunne reprimanded the uncontrite Coroner in a low tone, saying, "You ought to be ashamed of yourself for making such a silly return." The court ordered Walsh to try again, and when Shortridge intruded with an attempt to question the witness, Dunne cut him short. The lawyer, with insulting unctuousness, declared that it certainly was his intention to question Walsh, and Dunne held him in contempt and sentenced him to serve twenty-four hours in the county jail. This took the wind out of Sam's sails, he became meek, and as court was adjourning he supplicated: "Would you stay that matter until tomorrow—that little matter?"

"No stay at all," said Dunne, and passed into his chambers.

Sheriff O'Neil instructed his deputies not to arrest Shortridge, and

a sympathetic attorney who had suffered the same punishment from
Judge Dunne a couple of years before volunteered to show him how he
might evade incarceration. Eventually, through appeals to other
courts, Shortridge did avoid going to jail; but he was more respectful
toward Dunne from then on. The city hoped the new policy of
severity would be extended to other pestilential lawyers.

In the midst of Coroner Walsh's infructuous searchings, Mayor
Schmitz appeared before Judge Dunne to enter his plea on four
counts of extortion. He had crept into the city by a roundabout route
the day before; no reception committee was at the railroad station
(he had been threatened with a welcoming barrage of eggs), only
a few true friends. In a voice so faint it was inaudible—his attorney
had to repeat the words for the benefit of the Judge—the Mayor four
times pleaded "Not guilty." No one asked him if he knew the whereabouts of Ruef; in fact, in the furor over the boss's vanishing, the
Mayor found himself decidedly playing second fiddle.

On Friday afternoon, Coroner Walsh reported that his search for
one of the city's most easily recognized citizens was still fruitless.
Where had he looked? Why, he said, in all the better hotels and
barrooms,—the Dorchester, Majestic, Savoy, Little Palace, Taît's,
the Poodle Dog, Marchand's, Techau Tavern. Then he had visited the
roadhouses, and out at the beach,—Uncle Tom's Cabin, Sheehan's,
Dibble's, a liquid itinerary. And everywhere he had asked the same
question: "Have you seen Ruef?" At 11:35 P.M., he went to Ruef's
home and looked in the boss's bed; it was empty.

Thereupon Dunne disqualified Walsh as patently biased, and at
4:00 P.M. appointed an elisor (a minor court official usually employed
to run the bench's errands) with authority to arrest and hold the
fugitive. The man chosen was William J. Biggy, a former police commissioner and chief of police in the Phelan regime and a well-known
anti-Ruef man, whose pride was his reputation for inflexible honesty.

At seven o'clock that evening, Biggy and Burns arrested Ruef in
a roadhouse in a deep, wooded ravine off the main road a mile south

of Golden Gate Park. The name of the discreet hideaway was the Trocadero. Burns had led Biggy directly to the place.

They went upstairs, and Biggy rapped on a closed door. It opened, and Myrtile Cerf peered out. Biggy pushed past him, followed by Burns and detectives. Beside the window sat Abe Ruef in a rocking chair, waiting for his supper; Cerf had mistaken Biggy's rap for the waiter's.

The boss quickly overcame his surprise. "Glad to see you," he said with aplomb. "Will you boys join me in a drink?"

A suitcase and a few articles of clothing were the only luggage. These were bundled together and the party headed back to town. It had rained all day, a steady, fine drizzle, and the pavement, houses, and trees slid past mournfully in the headlights' glare. Ruef sat between Burns and Biggy in the back seat of a hooded touring car; in front rode the chauffeur and Burns's son, George, the other detectives following in a second machine.

They drove directly to the Red House, where Burns went inside. Heney was attending the Bar Association meeting on Hebbard, but Langdon and Dunne were reached by telephone, and the question of where to lodge the prisoner was debated; in either the city prison or the county jail he would be among friends and his escape might be counted on. The discussion went on for an hour and a half, while Abe sat patiently in the automobile. The rain sifted down and the headlights glimmered bleakly on the whitish tomb of Thomas Starr King, the Civil War preacher-orator, in front of the Unitarian church next door. Several newspaper photographers huddled on the porch of the house, waiting for Abe to alight, but the boss and his guards sat there. A passer-by glanced into the car and laughed: "Scratch you from the Burns handicap!"

Burlesqued Ruef: " 'Twas such a night as this at Waterloo."

Finally, Judge Dunne approved an arrangement whereby the prisoner would be taken for the time being to the Little St. Francis Hotel, where that afternoon Biggy had reserved a room for himself. Burns came outside and told Ruef. Abe indicated the rain, and condoled: "The very heavens are against you."

"Or against you!" came Burns's chuckle.

At the St. Francis, Biggy registered the distinguished guest and was assigned room 119, in the corner of the little wooden building nearest the Stockton and Post streets angle of Union Square. Ruef at once used the wall telephone to call his friends.

"Hello, this is Ruef. Say, I'm here at the St. Francis. Room 119."

News photographers entered, and for a moment the mask dropped and Abe shouted: "Get out of here! All of you! I've got the right to put you out and I won't have you here!"

"Oh, be a good fellow, Mr. Ruef," coaxed Biggy.

"You be damned!" Ruef snapped, and snarled at a tallish photographer: "You're a big son of a bitch, that's what you are!"

"I wouldn't call you that, Mr. Ruef," the man answered.

"No, because you never had any occasion!"

But the boss soon recovered his good humor, ordered drinks for everybody, and posed for the cameramen, keeping up a patter of jokes.

"How long had I been out at the Trocadero? Oh, I had been there about an hour and a half, anyway. We were just preparing to come into town when Burns arrived with Biggy and forty-eight other guards. I could have ducked the bunch—or licked them single-handed —but what's the use? Now if you fellows will form a hollow square at the finish, maybe you can help me escape."

By now, friends were arriving, and the two bottles of beer and several ponies of whisky sent over from the grill across the street were insufficient to go around.

"Never mind," said Abe genially, "I'll order more."

Carefully, he looked over his quarters.

"How many rooms have we here? Why, we've hired the whole floor! We're going to live well,—as long as that $100,000 lasts!"

For publication, he dictated a dignified statement contending that he had acted in good faith throughout, believing the proceedings before Judge Hebbard had superseded Judge Dunne's authority, and had merely gone away for a few days of needed rest. And he justified his efforts to escape from Judge Dunne's jurisdiction with the words:

I had been advised that Dunne practically contracted to pack a jury. I am willing to be tried on this infamous charge, of which I am not guilty, but I want a fair judge and a fair jury. I do not propose, if it is at all possible, to go up against a stacked jury and a prejudiced judge. Dunne has made insolent and unfair remarks to the attorneys without provocation; he has referred unfairly to the mayor, during his absence; he cast slurs upon him and has not refrained from doing the same to me. Innocence will avail nothing against such a combination of judge and prosecution,—the latter of which is openly being paid out of private funds to achieve private results.

At 11:30, Ruef prevailed on Biggy to take him out for a midnight supper. Away the crowd went—Burns, Biggy, two detectives, and Cerf—to a Fillmore Street café, where they were joined by Samuel Shortridge. At sight of his counsel, Ruef exclaimed gaily: "Well, I'm glad to see someone else who is in trouble! I've just learned that you are billed for a twenty-four-hour stint in the county jail!"

Shortridge winced; he often winced under the boss's sarcasms.

By 2:00 A.M. Ruef was in bed at the Little St. Francis, with Biggy snoring in the same room.

Late that night Heney called at the hotel, and received from Burns the full story of the arrest.

13 End of the Preamble

The captured boss's legal squadron wheeled into action to extricate him from Biggy's custody. Fairall applied to Judge Dunne for Ruef's release on bail. Judge Dunne refused. Fairall and Shortridge then petitioned the United States District Court for a writ of *habeas corpus*. And in Sacramento, the boss's cohorts worked frantically to provide some last-minute avenue of escape; for when Ruef disappeared, the Senate, taking fright, had *rejected* the change of venue bill,—and adjournment was at hand.

The grand jury looked into Abe's flight and elicited from Myrtile Cerf that he had been in telephone communication with persons unnamed while in hiding; Cerf loyally refused to divulge their identity. Ruef's chauffeur told the jurors he had taken the boss to the Trocadero at 11:00 P.M. Tuesday, driving right past the Ingleside county jail where Sheriff O'Neil was "looking for Ruef." The chauffeur had told nobody about the trip, he said, because nobody had asked him,— including the Sheriff and the Coroner.

Settled in a comfortable room, with a sophisticated menu and

wine list at his command, with permission to receive friends and relatives, the delicately incarcerated boss tried to keep a light heart, but
the sight of the guards roweled him. Two Burns detectives were always
in the room and two more in the hall outside, and the boss was allowed
to talk with visitors only in the presence and hearing of these
detectives.

"I feel as jolly as a clam at high tide," Abe maintained gallantly. "I
am living on the best the land affords, and I have been shown every
consideration by my captors. But it is not always pleasant to be a bird
in a gilded cage."

Glimpsing his face in the mirror, he grimaced; he seemed more
worried than at any other time since the prosecution began. But he
could still banter, telling reporters with airy nonchalance: "In my
little vacation, which Burns and Biggy brought to an abrupt ending,
I gathered material for a comic opera. I shall call it, 'The Troubles of
a Political Boss.' It will be a laughing hit."

On the Sunday after his arrest his lawyers seemed to have brought
cheerful news, for he poked fun at everybody. From his luncheon
bill of fare, reporters deduced that he was not being scrimped:

Toke points
Astrakhan caviar
Planked smelts
Fried sweetbreads
Squab
Chicken
Lobster salad
Biscuit Tortoni
Cocktails and wine

(The bill for this 1907 Lucullan snack, provided by one of the
most expensive restaurants in the city, totaled $5.15.)

During the day Ruef's father and sisters visited him, with Charlie
Haggerty and Myrtile Cerf. Schmitz did not call. The boss was never
out of sight of the detectives, but he still had hopes of wriggling out
from under Judge Dunne's thumb.

"If I were on the bench and a prisoner objected to being tried
before me, I would withdraw," he said petulantly. "Dunne should do
the same."

In court on Monday morning, Dunne heard Henry Ach argue that further proceedings there would be utterly illegal, in view of Judge Hebbard's action.

"Do you mean to say that, following the letter of the law, when one branch of a court has a prisoner on trial, a co-ordinate branch of the court may release the prisoner?" asked the Judge.

"It's the letter of the law, whether it's the spirit or not," was Ach's reply.

Again Dunne refused bail, and ordered Biggy to produce the defendant for trial two days hence.

This seemed to cast Abe down, and his attorneys were plainly disheartened. Schmitz had been in the courtroom when the Judge ruled, and his manner toward his co-defendant was cool. The Mayor looked pale and shrunken; his face was creased with lines of worry as he conversed in whispers with Police Chief Dinan, his faithful escort.

That day Heney, Johnson, and Langdon succeeded in plugging three more legal loopholes through which the accused pair were attempting to scuttle: in the federal District Court Abe was denied *habeas corpus;* the State Supreme Court refused to order Judge Dunne to desist from trying Schmitz and Ruef; and the State Court of Appeals listened to Shortridge's argument on behalf of still another petition to free Ruef—and after a brief interval denied it.

To crown the defense's disasters, the Legislature adjourned. No help from that quarter.

Thus, on Wednesday, March 13, 1907, the trial of Abraham Ruef at last got under way.

A crowd gathered outside Temple Sherith Israel when the boss arrived with Biggy in the fine red automobile which Spreckels had placed at the elisor's disposal. The exiguous courtroom—a former classroom in the Temple School—was crammed, with standees on the desks craning for a view of the boss brought to bay. Before the session got under way, Schmitz and Ruef held a long and apparently cordial chat. Then Judge Dunne continued the Mayor's trial for three weeks, with the understanding that it would follow Ruef's, and Eugene departed with a smile of relief.

Despite Ach's stigmatizing the action as "tyrannical and arbitrary,"

Dunne remanded the prisoner into Biggy's custody for the duration of the trial. All roadblocks to orderly execution of justice upon trickster Abe seemed battered down, and upon his return to the St. Francis he looked depressed. Yet should a reporter tap at his door, he would regain his vivacity.

"This is the first time that I have really taken a rest," he confided. "While the lack of exercise is keeping my appetite down, I believe the sojourn in this palatial little home will do me a world of good. What's the use of worrying? Of course, I am separated from my family, but we all look upon it as an enforced vacation,—and the best part of the affair is that some other man or men must pay the bills."

Sarcasm superseded affability when he reckoned this cost: "Yes, they have put on five extra guards—George Burns, here, and Mr. Sullivan—two in that room—and another—where is McCarthy? Oh, there he is, under the bed. No, here he comes down the hall. Five guards at $5 a day each,—that's $25. Biggy should be worth at least $6 a day, but I think he draws a hundred,—that makes $125. Put down $25 a day for board, meals, and sundries,—a good total of $150 a day. Thirty of these days make a month's stay here cost some person $4,500. Now, this trial is expected to last six months, so there you have a good total of $27,000 to be paid by somebody or somebodies.

"I intended to make my spectacular getaway for the benefit of the newspapers and the cameramen last evening, but the rainy weather spoiled the program. Moreover, every window and skylight here is securely fastened; I reconnoitered them all. So I can't see why all the guards are necessary, unless it be that someone recognizes a good thing and is laying extra hands on the payroll. But I have no complaint. I retire at ten o'clock; it used to be two or three A.M. I read the papers and other dime novels, and I seldom hear politics discussed, which is a relief.

"Judge Dunne? Well—whenever I discuss him, I am forced to ring for the waiter."

As a scamp, he could still make the town laugh.

A number of millionaires over in Pacific Heights laughed with the rest. They were not "cheap politicians," but men of substance and respectability and power in the community. They knew Abe was not going to talk. They felt secure.

Second Book

The City at War

A people so full of contrasts and so extreme in all their doings, so much guided by their emotions and so little by fixed principles, always behaving better, or worse, than one expected of them ... the best qualified to become ... the object of admiration, of hatred, of compassion, or alarm—never of indifference.

—ALEXIS DE TOCQUEVILLE

PART ONE

"Surely the serpent will bite without enchantment; and a babbler is no better."

1 Burns at Work

One day Francis J. Heney received a telephone call. An unfamiliar voice said: "I am the son of Dr. Handy, of Arizona, whom you remember. I want to see you on particular business."

In the old West, when the son of a man you had killed sent word that he wanted to see you, it was time to shift the gun. Heney shifted his; but he met young Handy alone. The latter, sitting down peaceably, told a story.

Six months after Dr. Handy's shooting, his wife died, leaving five children. The eldest boy was taken into the home of his father's sister, a woman of her brother's harshness and determination, and through the years she had preached that Heney murdered the boy's father. Twenty years later, young Handy was in San Francisco, driving a horse-truck for the city. Abe Ruef discovered him, sent for him, took him to lunch, and made a proposal.

171

"I want you to go down to Arizona and get Heney indicted for the murder of your father," said the boss. "I'll send down there; we'll take care of you and pave the way."

Young Handy asked for time to think it over, and telephoned Heney.

Heney already knew that an assistant city attorney, Howard Harran, a Ruef appointee, had spent weeks and some $20,000 in Arizona trying to procure an indictment; Heney's brother, Ben, still lived in Tucson and kept him informed.

"I thank you," the prosecutor said. "But why do you tell this to me?"

"Mr. Heney, I was brought up to believe that it was my duty to kill you, that I was no man unless I did. But after I grew up, I went back to Arizona. I talked with old friends of my father and with old friends of yours, and I looked over the testimony at the investigation. And I concluded that not only were you justified, but that I owe you a debt of gratitude for what you did for my mother. I said then if I ever had a chance to help you out, I would do it. Here is where I make good. Shall I go down to Arizona and find out what they are doing?"

Heney thanked him again, but told him not to bother. Later, when an unfriendly newspaper obtained a statement from the aunt calling Heney a murderer, the slain man's son repeated his story to the San Francisco *Call* just as he had told it to Heney.

This encounter was only one incident in the maze of crosscurrents and intrigue which already surrounded the graft investigation. About these hidden currents the public knew nothing. Heney, a politician by temperament, was sharply aware of the necessity of retaining public support; he had promised "big things," the grand jury had expected to receive "big" evidence, and when fulfillment of this promise kept being deferred month after month, the public and the jury grew restive,—and Heney worried.

The French restaurants extortion indictments against Ruef and Schmitz verged on more or less accepted police graft; even the perjury indictment of Police Chief Dinan fell short of the mark the prosecution had set up: not one case of bribery had been developed, and a feeling was growing that such meager results hardly justified so much noise and effort. But bribery is one of the hardest crimes to prove. A bribe is passed in secret; only two parties usually are involved; there seldom are witnesses; and care is taken to leave no trace. Hence, unless either the giver or the taker of the bribe admits the transaction, it is almost impossible to obtain legal proof.

Ruef had pointed to this dilemma of the prosecution when Heney took office. Referring to the rumors about a bribe in the United Railroads trolley deal, the boss said triumphantly: "You see that Tirey Ford denies any money was paid. The supervisors will deny it. I will deny it. And where else are they going to find anyone to summon who could tell anything about it?"

Where, indeed? The obstinacy of facts seemed to be threatening the prosecution with defeat. As Heney was to recall: "From October, 1906, until March, 1907, we labored every day trying to get evidence of the graft that we all were satisfied existed in San Francisco, without getting anything. For five long, weary months we labored until midnight and after midnight, sometimes until two and even three o'clock in the morning, struggling to work out a case."

Spreckels began to doubt Heney's ability to deliver. Heney grew doubtful that Burns could pin down the facts. Burns himself was wavering. Outwardly, all three professed confidence, and Spreckels informed men of his acquaintance whom he suspected of having bribed city officials, or consenting to bribery, that since they were certain to be involved they might better become witnesses for the State and escape punishment. These friends smiled and urged him to keep after those rascally politicians.

Fremont Older worked closely with Burns in the devious hunt, and did happen on one instance of bribery which he believed could be made to stick. It concerned the so-called "fight trust," a consortium of prize-fight managers who had paid Ruef $20,000 to obtain a monopoly of fight permits, which were issued by the board of supervisors. But Heney let this matter lie while he concentrated on the French restaurants case.

Burns deployed every trick in his capacious bag. He was shadowed continually by sheriff's deputies, city detectives, attorneys, the sporting gentry, businessmen, and reporters, and against all these he played a game of cunning. He maintained a network of counterspies. He would drop misleading remarks for city detectives to overhear and pass along. Sometimes he would disclose developments calculated to

spread consternation in the opposition ranks. He would call openly
on directors of public-service corporations when he knew they were
not in their offices. He subverted their chauffeurs and household
servants; when they bought his agents, he passed out phoney tips for
these double spies to transmit. In the whole Schmitz administration
he found a resemblance to a petty ducal court,—everybody had a
spoon in the gravy, and everybody suspected everybody else of
cheating, and Burns played with virtuosity on this mutual distrust.
Learning, for instance, that each supervisor had his allotted source
of graft, he started whispers that other supervisors were cutting in;
then his agents would confidentially sound out the separate members
on whether each was "getting his pinch." If Burns heard about some
private kudos being knocked off by the Mayor, he would make sure
Ruef was told; and whenever he suspected the boss had taken a fee
without splitting with Eugene, the word leaked back to Schmitz by
mysterious routes. This tactic Burns called "pouring in the poison";
his objective was to demoralize the administration and bring about a
break in its ranks. But at every point he was frustrated by the perfection of Ruef's control.

When Gallagher dismissed Maestretti, Burns saw an opening:
Maestretti was "sore as a boil," hot for revenge upon the boss and
the Mayor who had double-crossed him. Allied with Maestretti in
business and intimate with the Ruef coterie was Golden M. Roy,
a jeweler who also operated a restaurant on Van Ness Avenue and
was a partner with Maestretti in the Dreamland roller-skating rink.
Roller skating was at the peak of its vogue, and Dreamland was the
largest and most profitable rink in the city.

Older undertook to test the ice in regard to Maestretti. Dropping
into the Dreamland office one day, he invited the partners to come
over to the prosecution; as insiders, they probably could reveal a great
deal about the graft operations of the machine, Older thought, and he
frankly advised them to join the side that was going to win. As he was
leaving, Older was taken aside by Maestretti and warned not to trust
Roy; the jeweler, he was cautioned, was Ruef's man.

This nibble at the bait Burns shrewdly interpreted to mean that
Maestretti was ready to defect, but wanted to claim all the benefit
that might accrue from such action for himself. Thereupon Burns
paid a call upon Roy,—and instantly recognized him as a fugitive

from an Oklahoma forgery charge (a bankruptcy matter) of ten years back; his name then had been Moritz Roy Golden. Since coming to San Francisco, Roy had prospered, married, and reared a family, to whom he was deeply attached. Burns said nothing, but he told Older the facts.

When in pursuit of news or serving what he currently considered a noble cause, the *Bulletin* editor cared little for means and everything for results. He decided to use coercion to force Roy to help. He had the Oklahoma story set in type, pulled a single proof, and sent for the jeweler.

Roy walked into Older's office with a patronizing, "What can I do for you!"

"You can't do anything for me," shouted the editor, "but I am going to send you to the penitentiary!" And he held up the proof.

Roy read it and turned pale. When he finished, he said: "What do you want me to do?"

"Tell the truth."

Burns then entered from the next room and Older stalked out.

In a little while, Burns came out and said that Roy wanted to consult his friends before he started talking.

"It isn't friends, it's a friend," snorted Older. "He wants to see Ruef. I don't think we ought to let him."

"No," Burns disagreed, "I think it best to let him see his friends."

Roy went to his home, remained there without communicating with anyone until midnight, then telephoned to Burns that he was ready to co-operate. From that moment on, Roy's assistance to the graft prosecution was daring, ingenious, and unreserved. Whether coercion had been necessary to bring him to this decision, Older never knew; all he knew, and recounted later with compunction, was that he did use threats.

Neither Roy nor Maestretti, however, could vouch personally for anything that formed proof of bribery of the supervisors; they merely knew the hearsay in that connection. But at Roy's suggestion, Burns set about trapping some of the "boodle board" into accepting a bribe, and thus frightening some or all of them into revealing the big graft. An opportunity arose through a campaign against skating rinks which had been launched by a crusading Catholic priest; the places, he preached, were hotbeds of immorality, recruiting grounds for sin. Innocent girls, he declared, were being ruined by the depraved males they met there. When other clergymen took up the cry, Burns seized on the agitation and drafted an ordinance forbidding roller-skating rinks to admit any girl under eighteen years of age, unless she was accompanied by her mother. No better rule could have been devised to put the rinks out of business, and Burns had the ordinance passed to Mayor Schmitz by a roundabout channel, with the intimation that it would stop the mouths of the crusaders and also would strike back at Maestretti, part-owner of Dreamland Rink. Burns expected Schmitz to consult Ruef about the matter, and, sure enough, when the ordinance was introduced before the supervisors, it was in a copy bearing Ruef's interlineations.

Tom Lonergan, the bakery-wagon driver, was chosen by the prosecution as perhaps the likeliest to be lured out of line. The stage was set in Roy's office at Dreamland. Burns borrowed a gimlet from a grocery store and bored three holes in the door connecting with an inner office; then Roy placed two chairs where they could be seen through these peepholes. The action was rehearsed with Older and Burns stationed at the gimlet holes: sitting in one of the chairs, Roy pretended to count out money to the occupant of the other chair, repeating agreed-upon lines.

"A little to the right. A little louder, Roy," the prompters coached. At last it was letter-perfect. Older scoffed that the scheme was too stagey, too melodramatic to succeed, although Roy was sure it would go off exactly as planned. Burns and Older remained skeptical, but Roy—tall, dark, and nerveless—was confident. He sent a message to Lonergan, saying he wanted to see him, and Tom arrived by appointment at a time when Burns, Rudolph Spreckels' secretary, and a stenographer were posted at the gimlet holes. Roy motioned Lonergan to sit in the strategically placed chair, and when Lonergan shifted it slightly, the imperturbable Roy pulled it back into range.

"Tom," the jeweler began, "we skating-rink men have made up a purse to have that ordinance killed, and we want you to protect us thereafter. Will you stand in?"

"Sure."

"Well, here's your money." Carefully, in sight of the hidden witnesses and in a loud, clear voice, he counted out marked bills. "Fifty, one hundred, two hundred, three hundred, four hundred, five hundred. That right?"

"That's right. Five hundred plunks. I'll be your friend as long as you live, Roy."

For the benefit of the concealed witnesses, the jeweler made the purpose of the bribe unmistakably clear, repeating: "There is no writing, of course, so it must be understood between us, Tom, that you accept this money and you agree in consideration of it to vote against the ordinance. Is that understood?"

"That's understood."

"And there'll be other things," Roy added significantly.

"Well, you can depend on me for anything you want. Coffey [the hack man] told me to pick up his, too."

"Oh, no. You tell Coffey to come get his himself; I want an understanding with each one of you."

After the supervisor had gone, Burns hurried to Heney with the evidence. A detective soon reported that Lonergan had taken his boodle directly home and given it to his wife, who had placed it in a safe-deposit box.

This transaction occurred in February, 1907, while Mayor Schmitz was in Washington on his Japanese peace mission, telling reporters who wanted to know why President Roosevelt called him the "bassoon mayor" that he really couldn't guess, because he knew very little about music; and while Ruef was springing legal ambuscades in his fight to avoid trial.

A couple of days after Lonergan succumbed, Supervisor Walsh accepted $500 before the gimlet holes. Then Dr. Boxton, the dentist, joined the parade, but for him the action was transferred to the front parlor of Roy's home, out on Clay Street, overlooking Alta Plaza. Burns and his witnesses watched from the darkened back dining room through a chink in the double doors, that had been left slightly ajar.

Roy begged off from trapping Gallagher, who was his friend, but in order to preserve the appearance of a general bribery, he offered Gallagher $1,000 privately. But Big Jim stood on friendship: Roy was one of the boys, he said, and the supervisors would kill the ordinance for nothing. At this Roy feigned annoyance, protesting: "If it was my money I'd see you in hell before I'd give you a cent. But it's a fund. All the rinks contributed, so you boys might as well take it."

Gallagher asked whether any of the other members of the board had already taken money, and Roy admitted they had, but refused to say which ones. "You wouldn't expect me to tell on you?" he objected reasonably.

Thinking it over, Gallagher suspected Lonergan, and when Tom was questioned and admitted his indiscretion, Gallagher marched him to Ruef on the double-quick, the way he would have hustled a suspected carrier of some deadly disease to a doctor.

"Give it back," Ruef ordered. It was probably a trap set by Burns, he warned; Roy must have turned stool pigeon.

When this was reported to Roy, he stormed into the boss's office and upbraided him so sharply Abe conceded that he had been misled, and apologized.

Lonergan did not give back the $500, but unwittingly he rendered useless the prosecution's efforts by breaking the chain of evidence they were forging. Sometime previously, Burns had provided a partner with whom Tom opened a small electrical supplies shop (Spreckels put up the capital), and it had been arranged that directly after Lonergan accepted the bribe from Roy, the partner (a Burns detective) would ask Tom to cash a $200 check, expecting to receive some of the marked bills. But Tom cashed the check in gold.

At this setback, Roy proposed to trap Lonergan a second time. Burns doubted the trick would work again, but said Roy, "He'll eat it up."

The second attempt was pegged to a faked ordinance to regulate the storage of petroleum inside the city limits. To insure foolproof identification, an acrostic was worked into the first letters of the third, sixth, ninth, and twelfth lines of the original draft (framed in Heney's office) spelling "F-A-K-E."

This ordinance Roy showed to several supervisors, representing that he was financially interested in its enactment. Then he invited Lonergan to his house.

This time Tom was suspicious; his wife had warned him that the business smelled fishy, and he looked around the parlor carefully before he sat down, even glancing toward the double doors behind which Burns and the two witnesses were stationed.

"I have the oil ready for you," said Roy facetiously, counting out $500.

With the money in hand, Tom walked over to a picture on the wall near the dining-room doors.

"What's this a picture of, Roy?" he asked.

"That? Oh, a picture of my family."

"And what's in here?" said Tom, taking hold of the double doors.

They were flung open and out stepped Burns. In a flash Lonergan shouted: "I want you to arrest this man! He bribed a supervisor!"

"Yes, I saw him do it," Burns assented. "But did you tell me to arrest him when he bribed you down at the skating rink?"

Lonergan denied that trespass, but Langdon and Heney were sent for, and in a second-floor bedroom of the house they and Burns worked all afternoon trying to persuade the supervisor to make a general confession; otherwise, they told him, he would be tried for the bribes he had taken from Roy. His obstinate refusal puzzled them, until it dawned on Heney that the man was afraid he would have to refund the money he had received. Reassured on this point, Tom relaxed and started talking.

What he told was exactly what the prosecution had been striving unsuccessfully for months to establish. He told of taking bribes from the "fight trust," from the Home Telephone Company, from the United Railroads, from the gas company, from the Pacific States Telephone & Telegraph Company, and of money promised in connection with the Parkside and Ocean Shore deals. He gave dates, amounts, names, and described how the payments were made; it was a capsule history of corruption from the time the supervisors were elected.

Meanwhile, downstairs, Roy telephoned to Supervisors Boxton and Walsh, inviting them to the show. He also invited Spreckels. Walsh arrived incoherently drunk, as a result of too prolonged fraternization with a Burns agent; but he was brought back the next morning, and in a full confession confirmed Lonergan in all essential points.

But Boxton balked. Better educated than the other trapped men— he was dean of the dental department of the College of Physicians and Surgeons—he refused to admit anything unless all the supervisors confessed. Even when Spreckels urged him as a friend (Boxton had been Spreckels' dentist), he resisted. The attempt lasted until midnight; then he was permitted to go home, but was kept under surveillance.

Lonergan and Walsh had named Gallagher as the go-between who handed them their bribes. Gallagher, therefore, was the witness who could lead the prosecution to the source of the bribe money, and if this source was Ruef (the prosecutors were certain it was), Gallagher's confession would be the key that would produce the needed proof. Walsh and Lonergan had been won over by the promise that they would not be indicted as long as they told the truth; a similar offer, perhaps, might avail with Gallagher. The point was ticklish, and all day Friday, March 8th, the issue was debated at the Red House with the uncomfortable realization that a misstep could wipe out the tenuous advantage that at last had been gained.

Then Abe Ruef was arrested and locked up in the custody of Elisor Biggy. That played into the prosecution's hands, because now the boss was isolated from his puppets; and left leaderless, these might be persuaded or panicked into making a general confession.

This danger was apparent to the boss, and in his luxurious prison at the Little St. Francis dark circles appeared under his eyes, his skin grew sallow, he seemed preoccupied, and his conversation lagged. He knew the supervisors were weak, greedy, and susceptible to blandishments, and what they might do or say now that he could no longer control them, he dreaded to think. No message came from trusted sources, while Burns industriously spread the most alarming rumors of impending defections.

The prevalency of these rumors led the press, watchful but not yet aware of what was secretly happening, to presage some major break in corralling the "big stuff" which the prosecution had been consistently promising. Nothing definite could be learned, but the air grew tense with expectancy.

2   "The Treaty of the Presidio"

One point worrying Boxton was how much reliance he could place on the District Attorney's offer of immunity in return for a confession. He was allowed to consult a lawyer, Henry M. Owens, who assured him that while immunity agreements had no standing under California law, custom and practice did sanction them, and Boxton would do well to trust Langdon's word. Still Boxton hesitated, unless all the supervisors confessed.

After two days of discussion, Owens went to Gallagher and said that Boxton had admitted everything to him, and that Lonergan and Walsh had implicated Gallagher in their confessions to Burns and Heney. Gallagher had been fearing some such catastrophe since the boss was arrested; he had been unable to reach Ruef himself, although Abe had relayed word through his sister to "sit on the lid." The lid, Gallagher fidgeted, "was getting a little warm," and so he told Andy Wilson, the railroad commissioner, when they put their heads together to plot a course of action. Wilson realized that he also had been compromised seriously by Lonergan and Walsh.

Gallagher asked Owens to find out whether the prosecution would grant immunity to all the supervisors in return for their confessions; but Owens preferred to have Gallagher treat with the prosecution directly. Big Jim shied away from meeting either Heney or Burns, but did consent to talk with Rudolph Spreckels; he suggested that they meet on the grounds of the Presidio, the spacious, park-like United States military reservation lying within the city of San Francisco; its remoteness and seclusion, he believed, would insure privacy.

In a council of war with Langdon, Heney, and Burns, Spreckels was authorized to offer Gallagher immunity in return for his confession and later testimony. Spreckels then met Gallagher at the Presidio and the two men negotiated, Gallagher admitting nothing, promising nothing, but making clear that he would not consider immunity for himself only; it must be a package agreement covering the entire board.

On his side, Spreckels made quite a speech about the aims of the prosecution. They were not motivated by vindictiveness, he emphasized; in fact, they hoped to cause as little harm or distress as possible compatible with smashing the system of public corruption. In his judgment, the real guilty parties were the public-service corporations: elected officials and political bosses might come and go, but the corporations remained, and they tempted poor men to betray their trust. For that reason, he felt, it was more important to punish the people at the sources of corruption than to punish officials or bosses, and he believed that the District Attorney would be willing to grant general immunity to any of the supervisors who would make a full and truthful statement of their unlawful transactions in office, and would repeat the truth on the witness stand. But he made no binding promise.

In a second Presidio conference, Spreckels conveyed to Gallagher the definite offer of the prosecution to grant immunity all around, in return for confessions and testimony about the bribery. It was for the supervisors to decide, and Gallagher called a caucus for the evening of Wednesday, March 13th,—the day Ruef's trial at long last got under way. Events during that day greatly increased the supervisors' agitation, for word of the break in their ranks was leaking out.

That morning the *Chronicle* had published a statement, buried in a prolix account of grand jury doings, to the effect that the graft investigation was about to take a startling direction as a result of evidence against the supervisors obtained "within the last ten days.'

...A sensational disclosure [the report read]...which shows that during the past months William J. Burns and his corps of detectives have accomplished some splendid work in uncovering corruption among city officials has become public. Within a day or two Francis J. Heney will present evidence to the grand jury that Supervisors Charles Boxton and Thomas F. Lonergan, in the presence of three hidden witnesses, each accepted a bribe of $500 from G.M. Roy, one of the principal stockholder in a skating rink, in return for granting special favors to the management of that rink. The testimony of these witnesses, all of whom are in the employ of Burns, it is believed, will be followed by indictments for bribery against the supervisors.

More sensationally, the *Chronicle* stated that the coming disclosures would probably bring about the indictment of Patrick Calhoun and Thornwell Mullally of the United Railroads.

This transpiring of what was afoot alarmed the prosecutors, and that afternoon the *Bulletin* carried agitated denials that there was any truth in the *Chronicle* report whatever. The counterblast was almost overdone in emphasis:

... The reported bribery of Supervisors Boxton and Lonergan [said the *Bulletin*] ... is vigorously denied by the district attorney, his assistant, Mr. Heney, special agent Burns, and, in fact, by everyone whose names are directly or indirectly involved in the alleged transaction. Nothing of the kind occurred. Even G.M. Roy, who is supposed to have laid the trap for the supervisors, indignantly denies that he ever heard of the matter, and is preparing to bring an action for libel against the publishers of the canard.... The denials of Heney and Burns are equally strong. They were vehement in their statement that the publication was a tissue of falsehood and utterly reprehensible.

Coming through Older, this cover-up statement should have been convincing. Nevertheless, chills skittered up and down numerous spines at the prospect that Patrick Calhoun might be haled before a jury.

Amid such crosscurrents, the supervisors gathered for their last caucus. Gallagher outlined to them the alternatives: confess and receive immunity, or deny everything and take a chance. Lonergan and Walsh had confessed, he said, and Boxton was willing to do so. Boxton said he thought they ought all to be in one boat, while Wilson observed that he had always taken orders from Ruef, but in view of Ruef's arrest he saw no reason why he should sacrifice himself needlessly.

But most of the men said they preferred to deny and let the prosecution try to prove the charges.

"Very well," Gallagher ruled. "Any one who wants to take that attitude will be excused from further discussion."

He waited, but nobody budged. Then he put the matter to a vote, and the sullen board unanimously elected to accept the prosecution's terms for immunity. It was total surrender.

Once more Spreckels and Gallagher met in the rustic seclusion of the Presidio and worked out a formal compact. In return for revealing the whole truth about their illicit proclivities and testifying when required, the supervisors were to be guaranteed that they would not be prosecuted, nor would they have to return the bribes. George Duffey (who had resigned from the board when he became public works commissioner) was excused from making his confession for the time being, because Mayor Schmitz would dismiss him the

minute he defected; his job and salary thus were saved. Supervisor
Nicholas was accorded a special dispensation, also: namely, that if
he fulfilled his bargain the kickback indictment against him would
be dropped. Gallagher inquired about including Ruef in the round
robin, but Spreckels replied that he had no authority to negotiate in
respect to the boss.

This agreement (which in the annals of the prosecution became
known as "The Treaty of the Presidio") was embodied in two copies.
The supervisors signed both these, Langdon and Heney withholding
their signatures but promising that they would sign after the supervisors demonstrated good faith: Heney was sure all would be worked
upon to repudiate their surrender, and he insisted on retaining the
power to revoke the contract if they backslid. Both copies were placed
in escrow: one with Spreckels, the other with the lawyer Owens, who
throughout had served as an intermediary.

Sixteen of the elected Union Labor supervisors signed this im-
munity agreement. Duffey was not required to sign, and Sanderson,
who was gravely ill, signed separately in suburban Palo Alto later.
Two incumbent supervisors (the labor leaders O.A. Tveitmoe and
J.J. O'Neill), who had been appointed to fill the vacancies left by
Wilson and Duffey, were not affected.

On Saturday, March 16th, in Burns's rooms at the Gladstone
Apartments, Gallagher and his fellow culprits made their deposi-
tions,—and the "higher-ups" whom the prosecution had been eyeing
as their principal quarry were implicated by name and in detail.

At two o'clock Sunday morning, lawyer Frank Murphy appeared
in great agitation at the Little St. Francis, awakened Biggy, and insisted on seeing Ruef at once on a matter of the utmost urgency.
Murphy had brought word of the supervisors' appalling capitulation.

3 The Roof Falls In

Supervisor Wilson had succeeded in transmitting the news to
Murphy only around midnight Saturday; all that afternoon he had
been boxed off by hovering Burns agents.

When Murphy blurted the tidings, Ruef all but collapsed. But he clung to hope: he would never believe the report, he cried, unless Gallagher himself told him it was so. Gallagher was sent for, and soon arrived with Wilson. The two henchmen, inwardly rejoicing at their own freedom, were ushered into the boss's bedroom. Abe addressed Big Jim.

"I want to learn from your own lips," he said, "if what I have heard is true regarding your making a statement to the prosecution."

Gallagher confirmed his chief's worst fears, and the recriminations flew. But gradually Abe mastered his dismay, contenting himself with the acid remark to Wilson, as the two "immunized" men were leaving, that if he had been in Gallagher's place he would not have made any such statement.

"You can never tell what you would do until you are in Gallagher's position," Wilson replied defensively. "We discussed the matter fully for two or three days before we took that step."

During Sunday every lawyer on both sides passed in and out of the Little St. Francis. Shortridge and Ach seemed depressed. Heney called several times and spoke with Burns, but did not see the prisoner. Abe's father and the sister who served as his secretary, Mrs. Henrietta Sittenfeld, called twice. Politicians, friends, hangers-on streamed in and out, but the guards turned away political pals, including George Keane.

Through the screen of excited secrecy filtered reports that Ruef's nerve was breaking, that he was beset by fears, that he was about to take some sensational action. Heney needed to move swiftly, for at any moment the newspapers might detonate the shocking fact of the supervisors' swinging over to the prosecution at the price of going unscathed, and that would precipitate a struggle to hold these indispensable witnesses in line. Therefore Heney decided to bring the supervisors before the grand jury immediately and so make sure they would not be tampered with before their testimony was in the record.

This mass testimony was given on Monday, March 18th, two days after the Gladstone confessions. It was a day of rain and gales. The grand jurors assembled at an hour's notice, began to hear witnesses at 11:00 A.M., and continued in session until 1:00 A.M. Tuesday morning. One by one the supervisors were taken into the guarded room,—and through the Tenderloin and in banks and clubs the wildest apprehensions were churned up by rumors that they were "telling all."

Gallagher, however, seemed unperturbed as he passed serenely into the grand jurors' presence and emerged smiling. Confess? No, he assured reporters, he had not confessed, he had nothing to confess. Questioned about a report that he had been talking with Spreckels during the previous week, he brushed aside the thought as "absurd and ridiculous." He also blandly denied that the supervisors had met in secret caucus and signed affidavits admitting their guilt. The reporters were more than puzzled,—they were dumfounded by this airy unconcern.

Mamlock, McGushin, Coffey, Kelly, Phillips, Walsh, Harrigan, Nicholas, Boxton, Lonergan,—all testified. Lonergan, displaying a week's growth of beard, growled that Burns had rousted him out of a sick bed, and in perishing weather. Phillips said he had been unable to comprehend what the grand jurors were driving at when they quizzed him, and Mamlock grunted that only "unimportant questions" had been put. Laughter penetrating the closed door of the jury chamber was prompted, the reporters later ascertained, by "Gassy" Kelly's remark, as he sank into the witness chair: "All I'm asking for, your honors, is clemency." He was let off lightly and departed looking almost hopeful.

The moment the grand jury was summoned, Ruef had been placed incommunicado. His telephone was disconnected, lawyers and visitors were turned away, packages arriving for him were rummaged by guards. He was permitted to see only one newspaper,—an early edition of the *Evening Bulletin* splashed with a big headline: SUPERVISORS CONFESS! It gave no details. Throughout the hotel (where his continued presence was embarrassing both the management and other guests), the wildest surmises were bruited.

Heney, for his part, was radiant. Since Judge Hebbard's outrageous interference he had been discouraged, but now he seemed unable to contain his joy. He shuttled almost gaily in and out of the grand jury room, a place where he was always at his best.

"You can feel the truth there," was his way of expressing it. "You can see it—or you can see a lie—in the expression of a face, the

flutter of an eyelid, the passing of the tongue over the lips of a witness. These are not evidence,—but a jury of fair men, not lawyers,
who want the truth, can get it in a grand jury room. And a witness, uninfluenced by counsel and a watching judge, feels more like
telling the truth there; and when he does, he tells it all, humanly,
truly, not alone the facts, but the circumstances, the man-to-man
relations, the extenuations. The very spirit of truth is in a fair grand
jury room."

For the press, Heney had a wide grin. "The events of the last few
days have been very satisfactory to the prosecution," he confided
cockily. "We hope very shortly to make good on all the promises we
have given."

Despite the secrecy of testimony and light-hearted denials by
supervisors, the public learned almost immediately that the shame-
faced, strutting "boodle board" was implicating some of the "best
people" of San Francisco,—bankers, merchants, corporation directors.
The *Chronicle* dressed its front page with large pictures of Ruef,
Schmitz, and Patrick Calhoun, over the caption THREE PARTICULAR
AND NOTABLE TARGETS OF THE PROSECUTION.

Thornwell Mullally, spokesman for the absent Calhoun, issued an
instant disclaimer of guilt: "I am authorized to state in the most
positive way that neither Mr. Calhoun nor any official of the United
Railroads ever paid or authorized anyone to pay one dollar to an
official."

Nevertheless, when the grand jury reassembled Tuesday forenoon,
indictments were forecast, and at Temple Sherith Israel lawyers and
judges talked of little else. Presiding Judge Coffey, to whom the indictments would have to be reported, remained in his chambers until
late, then left word where he could be reached during the evening.

Around town the supervisors were strangely chipper. Guilt? They
knew nothing about that; certainly they had nothing to worry about.
Said Gallagher: "I never testified to anything that would incriminate
myself or any other supervisor. I don't know anything of that nature."

But Heney quite as flatly told newspapermen: "All the supervisors
told all they know, under oath. At two o'clock tomorrow, over seventy
indictments will be returned against city officials and bribe-givers,
and this will be simply a start."

Abe Ruef had regained his composure. The shock had almost unnerved him, but he rallied, and on Tuesday was allowed to read all the newspapers. He also was permitted to see his lawyers and family. And he had a long talk with Burns and afterward seemed to be in better spirits, even intimating that he also might make disclosures.

"I have been thoroughly informed of everything the supervisors are reported to have told the grand jury, and I have no comment to make at this time," he said crisply. "Later, however, I will issue a statement which will furnish more sensations in connection with municipal graft than anything that has been made public."

Although his face was yellow and haggard, he spoke cheerfully, and during the evening repeated his apparent purpose to confess: "They tell me that those whom I thought were most faithful to me have betrayed me. Well, I have nothing to say. They say I am accused of getting $200,000 from the United Railroads for securing the passage of the trolley franchise, and I have nothing to say. This afternoon, I am informed, the grand jury has brought more indictments against me, and in regard to that I have nothing to say. But I shall have a good deal to say later on, when the time comes."

One report did upset him: a rumor that Schmitz had fled the country. Burns reassured him that Eugene was still in town, but the boss refused to be convinced.

On Wednesday the dam burst. All that day Cobb, Heney's partner and legal assistant, wrote indictments at the Red House. At 2:00 P.M. the grand jury met. At four o'clock Cobb walked around to the grand jury's rooms carrying a canvas-covered suitcase filled with documents, and for an hour Foreman Oliver signed indictments.

At 5:15 the jurors filed out, led by Oliver carrying the heavy case. Heney, Burns, Langdon, and Oliver rode to Temple Sherith Israel, while the grand jurors walked the intervening nine blocks leisurely. Presiding Judge Coffey was waiting. As the jurors arrived, they took seats, filling the little chamber.

Court Clerk J.P. Callaghan polled the jury and seventeen answered to their names. Judge Coffey asked if the jury wished to report.

"Yes, your honor, we have a partial report to make," Oliver replied, then set the suitcase on the table in front of the bench and unfastened the snaps. A half-bushel of tightly wedged indictments popped up. Oliver carefully sorted them, handing one set to the Judge and retaining the duplicates for the District Attorney.

In tense silence Judge Coffey examined each paper. There were sixty-five indictments against Abraham Ruef, and ten against Theodore V. Halsey, lobbyist and "outside man" for the Pacific States Telephone & Telegraph Company.

When he read Halsey's name, the Judge glanced toward the jurors and mildly wondered, "Would any of you gentlemen like to take a trip to Manila?" Halsey was known to be in the Philippines on business.

After scrutinizing the papers a second time, Coffey peered over his spectacles and inquired what would be the amount of bail. Langdon whispered to Heney, then replied that $5,000 cash or $10,000 bond on each count ought to be sufficient.

A murmur ran through the courtroom: "Six hundred and fifty thousand dollars!" With the bonds he had already posted, Ruef's total bail would be three-quarters of a million dollars.*

Judge Coffey hesitated, then turned to the clerk and ordered bail to be entered in that amount.

Heney nodded with satisfaction. "I guess that will hold him for a while," he grinned.

Coffey asked if that was all.

"Yes, all we care to report for now," responded Oliver.

The Judge stood up and walked away.

The city went wild with excitement, as across the nation and overseas the news flashed that Abe Ruef faced the greatest aggregation of charges since the exposure of the infamous Tweed Ring in New York City. Heney was triumphant.

"If Ruef is convicted on every count of the indictments to be returned against him," he crowed, "he will serve nine hundred years in prison!"

Langdon, for his part, made clear that graver accusations, involving community leaders so far only gossiped about, were in the making.

* To appreciate the equivalent in today's dollars, multiply by three— $2,250,000.

"The public has little idea of how widely the ramifications of municipal graft in this city extend," he declared. "It is impossible for us to forecast where the investigation will end. Many of the highest social and business standing in the community, who pose as pillars of church and society, are implicated in this scandal. In each case the prosecution will follow them to the end, and expose them in their true light to the world."

Heney now estimated that two years of hard work would be required to finish the job, and when it was completed, he predicted, "the whole social and political fabric of the state will be overturned."

The popularity of Heney and Spreckels soared; even some of the "pillars of church and society" said to be on their list of culpable "higher-ups" felicitated them on their achievement and urged them to keep up the good work. Langdon warmly acknowledged the community's immense debt to Spreckels, saying that it would have been impossible to have carried through the investigation had it not been for his generosity. All over the state, praise for the prosecution team resounded, and the Los Angeles *Times,* in a eulogy of Spreckels, instructed San Franciscans how civic services should be honored:

... The most bewildering thing in the world to a crook is a genuinely unselfish man.... That able crook, Abe Ruef, had foreseen everything else, but Rudolph Spreckels was beyond his wildest imagining. That a man should open his purse and give $100,000 to save the name of his city "without getting anything out of it" was more than his cramped little soul could comprehend. San Francisco has a monument to a great sailor who sank a fleet at Manila Bay [Dewey], and another to a teller of sweet stories [Robert Louis Stevenson]. But it needs one more to tell the generations to come of a new man, who, to save a city's honor, gave of his substance, "without getting anything out of it."

4 "A Little Sauterne"

The least excited person in all the upheaval seemed to be Ruef. He appeared strangely optimistic. When informed of the nation's shock and disgust, he laughed light-heartedly, "That's quite a joke!" And his lawyers, in a sudden about face, withdrew an application they had made to the State Supreme Court for a transfer of their client to jail; the boss apparently was reconciled to Elisor Biggy as jailer. Rumors that Abe was about to confess gained in force and credibility.

Meanwhile Mayor Schmitz, who had been turned down by the Supreme Court on *his* plea to take the French restaurants case out of Judge Dunne's hands, walked the streets lugubriously in custody of a deputy sheriff, raising further bail. His office and home were under constant watch to forestall flight, and the scowl upon his handsome face grew blacker by the hour, as fresh revelations poured out.

The events were of too engrossing interest for rules of secrecy to have any force: the newspapers published the most zealously guarded testimony, readers avidly perusing veracious accounts of what the supervisors had confessed.

Tom Lonergan had been the first to traverse the booby-trapped ground of self-incrimination in his statement at the Gladstone Apartments.

Detective Burns had led off with: "The first caucus you had, how long was it after you were elected?"

"By George, I don't remember, Mr. Burns."

"What was the first agreement made with reference to acts of the board in their relation with Ruef?"

"It was that all men on the board were to be treated equally."

Heney interposed: "And that whatever money was taken, there was to be an equal division?"

"All were to be treated equally."

"And who was to handle the money?"

"Gallagher."

"Do you remember that Schmitz and Ruef were both present?"

"In the early caucuses Schmitz and Ruef always attended."

The first bribe had come from the "fight trust." Immediately after the new board was sworn, in January, 1906, Eddie Graney, the "Honest Blacksmith" (he had risen to fame as the first man daring to referee a prize fight in a dinner jacket), came to Ruef at the Pup and in a private room proposed a way to "organize" the chaotic fight-dates situation, in which every manager had to scramble for what he could buy, bulldoze, or wheedle out of the supervisors. Let the four principal managers—James Coffroth (he was secretary to the judges of the Superior Court), Morris Levy, Willis Britt, and himself—combine, said Graney, and call themselves the Consolidated Association of Athletic Clubs, retaining the boss as attorney; and in return receive all the dates for professional boxing matches during the coming year. It was a neat arrangement, which Ruef accepted, taking the retainer; the supervisors followed "program" and split the dates among the four favored entrepreneurs. For the counsel fee each of the managers contributed $5,000, or each was supposed to; but Britt griped about paying so much, and Ruef consented to take $18,000 instead of the agreed $20,000.

Half of this sum he handed to Gallagher without instructions. Half of the remainder, $4,500, Ruef said he gave to Mayor Schmitz (although Schmitz denied receiving it), and $4,500 he kept for himself.

The supervisors awarded the dates, and shortly thereafter Gallagher handed to each member of the board an envelope containing $475. Divided equally among eighteen supervisors, $9,000 should have given each man $500, but Gallagher had deducted a five-percent "commission." This did not sit well with Andy Wilson, who was sharp for perquisites; he inquired around and raised so much fuss that Gallagher kicked in the extra $25 to everybody who asked for it. But Ruef and he decided that in the future he should be allotted a larger share. The "equality agreement" had gone by the board at once.

Other complications arose from this trial balloon pay-off. Supervisor Rea, who was sufficiently prosperous so that $475 did not represent an important sum to him and who was, besides, a reasonably honest man, suspected an attempt at bribery and hurried to Schmitz with his suspicions. The Mayor was incredulous: he couldn't credit that anybody would try to bribe a supervisor. Hadn't Gallagher said something about a "campaign contribution"? Rea recalled that he had, and Schmitz told him to keep the money, but the next time anything like that happened to come and tell him.

Then Willis Britt, having secured his dates, demanded his money back. Although he had contributed only $3,000 to the fund, he contended he had paid $5,000, and he wanted it all back under threat of exposing the frame-up. Rather than cause trouble, Ruef paid him, —which left the boss with a net deficit of $500. However, he was satisfied; the transaction had tested the method of remitting to the board, and had brought out the feeling of each member. Rea's excessive agitation was laid to political inexperience.

Setting the gas rate provided the next windfall. The supervisors fixed the rate that was charged consumers annually, and the rate had been $1. The Union Labor Party platform (written by Abe Ruef), on which the board had been elected, called for 75-cent gas. The San Francisco Gas Company had just been merged into a consolidation of power concerns in Northern California named the Pacific Gas & Electric Company, of whom a leading stockholder and director was Frank G. Drum, widely known clubman with a diversity of financial connections. In January, Drum quietly retained Ruef as a P.G.&E. attorney at $1,000 a month; hence, when the matter of voting a new gas rate came before the supervisors, Ruef was in the dual position of boss of the board and unacknowledged counsel for the gas company. He proposed an 85-cent rate, and the issue was canvassed in the Sunday caucus, without any mention of money or similar crudity; for the benefit of the minutes, all such discussions were always kept on a high ethical plane, but everybody (except a greenhorn like Rea) knew that money, and how much, was the nub and the rub. Some of the supervisors muttered that this looked like "more of Ocean Shore" —the deal in which the board had given something for nothing—and Ruef faced opposition; but providentially a P.G.&E. substation burned down just then, with an attendant half-million-dollar loss to the company, and this furnished a pretext to vote the 85-cent rate.

But before the rate was approved, Ruef told Drum that in order to protect the company's interests, he would require an additional fee of $20,000. Drum paid, in currency, and the boss handed $13,500 of this to Gallagher and $3,000 to Schmitz (he said, and the Mayor denied). Gallagher, in turn, dispensed $750 to each of sixteen supervisors and kept $1,350 himself. He gave nothing to McGushin, who was a stern advocate of municipally owned utilities, but gave Rea his share. Again Gallagher neglected to identify the source of the money, and Rea hurried off to the Mayor with the cash in hand, as proof that someone was trying to ruin him. He said he wanted to resign, but Schmitz talked him out of doing anything so foolish.

"Put the money in your pocket and say nothing," the Mayor advised. "Just keep quiet. I'll let you know."

Rea segregated the money in a separate bank account and waited, but he never heard a word more on the subject. And Gallagher scratched his name from the pay-off list.

A neat touch in this transaction was the subterfuge by which the P.G.&E. directors concealed the bribe in the company's records: the directors voted themselves a salary increase that came to just the amount of the bribe,—and at the next meeting cut their pay back to the previous figure.

The Home Telephone Company franchise bribe was handled differently. Abram K. Detwiler, the Ohio capitalist who was promoting Home Telephone companies over the United States, utilizing local capital, met Ruef in Gallagher's office in January, 1906, just after the new administration had taken over. The two liked each other at once; both were physically small, both vital and quick-witted, and both knew exactly what they wanted. A bargain was struck,—Ruef to be employed by Home as attorney at a fee of $125,000, of which $25,000 was to be paid at once and $100,000 when the franchise was obtained. Behind drawn shades in Gallagher's office at City Hall, Detwiler gave Ruef the $25,000.

Ruef already was attorney for Home's competitor, the Pacific States Telephone & Telegraph Company, which had voluntarily raised his retainer again, to $1,200 a month—more than the company paid its distinguished general counsel, E.S. Pillsbury. During the recent election campaign, Pacific States, through its lobbyist T.V. Halsey, had contributed heavily to Schmitz's opponent, but had played safe by also helping Boxton and Nicholas financially. After the election, Coleman and Boxton were put on the Pacific States payroll to spy on the actions of their fellow board members.

Halsey and his assistant, John Kraus, quickly scraped acquaintance with the new supervisors, took them to lunch and on tours of the company's installations, explaining the disadvantages of permitting two telephone systems in the city,—double expense and half the service. Lonergan was introduced to Halsey by a mutual friend; fortuitously it happened on the sidewalk in front of Delmonico's, and

Halsey proposed that they adjourn inside for luncheon. In a private dining room, they lingered an hour and a half over a meal such as the bakery-wagon driver had never eaten; the talk was genial and general, and they drank "a little sauterne wine" (Lonergan's words) afterward. Halsey insisted on paying the check.

In February, Halsey called Lonergan to his office and solicited his friendship for Pacific States, again adverting to the waste and nuisance of competitive telephone systems. Lonergan was "deeply impressed" with the service provided by the present company, he said, and he felt he could be its friend; to which Halsey replied that it would be to Tom's advantage to remain steadfast in friendship—$5,000 worth, in fact—with another $2,500 the second year of his term. As earnest, he handed the friendly supervisor $1,000 in bright bank notes.

Then Supervisor Coffey trod the same remunerative route. Kraus and Halsey dropped past his hack stand and invited him to have a drink in a nearby tavern, where they inquired solicitously whether he found the telephone service satisfactory. Indeed it was, Coffey responded, although he only printed the number of the drug-store's phone on his business cards by their kind permission, but the phone at home rang clear and loud. Coffey was shown over the company's exchanges, was let in confidentially on costly improvements being planned, and was impressed that Pacific States placed a high value on friendship. He, too, was treated to a luncheon, only this time Kraus picked up the check, Halsey having pleaded another engagement.

In view of this solicitude, some of the supervisors were mystified when Gallagher introduced Home's application for sale of a competitive franchise at the caucus on Sunday, February 18th; they wondered which side they were supposed to support. When they appealed to Ruef, he replied elliptically that it was "usually safe to follow Gallagher." No mention of money was made, although most of the members present thought about nothing else. Finally the matter was set over for further consideration.

The next day Halsey heard about the debate from the informers Boxton and Coleman, and moved to block Home's maneuver. Without consulting Ruef, Halsey appealed to Frank Drum, who was a director of Pacific States as well as the gas company, for a place where he could meet the supervisors discreetly. Drum's office was on the ninth floor of the Mills Building on Montgomery Street, the Wall

Street of the West. There was an empty suite of rooms on the seventh floor, and this Drum rented for a few days. Then Halsey telephoned to a number of supervisors and asked them to meet him in this suite at strategically spaced intervals on Friday and Saturday of that week.

The suite comprised two rooms, one overlooking Bush Street, the other, a corner room, overlooking Bush and Montgomery; the suite thus was easily identifiable later. The callers entered the room facing Bush Street, which was Spartanly furnished with a table and two chairs; the second room had even less furniture. Halsey and Kraus alternated as greeter.

When Lonergan arrived, Kraus was behind the table; he asked whether the company could still count on Tom's friendship, and when the latter said yes, handed him a sealed envelope. No reference was made to Home's application. Lonergan volunteered that Coffey was a true friend, but Kraus replied that they already had the friendship of most (he meant a majority) of the supervisors and suggested that Lonergan leave by the other room. When he got home, Lonergan looked inside the enevelope; it contained $4,000.

Tom had not known that Mike Coffey was already on his way to the Mills Building. When the hack driver arrived, Halsey was waiting.

"How do you do, Mr. Halsey," said Coffey. "Did you telephone for me?"

"Yes," answered the urbane Halsey. "I want you to be friendly with the company." He slid a slim packet across the table. "I'd like you to have that for your friendship."

Coffey claimed that he did not open the envelope for several days; when he did, he found $5,000 in currency inside.

Altogether, eleven supervisors walked through the suite that Friday and Saturday, each receiving an envelope, and most of the envelopes held $5,000; in all, some $50,000 was handed out in the sentimental name of friendship, the virtue which Abe Ruef extolled above all others.

Wilson collected his bribe Saturday morning, then became uneasy, and during the afternoon hunted up Ruef. Abe enlightened him that the administration was backing the Home company, and he ordered Wilson and Gallagher to round up all the men who had succumbed to Halsey's blandishments and bring them to the Pup that evening. There

Ruef gave them a dressing down and demanded their support for Home.

The caucus the next day was stormy. McGushin, a strong union man, opposed Home's system because its dial telephone (Home held the patents on this service) would knock out jobs. Rea, of course, was ignorant of the real drama, while Boxton protested that he had been on record for years against a dual telephone setup. At length, an accommodation was reached: Home's application for sale of a competitive franchise should be approved, with the few opponents abstaining.

On Monday, March 5th, the ordinance received final approval; Boxton, Rea, Walsh, and Sanderson voted against it, and McGushin was allowed to pass.

At the Pup that night, Ruef bragged that "Halsey tried to steal my supervisors away from me, but I taught him a lesson." He was not surprised when Halsey burst in and charged him with ingratitude.

"You mean to tell me that your company paid those supervisors for their votes?" asked Abe in mock astonishment.

"Certainly, and you know it!"

The boss shrugged, then diagrammed for the lobbyist the errors he had committed: first, he had tampered with the supervisors' fidelity to the administration; second, he had gone behind Ruef's back; third, he had tried to buy votes, a crudity that could not be tolerated, since it might well land everybody concerned in prison. As a sop to Halsey's injured dignity and trembling for his job, Abe half-promised to get the supervisors to refund the money, or at least some of it.

Shortly after the ordinance was voted, Detwiler passed to Ruef $100,000, the balance of his fee. In Gallagher's office, Abe counted out $62,000 of this for the supervisors; then he paid Schmitz $30,000 (the Mayor again denied this), and kept $33,000 for himself. This ate up the whole $125,000 "attorney's retainer."

Gallagher now was confronted with a nice question of ethics and justice: how to divide the bribes equitably? Share and share alike was the rule. Yet eight supervisors had taken money from Halsey to vote *against* the Home franchise, then had voted *for* it,—and their votes had put the ordinance across. Having betrayed the administration in the Mills Building, they had rallied to its support when the ballots were cast. To how much, from whom, were they entitled?

Three others had "seen Halsey" and kept their bargain with him, voting against Home's application and throwing down the administration. Should they be rewarded equally?

Four stalwarts had not visited the Mills Building, had not even been invited there, and had voted loyally for the Home franchise; surely they should not be penalized because of Halsey's oversight, neglect, or mute recognition of their rock-ribbed integrity?

The two supervisors who had voted—or would have voted—honestly against the competitive system—McGushin and Rea—presented no problem; they were simply dropped from consideration.

After weighing the degrees of turpitude involved, Gallagher cracked the conundrum mathematically.

The eight who had taken Halsey's money and then betrayed him were told to refund half (a few of them did), leaving them, theoretically at least, $2,500 apiece from that source. Each of these eight, in consideration of their votes when the pinch came, then was awarded $3,500 of Home cash, making their total recompense, earned and unearned, $6,000 per supervisor.

The four regulars who had voted for the Home ordinance and taken nothing from Pacific States were each given $6,000 out of the Home kitty.

The three who took Pacific States money and delivered honorably, bucking the administration, were given nothing more: they had their $5,000, or as much of it as their consciences allowed them to retain; no accounting was ever required.

For his own services Gallagher pocketed $10,000.

And the two crypto-honest men were classified *non est* and ignored.

This ingenious solution disposed of the $62,000 Gallagher had received from Ruef. The pay-off was complicated, but by it, loyalty was rewarded, double-dealing reproved, and justice affirmed.

Formal sale of the new franchise was set for April 23rd. How, before that date, the earthquake and holocaust disrupted all plans and how, in spite of the calamity, the sale was greased through, has been related. A topping to the jest was applied when the Home representatives, who had brought $250,000 from Los Angeles, for use in the bidding, got the franchise for $25,000, to their embarrassed surprise. At a hint from Ruef, they donated $75,000 of their unused

cash to relieve the distress of disaster victims, and were showered with
gratitude by the deluded citizens.

Most intense public interest focused on the bribes which the
supervisors so blithely confessed having taken for granting the overhead trolley permit to the United Railroads. This transaction was
sketched in outline in the supervisors' disclosures; parts of the story
had become apparent long before; the complete picture would emerge
later, after further delving. In summary, it ran thus:

When the Union Laborites captured the city administration in
1905, Tirey L. Ford notified Ruef that his company intended to push
its demand for the overhead trolley permit vigorously before the new
supervisors. Ruef reminded him that popular sentiment against trolley
wires had been worked up to an extraordinary pitch; to which Ford
replied that of course the United Railroads would expect to pay Abe
a special fee for legal services in framing the franchise; this would be
in addition to his regular monthly retainer. Ford mentioned $50,000.

Ruef laughed and said the United Railroads would be ashamed to
deal with so cheap a lawyer; why, in the East a corporation thought
nothing of paying an attorney hundreds of thousands of dollars for
comparable services. He mentioned $250,000. Ford thought $150,000
might be equitable, and they compromised on $200,000, to be paid
when the franchise was granted. Not a word was uttered to indicate
that any portion of the fee was to be split with the supervisors. As
Abe himself put it, "Neither of us would ever dream of mentioning
such a possibility." Both men were capable lawyers and understood
the utility of silences.

The cry for public transportation after the April disaster smoothed
the way for Calhoun. In the struggle to revive the city's commercial
life, Ford, Mullally, Ruef, and Calhoun worked side by side, and
generous assistance to the survivors during the first terrible weeks of
suffering brought the street-car company much good will. Ruef himself acknowledged his obligation in this respect: several days after the
fire, Ford had dropped into Abe's improvised office on Pine Street,
close by the smoking ruins, and invited him to take advantage of the
free hot lunches the United Railroads was serving at its barns. (Abe's
office comprised the kitchen, bare except for an empty grocery box,

and the bathroom of a small flat; for private talks, Ruef took callers into the bathroom.) A decent meal at that time was almost unprocurable, and Ruef accepted Ford's invitation gratefully.

On April 27th, Mayor Schmitz handled the controls of the first street car to cross the burned district, and the United Railroads reaped more good will. On May 14th, the trolley ordinance was started on its way through the board of supervisors. It was then that the *Examiner* suddenly turned hostile. UNITED RAILROADS WOULD TRY TO LOOT THE CITY! it headlined, and when Schmitz protested lamely that the proposed permit was a temporary measure, the paper hit back with the truth, namely, that the grant was for twenty-five years. The Mayor retracted his "mistaken impression," and on May 21st the ordinance received final passage, while the *Examiner* screamed: SCHMITZ DELIVERS THE CITY'S STREETS TO THE LOOTERS!

"To hell with the *Examiner*," said Ruef, and on May 24th the Mayor signed the ordinance.

Ironically, the other newspapers at that moment were lukewarm in their opposition to the trolley grab, the *Bulletin* even chiding the *Examiner* for fomenting disunity when all elements should unite to meet the emergency.

Before the final vote, Gallagher and Wilson, at Ruef's behest, sounded out the supervisors and reported that they all favored the trolley anyway as the speediest method for getting the cars running, even McGushin sinking his hatred of every private utility in view of the need for transportation. However, Wilson argued that the members still were entitled to compensation for the roasting they were taking in the *Examiner*.

On the day Mayor Schmitz signed the ordinance, Tirey Ford and his assistant, piously prim William Abbott, bore away from the United States Mint the two bundles containing $50,000. The day before, Patrick Calhoun, who was then in San Francisco, had transferred $200,000 to his credit from the East; Ford had presented Calhoun's written order to withdraw $50,000 of this. The Mint had only gold coin, and $50,000 in gold weighs about one hundred eighty pounds, a burden for six stout pallbearers. But the disaster relief committee was housed in the building (one of the few downtown structures left standing and habitable), and they had the paper currency that was coming in by mail from sympathizers all over the world. Mint officials exchanged gold for this currency, most of it in bills of small denominations, and gave the money to Ford.

The next day, Ruef drove to the legal offices of the United Railroads in a car barn at Oak and Broderick streets. Ruef's "Green Lizard" automobile, because of its vivid color and its ubiquity, was easily recognizable, but he had called on Ford many times during the crisis and he had no suspicion that this one call would attract special attention; he told his driver to park in front of Ford's office and wait.

Ford apologized for the bulkiness of the two parcels on his desk, but Ruef laughed and said that his car could haul a bigger load than that. Since he had no office safe, Abe had been carrying valuable papers back and forth from his home in shirt boxes, which he thriftily picked up at a cousin's haberdashery on Fillmore Street. On his way to Ford's office he had picked up one of these boxes, and into this he packed one-half of the bills, and carried it and the second parcel, wrapped in a newspaper (a *Bulletin*), out to his automobile. A Burns detective watched him drive away.

By an odd circumstance, some of this very currency reached the hands of Rudolph Spreckels. Some while previously, Supervisor Rea had leased a property belonging to Spreckels, and after the fire, when cash was scarce, Ruef lent Rea $3,500, which he used to make a payment on the lease; the money Spreckels received was in tattered, frayed, crumpled $1, $2, and $5 bills.

Ford withdrew the balance of the $200,00 on two further trips to the Mint,—$50,000 in July and $100,000 on August 23rd—and on these occasions he was given currency in large denominations,—$50 and $100 bills.

In July, Ruef handed Gallagher $45,000 (this was after he had received the second installment), and in August, $40,000. Equally divided, this $85,000 would have given each supervisor (there were seventeen sharers, Rea, of course, being counted out as unreliable) $5,000. But Wilson objected that he ought to have something additional, say $10,000, for having felt out the supervisors ahead of time, and Gallagher figured his services were worth at least $15,000. This cut the fifteen others down to $4,000 apiece, which was distributed in two installments of $2,000 each, both in currency,—the first payment in bills of small denominations, the second in $50 and $100 bills.

Of the balance, Ruef swore that he gave Mayor Schmitz $50,000 and kept the rest (which he persistently miscalculated at $50,000) for himself. In this case again, Schmitz denied he had received a penny.

The Parkside affair differed from the other cases canvassed by the confessing supervisors in that it brought the supervisors into direct, open touch with the corporation's representatives, and it revealed Ruef as making the overtures. It also showed both board and boss at their greediest. The Parkside Realty Company, as has been recounted, acquired an extensive tract south of Golden Gate Park, comprising some four hundred acres, nearly one-fifth of the entire Sunset district. To attract buyers for its home sites, the company needed public transportation, and when the United Railroads declined to build a spur line to the area, the Parkside directors reluctantly undertook to build their own. Early in January, 1906, just as the new supervisors were settling into their seats of office, the directors applied for a permit to construct a street-car line along Twentieth Avenue, connecting with the United Railroads line at Golden Gate Park.

At the next Sunday evening caucus, Mayor Schmitz told the members that he had inspected the Parkside acreage with the company president, J.E. Green, and had already promised that the franchise would be granted; building up that empty section of the city would create jobs, put a big payroll into circulation, and nicely fatten the tax rolls. To Ruef, the Mayor observed privately that granting the franchise would procure the political friendship of William H. Crocker, head of the powerful Crocker-Woolworth Bank and a principal Parkside stockholder. The boss was annoyed that Schmitz had pledged his word without consultation, and also was nettled at the thought of the profit the Parkside crowd stood to reap from the lots Ruef had sold them *au bon marché*. For a while he tied up the legislation in spite of strong efforts by Green and others to pry an enabling ordinance out of committee.

Hoping that a personal inspection might convince the supervisors of the desirability of the project, Green escorted a dozen or so of them on an automobile tour of the tract one rainy Sunday morning. Later, to escape the dreary weather, the party was entertained by Green at luncheon in a resort called the Casino. The restaurant was cozy, the food was excellent, the champagne abundant. There was speech-making and drinking of toasts, and Supervisor Boxton, in fine fettle, made a speech that was destined to be embalmed in the record as the "Black Flag Speech," it was so nervily piratical. Supervisor Coleman on the witness stand recalled that it went as follows, Boxton declaring with mock gravity:

Mr. Green should bear in mind that we are the city fathers; that from the fathers all blessings flow; that we, the city fathers, are moved in all our acts by a desire to benefit the city, and that our motives are pure and unselfish. . . But it must be borne in mind that without the city fathers there can be no public-service corporations. The street cars cannot run, lights cannot be furnished, telephones cannot exist. And all the public-service corporations want to understand that we, the city fathers, enjoy the best of health and that we are not in business for our health. The question at this banquet board is: *How much money is in it for us?*

Gallagher, who attended the luncheon, informed Ruef that "other ice had been broken than that which surrounded the cooling wine," and warned Abe that the supervisors really did want to know the answer to Boxton's unblushing inquiry.

This was in February, and Green grew impatient; he appealed to an associate, Gustav (Gus) H. Umbsen, to try to find out from Ruef why the franchise was being held up. Umbsen was one of the leading real-estate men in the city, and he was interested in the Parkside development because his company held the sole agency for sale of the lots. Umbsen had known Ruef intimately for years, and was agent for some of Ruef's properties. He had the boss out to his fine home for dinner, made inquiries, and got from the boss a shrug and the comment that he was "not the attorney." Informed of this, Green instructed Parkside's legal counsel, Walter B. Cope, a former judge, head of the San Francisco Bar Association, who had been Ruef's classmate at the University of California, to approach the boss with an offer to become a company attorney. Ruef told Cope that he would represent Parkside for two years at a fee of $50,000. This figure was beaten down to $30,000, and Green ordered the company's secretary, Douglas S. Watson, to draw two company checks for $15,000 each, cash them at the Crocker bank, and give the money to Umbsen, who was told to hold it until the franchise was granted. The checks were cashed in $1,000 bills, which Watson carried to Umbsen's office and dropped on Gus's desk with: "Here's the money." In Parkside's books, the bribe was covered up by a hocus-pocus involving a fictitious sale of land: some property owned jointly by Watson and Umbsen's brother was bought by Parkside for $30,000, the deed of sale was recorded, and then the land was secretly sold back to the two men for the same price.

On March 26th, the supervisors passed the ordinance authorizing sale of a street-car franchise to the Parkside area, the sale to be held May 7. But before that date, the disaster radically altered Parkside's plans.

The proposed franchise authorized construction of a line along Twentieth Avenue, which existed only as a surveyor's line on a map. Nineteenth Avenue, however, had been graded, paved, and designated a boulevard, on which street-car lines were prohibited by the city charter. The post-fire demand for housing, and the urgent need to build up the city again, moved the Parkside directors to let their Twentieth Avenue franchise lapse, and they applied instead for a new permit to lay the tracks on Nineteenth Avenue, in order to save time and expense.

Green appealed to Ruef,—who thus far had received no money, inasmuch as no franchise had actually been obtained. Ruef had alerted the supervisors through Gallagher that they might expect to get $750 each for their votes; now he told Umbsen, Green's negotiator, that since he had already done a great deal of work for which he had not been paid, he was in no mood to do anything further. At this, Green authorized Umbsen to give Ruef $15,000, half his attorney's fee. The boss took this, then demanded a fresh fee of $10,000. The Parkside directors bowed to this blackmailing, and raised to $25,000 the sum still owing Ruef. The latter thereupon conveyed to the supervisors that their cut would be $1,000 apiece.

At a luncheon with Parkside officials in Umbsen's home on Presidio Heights, where snowy napery and sparkling crystal provided a soothing contrast to the grime and dreariness of the fire-blackened downtown area, blueprints were spread out, Ruef recalled, "on Louis Quatorze divans and Louis Quinze chairs," and a way was devised to circumvent the legal obstacle to building a street-car line on boulevard-designated Nineteenth Avenue: the board of supervisors could simply change the designation. This scheme was in process of being realized, and the balance of Abe's augmented fee was in Umbsen's possession (Abe dunning him for it) when the supervisors confessed and upset the program. Subsequently the suspicion thrown over the whole Parkside project prevented the company from obtaining, for two more years, a car line which everybody favored and the public wanted. And the supervisors never collected any money,— Ruef having told Gallagher repeatedly that he himself had not received one cent.

The grand outline of these mercenary betrayals of civic trust, as divulged by the supervisors and substantiated by other witnesses, became fully known to the public on April 26th, a few weeks after the supervisors' entrapment, when the *Call* got possession of the transcript of testimony given before the grand jury by members of the "boodle board" and also by representatives of the Pacific States Telephone & Telegraph Company. This the *Call* published in full,—six pages of fine type. How the *Call* obtained the testimony it never disclosed, but its enterprise spurred its competitors to emulation, and reports, or what purported to be accurate reports, of evidence the grand jury was securing appeared regularly in the city's press thereafter until the public's appetite was satiated. The man in the street never doubted, after the *Call* published the transcript, that the corporation officers named, as well as Schmitz, Ruef, and the boodling supervisors, were guilty; the evidence was overwhelming to the lay mind, whatever it might be to the legalistic.

In the corporation briberies, Gallagher received a grand total of $169,350 from Ruef to be divided with his fellow supervisors, and more, much more, had been promised. The abortive Bay Cities water scheme alone held out the prospect of cutting a $1,000,000 melon of graft. And this was admittedly only a fraction of the sums Ruef and his machine extorted from all sources. The grand total of their boodle was never calculated at less than several millions of dollars, much of it collected in the critical "nine black months" just after the great fire.

5 "Good Dogs" and Dilemmas

Soon after the supervisors paraded before the grand jury there were rumors that they were to escape prosecution. The public was shocked.

"Current reports run that the supervisors have not only been vaccinated with a virus that renders them immune from indictment, but have been acquitted and declared innocent to that degree that they are to be continued in the offices which they disgraced," one newspaper commented. "Their gross betrayal of the public trust, according to rumor, is not to be met by indictments, actions for removal from office, or even a request that they resign and forever hide their criminal heads in the obscurity from which they sprang."

"It would be intolerable to have a mayor and a board of supervisors openly charged with flagrant venality presiding over the destinies of the city," stormed the *Chronicle,* and a revulsion of feeling against the prosecution was predicted. Yet the rumors proved to be true, and Heney was forced, on behalf of his colleagues, to justify what seemed an indefensible policy.

The prosecution was in a dilemma which they had not foreseen. In order to convict Ruef of bribery, the testimony of Gallagher, the bagman who passed the bribes, and of the supervisors who received the money, was indispensable, and it could hardly be expected that these persons would testify if they faced going to prison themselves; immunity was the price of their evidence. As for continuing them in office, this was to guard against Mayor Schmitz's filling their places (should they resign or be turned out) with his puppets. But Heney reassured the public that a change would be noted in the behavior of the boodlers.

"With the evidence we hold over them they will be 'good dogs,' " he declared. "If we forced their removal, Schmitz, who has the power to make appointments, would appoint another board over whom we would have no control."

But the spectacle of admitted crooks being allowed to remain in authority by their potential prosecutors was too monstrous for the country to tolerate; San Francisco was given up as incurably depraved. The "good dogs" tag was repeated from coast to coast and the supervisors, staunchly maintaining a puritan pose before the public—in the face of their published testimony before the grand jury —smarted under the epithet.

The day after Gallagher spoke his piece to the grand jurors, George Duffey burst into his office waving a newspaper. "Did you say anything like that to the grand jury?" shouted the commissioner of public works. "Did you accuse me of taking a bribe from you or, to your knowledge, from anybody else?"

"No," replied Gallagher. "It's a damn lie."

"And so it is, if he said it," Duffey flung to reporters; "but I don't believe he did."

"My skirts are clear," professed Coleman. "They always have been clear, and I intend to keep them so."

Professional actors could not have been more letter-perfect in their lines.

The "good dogs" proved their aptitude at learning new tricks when they purged the civic payroll of several Ruefites like Myrtile Cerf. George Keane, also, was made to walk the plank.

"The board agreed that the close political friendship that has existed between the board and Mr. Ruef must cease," Gallagher explained. "We are no longer to seek his counsel or take it. Mr. Keane has been identified thoroughly with Mr. Ruef's association with the board. When we called him before us, he stated that his political fortunes had been associated with Mr. Ruef and he did not propose to desert him now. Under these circumstances, we had no option but to relieve him from office."

"This board is going to be strictly independent," Coleman broke in. "We intend to act hereafter solely for the public good."

And "Gassy" Kelly went to loquacious lengths in scotching the horrid notion he ought to resign. "The present board has no intention of resigning," he declared loudly. "There is no chance for us to resign,—the grand jury won't let us." He was downright grieved by the imputations of moral obliquity. "We only did what other supervisors have done before,—pick up a little easy money at various times."

Yawned Ruef in his hotel prison: "When supervisors get drunk they will talk, they will tell stories."

But across the nation arose a chorus of lamentation.

"Pity San Francisco!" groaned the Los Angeles *Times*. "Governed by a legislative body whose members are self-confessed felons, laved in the purling waters of immunity!"

While three thousand miles to the eastward the New York *Times* professed pious horror: an "incredible chapter" was being written in San Francisco; and it mourned that the "saddest part of all" was the "complaisance, weakness, and cowardice of public spirit in the disgraced city."

To which the San Francisco *Chronicle* tossed back that "it would be more decorous for a New York newspaper reputed to be controlled by some of the very men we are after to keep silent in this crisis [rather than] seek to divert attention from the boodlers by attacks on those who are engaged in pursuing them." The *Times* the indignant *Chronicle* dismissed as "an unsavory journal" which had long since "outlived and disgraced a noble record [and] has become one of the most mendacious."

The attacks from afar became strident when the investigation reached beyond San Francisco, and a number of Los Angeles capitalists were subpoenaed to appear before the Oliver grand jury. These were the directors of the Home Telephone Company of California, headed by the company's president, Alonzo B. Cass, a man of large investments whom the Los Angeles press deferentially described as "a conscientious and active church worker." Cass came north with his colleagues believing Heney was bluffing; he walked into the grand jury room confident and rosy, and came out cringing and distraught, on the point of collapse. A millionaire who had underwritten Home's bonds heavily, he had been confronted with evidence that raised the specter of his own imminent indictment.

The directors were compelled to acknowledge that they had known about the $250,000 shipped from Los Angeles on a relief train for the purpose of corrupting the supervisors of stricken San Francisco. All departed fearful and careworn, and when they were summoned north again they unanimously refused to testify, pleading possible self-incrimination,—even after Heney announced that no indictments against them were contemplated yet.

This involvement of prominent men in the southern end of the state stirred the hackles of Los Angeles conservatives, whose most vocal organ, then as now, was the labor-union-hating *Times*. This newspaper assailed the motives of the graft prosecutors with sudden and congenial ferocity, and over the coming months and years was to intensify its venomosity.

San Francisco dances in glee upon the carcasses of the Los Angeles men who have been drawn into this terrible disgrace [the *Times* correspondent wrote with more vividness than restraint]. It diverts the fire . . . All the San Francisco newspapers can find to criticize at home is that some seventy-five indictments stand against the most prominent men in the city; that the mayor is in danger of going to prison; that the supervisors are self-confessed bribe-takers; that the head of the United Railroads is accused of bribe-giving; that a hundred scandals have been laid bare, covering slot machines, saloons, race horses, thefts in municipal offices, prizefight crookedness, and many, many other things. Yet in the face of these positive facts, San Francisco turns in pretended horror and points its finger at the Los Angeles telephone men for an extremely problematical offense. . . The whine going up that these wicked Los Angeles millionaires corrupted the virtuous San Francisco supervisors is certainly not without comedy. . . Good heavens! One would think that the telephone companies and the United Railroads *wanted* to pay bribes! . . Heney's original way of dealing with highway robbery is not to prosecute thugs, because there are too many thugs to catch. He is going to stop holdups by preventing people from carrying money!

The "wicked Los Angeles millionaires" were passed over, but soon after their appearance the grand jury voted thirteen indictments for bribery against Abram K. Detwiler, promoter of Home Telephone's schemes. Detwiler was reported to be in Cairo, Egypt, and in several other distant places simultaneously, although Burns always believed that for several weeks Detwiler remained hidden in the attic of his home in Toledo, Ohio, eluding the prosecution's watchers and eventually escaping abroad. He was never apprehended.

Also indicted was Louis Glass, vice-president and general manager of the Pacific States Telephone Company, Home's rival; he was accused of bribery on nine separate counts as the executive who authorized Halsey to bribe the supervisors in the two-day procession through the Mills Building. Glass was wealthy, respected, an able executive, popular in club and social life, and his indictment spread shivers through the most eminent circles. In the East at the time the grand jury acted, Glass shortly returned, was met by the sheriff and taken to the Family Club, where Judge Lawlor lived, made bond of $90,000, and was released pending trial.

On March 29th (Good Friday), Glass appeared for arraignment before Judge Lawlor and a throng of spectators at Temple Sherith Israel. Lawlor's courtroom was the main auditorium of the Temple, a lofty, domed chamber lighted religiously by stained-glass windows. Here and there glowed an electric bulb. The judge's desk touched the pulpit, and defendants and counsel occupied front pews; Glass sat beside a prisoner accused of murdering a policeman. When his name was called, Glass arose, pale and dignified, but his features were deeply coursed by lines of anxiety. The clerk put the formal question: "Louis Glass, is that your true name?" In a whisper came the response: "Yes, sir."

The nine indictments were read, taking nearly an hour. All the while Glass stood, shoulders thrown back and chin thrust forward, now and then betraying nervousness by nibbling a fingernail or absently trailing his hand back and forth along the top of the pew in front. His counsel obtaining a week's continuance to plead, the unhappy man escaped through a rear door.

To see one of the city's leading business executives arraigned as a felon posed a different problem from the legal castigation of politicians, and the moral issue was plainly perceived. In a somber editorial the *Chronicle* speculated:

... This touches all American society. Suppose some of our rich men are caught—men who have been influential among us and moved among their fellows as honorable—what will society do about it? Will their clubs and societies expel them? Will their acquaintances continue to take their dirty hands? Will anyone be seen walking with them or giving them social recognition? Will their innocent families find it endurable to live in a community where their fathers and husbands are pointed out as pariahs? ... In the determination of that problem the people of San Francisco will themselves be on trial.

Within a month, other men than Louis Glass who figured prominently in the social calendar were appearing, or about to appear, in
the court calendar as accused criminals; and Heney was forewarning
of difficulties that would be encountered. "It is hard to convict a rich
man," he cautioned several thousand students at the University of
California. "But history shows that when you convict one in high life,
you accomplish more than when you convict ten thousand of the
smaller fellows." Louis Glass, he promised, would be prosecuted re-
lentlessly, regardless of social position or political influence. Throughout his address, Heney referred to Abraham Ruef as "our fellow graduate," grinning as he spoke.

The curve of public sentiment was graphed by the *Chronicle,* and
in a month it reached this conclusion:

The social position of known corruptionists is not affected in the least.
There is a certain embarrassment when one who has not been found
out meets one who has just been exposed at the club or in society, but it
passes off after the first interview. The family may seek retirement for a
few days in deference to the prejudices of the minority, but in a month
it is forgotten—by the minority and everybody else. The civic standard
of San Francisco is municipal corruption.

6 "The House of the Velvet-Lined Box"

Ruef—the "unspeakable Ruef," denounced on all sides as arch-
villain—had indeed "got his second wind," as his attorneys put it, and
was fighting the prosecution step by step. And nobody underestimated
his dexterity as a legal trickster. The press he enjoyed mystifying in
regard to recurrent rumors that he would confess in exchange for immunity; his penchant for persiflage was irrepressible.

On the day the sixty-five bribery indictments were returned, a
newsman hurried to the Little St. Francis and asked the debonair
prisoner: "Has there been any offer of a compromise from the
prosecution?"

"My eminent and learned counsel, A. Ruef, has directed me not
to answer that question," replied the curly-haired boss, negligently

looking up from a game of dominoes with his brother-in-law, Aaron Altmann. "I do not even know that any new indictments have been returned against me, not having been informed in that matter by my eminent and very learned counsel."

The reporter assured him that he had seen the very documents, with his own eyes, in Presiding Judge Coffey's courtroom, and Abe thanked him courteously.

"Then I may believe that they are in existence. But I trust that the next news you bring will be of a more pleasant nature."

And he turned to dominoes, which, with solitaire, reading, and writing, were his diversions in captivity.

A preoccupation less agreeably engrossing was being provided by his lawyers, who had found that the "attorney's fee" dodge might work both ways; in fact, it was rumored that Ruef's lawyers were in league to milk him of every dollar possible on the general principle of reciprocity. When Frank Murphy showed up at the Little St. Francis with a bill of $840 for "automobile hire," Abe exploded.

"Eight hundred and forty dollars for an automobile for ten days! Why, that's nearly a hundred dollars a day for an automobile! You might at least have hired three while you were at it!"

Murphy flushed, assumed an injured tone, but calmed down and departed peaceably,—leaving another bill, from another lawyer, also for "automobile hire"—$400.

Ruef was able to pay. Burns had traced to him, only a few months previously, cash deposits in San Francisco banks of more than one million dollars.

But these *divertissements* were incidental to the main drama which unfolded on several fronts during March, April, and May as the court skirmishing continued.

On March 25th, Ruef's appeal to the United States Supreme Court was dismissed without explanation, although his attorneys said it was at their instance.

Two days later, the boss suddenly reversed his tactics and in Judge Dunne's court demanded immediate trial on the French restaurants extortion charges. This caught the prosecution by surprise, and Heney requested a week's delay; Judge Dunne granted the request, after heated arguments, noting that the defense already had created five months of delay on its side. At the same time Dunne rebuffed a plea that Elisor Biggy be instructed to hold his prisoner less strictly.

The sober-minded Biggy, who went about funereally attired in a Prince Albert coat and derby hat, had been hunting a more suitable place of detention for his charge, since both the taxpayers and the hotel management were complaining about the prolonged stay at the Little St. Francis. By a chance not exactly fortuitous, Burns managed, in the space-tight city, to rent the two lower floors of a dwelling at 2849 Fillmore Street,—a house Ruef knew well, because it was the former home of Mayor Schmitz. It was only a couple of blocks from Ruef's own residence, and he was ready with a counter-proposal.

"Why not," said he, "use my house and pay me the rent?"

But 2849 Fillmore got the nod. The evening before he was to be transferred, reporters found him in talkative vein. Biggy lay stretched on the bed, snoring.

"My daily bulletin to the press," Ruef announced with dry sententiousness, "is that my eminent and very learned counsel, myself, has as yet given me no instructions to take the public and newspapers into my confidence. You may say, however, something like this: 'Ruef still in durance vile—almost.' Or if you wish to enliven the paper: 'Ruef plays cards while Biggy plays bass-drum solos.'

"There is absolutely no truth in anything you see, hear, read, know, imagine, surmise, think, or believe about me," he went on. "The guards have not been changed, because I found them to be incorruptible to my offers of the candy you see over there on the bureau. The elisor, however, is taking extra precautions and has ordered several packages of flypaper strewn about the hallways to prevent my departure."

At eight o'clock the next morning, Biggy and a party of detectives in two automobiles removed Ruef to the Fillmore Street house. The hotel's bellboys gave Abe a singing send-off with their parody of a popular ballad, "Goodbye, Mary":

> *Goodbye, Abe, we're sorry to see you go;*
> *Goodbye, Abe, you've sure been giving us the dough!*

The boss was charmed. He departed laughingly, and during the trip, whenever a pedestrian recognized him and grinned or scowled, he smiled and waved back. The trip, he said, was practically like going home.

In the house at 2849 Fillmore Street, Ruef was to be held for the next ten months. Its current owner rented it to a German from whom Biggy hired the basement and first floor. Ruef's room was on the first floor, in front. Downstairs was the den Schmitz had fitted up, next to his private wine cellar, and this Biggy used for a dining room.

The city soon was thrown into convulsions of merriment by a discovery which Burns made. Ruef's room had been Schmitz's bedroom in the days when the Mayor was a dashing fiddler; and in that room, precisely where Eugene's bed had stood, the floor had been cut away and a box or chest, about two feet square, had been built into the space between the floor and the ceiling of the drinking parlor below. It had a hinged lid and was lined with worn plush; when covered by the carpet it was completely undetectable.

The "boodle box," the town christened this treasure lair, and jokes were passed about the plush lining, designed, it was said, to "deaden the clink of falling coin."

Mayor Schmitz haughtily insisted that the box had been constructed to hold his precious Cremona violin; but Burns invited reporters to try to fit a fiddle into the space, and several tried, but all failed. Abe, sitting in a rocking chair, watched. "More of Eugene's wisdom," he said, grinning.

Cynical though it was, the hilarity over the "boodle box" did give the volatile citizens a needed respite from the highly charged emotions of recent weeks. Just at that time the newspapers bulged with accounts of the sensational New York trial of Harry K. Thaw for the murder of Stanford White. Thaw's San Francisco counsel, Delphin M. Delmas, was making legal history with his "brainstorm" defense: Thaw, Delmas contended, was a victim of "dementia Americana,"— maniacal irresponsibility brought on by overnight affluence.

Wags suggested that Mayor Schmitz offer the "boodle box" as evidence of hopeless insanity; while the supervisors might plead "dementia Californiana." Poor Tom Lonergan—who had hidden some of his pelf in a mattress of his Clementina Valley home, which had burned in the fire—was said to be patently a sufferer from "dementia Clementina."

Ruef nudged the joke along, although deploring that he saw little hope for himself in a "brainstorm" plea; the jury, he feared, might return a verdict of "crazy but no fool." He laughed heartily at the evocation of burly, bearded Eugene, "snoozing above the boodle box, conscience-free, dreaming not of wealth, because his wealth was no dream."

7   "There's Hope Beyond"

In his "parlor prison" (the cost to the taxpayers of maintaining this establishment the newspapers crassly calculated as equivalent to the expense Great Britain had been put to in maintaining Napoleon on St. Helena) Abe lacked no creature comforts. When he broke a tooth—on one of Biggy's "wooden steaks," he contended—he was allowed to have special food sent in while he dickered with Biggy to fire the pigtailed Chinese cook and hire a French chef. His tailor called regularly (incidentally picking up a customer in Biggy), and on fine days the boss was taken for a walk or ride in the park; at other times Biggy and he cruised the bay in a launch. But these maritime picnics were discontinued when Burns got wind of an elaborately timed scheme to kidnap the boss and spirit him away to a shack in the high sierra. Always guards were within Abe's sight and hearing, and Biggy, a dull companion who spoke as seldom as possible, slept in the same room. Ruef chafed at the confinement; and as the weeks went by, at times an expression of deep melancholy settled over his face.

He had been indicted on November 15, 1906. Almost five months later, on April 2, 1907, a start was made at choosing a jury to try him. On this momentous morning four attorneys appeared in his behalf— Ach, Shortridge, Murphy, and Fairall—while the state was represented by District Attorney Langdon and the specially retained Hiram Johnson. Heney was occupied with the grand jury, but at the Red House he received hourly reports.

Now that the real fight had commenced, Heney was bubbling with good humor. His office was in the upstairs drawing room of the once elegant, now dowdy and faded mansion, and the old-fashioned carved furniture and pier glass in gilt frame between the windows contrasted incongruously with the utilitarian desk and telephone. The prosecutor was full of jokes equally inappropriate to a drawing room. When the telephone would ring, he would answer with a shout: "Burns? You mean that bum detective? He's right here!"

And he would push the receiver across to his indefatigable helper.

Meanwhile, in Judge Dunne's Temple school courtroom, notables elbowed notables. The Judge, an image of doleful anxiety, sat at the teacher's desk, while defendant, counsel, reporters (including writers from distant cities and overseas), and even floridly handsome Rudolph Spreckels squeezed into the pupils' seats. Behind the press group, listening with mouth agape, crouched Myrtile Cerf.

The contrast between the opposing attorneys was sharp: Shortridge solemn and unctuous; Murphy youngish, rubicund, wattled, slouching with half-closed, impudent eyes; Fairall rumbling belligerently, baiting Judge and jurors; Ach, with glittering eyes and snaky locks combed back from a narrow forehead, evoking visions of a Levantine trader. On the opposite side, Hiram Johnson, immaculately attired, fencing with Ach in coldly cutting phrases spoken through thin, severe lips. Langdon disappointed most of the out-of-towners,— they felt he looked "like a fallen cake;" but this appearance of ineffectuality was deceptive.

Wrangling over the make-up of the jury soon settled into a battle of wits that dragged on day after day, and Ach in particular incurred such repeated rebukes from the patient Dunne that the newspapers growled: "A great part of the community is getting into a state of mind in which they would rather see certain pestilential lawyers in jail than Ruef himself."

And still there was no end to the legal dodges the wily boss set in motion to halt, transfer, or miscarry the trial. Judge Dunne was confronted with a new demand for release on bail, and turned it down. Another *habeas-corpus* petition was carried to the State Supreme Court, which delayed ruling, to Ruef's fretful annoyance.

"It wouldn't take me long to decide a simple case of that kind," he protested while the learned judges dallied.

Often the courtroom gabble bored him and he grasped at trifling distractions, but these were few. One source of amusement he found in the daily parade of sightseers past the Fillmore Street house; he was flattered when riders on the bobtailed cable cars creeping up the hill craned for a glimpse of his windows, which often were lighted late at night. Of an evening he would sit pensively in the bay window, watching the lights shimmering on the water until everything blurred under the fog swirling in through the Golden Gate. When the frogs croaked mournfully in the hollow at the bottom of the street, Abe would muse: "When I was languishing in the sylvan retreat at the Trocadero the night birds lulled me to sleep. At the St. Francis we had the music of the soughing trees in Union Square, besides the wailing snores of Biggy. Now o' nights the frogs hasten us into the land of dreams. It reminds me of the good old French restaurant days which are no more. It also reminds me of the talesman in court today who said the only time he had been in a French restaurant was when he sold a basket of frogs for $1.50."

Flinging himself on the bed, he picked up a book lying half-read,—*The Duke of Devil May Care.*

"My reading has been so casual lately I don't know whether this is a novel, a history, or the Bible," he yawned.

His library of light novels had been selected craftily by Burns: *Half a Rogue, Won By Waiting, The Fighting Chance, The Malefactor.* After one hard session in court, where Ach's most fertile objections had been beaten down, reporters came upon Abe reading aloud to the stolid guards from a book entitled, *There's Hope Beyond.*

One caller at the "chateau," who surprised practically everybody, was Mayor Schmitz; the relations between the two men had been mystifying the town. Eugene knocked at his former front door, was instantly admitted, and had a long discussion with the boss in the "boodle box" bedroom. Schmitz shook hands cordially, but Ruef's tone in discussing the visit afterward hinted that the cordiality might have been assumed.

"We talked about the weather mostly," he said. "We may have talked about the trials. Come to think of it, yes, we did talk about the trials."

A guard reported that Schmitz had wanted Abe's advice on whether he should obtrude upon the meetings of the supervisors; he didn't like to, he said, but the sight of Gallagher lording it in the mayor's chair was infuriating. Schmitz also complained about the Burns detectives who were stationed outside his home day and night; such surveillance, he protested, was demeaning to a mayor of San Francisco.

At last the State Supreme Court, sitting in bank, listened to recondite arguments by Ach for removing his client from Biggy's custody. Ruef, he said, was being held under conditions of "mediaeval suffering." In rebuttal, Heney denied that the prisoner had been subjected to "barbarities," while Biggy testified that he had so far complied with the prisoner's every request as to procure him an icebox and wine cooler,—at Ruef's expense, of course. Justice Henshaw listened to the exchanges with a smile that was half a sneer, and while the court ordered some of the restrictions to be eased—principally that Ruef be permitted to see anyone he wished to—the defendant was continued in the charge of the Elisor. The first caller to take advantage of Abe's right of unlimited visitation was faithful Myrtile Cerf.

April 18, 1907, was a day of high significance for San Francisco. On that day—the first anniversary of the earthquake and fire—the jury box in Ruef's trial was tentatively filled, and counsel began to use their peremptory challenges.

To signalize the resurgence of the city, precarious though it still was, the streets were gay with flags and bunting, and the dome of ruined City Hall, held aloft on gaunt, stilt-like girders stripped of masonry, was gloriously illuminated. Several hundred citizens gathered in a banquet formally opening the rebuilt Fairmont Hotel, and the keynote of the speech-making was one of hope, determination, and confidence. Both Langdon and Heney reported on the progress so far made in cleaning up the city's reputation, and Heney's fiery prediction of retribution for all the guilty brought the crowd to their feet cheering, many jumping on their chairs to applaud the fighting prosecutor. That night marked the high tide of popularity for the graft investigation.

In court the next day, Ach moved to disqualify on the grounds of prejudice every juror who had heard Heney's speech. Judge Dunne, who had been present, ruled adversely to the defense.

Finally, on May 13th—one hundred and seventy-nine days after

Abe Ruef was indicted—the jury to try him was completed and sworn. Taking of testimony was to start on May 15th, and the public looked forward eagerly to that banner day.

But before the first witness could be called, Ruef electrified the city and the nation by dramatically pleading guilty.

8 "Sweating" the Boss

Of course, there was a catch to it, a catch that reached back through weeks of intrigue about which the public knew nothing.

After the flurry caused by the supervisors' confessions and Ruef's bribery indictments, San Franciscans settled down to let the prosecution take its course. The big sensations, it was felt, were over, everything thereafter would be anticlimax. Ruef, who had been jolted hard by the supervisors' defection, recovered quickly and entered upon a duel of craft and endurance with his captors.

The prosecution's principal agent in this contest was detective Burns, who long had specialized in inducing criminals to confess. William J. Burns looked anything but sinister: plump and jolly, he laughed readily, was an excellent yarn-spinner, and exuded friendliness. Mentally he was extraordinarily agile, and he was also a shrewd psychologist and accomplished actor. Only his piercing, intelligent eyes gave a clue to his sharpness. Ruef was a master of barter and guile, and he understood perfectly his importance to the prosecution, since only through him could they hope to reach the "higher-ups," the dispensers of bribe money. Thus the antagonists were evenly matched, and both entered into the test with confidence and zeal. When it was all over Ruef said frankly, "Burns is a great man," while the detective admitted that he had never enjoyed a prisoner as much as he enjoyed Abe.

Two days after the supervisors confessed, Burns informed Heney that Ruef might be persuaded to turn State's evidence, if granted immunity. Heney thereupon read the detective a lecture about the sort of man they were dealing with, at least, in Heney's view. Ruef, he said, was not, like the supervisors, a mere accessory or tool in the briberies; he had initiated them. He was a man of "extraordinary brain power, keen intelligence, fine education, good environment, great power of persuasion over men, dominating personality, great shrewdness and cunning, coupled with an avaricious disposition." Such was Heney's settled opinion, and to let Abe go free of all punishment, he said, would be "a crime against society."

Burns pointed out the prosecution's position: only Ruef's testimony could certainly convict Mayor Schmitz in the French restaurants case, and the Mayor, who was loudly protesting his innocence, was getting some people to believe him; in default of Ruef's testimony, he might convince a jury. Also, without Ruef's testimony the prosecution could not reach the corporation officials who had dangled and paid the bribes, since only Ruef had dealt with them, not the supervisors. In fact, on Ruef's co-operation hinged the success of the prosecution, and for his co-operation he would have to be paid; if the price was immunity, Burns thought they had no choice but to accept.

Heney was obstinate and wary; he refused to trust Ruef as to either motives or intentions. Although conceding that everything Burns said was true, he was adamant in his insistence that Abe must be punished. At last, with extreme reluctance, he authorized Burns to negotiate, but warned him to observe the utmost caution, inasmuch as whatever might be said, Ruef assuredly would use it against the prosecution later, if he could.

Burns's first tactic in "sweating" a suspect was to isolate him from friends and trusted sources of information; thus when Ruef ran away and opened the way for his arrest, he played straight into the detective's hands. The next step was to gain the prisoner's confidence, and at the Little St. Francis, Burns laid himself out to be obliging and congenial. His purpose was to discover how Abe's mind worked, and he spent hours in artful conversation, watching to see Ruef's reaction to studied remarks thrown out apparently at random. At last he believed he had caught the boss's line of thought: Abe, it seemed, was prepared to bargain for telling everything he knew, in return for freedom from prosecution, but had no intention of carrying out such a bargain. Anything Burns might find out through other channels the boss would admit, but he would volunteer nothing and conceal as much as he could.

"In other words," the detective twinkled to Heney, "he wants me to confess first."

This reasoning was sound, the developments showed: Abe did not intend to give any more than he had to, although promising everything. His ultimate hope—and it was a project as daring as it would be difficult to execute—was to insinuate himself into the good graces of the prosecution, discover their secrets, and employ these for his advantage. He dreamed of again becoming boss of San Francisco— a "good," reformed boss, perhaps, sincerely serving the city, for which he had a genuine fondness—with power and prestige enhanced; and he did not doubt that, given time and leeway, he could outwit his adversaries. But he worked under a temperamental handicap, in that he never trusted Frank Heney's word, motives, or objectives. He could not think clearly about Heney, any more than Heney could think dispassionately about Ruef.

Abe's demand for blanket immunity Heney unalterably opposed: Ruef must accept some punishment, however inadequate, Heney told Burns; how much would depend entirely on the extent to which Abe co-operated. Any other course, he said, would be ruinous to the prosecution and make a farce of the law. Judge Lawlor, in private discussions with Fremont Older, concurred in this view: Ruef must go to prison, if only for a token punishment, or the prosecution would be utterly discredited. Burns still believed that total immunity was the only bait that would hook the boss firmly, but he followed instructions; at no time during the long course of the graft prosecutions was William J. Burns's fidelity to his employers ever questioned.

On the day when selection of a jury to try Ruef began, Burns was accosted in a corridor of Temple Sherith Israel by the Temple's rabbi, Dr. Jacob Nieto, who retained an office in the building during its temporary secular occupation and came there every day. Nieto explained that he had known the Ruef family for years, and suggested that he might be instrumental in persuading the boss to tell the prosecution what he knew about the unsavory civic conditions,— "primarily for the welfare of San Francisco, and secondarily for his own peace of mind and for the sake of his parents."

Burns welcomed any assistance, for he was making little progress alone, and he arranged a meeting between Ruef and the rabbi that evening at "the house of the crimson-lined box." Dr. Nieto discussed the situation with Ruef "from a moral point of view," and Abe assured him that he had committed no offense under the law and therefore had nothing to confess; in fact, that to say he was guilty of misdeeds of which he was innocent would be not only morally reprehensible but plain perjury. The rabbi reported lack of success to Burns, but the latter encouraged him to keep trying.

This development perturbed Heney when Burns reported it. Heney had had one unpleasant experience with Nieto: while the Oliver grand jury was being empaneled, twice the rabbi had stopped him in the Temple corridor and remonstrated that in questioning prospective grand jurors, Heney was showing prejudice against Jews. Heney scoffed at this, replying that he simply wanted honest men on the grand jury, and whether they were Jew or Gentile meant nothing to him. The Oliver grand jury, in fact, did have Jewish members, and other Jews, both prominent and obscure, worked in close sympathy with the prosecution throughout.

The second time Nieto charged him with prejudice, Heney, whose temper always was razor-edged, replied with some asperity, and mentally he put down the rabbi as an ardent admirer of Ruef, who at heart would like to see the boss go free. Such was Heney's suspicion, and he enjoined on Burns the greatest circumspection in dealing with Nieto. The detective felt that the rabbi's motives were of no consequence, provided he could induce Ruef to "come through."

Dr. Nieto's next participation was, with the prosecution's consent, to take Ruef to see his parents in their nearby family home. Abe's father and sister called at Fillmore Street regularly, but his mother, Adele, was gravely ill, broken by the shame of her son's arrest. The reunion was highly emotional, Abe's mother embracing him and tearfully begging him to "do what the reverend gentleman asks," Ruef weeping and coming away deeply affected. But he stuck to his demand for complete immunity, and on April 8 Dr. Nieto came to Heney's office for a consultation. In order to elude newspaper reporters who congregated in the front hall of the Red House, the rabbi entered and left by a latticed rear gate in the alley that separated the house from the Unitarian church next door.

Dr. Nieto impressed upon Heney that he was not interested in Ruef as a person, "but only in the welfare of the community." Heney replied that his position was similar, that he held no personal animus against Ruef: "I always liked him and admired his ability, although I had contempt for his character."

But since the objective of the prosecution, undertaken at such cost and against such formidable obstacles, was to put a stop to civic corruption, Ruef must be punished, since he had been the principal agent in San Francisco's debauch of graft, Heney went on. Putting Ruef in prison, he contended, "would have a wholesome effect upon other political bosses for the next decade at least," and to put "a few captains of industry in prison with him" would have an even more salutary effect. Ruef's case was entirely different from that of the supervisors, he stressed; leniency was the most Abe could expect.

Dr. Nieto then asked Heney to state his conditions. Heney replied that he would agree to a generous degree of immunity for Ruef, in return for the fullest and frankest testimony regarding all bribery matters; but he would insist on holding some sort of club over the tricky boss which could be used if he reneged on his promise; and so, in the French restaurants case, Ruef must plead guilty to indictment 305, on which he was being tried. If he did this, then sentence would be postponed indefinitely while other trials were proceeding in which Ruef would be required to testify; and if he co-operated fully and honestly, when these trials were completed, the prosecution would use its best influence to obtain a token sentence on indictment 305, and all other indictments standing against him would be dismissed. On the other hand, Heney made perfectly clear, if at any time the prosecution found that Ruef was holding back information or otherwise not co-operating fully, the immunity agreement would be canceled and he would be sentenced immediately on indictment 305 and tried on every other indictment against him.

"I will not trust him without holding that power over him," was Heney's warning to the attentive rabbi.

These definite terms were conveyed to Ruef by both Nieto and Burns, but the boss clung to his stipulation for complete immunity before he would confess. And for a while neither side budged.

Confronted with this stalemate, Burns tried working on Ruef's fears, using the boss's ignorance of what was happening among his former associates. Alarming rumors were propagated which the

detective knew Ruef's visitors would transmit to him: Schmitz was
said to be dickering with the prosecution to turn State's evidence; the
"higher-ups" were reported to have decided to make Abe the scapegoat in hope of saving their own skins; new indictments were understood to be in preparation by the grand jury.

Authentic messages also came to Ruef, urging him to "stand pat,"
and Burns seemed to know just when such messages were delivered.
After such a relay he would inquire cheerily: "Get any 'stand pat'
message today? Those fellows want you to hold out, don't they?
Then you'll go to prison,—and protect them. Well, you'll make a
good fall guy, if we don't get them. By the way, none of your rich
friends have dropped in to see you, have they? That's funny...."

And off he would stroll, leaving Abe to puzzle and worry.

On other days Burns would affect indifference as to whether the
boss confessed or not, and would drop hints that an offer by Schmitz
to "squeal" was on the point of being accepted. The detective noted
that this seemed to upset Ruef more than anything else,—the thought
that Schmitz might anticipate him in getting something from the
prosecution.

One unlooked-for result of Burns's diligence in fomenting rumors
of Schmitz's impending defection was that Schmitz himself was taken
in: he sent an emissary to sound out Heney, proposing that he resign
and let the prosecution name a new mayor, in return for immunity.
This roundabout offer was never seriously considered; and public opinion would have been outraged by a barter so flagrant, because almost
everybody believed Schmitz had betrayed the people brazenly.

Burns resorted to unremitting surveillance in the attempt to break
Ruef's resistance. The boss was never left alone, even for a minute;
a guard was forever in sight, watching, listening, saying nothing.

"I want him to feel always that, waking or sleeping, a human eye
is upon him," the detective explained; "a cold, impersonal eye doing
its duty, with suspicion, without sympathy. Always, you understand,
day and night, and that's fierce."

By contrast, Burns would show up cordial and quick to oblige
with favors. Technically, Burns was a deputy elisor under Biggy,
but Biggy took orders from Burns, and this enabled the detective to
assume credit for an occasional easing of Biggy's rules. When, at a
whisper from Burns, the Elisor would reinstate certain galling regula-

tions, Ruef would beg the detective to intercede. It was a cat-and-mouse game, in which the odds were all in Burns's favor.

These tricks, kept up week after week, told on the boss, but they failed to wear him down; he would not confess until he received a guarantee of full immunity. Burns even tried one extreme form of preying on Abe's fears: a guard posted beside his bed would wake the boss and read from a notebook statements which he said Ruef had made in his sleep, incriminating admissions of the sort Burns wanted Abe to make. This would be repeated several times during the night, until Ruef would become almost persuaded that he really was talking in his sleep and would dread dozing off again. After such nights he came into court looking haggard; but even this torture did not destroy his determination, and Burns soon desisted.

Heney, who never believed that Ruef was acting honestly, had refused to deal with Henry Ach as Abe's spokesman in the immunity negotiations; but Ruef declared, after studying the roster of San Francisco attorneys for three days, that there was not another lawyer whom he could trust, and grudgingly Heney yielded; both Ach and Frank Murphy, of Ruef's counsel, Heney believed to be corrupt. Ach then joined the secret conferences at the Red House, and in the presence of Dr. Nieto and District Attorney Langdon revealed that he was advising Ruef to make the best bargain he could for turning State's evidence; because while the prosecution, in Ach's opinion, could not convict the boss in the French restaurants case, they were bound to get him on one of the bribery counts. Ach begged everybody present never to repeat what he was saying because some corporation officials whom Abe might inculpate were Ach's clients, and if the word got out that he had disclosed confidences, his reputation would be ruined.

Finally after weeks of sparring, Ruef consented at least to "think over" Heney's terms, including entering a plea of guilty to indictment 305.

9 Midnight Meetings by the Alley Gate

Toward the end of April, Heney had sent word that the boss would have to make up his mind quickly. Burns had roughed out an immunity agreement embodying Heney's safety clause, but in a fit of rage, real or pretended, Abe threw it back and swore he would never sign such a capitulation. Then he redrafted it, working in complete immunity, and Heney told Burns flatly that Ruef was not playing fair. Heney's stock of patience was giving out.

Dr. Nieto was planning to leave for Europe on the last day of April, and Ruef asked him to bring some other rabbi into the negotiations who could be a witness to what might occur during Nieto's absence. The choice fell upon Dr. Bernard Kaplin, rabbi of Congregation Ohabai Shalome at the Bush Street Temple. This was another inauspicious selection so far as Heney was concerned; the prosecutor was soon sizing up Kaplin as a man of little worldly experience, naïve and easily misled ("honest and unsophisticated"), who seemed to be (in Heney's words) "far more interested in finding out what would be done to Ruef, provided he pleaded guilty in the French restaurants case, than in the moral issue involved."

Kaplin told Heney that he had talked earnestly with Ruef about the French restaurants charge, "and he assured me that he is innocent, and that he took the money as an attorney's fee, and that he refused to take the case until the *Bulletin* abused him and challenged him to do it."

The falsity of this contention Heney knew, for he had consulted the *Bulletin* files and established that the *Bulletin* disclosed Abe's retainer *after* the boss had already pocketed the fee; to Kaplin, however, he merely replied that he had heard the testimony given to the grand jury and Ruef was guilty all right. But from that time on, Heney was convinced that Dr. Kaplin "was influenced by no motive or purpose other than that of getting Ruef off without any punishment if possible." He reiterated that Ruef must plead guilty to indictment 305 and take his chances on that before any immunity would be considered.

On the night of April 23rd, the alley gate at the Red House swung open for one after another shadowy figure as Nieto, Kaplin, Burns, Langdon, and Ach assembled for a critical conference. The jury selection in Ruef's trial was going forward steadily, the time before the start of testimony was narrowing down. This raised a legal point which Heney was determined should not work in Ruef's favor. Under California practice, a defendant was placed "in jeopardy" the minute the first witness was sworn; thereafter, should his trial be broken off, the prisoner could not be brought to trial again on that charge. This was in Heney's mind as the group huddled in the kitchen of the Red House.

The question of a written contract of immunity was canvassed. Both Heney and Ach had consulted the precedents and both knew that such a contract had no validity in California, but that judges usually conformed to recommendations made by a district attorney in whom they had confidence; and that these recommendations might be embodied in a written agreement, as a form of mutual memorandum and guidance for both parties.

As usual, Ach did most of the talking for his side. He indicated that Ruef was wavering because of doubt about the attitude of the judges before whom he would come; would they follow Heney's or Langdon's recommendations? There were four Superior Court judges hearing criminal cases—Lawlor, Dunne, Carroll Cook, and Mogan. Heney had made known that he would appear before neither Cook nor Mogan, whom he considered abysmally corrupt; that narrowed the field to Dunne and Lawlor, and Heney proposed that he and Ach should go to these judges and ask them whether they had confidence in Heney and what was their practice in regard to defendants turning State's evidence,—without mentioning Ruef in any way. But Ach begged off, he preferred to remain anonymous in the affair; and two hours of wrangling brought no concert of views. Still in uncertainty, the participants glided one by one through the alley gate and vanished into the darkness, unperceived by the news-gatherers swapping yarns in the front hall.

The next day, Ruef was unusually chipper in court.

"See that headline?" he snickered to a reporter, pointing to one reading: RUEF—GRAFTER. "That's libelous." He chortled.

The reporter held up a cartoon of Abe and Schmitz, and the boss studied it closely. "Yes, that's Gene, all right," he drawled. "But where's the union label?"

Had he got that French chef yet? he was asked.

"Nothing doing," Ruef grimaced. "I hope they find another treasure chest,—they gave me chicken that night."

And when Ach asked a talesman, "Do you know that Mr. Ruef stands charged with crimes that could send him to prison for nine

hundred to a thousand years?" Abe giggled openly. Burns, watching
him, wondered whether he had received some message of good cheer,
—or perhaps had made up his mind to "do business."

The clandestine parley of April 23rd was repeated at the Red
House three nights later, the participants again entering by the
garden gate and gathering in a back bedroom on the second floor.
Spreckels and Cobb, Heney's law partner, joined the group this time,
and the discussion of immunity terms went on until midnight.

Heney would not budge from his insistence on a plea of guilty
to indictment 305 and the fullest co-operation by Ruef thereafter, any
immunity agreement to be subject to revocation at the discretion of the
District Attorney upon the first indication of treachery or non-com-
pliance. The two rabbis, unfamiliar with the legal niceties in which
Heney and Ach dealt, asked the prosecutor to state his position in
lay language, so that they could make their own recommendations to
Ruef in good conscience; and for their enlightenment, Heney launched
into what he termed a statement of his "present intentions." These
in no sense embodied a set program, and what he was saying under
no circumstances must be repeated to Ruef, he stressed; it was confidential and for the rabbis' personal understanding only. These "present intentions," as put by Heney, boiled down to this:

Assuming that Ruef did co-operate with the prosecution fully
and freely, and assuming that Ruef's testimony secured the conviction
of highly placed corruptionists right up to Calhoun and Herrin and
perhaps higher,—then, when the question of sentencing Ruef on
indictment 305 came up, Heney might—just possibly might, he
repeated—recommend that the defendant be permitted to withdraw
his plea of guilty and substitute one of not guilty; and the prosecution
conceivably might go even further and urge that indictment 305 be
dismissed. Meanwhile, in conformity with the immunity agreement,
all other indictments would have been dismissed, or recommendations
for their dismissal would have been made by the prosecution. All this
was extremely speculative, based on the highly improbable assumption
of Ruef's sincerity, Heney said frankly; absolutely nothing was being
promised or even put forward as a basis for future hope. And all

present were honor bound not to reveal these random remarks to Ruef.

Lawyer that he was, Heney hedged his statement of "present intentions" with the sort of reservations another lawyer would know how to interpret; but the rabbis fuzzily gathered that the prosecutor's "present intentions" amounted to a conditional commitment. The meeting broke up in a spirit of truce, and the participants one by one faded into the alley darkness. Ruef's reaction remained to be plumbed.

The next day, Drs. Kaplin and Nieto advised Abe to accept the prosecution's terms, convinced in their own minds (they maintained later) that the required plea of guilty to indictment 305 was only a sham, which could be set aside later. Still Ruef hedged, saying the attitude of the judges bothered him, and he urged the rabbis to get personal assurances from Dunne and Lawlor that they would be governed by the prosecution's recommendations.

Once again, on the night of April 29th, Nieto, Kaplin, Ach, Langdon, Spreckels, and Cobb sidled through the alley gate and joined Heney in a final consultation at the Red House. The rabbis reported Ruef's hesitancy in respect to the judges. They proposed that Heney should go to Lawlor and Dunne, and in the rabbis' presence ask the judges what was their practice in cases of recommendations by district attorneys whom they trusted. Dr. Nieto reminded Heney that he was leaving for Europe in the morning; hence the interrogation would have to take place that night. Late as it was, Burns was dispatched to locate the two judges.

He found Lawlor in a theater. The judge demurred against meeting anybody that night, saying Heney could come to his chambers in the morning; but Burns explained the urgency and Lawlor agreed to drop by Temple Sherith Israel after the play; since it seemed evident that Heney wished to consult him on a subject pertaining to his judicial duties, he insisted that the meeting be in his chambers. Ruef's name was not mentioned.

Burns then went looking for Judge Dunne, and reached him at his home on Presidio Heights between eleven o'clock and midnight. Dunne objected strenuously to a meeting at that hour, likewise observing that Heney could see him in the morning. Again Burns urged the necessity of haste, without mentioning names; and although repeating that he would much rather hear about it in open court in the morning, Dunne agreed to come to the Temple. Burns offered him a ride in his car, but the judge preferred to walk.

At Temple Sherith Israel, meanwhile, Heney, Kaplin, and Nieto were waiting. When Judge Lawlor appeared, all four went into his chambers. After apologizing for intruding at that hour, Heney said: "Judge, we came here tonight to ask you what the practice of your court is in criminal cases in relation to the recommendations which may be made by the District Attorney?"

The rabbis listened carefully as the judge replied. He said he did not wish to know any particulars, but would state his practice in general. It was proper for the District Attorney to make recommendations in the cases of persons who turned State's evidence, he said, but the law vested the authority to determine such recommendations in the court; that such recommendations ought to be carefully considered by the court, and if they were in the interests of justice, they should be followed. He would not consider any case, however, until after full discussion in open court; if the application then appeared to be in the interests of justice, it was his practice to grant it; if not, to deny it.

With that, Lawlor excused himself and left the building.

It was a few minutes after midnight when Judge Dunne arrived, entering by the Webster Street door. Heney, Kaplin, and Nieto were standing just inside, and they all went into the office of the Temple secretary. Heney explained that he had come with the rabbis in order to have Dunne tell them "what your practice is as to recommendations of the District Attorney on behalf of defendants, or co-defendants, in criminal cases pending in your department, and also whether you have confidence in Mr. Langdon and in myself as his assistant."

"I have great confidence in you, Mr. Heney," responded the judge, "and in the District Attorney; and while I have confidence in the District Attorney, whenever a recommendation or suggestion is made by him in a case pending in my department, it is my general practice to entertain and be guided by it, provided, of course, it is in the interests or furtherance of justice."

"But, your honor," interposed Dr. Kaplin, who was showing

signs of excitement, "suppose a man pleaded guilty and afterward asked to change his plea?"

"You have heard what I have said, gentlemen, as to my practice," Dunne replied. "Of course, in all cases of such recommendations, and which I insist shall always be made in open court, whenever the District Attorney fails to convince me that he is well advised, or that good and sufficient grounds exist for his motions, it must be remembered that the final determination must always rest with me. I shall give great weight to any recommendations which you, Mr. Heney, or Mr. Langdon make."

With a courteous good night, Judge Dunne then withdrew.

The rabbis declined Heney's offer of a lift home and the prosecutor rode away, leaving the reverend intermediaries on the corner. The interviews with the judges had lasted only a few minutes each.

At two o'clock that morning, April 30th, Kaplin and Nieto assured Ruef, on their "sacred honor as men and ministers," that he could trust himself to the prosecution, that its promises "would be sacredly and absolutely kept."

Even that assurance was not sufficient to bring the boss to the point of confession. That forenoon, just before he caught the train East, Dr. Nieto was taken by Burns to Fillmore Street once more, to advise the boss for the last time that it would be safe to trust the prosecution. Nieto then left the city for several months.

All April 30th and May 1st, Burns toiled to get Ruef to accept conditional immunity and confess. On the night of May 1st the detective telephoned to Heney in great excitement, saying that Ruef seemed ready to talk, but was demanding an interview. Heney had gone to bed, and he objected that Abe would misrepresent anything that was said anyway, but finally he told Burns to bring the prisoner over. It was close to midnight when the pair arrived at Heney's apartment. The boss at once launched into a legalistic argument as to why he should be excused from entering the plea of guilty to indictment 305; only Heney's personal bias, he asserted, kept him from realizing that most San Franciscans would be glad to see him go free, provided he helped put some of the culpable "higher-ups" in prison.

"Ninety percent of the people would sign a petition for my release tomorrow," he swaggered.

Heney shook his head. "You fooled the people here a long time, Abe, but you can't fool them all the time, and now you are fooling yourself instead of them. Ninety percent of the people in this state want to see you in the penitentiary for life,—and that is what I am going to do with you, unless you make up your mind very quickly to undo some of the wrongs you have committed."

Unless Ruef accepted the prosecution's terms by 11:00 A.M. on May 3rd, Heney concluded, immunity would be offered to Patrick Calhoun,—who could, and probably would, cook Abe's goose to a turn.

May 3rd came, and just before 11:00 A.M. Ruef dictated a "preliminary statement" to Burns as evidence of good faith. In this he recounted his dealings with the United Railroads. The elated Burns hurried with the document to Heney's office, and was considerably deflated when the prosecutor pointed out that Abe had disclosed nothing they didn't know already: he had confessed having received $200,000 from Tirey Ford, but still referred to it as an "attorney's fee," and had said nothing about the money's being intended to bribe the supervisors.

Burns reminded Heney that in Oregon they had won confessions only piecemeal, a bit at a time, and Ruef at least had made a start. Heney referred the question to Langdon, Spreckels, and Cobb, and then, with their concurrence, drafted a form of immunity contract which Ruef could accept or reject. But he told Burns to impress on Abe that time was running out, that ten jurors had been chosen in his trial, and the prosecution was through haggling.

Abe had not finished squirming. He asked for an interview with Langdon, and got it, in Heney's presence, and threshed over the same ground, objecting to the wording of the draft contract, into which he wished to insert a proviso that he might withdraw his plea of guilty at a future date. Langdon informed him bluntly that he could accept the prosecution's offer or not, just as he pleased; they intended to waste no more time on him. By now the District Attorney was as fully convinced as Heney that Ruef was not acting in good faith.

On May 7th, Abe made further statements to Burns, outlining his dealings with the "fight trust," the gas company, the Parkside promotion, and the Home Telephone Company; he also told of giving Mayor Schmitz a portion of the French restaurants money and of receiving a regular share of the profits from the "municipal crib." All these matters had been ferreted out by Burns from other sources, but Ruef's statements were corroborative and therefore of value.

In this situation, still tentative and ambiguous, the immunity contract was signed on May 8th by Langdon, Heney, and Ruef. But Abe had managed to insert a stipulation of great legal importance, namely, that any future indictments which might be brought against him would be in the form of *joint indictments* with the other persons accused. And this clause was to become the heart of a furious controversy that was to swirl around this extraordinary agreement.

10 "Guilty Though Innocent"

Of all these furtive transactions, the city had no inkling. Ruef's trial moved exasperatingly slowly but inexorably, Abe continuing to harass the court by technical maneuvers, among them a demand for a change of venue on the grounds that he could not obtain a fair trial anywhere in San Francisco. This application, with its attached newspaper clippings, bulked a foot and a half high, and Frank Murphy earnestly begged permission of the court to read every word.

"No," sighed Judge Dunne.

But still time was consumed in hearing arguments, submitting affidavits, and other dilatory tactics, and all during this interim the prosecution remained in doubt as to what Ruef would do; he had made no real confession yet.

Then Burns played his trump: he appealed to Ruef's vanity and craving for attention.

Instead of routinely entering a new plea (a formality that could have been taken care of by simply handing a petition to the court clerk), why not, the detective suggested, stage the action like a show? Abe would star in a scene that would lift him to the place of civic hero and would echo in headlines around the world. Burns sketched the picture enticingly:

"The courtroom will be crowded, everybody will be watching you.

Don't tell anybody in advance, not even your own attorneys. Well, you might tell one. But pretend to tell him in court, and let him tell the others. They'll jump up and you can go off in a side room and have an agitated conference. We'll play innocent, our side, and you can come back all paralyzed. The attorney you tell might walk up and down, as though suffering and angry, while you read your statement. And that statement,—we'll make it a corker! I'll help you with it. You'll move the whole town to tears, even the judge will feel it. And Schmitz,—he'll drop in his tracks. Because I can give you this straight,—Mayor Schmitz isn't expecting you to spill the beans!"

To this lure Ruef succumbed, and he set to work drafting the monologue.

Then Judge Dunne denied the motion for a venue change and the twelfth juror was sworn, and Heney's opening statement and the commencement of testimony was set for Wednesday, May 15th. A final warning was relayed to the boss that he must plead guilty before the first witness took the stand, or the immunity contract would be canceled and he would be prosecuted on every indictment outstanding.

Ruef, meanwhile, without communicating with Heney, who thus was kept in suspense, was editing and re-editing his courtroom statement and rehearsing pose and gesture before the dresser mirror. Wednesday morning a barber shaved him and trimmed his hair and mustache, now streaked with gray, while the tailor delivered a new suit of conservative cut; half an hour was spent in arranging tie and settling curls. Then the manicured, spotless boss set off with Elisor Biggy for Sherith Israel.

Burns, who was by no means sure of his fish, had not told Langdon and Heney what was afoot; and when the court convened, the prosecutors were as much in the dark as the public as to Ruef's intentions.

Judge Dunne took his seat and began the opening formalities. Ruef was observed whispering to Henry Ach with great animation; then the latter arose and addressed the court.

"I am requested by my client, your honor, to say that it is his desire to have a conference with his counsel. I would like to draw your honor's attention to the fact that up to this time Mr. Ruef has not had a single opportunity to confer with his counsel alone. If the elisor, or the guards, were not in the same room, they were close by.

I think, in view of this fact, that we might be granted an adjournment until say two o'clock this afternoon so that Mr. Ruef may have the privilege of conferring with us."

Heney objected that "Mr. Ruef has always been granted privacy in his conferences with counsel." But at Langdon's instance, a recess of half an hour was called, and Judge Dunne offered the use of his chambers for the consultation. Ruef led the way out, followed by Ach, Shortridge, Murphy, and Fairall.

A couple of minutes later the door opened and Ach hurried back in, calling loudly for a glass of water and sending Myrtile Cerf to fetch a flask of brandy. The rumor spread that Ruef had fainted. Twenty minutes passed; then the door reopened and the five men marched out.

Ach looked flushed and angry. Flinging down his coat, he took a seat while the court was called to order; then he requested permission to withdraw as counsel for the defendant in consequence of a disagreement over the conduct of the case. In an injured tone, Shortridge made a similar request. Both attorneys were excused and stalked out of the courtroom. Murphy and Fairall stated that they were remaining, although they strongly disapproved of their client's contemplated action.

Then Ruef arose, and the scene was acted out exactly according to the prearranged scenario, while the spectators sat fascinated. Abe trembled, the veins stood out in dark lines on his sallow temples, and his voice was almost inaudible as he requested permission to read a statement. And falteringly, with tears in his eyes, he read from a sheaf of penciled, crosshatched, heavily interlined yellow foolscap held in quivering hands.

He was making this statement, he began, against the wishes of his attorneys, whom he thanked for their "services, fidelity, and friendship." His action was motivated by contemplation of the strain of a protracted trial, which he believed he would be "absolutely unable to bear"; already the effect upon "those whom I hold nearest and dearest has been so grave and severe that their health has been all undermined, they are on the verge of immediate collapse, and their lives are indeed now actually in the balance."

Pausing pathetically, he sipped from a glass of water to revive his strength, and shuffled the intensively edited sheets of paper uncertainly. Then he resumed: "I have occupied a somewhat prominent position in this city of my birth, where I have lived all my life, where are all my ties and interests, and whence, when the time shall come, I hope to pass into the eternal sleep. I have borne an honored name. In my private and professional life there has been no stain. In my public affiliations, until after the municipal campaign of 1905 and the election of the present board of supervisors, the abhorrent charges of the press to the contrary notwithstanding, no action of mine ever gave just ground for adverse criticism or deserved censure ..."

The courtroom was hushed. Judge Dunne listened with fixed attention. Ruef's voice failed, and again he sipped from the glass held by Myrtile Cerf. The 1905 election, he continued, was the cause of his downfall.

"A desire to hold together a political organization which had been built up with much effort did ... in a measure influence me to lower the high ideals for which I had hitherto striven. To offer excuses now would be folly. To make some effort at some reparation for the public good is, however, more than possible ... [and] will be a welcome task. I have decided that whatever energies or abilities I possess for the future shall be devoted, even in the humblest capacity, to restoring the ideals which have been lowered; shall, as soon as opportunity be accorded, be re-enlisted on the side of good citizenship and integrity ...

"In the meantime, I begin by an earnest of purpose—a purpose to make the greatest sacrifice which can befall a human being of my disposition—to acknowledge whatever there may have been of wrong or mistake, and so far as may be within my power to make it right ... Where duty calls I intend to follow, whither hereafter the path of my life may lead and however unpleasant or painful may be the result. I make this statement so that the court and the whole world may know at least the motives which have guided me in the step I am about to take."

At this point he swayed, his breath came fitfully, and he swallowed a gulp of water before reading the concluding sentences: "As an earnest I have determined to make a beginning. I am not guilty of the offense charged in this indictment. I ask now, however, that this jury be dismissed from further consideration of the case."

Here Heney sat up, alert and balanced like a fighter poised to spring.

Ruef's voice continued: "I desire to withdraw my plea of not guilty heretofore entered and to enter the contrary plea, and at the proper time submit to the court further suggestions for its consideration."

With these final words he sagged, gripping the back of the chair in front of him. In the stunned courtroom there was hardly a person who did not pity the little man in his humiliation; many who had known him when he held court at the Pup, jauntily humoring labor leaders and ordering men of substance around, hardly recognized the gray, chastened, broken figure. Abe pressed a handkerchief to his streaming eyes and stood waiting.

"If the defendant wishes to change his plea of not guilty to guilty," came Heney's voice, "the prosecuting attorney will consent to the discharge of the jury, as he requested; but we think that the indictment should first be re-read so that he may enter his plea as he wishes."

The indictment was read.

"What is your plea?" asked Judge Dunne softly.

"Guilty."

The plea was so entered and the jury was dismissed. Several of the jurors crossed the room and shook the boss's hand warmly. Cerf threw his arms around his leader and they sobbed together.

The astonished city suddenly was sympathetic. District Attorney Langdon hastened out to Fillmore Street with congratulations. "You did a manly thing," he declared. "I want you to know that anything the prosecution can do for you properly will be done willingly, gladly."

Biggy added his felicitations, and Ruef begged the reporters to make known that the elisor "has been as good to me as the law allows." It was a love feast, brightened by messages commending Abe's courage and virtuous resolves which were arriving by the dozens, seemingly from everywhere.

The reporters' commiseration, it was true, was rather dulled when they noticed that the boss was interested mainly in hearing how the public was taking the news. What were people saying about him? he asked again and again.

"I guess I'll be on the front pages tomorrow," he said complacently, while casting an eye over the bill of fare for the celebration supper Burns was giving that evening in Schmitz's old drinking parlor. The reporters tried in vain to get Ruef to explain what he meant by pleading "guilty though innocent." Although Abe knew, he wasn't telling yet.

PART TWO

"Be not righteous over much, neither make thyself over
wise: why shouldest thou destroy thyself?"

1 Battle in the Streets

When Abe surmised that he would be front-page news in the morning, his words carried more than ordinary significance, because the front pages of San Francisco newspapers had been pre-empted for weeks by the embattled progress of the bloodiest, costliest transportation strike in California's turbulent history. The antagonists were the United Railroads carmen's union and Patrick Calhoun. And the carmen were backed solidly by all the labor-union strength in the city.

As far back as mid-March, Mayor Schmitz had written to a police commissioner: "I received information a few days ago to the effect that on May 1st another street-car strike will take place. Of course, I intend to try to avert it if possible, [but] from all accounts it seems inevitable."

239

At the time, this seemed unnecessarily alarmist. There had been loose talk among the carmen, and Father Yorke was encouraging a walkout, although most union officials opposed such action. But afterwards it was recalled that Mayor Schmitz had written his letter just after he returned from New York, where he had been the guest of Patrick Calhoun.

The prospect of a street car tie-up was dismaying in view of the precariousness of the city's revival. The false prosperity of the first winter after the calamity had given way to depression and pessimism: San Francisco was entering upon its bitter "nine black months." The insurance cash had been spent, hard times threatened; already there were premonitions in the investment market of the "tight money" panic that was to scourge the nation later that year. Tempers had been rubbed raw by the accumulation of woes. Franklin Hichborn, a writer who lived through the stark period, pictured the depression as follows:

San Francisco was in a condition of confusion and discord. Thousands were still living in shacks erected in the ruins of the old city. The principal business streets were littered with building materials. There had come depression following the activity of rehabilitation and the pouring into San Francisco of millions of insurance money. Titles to real estate were confused if not in doubt, much of the records having been destroyed in the fire. Thousands found themselves forced into court to establish their titles. A little later the community was to suffer a visitation of bubonic plague. There were many authentic cases and some deaths. For months the city was in dread of quarantine. There were labor disturbances which for weeks at a time paralyzed industry. At one period between 7,000 and 10,000 iron-trades workers [key workers during the reconstruction] were out on strike. The telephone girls had been on strike since May 3. This alone threw the complex organization of a modern city into extraordinary confusion. The linemen struck. Telegraph operators in San Francisco and Oakland left their keys.

Amid such chaotic conditions, thousands of San Franciscans yearned for someone who would restore order, and this role Patrick Calhoun suddenly filled with magnetism, vitality, and masterly application of force.

Calhoun had come from New York to fight personally for the preservation of his properties, endangered by the graft prosecutions;

already United Railroads bonds were falling on the stock exchange.
He found the city's businessmen bemused or demoralized by the
frequent warnings of Francis J. Heney that the indictment of Louis
Glass of the telephone company was "only a beginning." Many rich
men knew they had grounds for fear, but all seemed a prey to in-
decision.

Then the carmen struck against the pleading of their union president and in defiance of warnings that the public would not tolerate
another transportation tie-up at so critical a moment. Calhoun had
offered the men a wage increase based on the sliding pay scale and
ten-hour working day then prevailing, but the union held out for a
flat wage and an eight-hour day. Calhoun replied that he would run
the cars with strikebreakers. On Sunday, May 5th, all street-car service
stopped.

The car barns had been barricaded and stocked provocatively with
food, cots, blankets, and ammunition. Two trainloads of professional
strikebreakers were brought into the city from the East under cover
of darkness, and were installed behind the barricades. On Tuesday,
May 7th, Calhoun sent out the first cars, manned by non-union
operators and guarded by rifle-carrying private police. Rioting and
bloodshed ensued such as had not been witnessed since the lawless
Fifties.

From behind fences and inside the uncompleted buildings that
lined the avenues, strikers and sympathizers opened fire on the cars.
Men and boys hurled clubs and bricks. At the Turk Street barn a
pitched battle was fought between strikebreakers behind a high
barricade and a swarm of carmen. Bystanders were caught in the
fusillade, two persons being killed outright and sixteen wounded, including a boy of thirteen shot through the chest. The pavement resembled a battlefield littered with casualties, and passing vehicles
of all sorts were commandeered to serve as ambulances in transporting
the victims to hospitals.

The police were helpless, Chief Dinan openly siding with the
strikers and doing nothing effective to restore order. Mayor Schmitz
contented himself with a proclamation calling on people to stay off
the streets, and refused to ask the Governor to send in state troops.
Calhoun stated that he would smash the carmen's union; it was out-
lawed so far as he was concerned; he would never deal with it again.

Day after day through the press he issued defiant "addresses to the public," declaring that union supremacy must end and blaming the "supine police" for the "reign of brickbats and bullets."

For months bloody guerrilla warfare flared and subsided, with intermittent violence, but little by little Calhoun extended the street-car service, winning support by his intransigence toward the hitherto all but impregnable unions. Arrogantly, he cruised the streets in an open automobile, daring the "lawless elements" to harm him; and in no time the business community was hailing him as "the man who saved San Francisco from labor anarchy" and "the man of the hour." Bankers, merchants, shippers, manufacturers, shopkeepers, and house-holders of all degrees—the influential, the propertied, and the genteel —lined up behind him, not only in San Francisco but across the nation; Calhoun's bucking of organized labor in San Francisco was making news. Letters and telegrams came by the thousands, praising his "unflinching courage" and his "mastery of the unwhipped mob."

In the uneasy city, theaters and churches which had closed when the terror erupted reopened and blessed his name. Hostesses, fascinated by his romantic lineage and lordly manners, intrigued for the privilege of entertaining him and his family, and his own sumptuous home at 2525 Webster Street, in the most fashionable part of Pacific Heights, was lavishly hospitable.

In time he made good his boast: the carmen's union was smashed, —with a final cost sheet reading: persons known killed, 4; wounded, 252; car windows broken by hurled missiles, 3,529; wages forfeited, $600,000; loss to United Railroads, in excess of $1,000,000.

This turmoil had repercussions on the graft prosecution. Precisely at the peak of Calhoun's burst of popularity, Heney brought him and Thornwell Mullally before the Oliver grand jury for questioning about the overhead trolley franchise.

There arose a ferocious outcry from the most vocal, if not the most numerous, elements of the public: Patrick Calhoun was their Bayard *sans peur et sans reproche*. He refused to testify. On what grounds, Heney asked, and the magnate replied: "I am aware that anything I might tell this body might be used against me."

He was excused immediately, and when Mullally took the same

defiant line, he also was dismissed without testifying. Heney announced they had turned down their first and last chance to tell the truth, and in a proclamatory counterblast Calhoun based their refusal to testify on "the broad constitutional right of every American that a citizen cannot be called as a witness [sic]." Again he "fully affirmed" that neither he nor any official of the United Railroads had "bribed anyone, authorized any bribery, knew of any bribery, or approved of any bribery," and said that Mullally and he looked confidently to "the justice, fairness, and common sense of the grand jury for vindication without offering one word in our own behalf."

William Abbott, assistant legal counsel of the United Railroads, took the same escape route. So did Tirey L. Ford. But other witnesses traced the United Railroads deposits and withdrawals at the Mint, and Ruef's former chauffeur, Alex Lathan, told the jurors about that trip to Ford's office when the boss came away with a shirt box under his arm. All "an infamous lie," Calhoun retorted.

But on May 25th the grand jury foreman handed to Presiding Judge Coffey nineteen indictments against Calhoun, Ford, Abbott, Mullally, Ruef, and Schmitz jointly, charging eighty-nine separate felonies. Also indicted again were Glass and Halsey of the Pacific States Telephone Company.

Lawyers of the first rank were on hand to represent the United Railroads executives when the indictments were returned,—A.A. Moore, a leading corporation counsel; his son, Stanley; and Earl Rogers, brilliant but eccentric criminal lawyer brought from Los Angeles, rated by many courtroom experts the ablest criminal lawyer of his day. The attorneys promised to produce the defendants the next day, and William H. Crocker and Henry T. Scott, president of the Pacific States Company, volunteered to go bond for Calhoun out of friendship and admiration for his civic services. But in order to avoid possible delay, Calhoun said he preferred to utilize a surety company. The bribery cases were assigned to Judge Lawlor's Department 11 of the Superior Court.

The city was half-aghast, half-jubilant. Tirey Ford stood high in the political and legal councils of the state, a man of hitherto unblemished reputation, whom everybody loved. His comment was

terse: "Conscious of my rectitude, I have no fear of the outcome."
Mullally, a bachelor widely popular among the younger social set,
said feelingly: "I am innocent." But Calhoun put forth a lengthy
"Statement to the American People," in which he not only reasserted
his guiltlessness, but boldly launched a frontal attack on the whole
graft prosecution; it was, he declared, merely a commercial conspiracy
engineered by Rudolph Spreckels for business advantage, and in proof
of the contention he harked back to the formation just before the
disaster of a rival street-car company by Spreckels, Phelan, and their
associates.

I charge [read the bristling pronouncement] that the motives of Mr.
Spreckels and his associates are selfish and injurious to the welfare of
this community, and that they seek, through the assassination of character,
to injure the United Railroads and further their own financial plans, and
that inspired strikes, violence, destruction of property, boycotts, and
these indictments are each part of Spreckels's plans to confiscate the
property of the United Railroads, to replace our street railways with lines
owned by Spreckels, and to that end to control the politics of San
Francisco. To my friends throughout the country I give assurance that
these indictments are not founded upon fact, that there is no evidence
that could justify them, and that my associates and I will be fully vindicated.

This rationalization of Spreckels' motive in financing the graft
cleanup was accepted with specious enthusiasm in clubs and board
rooms, and henceforth Rudolph Spreckels was bracketed with the
enemy,—union labor. Even Patrick Henry McCarthy's fulminations
against the prosecution as a scheme to destroy unions and the Union
Labor Party failed to shake this conviction, once it had been implanted
in the minds of the propertied, the socially conspicuous, and the rich.
San Francisco seethed in a vortex of passion and hatred, and the area
of hostilities widened when Heney struck once more and the grand
jury voted indictments against the directors of the Parkside and gas
companies.

The grand jurors had debated these indictments for several hours.
During the long wait, Heney, chatting with reporters, appeared
brimming with confidence. He predicted that men higher in the social-

financial scale than any yet named would be netted; already he was tasting total victory.

This time fourteen indictments for bribery—not extortion—were returned against Ruef, Schmitz, and three gas company directors: Frank G. Drum, Eugene de Sabla, and John Martin. All were joint indictments, in which the defendants were accused together. Another fourteen joint indictments, also for bribery, were returned against Ruef, Gus Umbsen, J.E. Green, and W.I. Brobeck in the Parkside franchise affair. Brobeck was an attorney employed by Parkside. All the newly indicted men occupied positions of prominence and power in the community and enjoyed the highest esteem in financial, social, and church circles. Wealthy friends competed for the honor of posting their aggregate bail, which was set at $1,260,000. This brought the grand total of all bail posted thus far in the graft cases to the not inconsiderable sum of $3,350,000.*

These fresh indictments shook the citadels of capital and conservatism. Although the alarm spilled over class boundaries, the most corrosive bitterness against the prosecution was observable among the "better element," where Heney and Spreckels were denounced as two of "the greatest rascals that ever forbore to let well enough alone." Spreckels especially was stigmatized as a traitor to his class, "a fanatic." In their clubs the prosecutors were ostracized, Fremont Older being made so uncomfortable at the Bohemian Club, where he had been a leading spirit, that he resigned. Lifelong friends snubbed Phelan on the street. Mrs. Spreckels and her daughters were stricken from invitation lists, and San Francisco's upper crust formed itself into a virtual adjunct of the graft defense. From Nob Hill to the Barbary Coast, passions were inflamed as they had not been since the white-hot hostility during the Civil War between the city's "Chivalry" and "Shovelry," as the Southern and Northern factions then were slanged.

The upheaval was not without diverting aspects. A visiting society matron bemoaned that at dinner parties "you dare not express any opinion for fear your companion may be under indictment; or if he should not be, you are sure his brother or best friend is, or his sister is engaged to one who is." One capitalist, who was not himself involved, was obliged to exert all his influence to prevent his attorney from going

*In today's monetary values, roughly $10,000,000.

to prison. And Gertrude Atherton, born into San Francisco society, which she shocked by turning professional writer, found the excitement "hysterical."

... Many men of the highest position, social and financial, shook audibly in their boots [she wrote]. They tried to joke. "When are you going up? No danger? Oh, you are out of it! Your position will be gone, you'll be a rank outsider! Besides, you'll be lonely down here!" But these jokes died for lack of vitality. Joking turned to vituperation. San Francisco became as a house divided against itself. ... Old friends ceased to speak, sisters cut each other, people entertaining were given to understand that one party or the other must be invited at a time, and one dame went so far as to demand the sympathies of her guests as they entered her drawing-room; if they declared for the prosecution, they were requested to leave!

It is true, society was not unanimously arrayed against the graft hunters: there were men and women of wealth and rank who rallied just as fiercely to the "regenerators of the city," which was a popular epithet for the prosecutors. Nevertheless, in this war of checkbooks and tiaras the friends of Calhoun and the indicted millionaires unquestionably enjoyed an edge, and tensions were stretched to the point of snapping. Heney and his bodyguard went armed, the cocky prosecutor seeming to court physical danger. Fremont Older received death threats in every mail.

More insidiously, speculation began to be heard in hitherto friendly quarters as to what lasting good could come from so radical an assault on established customs, deplorable though these certainly were. The newspapers detected "an obvious attempt to poison the public mind against the prosecution by denouncing it as a mere political move." In distant Chicago, the *Post* commented:

... The indications point to an organized cabal against the prosecution, a definite and powerful and fully equipped secret support of Schmitz. The existence of this cabal no one with commonsense can doubt. It makes the drama, the tragedy of San Francisco, trebly tense.

Against so much and so formidably entrenched wealth and influence (the indicted millionaires represented personal or corporate wealth exceeding $600,000,000, it was estimated) the San Francisco

Examiner cynically wondered what the efforts of one puny prosecutor could avail. But to doleful prognosticators, Heney replied with cackling, triumphant laughter.

Just five days after the city's venal boss had pleaded guilty to extorting money from French restaurants, Heney placed the city's handsome Mayor on trial for the same low category of crime.

2 Schmitz Meets the Jury

Had Ruef confessed? This question baffled all California after Abe's sensational espousal of the cause of righteousness in Judge Dunne's courtroom. Ruef did nothing to dispel the mystery. The day after his public act of contrition, he told the Associated Press:

"I have made no confession. I know much. Some things I shall tell. Some things I shall not tell. I changed my plea to guilty in court, yes; but I pledge to you my solemn word that I am innocent in these French restaurant cases. I will not say at the present moment that Mayor Schmitz is guilty of these charges that have been brought against him, or that he is innocent. I will say this: I wanted to break away from Schmitz before his re-election in 1905 and said to him: 'I am sick and tired of the whole thing and I want to get out. I can't stand for these labor union bums you have gathered around you and will appoint. They would eat the paint off a house!' The Mayor begged me to stay with him, and put up the argument that these fellows must be allowed their share or we could never hold the machine together. Unfortunately, there was all too much truth in that. I stayed with Schmitz and I stayed with the machine. But I myself never asked a dollar of any man, never took a dishonest dollar from the public."

Would he co-operate with the grand jury?

"I don't give a damn for the grand jury," he snorted. "When I have made up my mind in every particular as to how I shall act, then I'll be willing to go before the grand jury or William J. Burns or Heney or anybody they may appoint, and tell them what I've decided to tell."

Heney brought him before the grand jury that very afternoon.

To foreman Oliver, Ruef's swagger seemed more like that of

accuser than a man accused. Repeatedly he attempted to take over the
direction of the interrogation and elbow Heney aside, but without
success. He had entered the grand jury room pale but smiling; he came
out flushed and grave.

While he was on the stand, the *Bulletin* appeared with a huge
headline, RUEF INDICTS, and underneath said flatly that Ruef was implicating Calhoun, Schmitz, Herrin, Drum, Mullally, Ford, Abbott,
and Tevis (of the abortive Bay Cities water scheme). The article had
been written in advance, from notes supplied by Burns based on what
Ruef had told him in private discussions; the fact was that almost none
of the corporation officials whom the *Bulletin* named was being involved directly by Abe in his testimony. Repeatedly he refused to
concede that the $200,000 United Railroads payment was anything
but an attorney's fee. He did admit that when Ford handed over the
first $50,000 installment of this "fee," he jocularly remarked that it
was "a pretty good one." And Abe did confirm his previous statement
to Burns that he once gave Schmitz $1,200 of "municipal crib"
money, mentioning where it came from, and said the Mayor had not
spurned it.

The boss's aspersions on "labor union bums" caused ructions,
and the supervisors one and all denied that they would "eat the paint
off a house."

"Ridiculous!" croaked hackman Coffey. "Mayor Schmitz and
Ruef planned everything out. We did whatever the Mayor said. We
fellows can't be blamed at all."

"I don't think we led Mr. Ruef astray," was the retort of
Coleman. "It was the other way around."

The scowl on Mayor Schmitz's face deepened.

The Temple classroom assigned to Judge Dunne proved inadequate to hold the crowd determined to witness the Mayor's trial, and
for a temporary courtroom the Bush Street Temple—an exotic fab-
rication with Moorish-style minarets where Dr. Kaplin was rabbi—had
been rented. This provided a dramatically solemn setting for the
momentous hearing. At the front, Judge Dunne sat on the pulpit platform in a high-backed chair, against hangings of crimson and fluted
organ pipes. On either side arose enormous brass candelabra. The

Eternal Light depended over the Ark, its red-shaded flame glowing in the subdued light. Inside the rail, long tables had been set up for attorneys and reporters, and telegraph and telephone wires had been strung in. The vestry served for judge's chambers, and on a rough plank dais at one side was built a jury box. Velvet-cushioned pews accommodated five hundred spectators, and along the walls in letters of gold were Hebrew inscriptions enjoining virtuous conduct.

Schmitz was represented by all three members of the law firm of Campbell, Metson & Drew, assisted by John J. Barrett, the fire commissioner. Heney was seconded by Hiram Johnson and, less conspicuously, J.J. Dwyer. Toward Heney the Mayor turned a fixed sneer; for Spreckels he had a special glare of bellicosity. Out-of-town newspapermen were struck by Schmitz's Othello-like appearance: his dusky hair, luminous eyes, fierce mustaches, and beard trimmed to a smart Van Dyke, and his bombast and theatrical poses. "Fiery, good-looking, and rather dull," was the consensus. "Dull" was an adjective never applied to Abe Ruef.

The proceedings were marked by the now-to-be-expected wrangles between counsel over hairsplitting technical objections. Heney threw the courtroom into a genuine furor when he accused Chief of Police Dinan of using city detectives to shadow talesmen and intimidate witnesses,—at Mayor Schmitz's command, he added. Dinan did not deny the charge, but defended his action as "in the public interest." The other side was doing the same thing, he said: "Our men ran into Burns men who were engaged in the same line of work."

The grand jury looked into this new complication, and in short order indicted Dinan for attempted jury-tampering.

The jury box was filled on June 4th. On that day San Francisco was startled by a sharp earthquake, the most severe since the 1906 catastrophe.

It was understood that the State's star witness against Schmitz would be Ruef. Other prosecution witnesses, led by the former police commissioners Reagan and Poheim, testified concerning the Mayor's part in holding up the liquor licenses of the French restaurants until Ruef was signed as their attorney.

"In compliance with [the Mayor's] request, I assisted in holding up the French restaurants," Reagan swore. "I never knew a French restaurant existed in San Francisco until they were discussed in the police board."

Later, the Mayor pressed him to reverse his vote and approve the licenses, Reagan testified, on the grounds of political expediency. "He said many rich people visited these restaurants and others had money invested in them, and he could not afford to antagonize them. But I replied: 'I don't think that is right, Mayor; you first made me vote to close them up, and now you want me to vote to reopen them.'"

Whereupon Schmitz flew into a rage, banged the table, and yelled: "That's the way! I appoint my friends to commissions and then they refuse to do the smallest thing I ask them! Why, things that happen in a French restaurant might happen in the Palace Hotel!"

The Sunday afternoon showdown in Schmitz's Fillmore Street house, just after Ruef had taken the restaurant keepers' cash, Reagan recounted racily: "The Mayor took my coat and hat and escorted me downstairs, where he built a fire. He told me he expected [Commissioner] Drinkhouse in a few minutes. He treated me very pleasantly. Drinkhouse arrived a little later. The matter of the chairmanship of the police commission came up. The Mayor worked himself into a towering passion. He walked around the table several times and banged it with his fist. He said: 'It was reported to me last week that you would not vote for the man I wanted for chairman. I've a good mind to dismiss both of you now!'

"'You can have my resignation,' said Drinkhouse.

"I said, 'You can't have mine.'

"Then he brought out the whisky and cigars. Ruef and [Commissioner] Poheim came in at this time."

Asked Heney: "Was anything said about Ruef being interested in or representing the French restaurants?"

"Not in so many words that he was counsel for them. It was distinctly understood. Ruef said: 'Tom will vote for the licenses.' 'No, he won't,' said the Mayor. 'I'll throw Hutton out.'"

Within a week, Commissioner Hutton was removed on the grounds of immorality.

Then Ruef appeared before the police commission and submitted the regulations which he said he believed he could persuade the restaurant owners to abide by.

"I didn't pay much attention to them," Reagan said. "I didn't think the mover of them took them seriously."

Poheim testified that Schmitz told him he wanted a police commission which would take orders. "I secured the position of commissioner through Abe Ruef," Poheim admitted. "The day before my first commission meeting, he took me to Mayor Schmitz's house and I was instructed. Ruef showed me the papers in the restaurants case before the meeting."

The restaurant keepers testified that they had gone to Ruef because he was a political boss, not because he was an attorney or because they felt in need of legal counsel. The agreement on the fee was that it should be paid in currency and no receipt would be given. Until Ruef produced the contract, none of them had ever heard of the French Restaurant Keepers Association of San Francisco or known that they were members in good standing, and they never referred to it afterward.

Now only Ruef's testimony was lacking to the State's case. But suddenly Heney rested without calling the boss.

The defense, caught by surprise, obtained an overnight delay, and the next morning placed the Mayor on the stand.

While awaiting questions, Schmitz clung tightly to the arms of the witness chair. Then, in a resonant, vigorous voice he denied every damaging assertion made by his disgruntled former henchmen, Poheim and Reagan, until Heney asked: "Did Ruef pay you any part of the $5,000 that it has been testified he received from the French restaurants?"

This question the Mayor did not want to answer, and he stroked his black beard nervously while his attorneys argued; but the court ruled that he must answer, and he said: "I didn't know that Mr. Ruef got $5,000 and I got no part of it."

He denied that he had ever had a conversation with Ruef regarding a "fee" from the restaurant men, or had received any money whatever from Ruef.

Whereupon Heney called as rebuttal witness Abraham Ruef.

The courtroom was startled, and the crowd packed in the corridor outside surged against the doors and forced them open, soon clogging the aisles. Unknown to the defense, judge, or spectators, Abe had been kept on call in a side room. He entered, freshly shaved, carefully groomed, wearing a gray business suit. As he was sworn, his eyes wandered listlessly over the public and jury, but his characteristic flippancy flashed briefly when the clerk asked his address.

"My temporary abiding place is number 2849 Fillmore Street," he replied.

Schmitz glared but did not move a muscle.

Removing his topcoat, Ruef folded it neatly, laid it across the railing, and sat down.

Heney put one question to him, while Abe's hands fidgeted: "Mr. Ruef, in the month of January or February, 1905, in this city, at 2849 Fillmore Street, in the house then kept by the defendant, did you give him $2,500 in currency?"

There was a hush. Then the defense burst into objections, which continued until Judge Dunne announced he would defer ruling until the morning. Ruef seemed hardly interested in the debate.

That evening at 7:30 Burns picked up the boss and rode away with him in an automobile, returning at 11:30, and reporters made wild guesses as to where they had passed the intervening hours. But in court the next morning Heney cleared up the mystery: the prisoner, he said, had been spirited away to forestall an attempt by the defense to reach him and persuade him not to testify.

"All of which you say is a lie!" shouted defense counsel Metson.

Heney dared him to repeat that on the witness stand,—a dare which was not taken.

Ruef being recalled, he was instructed by Judge Dunne to answer, and Heney repeated the question: "Did you, in January or February, 1905, in this city and county, at the house of Eugene E. Schmitz, the defendant, at number 2849 Fillmore Street, give to Eugene E. Schmitz any money, and if so how much, and in what kind of money?"

After renewed objections had been overruled, Ruef answered: "I did—$2,500 in currency."

"Did you then and there tell him that it was his share of the money you had received from the five French restaurant keepers?"

"I didn't say to him that it was his share of the money which I had received from the French restaurants. I did say to him that I had received from the French restaurants the sum of $5,000, and that if he would accept half of it I should be glad to give it to him. I thereupon gave it to him."

He added that, early in 1906, he gave Schmitz $1,500 as his share of the second payment of $3,000 made by the restaurant men. His air in telling this resembled that of a child detected in some naughtiness.

Schmitz slumped in his seat, looking old and drawn. From his livid features the sneer had been erased. Ruef himself was pale, and he did not glance toward the defendant.

Heney turned over the witness to the defense, and attorney Campbell attempted to bring out that immunity was the price being paid for Abe's evidence. (The prosecution's contract with the boss was still a tightly guarded secret, the document itself lying in a safe-deposit box in the joint custodianship of detective Burns and Rabbi Kaplin.)

"It is a fact, is it not, Mr. Ruef," began Campbell, "that at the present time you expect these gentlemen connected with the prosecution to use what influence they have in your favor to secure for you leniency upon certain criminal charges now pending against you?"

"Upon my testifying fully and fairly to the truth in these matters, yes, sir," was the reply.

"Who is to be the judge, Mr. Ruef, as to whether or not your testimony is true, you or the prosecution?"

"Well, I shall insist that I am."

"What is their situation about it?"

"I presume they—knowing me as they do—that they will take my word . . . The testimony I am giving now is true. I expect the prosecution will believe it to be true, and expect that they will carry out what they have said, namely, that they will do what they can to assist in securing leniency."

Campbell brought out that in a discussion with Schmitz and the latter's counsel, in the parlor of the Mayor's Vallejo Street home one rainy afternoon shortly before Ruef's arrest, the boss had assured those present that he never gave the Mayor "one dollar of the French restaurants money."

"Now," said Campbell silkily, "were you telling the truth then?"

"I am telling the truth now."

"So you were not telling it then?"

"Well, that is the natural deduction, that I was equivocating about the proposition."

Heney looked grim: if this was an "equivocation," he wondered, in an audible aside, what would the boss consider a downright lie?

"Now I will ask you," Campbell bore in with sudden harshness, "if you are not now giving your testimony under the expectation and hope of immunity,—complete immunity?"

Ruef shifted uneasily and glanced appealing toward Heney, who objected to the court that "what his hopes or expectations may be is immaterial, incompetent, and irrelevant."

This objection Judge Dunne sustained, but he watched closely as Campbell continued to probe.

"Has Burns frequently awakened you at midnight to discuss your case with you?"

"Not since we left the St. Francis."

"Did you not at first tell them that you would not testify, and that if you did testify it would be to acquit the Mayor?"

"I didn't put it as strongly as that. I said that I didn't wish to testify. I said that if I gave all the facts, in my judgment the majority of them would be in favor of the Mayor."

(This statement was never amplified, and Ruef's insinuation was not clarified.)

Abe succeeded in getting into the record that he held a written contract with the French Restaurant Keepers Association (he had a copy in his pocket), and then was excused.

In closing, Hiram Johnson spoke first for the State. The acid-tongue attorney's forelock bobbed angrily as he exclaimed: "Ruef and Schmitz were Siamese twins, and it took a Heney to separate them! San Francisco had been good to this man." He pointed to the ashen-faced defendant. "San Francisco treated him kindly. She had a right to ask of him fairness, honesty, decency . . . He sold us out! . . . A bribe-taker, a brothel proprietor, a man who takes money from French restaurants! . . . He is sleek and he is fat and he is rich now. He lives over on the hill. He is living on the fat of the land. And now, rich though he may be, he is brought to bay! He betrayed us!"

Barrett, speaking for the defense, excoriated Reagan,—"$10,000 Tom," he called the ex-commissioner, referring to the insurance Reagan wrote on saloons and bawdy houses while he was a city official.

Heney summed up, and the jury retired.

Consideration of the verdict consumed all afternoon. Toward seven o'clock, Schmitz drove up to the Temple in the handsome red automobile provided by the city for his official use and inquired about the outlook. His counsel were nervous, and the Mayor gloomily drove away. At 8:15 he was back. The jury filed in and the verdict was handed to the clerk. In profound silence the crowd heard the clerk read . . . "Guilty." For an instant the silence held. Then from the rear of the room came a single, heartfelt, "Good!"

The members of the prosecution team glanced at each other significantly; the defendant and his attorneys were mute. Judge Dunne remanded the prisoner into the custody of the sheriff, discharged the jury with thanks, and retired. Schmitz continued to sit at the counsel table, lightly drumming his fingers, apparently dazed. The crowd was reluctant to leave, staring with merciless curiosity at the convicted Mayor, some even climbing on the pews to see better. The prosecutors stood up and shook hands all around. Still Schmitz sat, drumming on the table, while his lawyers whispered among themselves. At length, a janitor began to turn out the lights and push the spectators toward the doors. The prosecution party melted away, all except Heney, who remained eying the Mayor distrustfully, suspecting that Schmitz might try to bolt.

Soon the Mayor stood up and moved around the room vaguely; he seemed nervous, and his attorneys pressed around him closely. Suddenly the group darted through a side door, with Heney and the crowd in pursuit. An automobile was at the curb, and Schmitz and a deputy sheriff sprang into it and were whisked away before anyone could intervene. The car was driven to the Mayor's residence, where Schmitz and the deputy went inside. About an hour later they emerged and drove off together, and soon thereafter Julia Schmitz, sobbing, came out with one of her daughters and also drove away.

Where the Mayor spent that night remained a secret.

At 2849 Fillmore Street, in the gingerbread house from which Schmitz had fiddled his way to fame, there was a victory banquet, with detective Burns the host. There was music and flowers, toasts were drunk, and Ruef was the wit of the occasion. (Later the party was repeated, with Ruef as host and raconteur-in-chief.)

Upon learning, the next morning, that Schmitz was not yet in jail, District Attorney Langdon telephoned Sheriff O'Neil. "Where is the Mayor?" he demanded furiously.

"Where it doesn't cost $1,700 a week to keep him," came the cool reply, and the Sheriff hung up.

But when court convened, Schmitz reappeared. He was haggard and disheveled, and listened wistfully to his lawyers' plea that he be released on bail pending appeal. Official business required his presence in his office every day, the court was told, but Judge Dunne brushed aside this contention and ordered the prisoner to be taken to jail at once, cautioning the Sheriff that he must be treated precisely like any other inmate.

Eugene and his obsequious guard thereupon stepped into the flashy "red devil" car and tooled away toward the Ingleside county jail in the style and dignity befitting the chief magistrate of an opulent and fantastic city.

3   "Mayor, Mayor, Who Is the Mayor?"

Why Heney delayed until the very end of the Mayor's trial to call Ruef as a witness puzzled observers, especially when subsequently several jurors revealed that until the boss testified they had harbored doubts. Of Heney's problems, however, the public at large knew nothing.

Since signing the immunity contract, Ruef and Heney had quarreled. Directly after Abe pleaded guilty, Heney had called him to the Red House to discuss the testimony he would be expected to give in the trial of Schmitz and the indicted corporation men, and in the course of their talk had become convinced that Ruef was acting in bad faith and probably would continue to do so. Heney detected him in lie after lie; for instance, Ruef persisted in saying he had undertaken the cause of the French restaurants only *after* the *Bulletin* goaded him into it. Heney confronted him with the *Bulletin* file, and exclaimed: "You have been lying to us about your motives in accepting this pretended employment, which was, in fact, as clear a holdup as any highwayman ever committed!"

"What of it?" laughed the boss.

"This of it," retorted Heney. "You are an unmitigated liar, and I wouldn't believe you under oath in any material matter where you are not corroborated by reliable evidence. You have not told us all the truth in the United Railroads case. You have not told us all the truth in the gas rate matter. You have not told us all the truth in the Bay Cities water deal. You have not told us all the truth in the telephone franchise matter. You lied to us in the Parkside matter and I caught you in it before the grand jury. I don't believe you ever acted in good faith with anybody in your life. But you have overreached yourself this time. The immunity agreement is off,—and if I have my way, you will be prosecuted on at least one of each set of cases in which you have been indicted."

He ordered Burns to take the prisoner away and not bring him back, and from then on Heney refused to talk with Ruef or see him. And in his opening statement to the Schmitz trial jury, Heney had purposely refrained from saying that he would use Ruef's testimony, because he felt he could not trust the boss on the stand. When Schmitz took the stand unexpectedly, Heney yielded to the importunities of his associate counsel, Johnson and Dwyer, and called Abe in rebuttal; and by narrowly limiting his questions, he also limited the area of cross-examination permissible to the defense; he was playing safe. Abe did not know, either while he was testifying or afterward, whether Heney considered the immunity agreement still in force; he hoped, but the prosecutor gave no sign.

When the jury declared Schmitz guilty, Jere Dinan wept, and that evening one of the jurors was arrested on a pretext of beating his wife and tossed into the drunk tank overnight. The prosecution, for their part, immediately was confronted with still another problem created by their victory.

Under California law, conviction of a felony automatically disqualified an officeholder; the mayoral seat, therefore, was vacant. The supervisors were empowered by the city's charter to fill a vacancy in the mayor's office, and the "good dogs" were ready and eager to elect whomever they were told to elect; indeed, several of them were even humming hopefully, "It Might as Well Be Me." It was, of course, imperative that the new mayor should be favorable to the graft inquiry.

A struggle for power was precipitated when every faction in the city—political, racial, economic, social—pressed forward with its candidate. The behind-scenes jockeying became frenetic, one of the most insistent manipulators being William Randolph Hearst, who wanted his political lieutenant, J.J. Dwyer, to be appointed. But the prosecutors believed Dwyer was too closely associated with them in the public mind to escape the suspicion of being a mere mouthpiece, and they rejected Hearst's solicitations. This action cost them dearly, for from that moment, the publisher turned against the prosecution and through the *Examiner* became one of its most effective opponents, dealing in the dual weapons of scurrility and ridicule.

Meanwhile, the city had to have a chief executive in order that business might proceed, and Langdon directed the "good dogs" to elect one of their number temporary mayor. The choice fell upon Gallagher. To justify the expedient, the prosecution evolved a tenuous legal theory that the Mayor was "temporarily unable to perform his duties," and defined Gallagher's status as acting mayor. The two supervisors whom Schmitz had appointed and who were not involved in the briberies (Tveitmoe and O'Neill) cried out against their fellow members' lickspittle acquiescence, of course to no avail.

"What is the difference between Eugene E. Schmitz and James Gallagher?" shouted O'Neill; and all over the land that question was echoed with varying degrees of rage and frustration.

"San Francisco exchanges a rebellious and unconfessed crook for a high-class stool pigeon," was the scornful comment of the Los Angeles *Times.*

The Calhoun camp gagged at the spectacle of a "Mayor of Spreckelsville," and the influential weekly San Francisco *Argonaut,* a leading apologist for the bribe-givers which boasted that it circulated around the globe, sneered, "One rogue for another," and rated Gallagher "the cheapest pawn that ever figured in a big game."

In the Eastern United States, the press broke into jeremiads, the

New York *Times* groaning, "The position of San Francisco may not be entirely hopeless, but it is pretty nearly so."

The New York *Sun* gave voice to Wall Street's disapproval with the stern judgement: "It is a hard thing to say, but it is a just conclusion that at the present time investment in any San Francisco enterprise has become unsafe." Since the city was in desperate need of investment capital to regain its feet, this was a crippling arraignment.

The Philadelphia *Ledger* detected "something peculiarly sinister in the aspect presented by San Francisco . . . With reason for believing that a rascal occupies its mayoral chair, [it] does not care." And the austere and respected Springfield (Massachusetts) *Republican* administered a stinging condemnation that was quoted with approbation nationwide:

San Francisco, in the hour of its deepest shame, is still an American city, and the country must needs share in its degradation and stand before the world as sponsor for its conduct. With the conviction of Mayor Schmitz on the criminal charge of extortion, however, the country must experience a new feeling of disgust over the San Francisco situation. It would seem as if government by the people there had broken down, and that, in its relation to the ordinary sanctions of decent, orderly municipal government, San Francisco has become a moral bankrupt.

Chief target of the outcry in San Francisco, as the squabble over selection of a new mayor intensified, became Rudolph Spreckels,— the "Big Stick," he was called, in emulation of the pugnacious layer-down-of-the-law in the White House. The *Examiner* and other unfriendly newspapers lampooned Spreckels as a despot—"Emperor Rudolph I"—determined to rule through a puppet of his choosing. His very disclaimers of personal interest or selfish motivation were cited as evidences of cunning and insincerity.

"No man has the right to buy himself a position of moral authority," the *Argonaut* admonished, and the attacks became so virulent that Spreckels was stung into making one of his few replies to published abuse.

"I have no desire to dictate who shall contribute to the membership of the city offices," he said. "I started out in this graft prosecution to bring all guilty municipal officials to the bar of justice and have them punished. That is my single motive. I have no ulterior designs in this matter, regardless of what anyone may say to the contrary."

When reporters tried to provoke him into more extensive rebuttal, he referred them to the only press interview he had given on the subject of his participation in the graft inquiry, in which he had revealed his insight into some of the profounder issues at stake. This interview had appeared in the Los Angeles *Times* a month previously, after Ruef's courtroom recantation and Patrick Calhoun's indictment.

... I am not given to talking, especially to newspapers [he had said then]. What's the use? The newspapers have condemned me without a hearing. ... I do not want to be mayor. I do not want the franchise of the United Railroads. The peculiar position in which I have been placed is distasteful to me. It is quite to be expected that Mr. Calhoun and the rest of these men expecting indictment should make a bitter attack upon me. The reason is quite obvious.... Do you suppose that I enjoy prosecuting and bringing disgrace and public odium upon men who have been associated with me in business, and perhaps men who have been my dearest and best friends?... In instituting this graft investigation, I was actuated by a broader motive than the mere punishment of wrongdoers and the moral cleaning up of a city. Any man who thinks can see that this country is in danger of a revolution. Our menace is the growth of bitter class feeling. Poor men are coming to believe that very rich men may break the law when and where they choose. Some rich men, I am sorry to say, are coming to believe so, too. My greatest purpose in using my resources as a private citizen and bringing these rich corporations and rich bribe-givers to justice is to try to do something toward healing this terrible and growing breach between the classes.... I went into [this] resolved to let justice hit whomever was found guilty, be it my friend, my business associate, my enemy, or myself.

Even his detractors realized that he meant every word. For his part, he was teaching himself to expect misrepresentation. "It will be ten years before people understand me," he told condoling friends. Nevertheless, he was deeply hurt; but his monolithic resolution was not cracked, he did not waver.

Schmitz viewed the whole upheaval as a rump movement and refused to concede that he was not the Mayor. From the county jail (where he was comfortably lodged, not in a cell but in a warder's room in the administration wing), he "vetoed" Gallagher's election, declared Big Jim's seat forfeited, and appointed a successor supervisor; the "good dogs" received the warrant of appointment with howls of merriment. Schmitz signed vouchers on the city treasury, and rode back and forth to his lawyers' offices daily in the official red automobile. He telephoned the city auditor's bondsmen that he would hold them responsible for any monies paid without his authorization, tied up all payments for a while, and then was assured formally by the auditor that while Eugene undoubtedly retained "the title and honor of *de jure* mayor," Gallagher undoubtedly was "*de facto* mayor." But the city treasurer played safe and declined to cash any warrants unless they were signed by both Eugene and Big Jim.

On June 20th, Schmitz applied to the Court of Appeals for release on bail, pleading that he was suffering from an incurable kidney disease,—a surprise to his friends, who had always considered him exceptionally robust and healthy. Schmitz also warned that the course being pursued by Rudolph Spreckels would "produce riot and anarchy" unless checked. The court denied him bail and took their chances on anarchy.

One of Schmitz's attorneys had a curious consultation with Supreme Court Justice Henshaw at about this time, receiving from the Justice sage advice on the proper form to follow in wording the appeal from conviction; the Appeals Court was understood to be inclined to favor Schmitz, if the appeal were framed on certain lines.

This egregious participation by Henshaw in the conduct of the defense was overlooked in the multiplicity of excitements provided by Schmitz's disclosure that he intended to run for a fourth term in the autumn election.

"You may announce that I am a candidate for re-election this fall, and that I expect to win," he told the Associated Press and the bewildered nation. "I have already begun my campaign in a preliminary way." The interview was given in jail.

This incredible prospect provoked another convulsion of indignation.

"A suggestion that the people of San Francisco choose a mayor from the inmates of a prison is an opera-bouffe idea that Schmitz must have imbibed in the days when he led the orchestra," marveled the

Philadelphia *Press;* but the Philadelphia *Record* predicted that Schmitz "will get the greater portion of the regular party vote and the Union Labor vote."

Burns thought Schmitz a likely candidate for examination by a lunacy commission.

Smiled Langdon: "Eugene's training was theatrical, wasn't it?"

And Schmitz's own lawyer greeted him in court the next morning with, "Hail, Mayor, that was, is, and is to be!"

Eugene ignored the Macbethean satire and glibly outlined his plans to a swarm of reporters.

"You don't feel that the people's confidence in you has been forfeited or destroyed?" he was asked.

"I do not. To the contrary—and I believe my information is accurate—I feel that it is weekly becoming plainer to the people of San Francisco that I am the object of a political instead of a moral prosecution, and have been notoriously deprived of a fair trial. I was convicted by a jury, ten of whom were pledged to find me guilty, and two of whom were jibbed and cajoled into voting me guilty. I have no fear that the higher courts will sustain the verdict. Until they do and the last resort the law affords for justice has been exhausted, I will fight my persecutors every inch of the way. I ask no quarter. I want no mercy. I demand justice. The issue on which the fall campaign will be decided is 'prosperity.' Nothing else."

He said he would call for a $50,000,000 bond issue for civic improvements on a grand scale; and, of course, he would run without Ruef's support.

The speech was virtually a valedictory,—for two days later, Judge Dunne sentenced the pale and hollow-eyed Eugene to five years in prison.

Passing of sentence had been postponed several times, and when Judge Dunne called the case on July 8th the crowded courtroom expected another postponement. Instead, the Judge inquired whether the prosecution intended to press the other indictments against the defendant. Langdon replied that there were so many graft cases pending, trial of the additional charges against Schmitz could not be scheduled yet, and the prosecution would have no objection to imposition of sentence at once.

A thrill ran through the room, and in a suddenly penetrating voice Judge Dunne called: "Eugene E. Schmitz, stand up."

The Mayor's face turned chalk white. He arose and stood swaggering, hands in pockets.

"Eugene E. Schmitz," began the Judge, "you have heretofore occupied the highest office the city of San Francisco can confer on one of its citizens. You were elevated to that position because of the confidence and trust imposed in you by the mass of..."

Schmitz flushed and broke in angrily: "I am here to receive sentence at your hands,—not to be humiliated by a lecture which the newspapers can repeat in print! As an American citizen I demand my rights, which I am entitled to, and that is a sentence and not a lecture!"

Imperturbably Dunne resumed: "You were elevated to that position, I say, because of the confidence and trust reposed in you..."

Here Schmitz's attorney, Metson, sprang up, shouting: "We are here to take sentence, not to be lectured! We..."

At last Dunne's temper snapped, and he shouted back: "Mr. Metson, if you interrupt these proceedings again I will send you to jail! You would be in far better business if you were here begging for a day in court to answer the charges that you have willfully and improperly attempted to tamper with a juror in this case!"

Gasped Metson: "I take exception to the remarks of the court, addressed to the defendant, and to the improper and uncalled for insinuation of the court against myself!"

But Judge Dunne had regained self-control, and he turned back to Schmitz, ignoring the sputtering attorney. "You were elevated to that position because of the confidence and great trust reposed in you by the mass of people. You have, by your willful, criminal act— so a jury of your fellow citizens has declared—broken that confidence and betrayed that trust."

Again Schmitz protested the "lecture," while from the rear of the room came hisses.

"Therefore," Dunne continued, "it may be said that the penalty which the law permits in this case is insufficient to meet the demands of justice. It may be suggested, however, that by your conviction you will lose the respect and esteem of all good citizens and men; that you will suffer the humiliation of knowing that your career of hypocrisy, duplicity, and dishonor . . ."

"Have I any rights as an American citizen?" bellowed the enraged defendant, purple-faced and quivering with wrath, his eyes glaring, his voice at times so muffled by passion he could hardly articulate. "I'm not asking any leniency at the hands of this court! I am prepared to receive sentence! I ask that your honor do your duty and pronounce it, and I be not further subjected to humiliating and degrading remarks,—which the papers are copying and will repeat! I say, if your honor has any self-respect, you will proceed with the sentence!"

Judge Dunne went on with scathing forbearance: "It is not unusual for courts to be brought into contact with such brazen acts of effrontery as yours in the present moment. It is the duty of the court in such cases to view the conduct of a convicted felon with patience and toleration, not to say with pity. By your conviction you will lose the respect and esteem of all good men and citizens. You will suffer the humiliation of knowing, I say, that your career of hyprocrisy, duplicity, and dishonor has been exposed, and that you stand before those who believed in and honored you, morally naked, shamed, and disgraced."

"I deny that!" shrieked Schmitz. "The people of San Francisco know I was railroaded through!"

"Morally naked, shamed, and disgraced," came the implacable voice. "And it is in the knowledge of these things, rather than in any mere term of imprisonment in a state penitentiary, that the full measure of your punishment will be found. It is the judgment of this court that you be confined in the state prison at San Quentin for a term of five years."

It was the maximum sentence possible. Five times the Mayor and his counsel had interrupted the bench's excoriation, but at the close there was profound silence. Then the room rang with cheers. Men threw their hats into the air, waved their arms, stamped, yelled with joy. Schmitz turned pale again.

"If we had a sheriff worthy of the name, this exhibition would not happen," Judge Dunne remonstrated, but Sheriff O'Neill shrugged.

"We couldn't stop that, your honor," he said. Nevertheless, he did grab two men by the collar and propel them toward the door,— both of them Burns agents.

After court had adjourned, Schmitz dictated a statement for publication, reiterating that it had been impossible for him to get a fair trial from Judge Dunne.

"The animus nurtured in his heart for years came out this morning," was the bitter protest.

The return to Ingleside jail was in the city-owned "red devil" motorcar.

The sentencing of Schmitz ended the legal fiction that he was "temporarily unable to perform his duties." The prosecutors had been bombarded with more than a hundred proposals for designating a new mayor, but on none could a majority of the partisans unite, and in their extreme dilemma the prosecution again instructed the "good dogs" to elect a mayor. Supervisor Charles Boxton was dutifully chosen,—not acting mayor, but Mayor of San Francisco, to hold the fort pending a more acceptable solution.

Boxton surveyed his elevation with undisguised chagrin. "It is with a feeling of sadness that I take this office," he confessed. "I am sorry that they asked me. The only thing I can say is that I believe that during the short time I hold office, the people will have no cause to—" he groped for the right word "—to again find fault with me."

News of Boxton's promotion was received at first as a bad joke. Then a groan went up from the harassed, humiliated citizenry. The *Chronicle* published portraits of Schmitz, Gallagher, and the dentist side by side over the caption: "Three Boodlers Who Have Graced the Mayor's Chair Within One Month." And the *Examiner* gibed: "Having put our bribe-taking mayor in jail, and having put in his place a taker of smaller bribes, we have now substituted for Gallagher, Boxton, who differs from Gallagher principally in having sold his vote for less of the bribing corporations' money."

Mourned the New York *Times:* "The evil reputation of San Francisco is maintained."

And San Francisco's city treasurer refused to honor warrants for cash unless they bore the triple signatures of Boxton, Gallagher, and Schmitz.

4   A Poet to the Rescue

The day Boxton was elected Mayor, the District Attorney and he descended on Schmitz's rented office at Post and Franklin streets and personally carried out the cherrywood desk and ornate chair in which Eugene had functioned, uprooted from the front lawn the brass sign reading "Mayor's Office," piled the lot into a horse van, and carted it to new mayoral offices set up in a refurbished wing of the old City Hall. Then they discovered that the city seal was locked inside the desk, and they had omitted to pick up the keys.

Schmitz ruled this raid on municipal property "null and void," and vowed he would continue to pay his office rent out of his own pocket. Schmitz's secretary and usher, failing to report for duty to Boxton, were snipped off the civic payroll; Schmitz announced he would pay their salaries, too.

To settle the dispute over a suitable successor to Schmitz, pending the autumn election, Langdon called for an electoral convention representing every shade of public opinion; but this merely exacerbated the squabble.

"Boodler Boxton is still mayor, and the prosecution is in hysterics because its political schemes have gone all awry," taunted the *Examiner*.

Having begun by eschewing politics, the prosecutors found themselves being pushed into the political arena willy-nilly; and smarting under the nationwide derision that was being vented on the distraught city, they made their own selection,—a mildly distinguished elder citizen, widely and irreproachably known, Dr. Edward Robeson Taylor. As president of Cooper Medical College, Dr. Taylor was a prominent physician; as dean of Hastings law school, he was a legal authority; as an active poetaster, he was a leading light among the city's literati. He had served San Francisco in a number of quasi-official capacities, and since nobody knew anything in his disfavor, it was difficult to find grounds for opposing his nomination. The gentle scholar was sixty-eight years old; his roots reached back to San Francisco's beginnings.

His appearance was somewhat odd: he wore a tufted beard and his hair streamed out in a silvery halo, which fitted the nickname "Fluffy" given him by his students. His eyes twinkled humorously, he was never seen without a red carnation in his buttonhole, and his bearing was invincibly benign. The prosecution's intermediary had found him browsing in a bookshop, and there, after earnest deliberation, he had accepted the invitation to become mayor, deeming this service due to his greatly beloved and sorely beset city.

Dr. Taylor's selection was revealed at a meeting of the board of supervisors. When the clerk banged for order, Mayor Boxton being absent, Gallagher was elected temporary chairman. Big Jim took the chair and inquired what business was before the board.

"Well," said the clerk, "there's the ordinance to grade Buchanan Street."

"To hell with Buchanan Street," came a growl from the floor, and the clerk then read Boxton's signed resignation as mayor. This was accepted without debate and unanimously, terminating the unhappy dentist's interregnum on its seventh day. Nominations for mayor were declared open, and with an air of just having thought of it, Supervisor Mamlock sprang up and rattled off: "I take great pleasure to name Dr. Edward Robeson Taylor, a well-known citizen of our city."

The nomination was put to a vote and Dr. Taylor was declared elected.

The spontaneity of Mamlock's nominating speech being somewhat suspect, he was asked how he had hit upon his candidate.

"I dunno," responded Max. "I never heard of him before. The 'Big Stick' [Langdon] came around and told me to nominate Dr. Taylor. I said, 'Who the hell is Taylor?' And the 'Big Stick' says, 'Never you mind who Taylor is; all you got to do is nominate him.' So of course I done it."

The poetic Mayor's troubles started at once. Although generally his selection was approved, the *Examiner* launched upon a campaign of what might best be termed laudatory pejoration. On one page it saluted Dr. Taylor as upright, kindly, and lovable, and on another page it lampooned his literary avocation and made sport of his appearance,—both subjects ready-made for caricature. A typical cartoon depicted the Muse of Poetry kicking the Muse of Music,— Taylor being Poetry, and Schmitz, Music.

The *Examiner* described the new Mayor as "a mildly poetic gentleman who wears his hair in ruffles," and surmised that he was hesi-

tating in the choice of a new police chief between Black Bart, the
doggerel-perpetrating highwayman, and Joaquin Miller, flamboyant
self-styled Poet of the Sierras, who paraded through drawing rooms
in miner's boots and a red shirt, bragged about backwoods exploits
for the most part fictional, and doted on the adulation of silly women.
As for executive policy or a future crisis such as renewed street-car
violence, the *Examiner* guessed they would be met with tasteful
proclamations from City Hall in iambics patterned on:

> *Pine not, nor fret;*
> *The rain will fall,*
> *The sun will shine,*
> *The flowers will bloom....*

The quotation was from one of the Mayor's less felicitous frenzies.

Animated, it averred, by a desire to raise the cultural level of its
readers, the *Examiner* gave over the better part of a page to repro-
ducing Dr. Taylor's poems, and offered a $10 prize for the best
criticism. Every buffoon and wisecracker in town responded, and the
Examiner published their critiques,—all in the cause of disseminating
culture. The verdicts ranged from a forthright "Bum!"—and the
comment that the title of one effusion ("The Axe") expressed succinctly what the author deserved to get—to the giddiest praise
limping in meter and spavined in rhyme. One professed admirer included in his metrical tribute this practical foresight:

> *The poets do not graft;*
> *They poor and honest be.*
> *We both are of the craft,—*
> *So save a job for me.*

On the day Dr. Taylor was inducted, the *Examiner* headlined the
event: POET TAKES OFFICE AND QUOTES OMAR. It published a mock
interview, in which the reporter pompously sought the new executive's
views on civic issues, such as an adequate water supply, municipal
bonds, and so forth, and the Mayor replied in silly limericks. Minding
themselves, they said, that the Mayor had a rival prosodist on the
city payroll, Supervisor Pat McGushin, the *Examiner* jokesters hustled

around to the "drinking emporium" of that gusher of soggy verse and ordered a couplet as chaser to their beers. Pat kept his poetry on tap and ad lib spouted the following:

> *No matter what the boys confess,*
> *I'm still at Fulton and Van Ness.*

This was good, very good, his visitors conceded, but surely he could soar more loftily if he gave his Pegasus rein? They ordered another round of beers. After ruminating a moment, Pat fixed his eyes upon the ceiling and eructed this quatrain:

> *First a Ruef was o'er this town,*
> *And then a Heney tore it down.*
> *A Taylor now has come to patch*
> *The holes in San Francisco's thatch.*

The applause of the entire bar rewarded this, and the reporters ordered more beer. Not to seem niggardly, McGushin favored all within earshot, even those hard of hearing, with a rendition of a composition of which he was most proud, cooked up before the fire for a banquet honoring Ruef. It was entitled "California," and apostrophized the state:

> *Famed in peace and famed in strife!*
> *Thy sons are famous in all walks of life!*

("That's two lines, not one," the bartender interpolated, then resumed with basso-profundo sonority.)

> *Thy future poets can for ages sing*
> *Of modern giants famous in the ring!*
> *Famed politicians, too—here's the convincing proof—*
> *The Golden State produced Abe Ruef!*

Unable to smother their enthusiasm, Hearst's legmen hustled back to their office to enshrine these outpourings in printer's ink, and so they appeared, for comparison with Mayor Taylor's. A secondary feature pondered the pertinent question as to whether Schmitz was not really preferable to Taylor, because there were so many rhymes for Gene's patronymic ("snits," "nits," "nitwits" came to mind) and so few for the fuzzy-haired doctor's ("sailor," "jailer," and "squalor" were all the editors could rustle up, although they admitted that their poetic faculties were rusty).

The satire was cruel, but the good Doctor proved to be surprisingly resilient. He jogged along serenely, his first preoccupation being to assemble a board of supervisors to replace the "good dogs," who had outlived their usefulness in office.

From jail (where one newspaper said he was now occupying a suite of three rooms and bath, and printed a diagram of the lavish layout) Schmitz continued to shoot arrows of dissent, in particular refusing stubbornly to surrender the municipal automobile; the public giggled that Gene seemed to believe that whoever rode in the red "buzz wagon" really was mayor. At Schmitz's instance, Police Chief Dinan posted six policemen in the garage to prevent a duplication of Langdon's seizure of Schmitz's office furniture; Taylor laughed and contented himself with a rented conveyance. Meanwhile, the rhymers' itch spread by contagious versifying at City Hall continued to be scratched in public. Typically, "The Ballad of Sheriff O'Neil's Jail" lamented with the voice of the discomfited Eugene:

> *They've taken away my high-backed chair,*
> *They've taken the office from me,*
> *My plush-lined box where I kept my rocks,*
> *And also my fiddle-de-dee.*

> *I managed to hold a small sum in gold,*
> *And to skip with the office seal;*
> *But grief and dismay! They've taken away*
> *My pretty red automobile!*

Mayor Taylor with quiet persistence selected new supervisors and persuaded them to serve; his "roll of honor," he called it, comprising outstanding business and professional men; the representatives of labor had refused to co-operate in supplanting the crooked Union Labor Party regime.

Spreckels sighed with relief. "Now that Mayor Taylor has assumed office," he said, "it is about time this 'Big Stick' talk was dropped. I have not attempted to give him one word of advice concerning any municipal appointments or the conduct of his office, and I don't intend to."

Some of the "good dogs" rebelled at being driven out of the limelight, and Lonergan brashly announced he would seek a second term. This provoked another popular jingle, of which the pie-wagon driver was half proud:

> *I must admit, like all the rest,*
> *That I was handed mine;*
> *I told the jury all I know,*
> *But no, I won't resign.*

> *As long as I escape the jail,*
> *And dodge the grim elisor,*
> *I'll still be Tommy on the job,*
> *And die a supervisor!*

McGushin also was refractory and improvised unprintable stanzas objecting to his demotion.

On Monday, July 29th, Gallagher circulated word that all must attend a farewell caucus, but it took a posse of Burns men to round up the mavericks. The newspapers outdid themselves in contemptuous ridicule of this final appearance. By six o'clock that evening, it was written, all but four of the "good dogs" had been "kenneled in an anteroom,—the queerest alcoholic curio shop since the Keeley Cure became popular." "Gassy" Kelly, having "disguised his voice by swallowing a corkscrew," demanded that he be permitted to write his resignation personally, but he was dissuaded.

At 9:30 P.M., Mayor Taylor arrived with the incoming board, and the "good dogs" were herded to their seats. One by one, they then resigned. Over and over, Taylor's voice droned, "Mr. Clerk, have you another resignation?" And as each was accepted, the successor was sworn in and ushered to a seat beside the departing member. It was like a game of solemn musical chairs, with Gallagher, "good dog" to the last, acting as master of ceremonies,—calling "go" and "stop," offering the appropriate motions, requesting Sergeant-at-arms Burke to escort each new supervisor to his place. The formalities dragged along until nearly midnight.

Toward the close, the Sergeant-at-arms passed rapidly along the aisle and dropped on each new member's desk an envelope. Matt I. Sullivan, one of the city's leading attorneys, opened his, and inside found two $20 tickets to a prize fight. Sullivan addressed the chair: "I observe that about $600 worth of graft in the shape of prize-fight tickets has been distributed to the members of the board. May I ask if your honor has received his share?"

Mayor Taylor nodded and laughed. "I received mine ahead of time, and they are already on the way back."

Sullivan moved that the Sergeant-at-arms be instructed to return the tickets "to the donors—not to his friends," and sheepishly Burke retrieved his error. Old tricks are hard to unlearn, the public chortled sourly when they read accounts of the degrading valedictory under headlines like GOOD DOGS YELP FOR LAST TIME. One inland journal frankly congratulated the metropolis on having "shaken itself free of fleas."

Schmitz, of course, "nullified" Taylor's appointments and named his own board,—some of whom accused him of trying to ruin them politically. But Eugene continued to contest the issue until August 19th, when the State Supreme Court ruled that Taylor was legally Mayor of San Francisco. The decision came through just as Schmitz was entering Temple Sherith Israel for a court appearance; he held a whispered sidewalk consultation with Chief Dinan; then, taking a slip of paper from his pocket, he rested it against the wall of the building and wrote out his last "official" order,—instructing Jere to surrender the red municipal automobile. Soon thereafter, Dinan resigned as chief of police, and William J. Biggy, the elisor, was named to succeed him.

The city was jubilant: the crooked Mayor had been removed, his crooked police chief was out, the boodling supervisors had been replaced, the boss's power had been broken, the publicly condemned givers of corporation bribes had been indicted, and honest men were installed in office. The graft prosecutors had piled up a record of successes. Their real fight lay ahead.

5 "As in a Glass Darkly . . ."

Twenty-four hours after the change-over in city government, the trial of the first of the asserted bribe-givers, Louis Glass, ended. Glass was executive vice-president of the former Pacific States Telephone Company (previous to his indictment, this company had merged with the Pacific Telephone & Telegraph Company), and his was one graft case in which Abe Ruef was not directly implicated. Eleven supervisors had confessed that Theodore V. Halsey, Glass's brother-in-law and lobbyist for the Pacific States company, bribed them to vote against the Home Telephone Company franchise, and evidence given to the grand jury by the company's officials indicated that Glass had drawn the bribe money from the company treasury and authorized Halsey to pay it. Glass's trial was held before Judge Lawlor, a jurist learned in the law, vigorous, and respected.

A key witness before the grand jury in April, 1906, when supervisors were tumbling over each other in haste to confess, had been Emil J. Zimmer, Pacific States auditor and confidential secretary to the president. Zimmer had testified that at the time of the asserted bribery, Glass alone possessed authority to approve expenditures by Halsey, and that just before the bribe payments, he (Zimmer) had drawn checks for large amounts at Glass's order, cashed them, and handed the money to Halsey; Zimmer did not know to what use the money was put. He also had cashed vouchers for Halsey marked "special expenses, as per detail on file," although the only file appeared to have been Glass's memory; on the company books these outlays were charged to "Reserve for contingent liabilities," and after making the rounds of multiple double-entry, wound up under the heading "Legal." Zimmer estimated that Glass might have withdrawn as much as $70,000 of company funds without making any accounting during February, 1906, the month in which the bribes were passed; eleven supervisors had testified to having received some $50,000

at that time. Zimmer's grand jury testimony had been given only after
Heney reassured him that in carrying out the orders of his superior
he could not be judged guilty of any criminal act, and on Zimmer
Heney had relied to establish that Glass, and nobody but Glass, could
be held accountable for the withdrawal of company funds for any
purpose not plainly shown in the books.

Glass and Zimmer both were career men in the company, Glass
having started as a telegraph operator and Zimmer as an office boy.
Glass was reputed to be an able executive and the company stood by
him loyally, engaging high-powered counsel, headed by the most-
publicized criminal lawyer in the United States at that moment, the
astute Delphin M. Delmas, who had just scored a dubious victory in
New York City by securing a hung jury in the Thaw murder trial.
Delmas, who was conscious of his striking resemblance to Napoleon
Bonaparte, wore a silk hat and morning cutaway, or a straw boater
and white flannels, to court, and was a master of legal argument.

In the public mind there was no doubt of Glass's guilt, so much
of the grand jury testimony had been published.

The trial opened with the now familiar assault on the validity of
the grand jury, the supposed insufficiency of the indictments, and the
qualifications of Judge Lawlor to try the case. Weeks were consumed
in tedious in-fighting, to the disgust of the public, the *Call* expressing
popular feeling exactly when it commented:

... Anything to delay trial and judgment is the policy of the accused
bribe-givers. Every day's proceedings in the trial of Glass provides ample
proof to the most skeptical citizen that the last thing desired by the men
charged with debauching the boodle board of supervisors is prompt determination of the issues on their merits, and every pettifogging move for
delay, every cunning attempt to betray the court into technical error is
confession of a case too weak to be given to a fair jury on a plain showing
of the facts.

One visitor to the city marveled at the spectacle of "so many
innocent men moving heaven and earth to prove that they are innocent."

The Glass case preliminaries were spun out coincidentally with
the trial of Schmitz before Judge Dunne, and it was not until the
Mayor's sentencing that selection of the Glass jury got under way.

Contrary to expectations, jurors were passed quickly, and on July 9th (the day Supervisor Boxton became Mayor) the panel was completed. Glass was being tried on the specific charge of bribing Boxton, and the new Mayor's first day in office was spent on the witness stand telling how he sold out the city for $5,000. It was a distressing and unedifying spectacle. During the months ahead, San Franciscans were to hear stories of bribery from supervisor after supervisor, but Boxton's courtroom confession was the first, and it was sensational.

The new Mayor felt his humiliation. At first he pleaded that municipal affairs would leave him no time to appear in court; but Judge Lawlor ruled he must testify, and before an audience thronging the auditorium of Temple Sherith Israel he took the stand. Twice during the day he was excused to return to City Hall and preside at caucuses, and thereafter for two days he shuttled between his office and the courtroom, where neither Heney nor Delmas showed him the least mercy.

In an irritated, bored tone he recounted taking $5,000 from Halsey in the bare room in the Mills Building. Heney drew out that he had also been on the Pacific States payroll at $100 a month to spy on his fellow supervisors.

"I kept Mr. Halsey informed as to how they would vote," the Mayor admitted with a blush. "I didn't ask them, but I found out all right."

That "purity affidavit," he protested, he had signed at Schmitz's insistence. "It was expected. That was what the administration expected of us." Self-assured and quick-witted at the start, when Heney pilloried him as a perjurer devoid of honor public or private, and he had winced repeatedly under the satire of Delmas' urbane cross-examination, he was in tears. Delmas addressed him with punctilious courtesy, employing his full honorific, "The honorable, the Mayor of San Francisco," or simply "Mr. Mayor"; and in this capacity Boxton was compelled to relate how his election had come about.

He began with the unavailing disclaimer: "It was through no fault of mine!"

"Order! Stop laughing in court!" bailiffs barked, while Boxton hung his head and sighed.

"That office was thrust upon you?" Delmas purred.

"I don't know that it was thrust upon me, but I certainly didn't want it. Somebody had to take it."

He had been called into a committee room, he said, where Gallagher and Langdon were talking, and "Mr. Gallagher said it was necessary immediately to select a mayor from among the members of the board of supervisors, and he asked me if I would accept the honor. This was the first I knew of it. I agreed, and a few minutes later, at a meeting of the board, I was elected. Then Mr. Langdon took me to the auditor's office, where he took a $25,000 mayor's bond from his pocket and the auditor approved it. Then Mr. Langdon and I and a newspaperman had lunch together—a very humble lunch —and afterward the District Attorney took me to the county clerk and I was sworn in. Then I came here, where I was to be witness against Mr. Glass on the bribery charge."

"Order! Stop laughing in court!" shouted the bailiffs, and Boxton, excused for the nonce, staggered to a front pew and crumpled in an agony of shame.

The next day he sobbed and dabbed at his eyes while telling about accepting the boodle from Halsey,—and later counting it carefully. Asked by Heney to whom he gave the $5,000, he begged to be spared. Heney thereupon called Mrs. Boxton, who testified without visible embarrassment that her husband had handed her the envelope containing $5,000 in currency.

Other supervisors followed with similar testimony—Lonergan, Wilson, Coffey, Nicholas, Mamlock, Furey, Phillips, Walsh, and Coleman—all telling of their trips to the Mills Building and pocketing Halsey's money at the very time they were preparing to betray him by voting for the Home franchise.

Nicholas, who had joined the penitential procession at the price of having the furniture kickback case against him set aside, told the jury that on the day Halsey gave him $5,000, he had hunted up Ruef, and the boss said: "Halsey's a damn fool. Keep the money." Then Ruef instructed him to vote for the Home franchise.

Lonergan grew garrulous in recalling his dealings with Halsey and John Kraus, Halsey's assistant,—the sauterne luncheon and other convivial interludes. And Coffey's conscience was a striking exhibit: without the slightest uneasiness, the hack driver said he took pay from both sides in the telephone affair, and justified his duplicity by the naïve reservation: "I made no promise to vote one way or the other when I accepted the money."

Glass listened to this testimony with an air of dignified weariness, most of the time sitting in bored silence; now and then he leaned his head on the back of the pew in front in an attitude of prayer, but actually he was reading a book, which he carefully kept out of sight of the Judge and jury. Many fashionably dressed, socially prominent women were present day after day, following the proceedings avidly, thrilled by the daring slanginess of Heney and the deadly suavity of Delmas.

The prosecution's task was to link Glass with the bribes passed by Halsey. A complication confusing the picture of events was the fact that the president of Pacific States, John I. Sabin (brother-in-law of Glass and Halsey), had died in October, 1905, and Henry T. Scott had been elected to succeed him in February, 1906, the month of the briberies. But Scott had not assumed his duties immediately, although he bore the title and nominal responsibility; for several weeks in the interim, Glass had acted as president.

After the supervisors had testified, Heney called Zimmer, and to the prosecutor's amazement the sleek, discreet auditor, who looked like a high-class butler, refused absolutely to testify. Judge Lawlor ordered him to take the stand; still he refused, not because of possible self-incrimination, he explained, but because he had come to feel that the testimony he had given before the grand jury—on which, in large part, Glass had been indicted—was "insufficient," and conscience would not permit him to repeat it. The court admonished him on his rights and duties, but he refused to answer any questions.

Heney was quivering with anger; he charged that the defense had got to the witness and persuaded him to keep silent. Delmas denied ever having seen the man before, and as Heney's manner grew more excited and his arms flailed, the defense spokesman icily drew the court's attention to the spectacle of a prosecutor "with face flushed with blood and the veins of his temples swollen with malice and revenge, and with a voice vibrating with passion,—a human bloodhound."

"I am indignant, it is true," Heney roared, "but at the way my city has been crucified!"

"A human bloodhound," Delmas repeated, without raising his

voice, "ready to sell his services for blood money wherever they may be required." And he deplored "a certain fiendish and insatiable desire to inflict pain upon others, which seems to characterize the learned gentleman from Arizona."

Judge Lawlor instructed Zimmer once more to testify, and when the latter point-blank refused, sent him to jail for five days for contempt. Zimmer left the courtroom with the air of a man whose mind was made up.

At the expiration of five days, he was brought into court again and ordered to testify. He repeated his refusal, and Lawlor fined him $500 and sent him back to jail for another twenty-four hours. The fine was paid, the new sentence served, and a third time Zimmer defied the court; whereupon Lawlor returned him to jail for another five days.

Compelled to proceed without him, Heney produced his remaining evidence and on July 24th rested.

"That is our case," he said.

In mellow tones Delmas responded, "And it is ours," and offered to submit the case to the jury without a closing argument.

Objected Heney, "Mr. Delmas rather ostentatiously yesterday said the defense would introduce some witnesses!"

"What covert insult is intended by the learned counsel I do not know," mellifluously responded the Napoleon of the bar, "and from its source, I do not care. When I said there would be witnesses, I assumed there would be a case to meet. There being no case, there is no necessity for introducing witnesses."

Thus Louis Glass was not to deny under oath his complicity in the bribing of San Francisco's "boodle board"; his refuge was silence.

Into Heney's jury speech flowed all the fire of his devotion to the cause of purging San Francisco.

"We are not able to carry out our promise that we would prove by Zimmer that Glass instructed Zimmer to draw the checks and take them to the banks and secure currency and hand it to Halsey," he admitted. "But there is only one inference to be drawn from Zimmer's refusal to testify, and that is because his testimony would tend to incriminate Louis Glass. Who had a motive in getting Zimmer not to testify? Nobody but Louis Glass.

"There has been some talk about human bloodhounds. There will be some talk, possibly, about extortion. Was the company held up? Held up from the right to give you the poorest service possible? Yes, I guess they were held up from that. The moment the Home Telephone Company endeavored to get in here, these people—these respectable broadcloth wearers, these highest members of society—deliberately went into the field and commenced to debauch your supervisors, undermine your government, corrupt your officials so that this city will have disgrace upon it for all time as the worst-governed city in the United States! At whose door should you lay that? Not at the door of the poor devils who accepted their filthy money, but at the door of those men who went out and invited these poor fellows to lunch,—with a little sauterne after.

"Louis Glass, the unconfessed, made Boxton a criminal, made Nicholas a criminal. He is the man who made the bakery-wagon driver, Lonergan, a criminal, the man who made every one of these supervisors a criminal, who paid them and created an appetite for more money, and thus led them on and on until they sell your city and mine to the public-service corporations, who took from your city, when it was in ashes, rights worth thousands of dollars. Oh, if it were not that I love my country, these conditions would fill me with disgust and I would vomit in reply! Why, at the height of our tribulation, debauch us before the civilized world by making criminals of our poor and weak officials?

"Who signed those checks?" he pounded home his pivotal contention. "Glass did. You may go round and round, like a dog chasing its tail, and each time you come back, back to Louis Glass!"

In reply, Delmas eschewed dramatics and developed a subtle argument which was designed to raise the wisp of a shadow of uncertainty in the jurors' minds. Glass, Delmas reminded the jury, must be proved guilty beyond all possible doubt. The prosecution had maintained that Glass had authorized the bribe payments, and had signed the checks for the cash,—but had the prosecution, Delmas asked, proved beyond a possibility of doubt that Glass was the *only* person who could have done this? Then, in a conversational tone, he followed a trail of elimination that parodied the prosecution's logic. Scott had been elected president of Pacific States by the time the payments were made, and certainly he possessed authority to draw checks.

"Mind you, gentlemen," the caressing voice lulled the jurymen,

"I do not want you to understand that I am charging Mr. Scott with crime. That is no part of my business. I am assuming, on the theory of this prosecution, that a crime was committed, and I say that you yourselves, Mr. District Attorney and your attendants, have undertaken by a process of elimination to show us that Mr. Scott could not have committed this crime. It is sufficient for us to show you that he could, without charging that he did."

Another possibility which Delmas opened up was that the money might have been supplied by either one of two Bell Telephone system officials who were in San Francisco during the month of February, 1906, although again care was taken to impute crime to neither of these startled and not at all pleased gentlemen. For several hours Delmas spun his gossamer threads,—not disputing that the supervisors were bribed, but contending that some person other than Glass conceivably might have authorized the bribery.

In rebuttal, Heney repeated stubbornly, "Zimmer and Glass between them did it." Alluding to the ripples of admiration which had greeted his celebrated opponent, known as the "fashionplate of the bar," the one-time cowhand reminded the jurors that "it doesn't make any difference about my dress, my gestures, and my style."

The jury left the Temple in the four-horse tallyho which had been provided for their transportation, and drove back to their quarters in the Fairmont Hotel to weigh their verdict. Sixteen ballots were taken, and after forty-seven hours of deliberation, on Sunday, July 28th (the day before the "good dogs" were sent "yelping to the city pound"), they reported to Judge Lawlor that they were deadlocked at seven for conviction to five for acquittal. The Judge dismissed the panel and declared a mistrial.

A newspaper poll of the jurors disclosed that Delmas' ingenious argument had been the determining factor, having raised the ghost of a doubt in five jurors' minds; all twelve men believed that bribery had been proved, but five felt it had not been fastened ineluctably on Louis Glass.

After a lapse of two weeks, the undaunted prosecutors placed Glass on trial again, this time for bribing Lonergan. Again Zimmer refused to testify, but now on the grounds of possible self-incrimination. However, through other witnesses, Heney succeeded in establishing that only Glass possessed the power to sign company checks at the time the bribe was passed. The new company president, Scott, himself testified that he had not assumed office and was absent in the East during much of the period in question; the Pacific States' treasurer testified that notifications to the banks that Scott's signature was to be honored did not go out until a date later than that on which Lonergan accepted his bribe; and the minute books of the company showed that during the critical weeks, only Glass, or Zimmer for him as his confidential secretary, could sign checks.

For his summing up, Heney produced, over the vigorous objections of the defense, a huge chart on which was traced the course of six company checks, cashed at different banks within the period, which totaled $50,000,—and alongside this, the list of eleven supervisors and the amounts they swore they had received, which also totaled $50,000. With the help of this visual evidence, the lack of Zimmer's testimony was overcome.

Delmas attempted to repeat his *tour de force,* but, like a soufflé, it would not bear reheating; and after twenty-five minutes of deliberation the jury voted Louis Glass guilty.

In this trial, Heney's closing argument was conceded on all sides to have been superlatively brilliant. Two thousand spectators jammed the Temple auditorium to hear him, even the organ loft being filled, while a thousand more clamored outside, climbing up to the door lintels and pulling the windows open in order to see and hear. One woman perched on a stack of chairs in the corridor and watched through a transom. The justice of the verdict was applauded by most of the public (although not by the well-heeled and socially foremost) and by nearly the entire press of the state.

Five days after Glass's conviction, Judge Lawlor sentenced the immaculately dressed defendant to five years in prison. Glass heard the sentence as in a daze, and as he was led away he was heard to murmur: "I am entirely guiltless. I have no other reply."

That was on September 4, 1907.

At Ingleside county jail Glass joined ex-Mayor Schmitz, and was similarly lodged in a comfortable, twelve-by-sixteen-foot warder's room, with a view of the vegetable garden, special food, and more or less the run of the place. Both distinguished inmates were irked by their accommodations, however; Schmitz especially complaining that his bed was too short for a man of his stature,—his feet hung out.

6   Marches and Countermarches

Louis Glass, jail inmate, was dropped by none of his clubs. He continued to be listed as first vice-president of the Pacific Telephone & Telegraph Co. on leave of absence. Zimmer was tried on a misdemeanor charge for his refusal to testify, was convicted, and sentenced to six months in jail. He appealed, and after a long delay, while he was traveling in Europe, the conviction was set aside. He retained his position as second vice-president of the P.T.&.T. until 1912. But John Kraus, Halsey's assistant host at sauterne luncheons and similar jollifications with supervisors, in November, 1908, while aboard the liner *Adriatic* between Cherbourg and Queenstown, cut his throat in terror of arrest and imprisonment upon return home.

Halsey had been placed on trial before Judge Dunne, while his superior, Glass, was before Judge Lawlor. The usual delaying tactics were invoked, road blocks were thrown in the way of choosing a jury, and clashes between opposing counsel became so vitriolic they once degenerated into a free-for-all that left the defendant kicking on his back on the floor. Hiram Johnson had got in the first blow and was fined $20 by the court for provoking the scrimmage. The jury was still incomplete when Halsey was stricken by appendicitis, underwent an operation, and entered a period of convalescence that stretched into weeks, then months, then years, during which medical affidavits repeatedly assured Judge Dunne that the defendant was physically incapable of standing trial. Dunne did not doubt that Halsey was ailing, but believed the cause of his incapacity was his predicament.

Victory in the Glass trial elated the prosecution; it proved, they asserted, that in spite of dark forebodings, the city's rich men were not exempt from the law.

"Now they will all fall!" crowed Langdon.

"This is a vindication of the jury system," glowed William J. Burns.

Heney, who had borne the brunt of the fight and was pleased by his difficult triumph, did not gloat over netting the first "higher-up." His duty as prosecutor he understood and would fulfill, but he did not relish the pursuit of men whom he had known as friends and some of whom he admired. This feeling he had made clear in a conversation with Rabbi Nieto months before:

"Don't imagine this is a pleasant task to me," he had said. "It is far from being so. It involves men like Frank Drum, whom I liked and respected as a friend for years, and who has quite recently paid me a good attorney's fee for services performed for a company represented by him. I have met Patrick Calhoun socially, and greatly admire his ability. I wish there were some other way to secure a proper deterrent effect without causing these men and their innocent families to suffer; but unless the laws are enforced, Doctor, our republican form of government cannot continue very long. It is not sufficient to punish the poor man, who has no friends or influence. The people will lose respect for the courts and the law unless the rich and powerful can be made to obey the laws."

Heney's task was aggravated by fresh obstacles that sprang up to impede every forward step taken by the prosecution. There was, for example, a sharp falling off of support by the press. Of San Francisco's four major newspapers, the *Bulletin* continued to serve as the accepted mouthpiece of the prosecution, and the *Call* remained loyal in spite of the personal coolness between its proprietor, John D. Spreckels, and his brother, Rudolph; John D. went out of his way to emphasize that the *Call's* support was for the cause of clean government, and was given irrespective of family connections. The *Examiner* was openly obstructive, continually subjecting the prosecutors to scorn and belittlement; where it could not condemn, it remained silent. But the trickiest shift in attitude was executed by the *Chronicle,* where the tenor of its editorial comment differed from its news reports. For example, its editorial-page observations on the conviction of Louis Glass could not have been more gratifying to the prosecution or expressive of the feeling of the great majority of its readers:

The moral evidence in the possession of the country leaves no doubt of the justice of the verdict convicting Glass, and in spite of the willingness of Zimmer to go to jail to save his superior, the chain of legal evidence was in the end successfully connected.... There is no possible ground of sympathy for Glass...It was a dirty mess, and the public will rejoice when all the guilty men are where Glass and Schmitz are now.

But counteracting this ostentatious approval, the accounts of day-to-day developments in the graft investigation, as reported by the *Chronicle,* tended subtly to undermine public confidence in both the motives and the ability of the prosecutors. Heney, especially, was caricatured, his mannerisms and occasional bellows of indignation being exaggerated so as to convey by indirection an impression of an uncouth booby and braggart, a relic of the range, a bombastic and hypocritical shyster. This left-handed denigration the *Bulletin* called the "stiletto attack," and it became increasingly irritating as well as being detrimental to the cause of municipal fumigation.

A more direct difficulty with which Heney had to cope was Abe Ruef. In spite of the boss's testimony against Schmitz, Heney felt certain that Ruef was playing neither squarely nor fairly. Ruef refused to implicate Calhoun or any of the United Railroads officers in a way that could be construed as bribery under the statute; he stuck to his assertion that he had been paid an attorney's fee, that was all. In the other cases, he was just as slippery and forgetful of essential details. Burns worked on him constantly, and in his appearances in Judge Lawlor's or Judge Dunne's court (where the formalities attendant on the multitude of graft indictments frequently required his presence), the boss often looked old and careworn. The tedious sessions he wiled away by reading newspapers or chatting flippantly. Every two weeks his sentencing in the French restaurants case was set over with reciprocal courtesy.

"You don't mind, do you?" Judge Dunne would inquire, and the boss would respond agreeably, "Certainly not."

When Abe's "Green Lizard" motorcar, familiar to the whole city, was sold, Ruef got fun out of pretending that he had disposed of it to a theatrical troupe appearing in George Broadhurst's drama about municipal graft, *The Man of the Hour.*

"Yes," Abe would joke, "I've loaned it to *The Man of the Hour,* where it will appear on the stage in familiar surroundings. When its stage days are over, it will be sent to the Smithsonian museum in Washington as one of the greatest reptiles living,—outside of certain other parties."

But it did seem to him that bringing a play about graft to San Francisco was superfluous.

Time after time Heney lost patience with Ruef's wriggling, and threatened to tear up the immunity contract. Abe's "immaculate gall" infuriated him. "I don't know his equal in this respect," Heney growled, "unless it be his leading counsel, Henry Ach!"

In court, Heney was forced to resist weeks-long attempts by the defendants in the trolley, gas, and telephone cases to have their indictments set aside on technical objections, some of them so trivial as to incur the court's rebuke. For the indicted United Railroads quartet, attorney A.A. Moore advanced the contentions (among a host of others equally substantive) that Calhoun, Ford, Mullally, and Abbott had been (1) improperly summoned before the grand jury, and (2) were not allowed to testify when they got before the grand jury, and (3) that calling them there was "hounding" and "doing everything possible to prejudice them before the grand jury."

To this nonsense, gravely argued with enormous verbosity by defense counsel, Heney listened, growing redder and redder in the face. At last, in a burst of unsuppressible wrath, he cried out:

"After the supervisors confessed and sixteen of them testified that they had been paid $4,000 apiece to vote for the trolley franchise, these defendants thought in their own minds that they were so connected with the crime that Patrick Calhoun, Thornwell Mullally, and Tirey L. Ford each made a public explanation in the press, denying that they had bribed a public official! A crime had been committed, and the first question to be asked was: who had a motive? The supervisors testified that they received the money from Gallagher, and Gallagher testified that he received it from Ruef. Did Abraham Ruef own the trolley lines? The question arose as to who had the motive. Ford and Mullally came to me personally and told me they had not bribed a city official. Wasn't that an explanation? If, under the circumstances, the grand jury had *not* called them, then you would have heard the cry that this was a conspiracy to destroy the good name of Patrick Calhoun!

"If it had been a poor, ignorant man—or a helpless woman," he went on, his voice rising in shrill passion; "if the grand jury had dragged her from the jail and compelled her to testify against herself, and she had not known what her constitutional rights were, it would have been a different picture. But these four gentlemen are learned in the law. One of them [Ford] has been attorney general of this state, another [Abbott] was his assistant in that office for four years. Mullally is an attorney, and Patrick Calhoun is an attorney whose mind is equal to that of any man's in California. Advised of their rights? Why, they came in there on a subpoena which Ford has declared in his own affidavit was faulty and ineffective. They came in on a defective process, which they knew to be defective, and they refused to be sworn and they were not sworn, and they left the grand jury room without having answered a question, for the purpose of coming solemnly here to get these indictments set aside on the grounds that their constitutional rights had been invaded! They knew they didn't have to go; but they went, and they refused to testify; and now they want the indictment set aside because their great constitutional rights have been tampered with!"

Murmured A.A. Moore: "Jesus stood by with His mouth shut, and they made a case against Him."

Then with lofty eloquence he claimed a rich man's right to equal consideration with a poor man before the law, saying: "A constitutional right is a broad mantle which covers all human people, whether they are poor women or corporation officials learned in the law."

Ex-Mayor Schmitz, who was present in court as a co-defendant, listened appreciatively to Moore's hairsplitting. He believed it. And so the wrangle continued, weary week after weary week, until, on September 7th (three days after he had sentenced Louis Glass), Judge Lawlor swept aside the mass of demurrers filed by the battery of defense lawyers, and all the defendants in the gas rate and trolley cases—Calhoun, Ford, Abbott, Mullally of the United Railroads, and Drum, De Sabla, and Martin of the gas company—pleaded not guilty and demanded separate trials.

Ford's trial began at once.

7 Ford on Trial—And a Kidnaping

Chief counsel for the eminent and widely admired Tirey L. Ford was Earl Rogers, an expert at baiting a witness or goading an opposing counsel. Assisting Rogers were Ford's brother-in-law, Lewis F. Byington, the former District Attorney; R. Porter Ashe, a highly connected attorney and social figure whose specialty was jury investigation; Alexander King, a Georgia attorney, long a close friend of Patrick Calhoun; William Abbott; and Stanley and A.A. Moore. This array of talent was opposed by Frank Heney and such assistance as could be spared from the District Attorney's staff.

Public interest was intense, and crowds fought for places of vantage in the courtroom. The upper circles of San Francisco society were plentifully represented.

The prosecution faced the necessity of proving that Ford gave Ruef $200,000 for the purpose of bribing the supervisors to grant the overhead trolley permit. It would not be sufficient to show that the supervisors received money from Gallagher, who received it from Ruef, who got it from Ford; to prove bribery against Ford, it would have to be shown that Ford and Ruef understood between them at the time of the payment that it was to be used to corrupt the board. Only Ruef's or Ford's testimony could establish this positively; therefore, it was foreseen that the curly-haired boss's testimony would provide the sensational climax.

The jury was formed with comparative celerity, and was packed off in the court's tallyho to the Fairmont Hotel, resigned to a long sojourn in strict confinement there.

Ford was on trial for bribing Supervisor Lonergan. In his opening statement, Heney said that he did not expect to prove that Ford bribed Lonergan personally, but that the offer of a bribe was made to Lonergan by Supervisor Wilson, who was authorized by Gallagher; and that through Gallagher, a bribe had been offered to each supervisor by Ruef, who was authorized by Ford. The transfer of monies through the Mint, in the weeks immediately after the earthquake and fire, the prosecution promised to trace in great detail, and Heney briefly sketched the sequence.

On May 29, 1906 (just after the trolley ordinance was voted by

the supervisors), the United Railroads had on deposit at the Mint
$175,000 to the credit of Thornwell Mullally. This money had all
been withdrawn either by Mullally or by the United Railroads
treasurer, George E. Starr, in coin, entered in the company records,
routed to the proper company officials, and disbursed for legitimate
business purposes. The only other United Railroads money passing
through the Mint had been one deposit of $200,000, transferred from
the East to the credit of Patrick Calhoun on May 22nd (the day
after the trolley ordinance was passed); this had been withdrawn by
Ford, not in coin but in currency, in three installments, on May 24th,
July 31st, and August 23rd. Not one dollar of this $200,000 appeared
in any available record of the corporation, not one entry indicated that
this $200,000 had been deposited or withdrawn, and none of the
company's directors knew about this $200,000, except the three
directors who were indicted,—Ford, Calhoun, and Mullally. Abbott,
although not a corporation director at the time, had participated in
the transaction.

The first witness was Tom Lonergan, whom the newspapers
pictured as a cheerful sort of liar. Under Heney's quizzing, Tom
listed the bribes he had taken while in office, and told where the
money went: he had lent two friends $200 each, gave another friend
$300, and several hundred dollars had gone up in smoke in the great
fire. He gave his testimony in an even tone, and now and then con-
vulsed the spectators with droll admissions.

Rogers attacked the witness for having signed the famous "purity
affidavit," in which he disclaimed ever having committed a felony
or knowing any supervisor who had. Tom said he had signed that because George Keane told him to.

" 'Tom, there's a paper across the street for you to go over and
sign; all the boys are signing it,' " he quoted Keane as saying. He
added defensively, "I didn't read it."

"So you swear to things without being careful of their contents?"

"In this matter I did," the witness nodded.

Lonergan said that Gallagher had slipped the envelope containing
the first $2,000 payment into his wallet when he wasn't looking, and

about a week later, after he had heard that other supervisors were "getting their pinch," he accused Gallagher of holding out.

" 'Cut that out. That won't work,' " he said Gallagher answered. " 'I gave you that money.' I said, 'If you did, it's in my pocketbook now.' I felt in my pocketbook, and there in an envelope was $2,000 in currency!"

"Stop laughing in court!" bawled the bailiffs.

Lonergan got the second installment at Mowry Hall; Gallagher took him upstairs and handed him an envelope. When he got home he found only $1,500 inside, and he went right out to Gallagher's house and reproached him for trying to short-change a pal. Gallagher examined the envelope, guessed he had made a mistake, and forked over $500 more.

Heney interrupted the questioning to call the court's attention to a situation that had been worrying the prosecution: the presence in the courtroom of underworld characters, whom the *Call* had spotted and described as "the retinue of the trolley magnates... a motley train of gunfighters, professional plug-uglies, decoys, disreputable 'detectives,' thugs, women of the half-world, and the wolfish pack of gutter journalism."

Said Heney: "I have noticed about half a dozen of the most desperate characters in California, including Dave Nagle [who had killed a judge in a celebrated case] and Bogie O'Donnell and the 'Banjo-Eyed Kid' and three men who have reputations for killing prisoners at Folsom penitentiary, sitting in this courtroom, in close proximity to the jury. They were here the first morning of the trial and they have been here ever since, and they are supposed to be in the employ of the United Railroads."

A.A. Moore was indignant. "I take exception to the remark that we ever had in our employ any ruffians or persons of improper reputation," he protested.

"Including Luther Brown, whom I have seen sitting around here," Heney rejoined grimly.

Luther Brown, undercover agent and minor Los Angeles politician of some notoriety, had appeared in San Francisco at the same time as Earl Rogers and had assumed command of the United Railroads detective force, rapidly augmenting it to what the *Examiner* sarcastically termed "the proportions of a small army." Luther Brown was as full of guile and resourcefulness as his opposite number, William J. Burns.

The Judge ordered the pews immediately behind the defendant to be cleared and kept cleared.

Then Rogers sprang a surprise intended to destroy Lonergan's credibility irretrievably. Holding up a bundle of typewritten papers, he asked the witness whether he had signed them. Tom said yes, he had. The papers comprised an interview compiled by a man representing himself as a writer for an Eastern magazine which wanted to "set the supervisors right" with its readers. The supposed writer, it turned out, was Walter E. Dorland, a United Railroads detective, and in the interview Lonergan was quoted as saying he had voted the trolley franchise "for the good of the community," and nobody had offered him money for his vote.

"Oh, I wasn't under oath then," Tom tried to pass off the matter, but Rogers drove home: "You intended to make that declaration to all the readers of that magazine, didn't you?"

"I wasn't under oath," Lonergan repeated weakly.

Then Heney, in turn, brought out a more sensational matter,— an attempt to kidnap or compromise Lonergan on the eve of his testimony. Heney gave the details: Dorland was working for Rogers and Luther Brown, and for weeks had been making himself agreeable to Lonergan and his wife, taking them to expensive restaurants and on automobile rides, while pretending to gather material for the non-existent magazine. Thinking "there was no harm in it," Tom had scrawled his name to the purported interview.

Burns, meanwhile, had found out about Dorland, that he was on the payroll of the United Railroads; and the day before, he had warned Lonergan to telephone at once should Dorland show up again. That evening Dorland called and told Tom he was coming around in a car with "a couple of nice girls" to "make a night of it," and not to bring Mrs. Lonergan along this time. Lonergan telephoned Burns, who instructed him to stall for fifteen minutes, then go out and meet Dorland but to take his wife with him, and under no circumstances to get into Dorland's car; Burns had received a tip that something more than a gay evening was planned. He hurried to the scene, and from a distance saw Lonergan and his wife come out of their house and walk over to the automobile where Dorland was waiting with two women. Lonergan at the trial drew a laugh with his mimicry of Dorland's "dismay" when he saw Mrs. Lonergan, and said the under-cover agent mumbled some excuse and drove away. Burns saw a second machine follow Dorland's a little way; in this car were Luther Brown and the "Banjo-Eyed Kid." Burns trailed Dorland and saw him pick up another United Railroads detective, J.C. Brown, and drive to a disreputable resort, where J.C. Brown and one of the women stayed the night.

The plot, Heney told the court, had been for Luther Brown to meet Dorland and Lonergan at a roadhouse, where Tom would have been turned over to the "Banjo-Eyed Kid" for whatever disposition might be deemed expedient; or, failing this, to have one of the women, who had been brought from Los Angeles for the purpose, accuse Lonergan of raping her.

Heney's bombshell threw the courtroom into a furor, the defense angrily denying any participation in the asserted plot.

The opposition press sneered that the whole business was in-credibly silly. Wired its San Francisco correspondent to the Los Angeles *Times:* "There is not one word of truth in the childish tale that Luther Brown tried to kidnap Bad Man Lonergan. Everybody in San Francisco is laughing at the fake."

But four days later, Fremont Older, hated and admired editor of the *Bulletin,* was himself kidnaped.

Older was one of the most easily recognized men in San Francisco. For weeks—ever since Luther Brown took over the United Railroads secret service—he had been dodging traps. Women would telephone, saying they could give him valuable graft information if he would come to a certain apartment; day and night he was shadowed; the streets bristled with armed men working for Brown or detective Burns. Reports of terrifying threats and mysterious shots in the night were commonplace.

On the afternoon of October 27th, Older was at the Red House, chatting with Cobb, when the telephone rang. A man's voice said: "I am Mr. Stapleton. If you will come to the Savoy Hotel, I will give you some very important information."

He could not come to Older, the caller explained, because he was being watched. The Savoy Hotel was on Van Ness Avenue, a block and a half from the Red House. Older had accepted many such dubious summonses in his quest for graft evidence, and he reasoned that the risk in broad daylight, on one of the busiest streets in the city, would be slight. But as he was leaving, he said to Cobb: "This may be a trap. If I'm not back in half an hour, you may be sure that it is. Tell Spreckels."

Older walked along the downhill block on O'Farrell Street to Van Ness, passed St. Mary's Cathedral, and turned south, when he noticed an automobile draw up to the curb. There were four men in it. Two of the men got out and accosted Older, one identifying himself as a Los Angeles constable and flashing a warrant for Older's arrest. The warrant was endorsed by Judge Carroll Cook, and the constable ordered Older to get into the car. The editor, not wishing to resist a lawful arrest, obeyed. The car started west toward the beach, Older demanding an opportunity to call his lawyer and arrange bail; he was assured that they were taking him to Judge Cook's home for this purpose. But when the machine entered Golden Gate Park and then turned southward, out of the city, Older became alarmed. His alarm became fright when he observed, in an automobile keeping about two hundred feet ahead as though acting as guide, Luther Brown and R. Porter Ashe, the Calhoun-Ford lawyer. He tried to stand up to attract the attention of pedestrians, but the man beside him pressed a pistol against his ribs and threatened to kill him if he made an outcry.

The car took him to Redwood City, some twenty miles south of San Francisco, stopping only once to turn on the acetylene headlights as darkness fell. Older was held prisoner in the auto until the overnight express to Los Angeles, the Lark, pulled in; then the two constables took him aboard and locked him in a Pullman stateroom that had been reserved. Luther Brown and Porter Ashe got aboard the train separately. Older spent the night in an upper berth, his two guards in the lower berths of the locked stateroom, while the train roared southward.

Meanwhile, Cobb had spread the alarm, and San Francisco was being ransacked for the missing man. Several members of the prosecution had arranged to dine that evening at the restaurant run by Golden M. Roy on Van Ness Avenue, a couple of blocks from where Older had been seized; Mrs. Older arrived, and for a while supposed that her clue-hunting husband was on one of his news chases and would show up later. But at the next table, Phelan and Heney and his wife seemed preoccupied, and at length they told her about Fremont's vanishing; Police Chief Biggy's entire force was scouring the city but had learned nothing. In a state of nervous collapse, Cora Older went back to San Rafael and waited for news.

Aboard the Lark, a young San Francisco attorney overheard Luther Brown and Porter Ashe in the dining car talking about an important arrest, and Ashe boastingly mentioned Older's name. Although he knew nothing about the excitement back in San Francisco, nor that Older had disappeared, the attorney gathered that the editor was in some imminent danger. Getting off the train at Salinas, the next stop, he telephoned the San Francisco *Call*. The *Call* immediately informed Heney and Spreckels, and by 1:00 A.M. the story was in type in the *Call* composing room and Mrs. Older was reading it in a proof rushed to her by messenger.

Spreckels got on the telephone to Santa Barbara, where the Lark was scheduled to stop early in the morning, and legal machinery started moving; a judge was routed out of bed to sign a warrant and attorneys were engaged. When the Lark pulled into Santa Barbara at 8:30 A.M., Older, looking out the window, surmised a wedding party had come to the station, so many people were on hand; really it was a crowd come to watch the sheriff's descent on the train, for the Santa Barbara morning newspaper contained an account of Older's vanishing and the projected action.

Older and one of the constables (the second had disappeared) were taken into custody by the sheriff on a technical charge of false arrest. There was an immediate court hearing, at which Older told how he had been denied an opportunity to make bail. The constable refused to testify, and the judge released Older in bail, which was at once posted by Franklin K. Lane, the student-days reform associate of Abe Ruef, who happened to be in Santa Barbara.

The intention behind the abduction attempt came to light in later testimony. In reporting Heney's exposure of the plan to trap Lonergan, the *Bulletin* had inadvertently confused J.C. Brown and Luther Brown, crediting Luther Brown with spending a night in a dive with a woman of shady character. Luther Brown really had spent that night at home with his family in San Leandro, across the bay from San Francisco, and he charged that he had been defamed. A compliant justice of the peace in Los Angeles, who incidentally owed his position to Brown, issued the warrant for Older's arrest, which had been served by the two Los Angeles peace officers.

But the scheme did not stop here: the plot, as it was afterward disclosed by underworld informants, had been to take the editor off the train below Santa Barbara, carry him into the hills, and kill him "while attempting to escape." Only the midnight call of the young attorney prevented execution of this plan.

The opposition press sneered at the "childish" affair, intimating that Older had got himself abducted in order to create sympathy for the prosecution. But the grand jury took a graver view and indicted Luther Brown and Porter Ashe for kidnaping, and Brown for subornation of perjury. Then the two constables turned State's evidence, —and after testifying before the grand jury, were compelled to beg an escort from Burns to get out of San Francisco alive! But the laughter of that portion of the press friendly to Ford's defense kept up, a typical gibe being printed by the Los Angeles *Times:*

... It makes the editorial bosom swell with pride to learn that it is considered an indictable offense in San Francisco to kidnap an editor,—any sort of editor. The action of the San Francisco grand jury shows that the law amply protects elk, mourning doves, and also editors,—all sorts of editors.

Patrick Calhoun denounced Older's narrative as "infamous," and declared it was "fantastic" to suggest that Luther Brown's libel action had "anything to do with persons accused of bribery."

Elsewhere, the outrage was reported with expressions running from astonishment to flat disbelief. The London *Times* gave two columns to the hair-raising yarn; and years afterwards an English dignitary, visiting San Francisco, remarked to Older that he had once read in the *Times* (which he had always regarded as a truthful

journal) "an incredible story about your interesting city—the kidnaping in broad daylight of an editor. He was taken away in an automobile
at the point of a pistol."

"Why," grinned Older, champing on his cigar, "that's a true story.
I'm that editor."

8 A Network of Evidence

Amid such excitements, the trial of Tirey Ford went forward in
jerks and jitters. Armed men haunted Judge Lawlor's courtroom,
Heney and Rogers both packed pistols, and the bitterness between
opposing counsel became explosive.

One by one, nine ex-supervisors told of taking the trolley bribe.
Gallagher, as chief witness for the State, gave his testimony in un-
emotional, matter-of-fact detail; he said Ruef had discussed the over-
head-wire franchise with him before the 1906 fire and the boss had
asked him to sound out the supervisors, and that it would be worth
$4,000 apiece to them. Wilson brought word that the members would
take this sum, although he himself held out for a bigger slice, finally
setting at $10,000; Gallagher was cut in for $15,000. All this
Gallagher swore he reported to Ruef about a week before the ordinance was passed; later Ruef handed him the money, and he distributed it among the supervisors in the agreed ratio.

This testimony was crucial to the prosecution's case, because it
established that the supervisors were offered a bribe *before* the
ordinance was passed. The significance of this point became clear
when Wilson and Coffey took the stand and blandly denied that they
had heard any talk about money until *after* the ordinance had been
voted. This conflict with the testimony the two men had given before
the grand jury resulted in their being promptly indicted for perjury.
Wilson thereupon begged permission to "correct" his testimony, explaining that he had been suffering from carbuncles and was dizzy from
a pain-killer when he testified. He was permitted to make the alteration
and confirmed Gallagher in every respect. But Coffey, for whatever
reason, stuck to his new story, and eventually he was tried for perjury
and convicted. It was remarked at his trial that the lowly hackman's

lawyers were attorneys closely associated with the high-priced counsel defending the indicted millionaires.

Under cross-examination Gallagher gave his opinion that the trolley-wire permit could have been passed without the payment of a dollar, inasmuch as the whole city wanted to get the street cars running again. Other members of the old board said they believed the same, although they had not scrupled to take a bribe to vote their convictions.

Rogers made great play with the furtive meetings between Gallagher and Spreckels on the grounds of the Presidio. Gallagher explained that he chose that meeting place because it seemed the most secluded of several proposed. "It never occurred to me that it was government property and that the laws of the state were not operative there." He denied that any of the meetings had been at night.

He also recounted having been given a note by Abbott for delivery to Ruef soon after the Oliver grand jury was formed, and of being unable to find the boss; so he took the note back to Ford, who invited him to read it; it was a warning that the grand jurors were investigating the trolley franchise and that their next step probably would be to trap the supervisors.

Harrigan, the grocer, Kelly, and Walsh all said they would have voted for the trolley franchise, bribe or no bribe. Walsh spoke in so low a voice he was scarcely audible, and Heney asked with mock solitude, "Are you weak this morning? Do you think you could carry $2,000?"

"No laughing in court!" bawled the bailiffs.

Boxton recalled that Gallagher always brought the bribe money to him: "I never had to trouble about going after it." The first installment of the trolley bribe Gallagher dropped casually on the back seat of his automobile, the dentist said.

Records of the Mint were introduced, and Mint employees told of making up several bundles of currency for Ford, the first ones in bills of small denomination. One clerk remembered the occasion with special clarity, because, as Ford and Abbott walked away with the money, "I said to Mr. Hawkins [a fellow clerk] that the packages looked as if they might be the supervisors' bit."

Several United Railroads directors testified they knew nothing about the $200,000, nor had they known of Abe Ruef's employment as a company attorney at any time in any capacity.

Charlie Haggerty, Ruef's office boy, testified that Ford and Mullally called at the boss's temporary office just after the fire; Haggerty was certain that Mullally was with Ford, because there was only a cracker box to sit on in the kitchen, "and when I came back after stepping into the hallway for a minute, Mullally had my box." Ruef and Ford, meanwhile, were confabulating in the bathroom.

Ford's confidential stenographer, Miss Celia McDermott, haughtily declined to give any information of importance, even after being admonished by the court. And the State was blocked in two other directions, when it developed that the United Railroads treasurer, Starr, had left the city, and that the corporation's cash book, which might have contained a $200,000 entry, had been sent East for auditing, outside the court's jurisdiction. Then Alex Lathan, "the shirt-box man," who had been Ruef's driver on the trip to Ford's office, disappeared, and Heney charged that he had been taken out of the state by Luther Brown's father-in-law. The defense scoffed at the imputation, but later developments proved it to be true.

Heney's final witness was Mrs. Henrietta Sittenfeld, Ruef's sister. When she took the stand, there was a murmur of admiration. Modishly attired and handsome, with black hair and flashing black eyes, she answered Heney's questions skillfully, denying that she had typed the official copy of the trolley-wire franchise. Abe's pride in her as she testified was evident.

Ruef had been in court daily, held in reserve as a witness. As the weeks passed without his being called, he fretted; often he appeared with bloodshot eyes, as though he had not slept. He wanted to be called, and was greatly disturbed when, on October 2nd, Heney suddenly rested without putting him on the stand.

The courtroom was startled, while the defense looked smug. Rogers grinned.

"Yes, I suppose the crowd is disappointed," Burns shrugged when the session broke up, "but we couldn't help it."

Standing just behind the detective on the broad marble staircase leading from the Temple auditorium to the street, Ford was the center of a crowd of the "best people" of San Francisco, eager to shake his hand and offer congratulations. Porter Ashe held a levy

on the steps; that same day he was indicted for kidnaping Fremont
Older.

The next morning, Judge Lawlor's courtroom was thronged again
with fashionably dressed men and women, chattering confidently as
they filed into the pews; the women glittered with jewels as if for the
theater. Down the center aisle strode Calhoun, leading in Ford,
Abbott, and Mullally, all indicted like himself; when he leaned across
the pew to whisper to the attorneys, his lavender necktie flashed
brightly. A little apart in the synagogue, unregarded, sat Abraham
Ruef.

Stanley Moore explained the three choices open to the defense:
put on a witness, rest their case, or move for acquittal on the ground
that no case had been made by the prosecution. They chose the last.
Ford would not take the stand, said counsel, nor would the defense
introduce one sworn word in his behalf.

The weather was hot (it was the hottest October in years), and
applause frequently cut the stifling atmosphere as the attorneys
summed up. A.A. Moore was sarcastic and solemn, referring to "this
Coxey's army of supervisors," "St. Lonergan the Guileless," "the
bathroom episode." Lonergan he described as hurrying to Roy's
house on the day he was trapped "with his eye cocked for boodle like
a duck looking for rain." Then, gravely, he warned the jurors against
joining a mere crusade against rich men: Ford, "a man full of years
and honorable," had exactly the same rights, he reminded them, as
any beggar.

Rogers worked himself into extraordinary excitement, extolling
the good work done by the United Railroads during the days of the
great calamity,—the food brought into the city, the men put to
work clearing away debris.

"Now their associate, Tirey L. Ford," he pleaded tremulously,
"who labored side by side and shoulder to shoulder through the days
that tried men's souls and nights of darkness and terror, is to be sent
to the penitentiary. Why? Because Rudolph Spreckels wants their
street-car system for himself! Are you going to stand for it?"

Spreckels, sitting beside Phelan and Burns, listened unmoved.

Why did not the prosecution put Ruef on the stand, Rogers demanded, and shouted: "Heney came from the same place in New York State I did. We came to San Francisco. He went to Arizona. So did I. But he went out in a different way. And, gentlemen of the jury—" he walked across and wagged a finger fiercely under Heney's nose "—when I coin the blood of General Ford, the blood of his weeping wife and his poor children, into dollars, you can come out and kill me!" He paused, and looking Heney squarely in the eye, hissed: "That is what you have done!" And turning, he rushed up the aisle and into the corridor, while the spectators gasped.

Rising to reply, Heney referred to Rogers' "condition." (The Los Angeles attorney's drinking habits were no secret among lawyers.) Then he added with a glint: "I am told that Mr. Rogers said the Irish are quitters. Well, here is one half-Irish who's no quitter,—as he will find out, if he keeps on with these cases."

Why was the prosecution keeping Ruef securely confined and away from meddling inquisitors? He answered the defense's repeated taunt: "Because we don't propose to have any interference with our witnesses!"

Byington was on his feet with a bitter interruption: "Is it not a fact that you have not sentenced Ruef for six months, and that you did not put him on the stand in this case, because he would not tell what you wanted him to,—because you knew his testimony would free an innocent man? You feared he would tell the whole truth!"

"He was here in the courtroom often," Heney retorted. "You could have talked to him."

"There never was a moment when one of Burns's armed guards wasn't within two feet of him!" blurted Byington.

Heney flushed. "That's a fact!" he cried. "We wanted to hear what you would say to him! We wanted to see how much you would offer him!"

Applause drowned out his words.

Heney adverted to the disappearance of the United Railroads cash book.

"That cash book and voucher book went to New York over a year ago, just about the time when the grand jury began an investigation of the trolley franchise," he said, "and about the time when

Ford sent the note around to Ruef warning him that the trolley matter was being investigated. The books have never returned."

Ruef he castigated as "the grafting chief of the forty thieves, a scoundrel and a rascal, warmed at the hearthstone and fed at the table of the man who bears the honored name of Patrick Calhoun,— whose associate and honored employee, Tirey L. Ford, we find sending a note to the boss thief warning him that the grand jury is investigating the trolley deal. If you have not sense enough to maintain your laws regardless of any man, then you are unfit to be free men, and unfit to have your children inherit freedom!"

The jury received the case on a Friday at 6:30 P.M. and sallied off to Nob Hill in their tallyho to consider a verdict, while Judge Lawlor relaxed at a performance of *The Merry Wives of Windsor*. He was not disturbed that evening.

The next day, after taking more than thirty ballots, the jurors sent word that they were deadlocked at eight to four in favor of acquittal. Because Sabbath services were being held in the auditorium of Temple Sherith Israel, Judge Lawlor received their report in the little downstairs room used by Judge Dunne, and then dismissed them. The prosecution at once moved for a new trial, which was set to start one week hence.

Ruef watched the dismissed jurors walk away with a wistful expression on his drawn face. The next day he was back in Lawlor's courtroom with his co-defendants—Calhoun, Ford, Mullally, Abbott, Glass, and Schmitz—for another legal formality. Glass showed no effects of jail confinement, but the ex-Mayor was the image of misery —cheeks hollow, hair unkempt, beard ragged—utterly changed from the magnetic personality San Francisco had once hailed as "the man of the hour." He looked ill and broken. He had just filed his appeal with the higher court, citing "gross irregularities" and bias by Judge Dunne, and asking a new trial.

9 "Clad in the Mantle of Decency"

Up to the last moment, Ruef had trusted he would be called as a witness in Ford's trial. He had sat in court day after day, watching

Heney, searching for some recognition, but the prosecutor ignored him. He sent emissaries to sound out Heney's intentions; Rabbis Kaplin and Nieto inquired why the boss had not been called, and Heney put them off, civilly but coldly. When Dr. Kaplin became persistent, Heney asked him not to come to the Red House any more.

The public remained mystified and suspicious, for without Ruef's testimony, the cases against the "higher-ups" were purely circumstantial; one word from Abe would make them positive. Ford's failure to deny his guilt under oath drew adverse comment: one word from him would have dispelled the enigma of the equivocal $200,000. In view of both men's silence, the jury deadlock was not unexpected, and the eight jurors who voted for Ford's acquittal indicated that Ruef's failure to testify had decided them.

Heney had made his suspicion of Ruef's potential treacherousness clear. Indeed, while the jury was out, he had explained his strategy to newsmen, saying: "When you are playing stud poker and have just one card in the hole, you are a fool to show that card before the other fellow bets. The case is complete as it stands. We didn't want Ruef to come on and tell some tale to suit the defense, and then let them go ahead with a lot of testimony to suit that theory." The outcome proved that as a poker player the pugnacious, wary prosecutor could not always win.

The public knew nothing about the weeks of haggling and twisting by the indicted boss which had preceded Heney's decision not to risk putting him on the stand. The point at issue, one on which no compromise could be attained, was the divergence between Ruef's and Heney's versions of what passed between Ford and the boss in connection with the $200,000 "fee." Ruef insisted that never was one word uttered that would indicate that Ford had any knowledge that the money was to be used for bribery. Heney ridiculed this, saying the United Railroads would never have given Abe $200,000 without a clear understanding that it was to be used to buy the franchise. Heney insisted that Ruef say so on the stand, and Abe balked at (as he phrased it) "committing perjury."

That Ruef was telling the literal, if not the essential, truth was possible: Ford and Abe were capable lawyers and aware of the necessity of discretion. Burns suggested to Ruef formula after formula that might satisfy Heney and still keep within the strict boundaries of truth; Ruef rejected them all.

A few days before the commencement of Ford's trial, Kaplin, Nieto, and Ach showed up with Burns at Heney's office and demanded that the prosecution make good its pledge under the immunity contract: let Ruef withdraw his guilty plea in the French restaurants case, and dismiss the other indictments against him; in return for his testimony. Heney smelled blackmail and replied vigorously: "We might as well understand each other. You know perfectly well that I did not at any time make any such promise to Ruef or you, or to anyone present, or to anyone on earth."

Then, as evidence of Ruef's continued bad faith, he listed the lies the boss had been caught in, and concluded: "Ruef tried to job the prosecution and he has only succeeded in jobbing himself into prison."

After this encounter, a belief that the prosecution, in its eagerness to convict Ford and Calhoun, was trying to compel Ruef to commit perjury became indelibly fixed in Rabbi Kaplin's mind.

Heney refused to trust Abe and did not call him, and characteristically said why publicly. During a political speech, when he was heckled with the query, "Why didn't you put Abe Ruef on the stand?" he shot back: "I'll tell you why! We didn't put Ruef on the stand because he wanted complete immunity! We had given him partial immunity, and when the Ford trial came up, he thought he was the whole show,—he concluded we couldn't get along without him! He thought he had us where he wanted us, so he said he wouldn't go on the stand and tell all he knew about the overhead-trolley bribery unless we granted him complete immunity! And I told him to go to hell!" (Later, Kaplin was to claim that Ruef had intended to satisfy the prosecution, and still stay within the bounds of truth, by replying to the question by Heney as to whether he had accepted the $200,000 from Ford as a legal fee: "Well, yes, that is what we called it," but by his manner and intonation conveying that both Ford and he were aware of the subterfuge. In this way no "untruth" would show in the transcript.)

Heney by that time was stubbornly determined, above everything else, to put Tirey Ford and Patrick Calhoun in prison,—"where they belong."

The second trial of Ford began on October 17th, and this time Heney said in advance that he had no intention of calling Ruef to testify. Again the boodling supervisors repeated their stories, but their memories were becoming blurred and Heney had difficulty in making them recall the dates of their talks with Wilson and Gallagher. Phillips had become pathetically confused. Furey remembered the amount of the bribe he received for his trolley vote, but was vague about the denominations of the bills,—a salient point in the State's case. Rogers tried continually to get the witnesses to admit that they had colored their testimony before the grand jury for the sake of gaining immunity, and succeeded in confusing them further.

At one point Heney threw the defense camp into an uproar by forewarning that Fremont Older was prepared to take the stand and testify that Ford had sent Lewis Byington to him with a bid for immunity,—if Ford should deny making the overture under oath. Flushing with anger, Byington shouted a denial from his seat in the counsel's pew, but he did not accept Heney's invitation to repeat the denial on the stand.

Byington taunted Heney with being "a little god who stands above the rest of the world. We are as much interested in the welfare of California as you are!" he cried. "There is a little red blood in the world besides yours! You're not the only honest man!"

"Well," blazed Heney, "if yours was only a little more red when you were District Attorney, Abraham Ruef would have been indicted and convicted in the French restaurants scandal long ago!"

Byington stared, shook his fist, and cried to the court for protection against "this man who insults everybody." Judge Lawlor recessed proceedings for the day to allow tempers to cool, stating that he would decide in the morning whether William Abbott, whom Heney had put on the stand and who was coy about testifying, would have to answer questions.

But the next morning there was no court session. The great money crisis of 1907—the "tight money panic"—had arrived, banks were closing and Governor Gillett invoked a statewide legal holiday to continue for the duration of the emergency. The courts could not function during such a holiday, and the recess was to last until December 2nd.

The interim was occupied with an activity as vital to the graft prosecution as court trials, namely, another municipal election. Mayor Taylor, who was serving by action of the board of supervisors, had been nominated for a regular two-year term by the Democrats. The non-partisan Good Government League (a member of whose executive committee was Rudolph Spreckels) also had endorsed Taylor, but the Republican nomination for mayor had been captured by an ambitious young attorney named Daniel A. Ryan. This split the opposition to "Pin Head" McCarthy, who was running for mayor on the Union Labor Party ticket; his nomination, it was said, having been dictated by Schmitz from the Ingleside jail. Sheriff O'Neil, the ex-Mayor's official host, was up to retain his job, also with Schmitz's blessing. The all-important office to the graft investigators, the district attorneyship, was a straight contest between Langdon, as the nominee of both Democrats and Republicans, and the Union Labor man, who seemed to have little chance.

The forces of wealth—the corporate interests—were openly active on McCarthy's behalf, the underworld and the upper world again joining hands to thwart a common threat to their privileges. The multiplicity of cross-currents set into motion by the tangled campaign bewildered even San Franciscans, while to outsiders the muddle became impenetrable.

The *Examiner* supported Langdon for District Attorney, but opposed Taylor, "that good old poet," whom it cartooned strolling, dreamily reading "Pale Poems for Pink People," while on his broad-brimmed hat roosted two loathsome birds—a vulture (Older) and a cormorant (Spreckels). The *Examiner,* after much straddling, finally plumped for Ryan for mayor.

McCarthy centered his fire on Fremont Older ("rotten Older" of the "boughten *Bulletin*") and rejoiced when a Union Labor band Pied Pipered an audience of workingmen away from Heney. The *Chronicle* added to the jumble by supporting Taylor and Langdon, but turning a frosty eye upon Heney's continuation in power and attacking Police Chief Biggy, a prosecution appointee. In 1900, when he was a police commissioner and acting police chief, Biggy had been removed by Mayor Phelan because of indiscretion in divulging police secrets and persistent ignoring of his fellow commissioners. The

Chronicle unearthed this long-forgotten "malodorous record" of the police chief and used it to belabor the prosecution.

The brannigan came to a head on November 5th, when the voters trooped to the polls in overwhelming numbers and triumphantly elected Taylor and his entire ticket. Langdon also snowed under his opponent. The Ford trial jurors, locked up in the Fairmont Hotel because of Judge Lawlor's apprehension that some technicality might invalidate the trial, should he permit them to go home during the holiday, cast their ballots with other good citizens; they had begged off dashing around to the polls in their tallyho and requested some less conspicuous conveyance. The Judge unbent and ordered hacks to be hired. The only real issue in the election, which once more focused national attention on San Francisco, was continuation of the graft prosecution, and the outcome brought hallelujahs of rejoicing from protagonists of reform across the country.

"San Francisco has redeemed itself!" jubilated the New York *Evening Post;* while the New York *World* warily conceded that "San Francisco has taken another long step toward self-redemption..." The New York *Sun* was delighted: "San Francisco is sane again; its good citizens have quite recovered from their temporary madness of fear." True, a residue of skepticism remained, as expressed by the Washington *Star,* which commented: "It remains to be seen how San Francisco, having purged itself of its corruption and given evidence of a desire to continue the good work, will hold up under the test of protracted performance."

At home, the future seemed bright. Exulted the *Chronicle,* after arrogating to itself the principal credit for the voters' resounding verdict: "Yesterday was the turn of the tide. It was the beginning of the ascent to nobler ideals and better days. Clad in the mantle of decency, the city stands unashamed before the whole world."

Then the legal holiday was terminated, and on December 2nd Ford's second trial resumed. But the prosecution, the defense, the jurors all were on edge, their nerves frayed by the weeks-long interruption. Judge Lawlor, picking up at the point where the trial had suspended, ruled that William Abbott must testify. Reluctantly, the witness then told of going to the Mint with Ford and bringing away a parcel which he had left on Ford's desk; that was the last he ever saw of it. What the money in it was used for he was not told and he did not ask.

Summations succeeded rapidly, and this time A.A. Moore employed a new argument, saying that even if Ford had given Ruef $200,000, there was no proof of bribery; it might have been an "extorted" payment, given because of Ruef's power over the supervisors, "who would 'eat the paint off a house.' Maybe Ruef split with them to keep them in line, but that was not bribery by the United Railroads. When Rudolph Spreckels made a bargain with these villains, he may have told them that what he wanted was the conviction of Ford, Abbott, Mullally, and Calhoun!"

In an extraordinary burst of candor, Moore struck at the professed civic zeal of the prosecutors and their associates. It was impossible for him to understand, he said, that any man would give his time and money "merely to correct the morals of San Francisco. It isn't in human nature that Heney and Spreckels should have done these things without a motive. I cannot imagine myself doing it. Possibly Heney expects glory, and place, and power. He may expect to become the King of the Muckrakers, and have his face emblazoned alongside the head of Rudolph the First, towering in juxtaposition to the cranium of Burns. But the feet are of clay. No man lives who would have given up his money and his time merely for the love of his country!"

There was no applause, but Heney was moved to a red-hot rejoinder. First, he ripped savagely into the pretense that the United Railroads men might have merely yielded to extortion: "If they had been held up, they would have come to me as soon as they learned we were investigating these matters and said: 'He held us up for $200,-000. We'll help you convict him.' Instead of this, Ford sent a note to Ruef telling him that we were going to investigate the trolley matter. Instead of warning Heney, they warned Ruef! When a man is held up, he doesn't wait a year and a half before he tells about it. But they liked it! They liked to be held up that way!"

Then the prosecutor's eyes flashed behind the academic-looking spectacles and his voice swelled as he bristled up to the jury box:

"Mr. Moore has told you that he cannot imagine Mr. Spreckels or myself acting in this matter without a motive. Moore will probably tell you that George Washington went through Valley Forge because he wanted to be known as 'The Father of His Country,' and that Abraham Lincoln was a false alarm, merely another Spreckels seeking to acquire some property that didn't belong to him. Oh, shame on American manhood that such a statement should come from any lawyer! I would rather give fourteen months of my time to save San Francisco from disgrace than to have the wealth of the Indies! While we were turning out the boodling supervisors and sending a corrupt mayor to prison, these men were sending notes of warning to Ruef,— and now they have the audacity to come here and tell you that we must have been actuated by false motives! My God! Is that the sort of thing that is to receive the approval of San Francisco?"

The jurors tallyhoed back to the Fairmont for dinner, and between dessert and 11:00 P.M. they balloted six times. At 11:30 they sent word that they had reached a verdict.

The courtroom filled swiftly. As the jurors filed in, Ford—a self-made man with a lifetime of achievement at stake—trembled like a man with palsy, and his lower lip visibly quivered. The clerk received the slip of paper from the foreman and read, "Not guilty." Ford's eyes gushed tears and he groped his way toward the jury box, choking out words of gratitude and clasping each juryman's hand.

Said Earl Rogers drily: "This is the beginning of the end."

PART THREE

"Therefore I went about to cause my heart to despair of all the labor which I took under the sun."

1 Schmitz Freed—Ruef Demands Release

On January 6, 1908, the new city administration took office, sweeping out the Union Labor Party regime from top to bottom. And on January 7th, Judge Dunne relieved Chief of Police Biggy of his duties as Ruef's jailer and remanded the boss to the custody of the new sheriff, Lawrence J. Dolan. The next day, Abe joined Schmitz and Glass in the Ingleside county jail. He was placed, not in a comfortable room like his predecessors, but in a cell, and Dolan promised that his two other distinguished charges would be similarly accommodated.

Two days later, on January 9th, the State Court of Appeals set aside Schmitz's conviction, ruled that the Mayor had not been given a fair trial, and declared the French restaurants extortion indictment invalid. As Schmitz's co-defendant, Ruef benefited equally from this decision. His plea of guilty became a nullity and the club his prose-cutors had held over him was knocked out of their hands.

The reasoning of the Appeals Judges threw the city—indeed, the entire nation—into a ferment of confused indignation. Justices Cooper, Hall, and Kerrigan, who comprised the court, cited the Penal Code's explicit definition of extortion as "the obtaining of property from another, with his consent, induced by a wrongful use of force, or fear, or under color of an official right"; and the next section of the statute, reading: "Fear such as will constitute extortion may be in-duced by a threat either: (1) to do an unlawful injury to the person or property of the individual threatened, or to any relative of his, or member of his family. . . ."

The keystones of the statute, the learned Judges ruled, were the words "wrongful" and "unlawful": grammatically they construed the adjective "unlawful" as modifying "injury" and not "threat"; and similarly, the "use of force or fear" was not enjoined, but merely the "wrongful" use of force or fear. Since the right to oppose the granting of a license to do business to an establishment believed to be foster-ing immorality belongs to every citizen, the exercise of that right was entirely lawful, and the incidental fact that the person availing him-self of that lawful privilege happened to be a public officeholder was wholly irrelevant, the Justices pointed out; being elected to office does not strip a man of his just rights of citizenship. The bringing of pressure to bear upon the police commissioners by the expression of an opinion or belief, however strongly entertained, was lawful, the court went on; hence any injury which might thereby be done to the restaurant proprietors would not be an "unlawful" injury, as re-quired by the statute, and therefore could not constitute statutory extortion.

"It is true that from a high standard of ethics it could not be claimed that one could extort money by a threat to do a lawful act," the opinion read; "but every wrong is not made a crime."

By extension, the restaurant men were deemed to have no grounds for complaint, because nobody had acted illegally against them, how-ever hostile might have been the intent; nor had they suffered property loss in consequence, because a license to sell liquor is not property in the usual sense, "but a mere permission granted by the proper au-thorities to carry on business."

This the learned court unanimously set forth, with more, much more,—for it found that Judge Dunne had erred prejudicially on five counts, including the employment of the elisor, and that Ruef's testimony that he divided the restaurant keepers' money with Mayor Schmitz was not proper rebuttal evidence.

Some lawyers professed to have anticipated the adverse decision, and it was obvious that Supreme Court Justice Henshaw, that blandly busy bystander, had prompted sagely from the wings. But to the plain citizen, the opinion sounded like the chattering of Bedlamites let loose, the Court of Appeals like three March hares glibbering in misjudgment; while across the nation this whitewash of the maculated Schmitz was greeted with hoots of execration. Everywhere, men and women of good will were staggered. Reported the New York *Press:* "Another earthquake might not have shocked San Francisco more." And the New York *World* voiced the general reaction when it stormed: "The decision shocks common sense! It insults decent public opinion! It means that a crook in office and a crook at his side represent a political interest that must be protected by law. . . . The cause of reform in California is hapless!"

One hour after the decision was rendered, Heney closeted himself with Langdon, Spreckels, and Burns; then hurried off to catch a train for Oregon, where he had been called to revive the lagging land-fraud trials. He maintained he was not downcast: even with the five extortion indictments dismissed, forty bribery indictments still stood against Schmitz and one hundred and twelve against Ruef.

Judge Dunne made no attempt to conceal his scornful disagreement.

"It is to be regretted," he said, "that the hearing of this appeal came before a court whose members have relatives and intimate friends against whom many indictments were returned by the same grand jury that returned these true bills. Judge Cooper's wife is a sister of Mrs. W.I. Brobeck. [Brobeck was indicted in the Parkside case.] Judge Hall is a brother-in-law of A.A. Moore, who defended Patrick Calhoun. I am satisfied that the evidence sustained the verdict. I will further say," he went on, his voice rising, "that the jury which returned this verdict, in accordance with the evidence and the law, will be remembered with respect and honor in the community long after the court which set aside the verdict has been forgotten."

Schmitz at once set about procuring his release on bail, while the prosecution carried an appeal to the State Supreme Court. In his seventy-eight-page petition for a rehearing, Heney excoriated Schmitz as "a conscienceless rogue and faithless official, a thief dressed in brief authority," and called on the highest court to find "that levying blackmail upon licensed businesses by the mayor and the political boss of a metropolitan community is a crime under the law of California, and should not go unwhipped of justice." Heney's analysis of the statute and of the Appeals Court ruling was extensive, and by so eminent an authority as Dean John H. Wigmore was applauded as well-founded and penetrating.

Ruef lost no time in taking tactical advantage of his new position: he demanded cockily that the immunity bargain be consummated immediately, all the indictments against him be dismissed, and in effect that he be taken into the District Attorney's good graces and be made privy to the prosecution's strategy and secrets, in exchange for testifying at the forthcoming trials of the indicted "higher-ups." With Heney absent in Oregon, this insolent ultimatum was served on Langdon; Ruef refused to co-operate unless his terms were met. The negotiations rapidly grew acrimonious.

The public, which had no inkling of the existence of the signed immunity contract, became restive and suspicious. Seeing the boss shuttle daily between the jail and Langdon's office, while apparent intermediaries scuttled in and out—saying nothing but betraying every indication of concern, agitation, and anger—reporters made wild guesses. The appearance at the District Attorney's rooms, at times when Ruef was there, of Rabbis Kaplin and Nieto especially was baffling, for their participation in the haggling that had led up to the immunity agreement had never transpired. The press, realizing that some sensation must be brewing, floundered in conjectures, many of them shrewdly close to the truth.

Ruef himself remained flippant and enigmatic. "My conference with District Attorney Langdon tomorrow will decide my future course of action," he told reporters one Sunday, then perorated: "Monday will decide the fate of nations!" And away he tripped to Langdon's office, light-hearted and airy,—so markedly so that, in

classical vein, he suggested that Mercury's wings might be sprouting
on his heels.

Back at the jail every evening he sedulously cultivated popularity
among the inmates, listening to their laments and giving good counsel
and at times a trifle of material help. He bought out the commissary's
stock of pipes and tobacco and distributed it gratis; he brought in a
phonograph and box of operatic records for the prisoners' recre-
ation; he ordered cake and cookies sent in. After months of surveillance and solitude, his starved ego expanded in the glow of the
ragtail but adulatory crew.

"You know, it's a relief to be here," he confided. "I don't have two
or three guards spying on me day and night, and I forget my troubles
by listening to those of these chaps."

Meanwhile, from the jealously guarded conference room at the
District Attorney's quarters came muffled sounds of argument. The
rumor spread that Abe was demanding to be restored to virtual
liberty as a private prisoner, with the right to move about the city at
will and transact business without hindrance, under the nominal watch
of a deputy sheriff. Another rumor had it that he was actually demanding a written contract guaranteeing him immunity!

This supposition so shocked the city that a chorus of protest went
up. Langdon (who was further distracted just then by the social
amenities attendant upon his ensuing marriage, dashing back and
forth between San Francisco and the home of his bride-to-be in
Modesto) parried all questions, but it was obvious that he was on
the rack. As for Ruef, day after day he capered, jaunty and smiling,
delighting in matching wits with newspaper inquirers, and always
ready for chat or badinage. Upon emerging from Langdon's office,
he might linger for half an hour guying his critics; then espying his
guard camped glumly in a corner, he would sing out, "I've been
looking for you, boy!" And off the pair would saunter, surrounded
by a cloud of newsmen.

Then there occurred a curious scene in Judge Dunne's courtroom.
Langdon, Burns, and Ruef arrived together while Dunne was in
chambers. After a long whispered conversation, Langdon stepped to
the Judge's door and tapped discreetly. He was admitted, and ten
minutes later came out, visibly agitated. Again he and Ruef whispered,

Burns leaning across the table to catch their drift, and Ruef seemed disturbed. Then the three men separated.

Ruef went directly to his office on Fillmore Street, where he spent most of the afternoon on the telephone, speaking with either Langdon or detective Burns; he seemed to be waiting for some message. At last, at 6:30, he called Langdon and barked testily: "This deputy sheriff is getting uneasy and says he must get back to the jail! I can't keep him here all night!" Thereupon, in his own automobile, he and the deputy headed back toward Ingleside, stopping along the way for dinner in a first-class restaurant.

The next day a report gained credence that Langdon had asked Judge Dunne to approve an immunity agreement with Ruef, and that the Judge had refused. Such talk so incensed Dunne that he adverted to it in court, with the comment: "It is astonishing to me that such an idea should occur to anyone,—that a district attorney should be running around trying to get a judge to sign a contract of immunity freeing a person accused of crime! The District Attorney knows that it would be useless to broach the subject to me."

"Is it likely that he [Langdon] will consult with you before closing any agreement with Ruef?" he was asked.

The Judge's underjaw thrust out. "You bet not!"

After this development, Rabbi Nieto broke silence with the intimation that "sensational disclosures" might soon be forthcoming.

"Unless the prosecution does the right thing in regard to Ruef, and does it within a short time, I will tell all I know of the affair, and it will be a startling story," Dr. Nieto declared. "I have served notice on the prosecution and I shall wait."

Ruef pretended to have no notion what Nieto might be alluding to. Queried over the telephone in regard to the rabbi's vague threat, he was unusually debonair. In reply to a question as to whether he expected to be released on bail, he answered that the jail cells were too short. Asked about his future plans, he observed that the air space was less than required by city ordinances. Pressed to say when he would talk with Langdon again, he stated that the sanitary conditions at Ingleside were "insufferable"—the board of health would have a field day if they would inspect the place.

Then Langdon ended the mystery by breaking off negotiations, canceling the immunity contract, and releasing for publication the text of the vexatious agreement; like Heney, Langdon had become unalterably convinced that Ruef never had any intention of acting in good faith, but on the contrary had been aiding the defense of the "higher-ups" all the while.

"That is just what got Ruef into trouble," the District Attorney explained grimly. "The other side not only knew about all these [immunity] matters, but they had been given information about other things."

Langdon announced that Ruef would go to trial at once on the charge of bribery in the Parkside affair.

2   The Battle of the Affidavits

Disclosure that a written contract had been in existence for months which assured almost freedom to the prime villain in the civic drama, and that Abe had made his celebrated guilty plea under the benign protection of this contract, starkly disillusioned a host of the prosecution's well-wishers; the outcry went up that this was "treason," an "act of betrayal" of the cause of justice, a subversion of municipal honor; and the contract was scourged and defended in a hurricane of public excitement which shrieked into hysteria. All parties concerned rushed into print with statements of self-vindication.

In the best manner of melodrama, Rabbi Nieto released his thunderbolt in the form of a full account of the midnight conferences with Judges Dunne and Lawlor held in the shadows of Temple Sherith Israel; he solemnly averred that Judge Dunne had agreed to let Ruef withdraw his "phantom plea" of guilty in the French restaurants case and substitute a plea of not guilty, following which the prosecution would recommend that indictment 305 be dismissed. The rabbi nimbly side-stepped making an accusation of deliberate deceit, concluding: "The prosecution states that Ruef has not lived up to his contract. Ruef declares he has. I have no means of judging who is right."

Nieto's rending of the veil of secrecy touched off a torrent of disputation, and before the billows of rhetoric surceased to foam and roar, sworn attestations had been submitted by Nieto, Kaplin, Heney,

Langdon, Burns, Spreckels, Ruef (a handful of affidavits; at one time he kept three stenographers busy), grand jury foreman Oliver, Police Chief Biggy, the landlord, a servant girl, and guards at the Fillmore Street prisonhouse, Ruef's sister and father, Judge Dunne, Judge Lawlor, Henry Ach, Dr. George Woodbury Bunnell, a retired University of California Professor of Greek and Latin who had taught Ruef, and a hoard of supernumeraries who cluttered the brawling scene.

Rabbi Kaplin would have none of the caution of his colleague, Dr. Nieto, but roundly accused the prosecution of bad faith, stating categorically that in the midnight parley Judge Dunne did make a definite promise regarding a future withdrawal of the guilty plea. This, Dunne in plainest language denied. The Rabbi retorted that "Judge Dunne knows well in his heart that what Dr. Nieto and myself stated about the midnight interview is the absolute truth." He charged Dunne with willful untruthfulness, and his sense of injury became so deeply ingrained that when Heney's recollection of the words spoken in the midnight encounter coincided with Dunne's, he asserted that Heney "would have shown a far greater respect to the court and the cause of justice by handing in any cheap detective story in place of his affidavit." The fiery prosecutor he called either "a mythomaniac or plain liar."

Dr. Bunnell told of having called on Ruef at the Fillmore Street house, alone and in the company of the rabbis, in an endeavor to persuade the boss to tell the truth, and swore that the impression he gained was that the two reverend gentlemen were more interested in getting Ruef off than in serving the public welfare; even though once, "in the corridor of Temple Israel, Dr. Nieto said to affiant, after affiant had remarked to him that Abraham Ruef was not telling the truth, 'Ruef is a liar.' "

Henry Ach hotly defended the rabbis, saying it was impossible to believe that these "two reverend gentlemen would, in order to carry out designs with Ruef, so deny their God as to bear false witness against the man from Arizona ... It is no longer a question of Ruef; it is a question of the prostitution of the office of the district attorney and the prostitution of the courts ... Ruef pleaded guilty because of the condition of his family. Through the machinations of the prosecution, his aged father and mother lay dying on their beds and his sister was on the brink of insanity..."

The lawyer piled horror on horror and strained at the limitations of invective: "Honeyed words were poured into Ruef's ears by these prosecutors, persecutors, and sweaters, until even he, cultured and refined lawyer that he is, felt his mind giving way. I will make it stronger: it was as if these persecutors said to him: 'If you do not say this or that, you will be murdered in your sleep in the night while in our custody'... By fraud and misrepresentation they took this man into the grand jury room and forcibly, probably with red-hot irons, invited him to make his own indictment... It is horrible! It is worse than your old thumbscrews, the Spanish Inquisition, being drawn and quartered!..."

William J. Burns quoted Ach in a different vein of eloquence as saying: "Ruef is the stingiest son of a bitch I ever knew. After all I've done for him, I've had the hardest time trying to get my fees. Why! Why! He hasn't even paid Judge Hebbard anything for what he did for him!"

Oliver swore that Ruef tried to give the grand jury the impression that he was "the savior of San Francisco and never committed any crime,—all the money he took was attorney fees, and he never asked for money from the persons accused of handing out the bribes." Oliver submitted as an exhibit the draft of a counter-affidavit which he said Ach had begged him to sign, and which could be given "an interpretation absolutely opposite to what is the truth."

Ruef's retorts ranged from the playful to the vitriolic. Bunnell he ridiculed, recalling their conversations as "largely, if not mainly, upon the subject of the psychological development of the mentality of parrots, especially as demonstrated by a particular parrot in the house of the said Professor Bunnell, and affiant and said Bunnell had several quite extended discussions upon the subject of said parrot and animals in general."

The kidnaping scares raised by Burns the boss called fakes, including one asserted plot by which Ruef was to have been spirited away from the Fillmore Street house and hidden in a cabin in the high sierra. The only mysterious person who ever called on him, Abe declared, "was a mysterious young lady who sent to affiant some letters and beautiful flowers," and if she was part of the plot, he

wouldn't have minded being kidnaped. Figuratively he thumbed his
nose at Burns's "habit of building fantastic theories and imaginative
occurrences and complaints under the slightest circumstances, and
without any foundation in fact . . . [and] conjuring up vivid stories and
theories of kidnaping and of connubiating and of conspiracies without
any foundation in fact." He also called Burns a liar.

For Heney his hatred was almost inexpressible. Heney had "deliberately and willfully falsified and fabricated facts and denied
truths . . . for the purpose of excusing misfeasance, malfeasance, lies,
unprofessional and improper conduct"; Heney was an "unreliable, vicious and malicious person . . . not a lawyer, but a bluffer, a faker, and
a man who simply makes noises . . . not assistant district attorney in
good faith, but the paid and hired employee of private capital for
public purposes and private malice and for the assassination of the
character of the citizens of this state." Heney was "guilty of homicide,
false swearing, inconsistent statements in court and out, under oath
and upon affirmation, conspiracy under the laws of this state to obtain
the conviction of innocent persons and the indictment of persons
without sufficient evidence, and of other maldoings and vicious acts
sufficient to discredit him before any court."

The spate of abuse poured through January, February, and
March, the legal point of it all being Ruef's attempt to avoid going
to trial in the Parkside case before Judge Dunne, in view, the boss
contended, of his loyal fulfillment of every obligation under the immunity contract; or at least evading trial until he had been restored to
the legal situation as it existed at the time of his arrest. This, of
course, would open the door to more months of delays while the
gamut of legal shenanigans was coursed again from the start.

During all this vituperation, Tom Lonergan died. A simple-
hearted, uneducated man, he had faded visibly since his downfall, his
thin frame growing more and more shrunken, his mind more bewildered. When neighbors on Sanchez Street shunned his company or
pointed him out with contempt, he could not comprehend why. His
speech had become rambling, and Burns suspected that he had been
poisoned; although the medical certificate said he succumbed to a
weakened heart.

At about the time of Lonergan's death, Judge Lawlor admitted
Louis Glass to bail. After bearing up bravely for a while, Glass had

deteriorated in jail, and at the bail hearing he appeared so enfeebled he could scarcely climb the Temple steps to Lawlor's courtroom; during the proceedings, he sat with forehead resting on the back of the pew in front of him, as though in prayer; this time there was no book. Upon his release he went to Southern California for a long convalescence.

On March 9th, the State Supreme Court unanimously upheld the Appellate Court's annulling of Schmitz's conviction, with the addition of a further reason for invalidating the indictment, namely, that nowhere did the document identify Eugene Edwards Schmitz as the Mayor of San Francisco or Abraham Ruef as a political boss in control of the municipal government. The wording used by the Justices was: "The indictment does not aver that Schmitz was Mayor, or that Ruef was a political boss, or that either of them had any power, or influence, or control over the police commissioners."

The furor engendered by this decision was more clamorous than that raised over the Appeals Court ruling. Press, pulpit, and public united in a stentorian snort of disgust. "A striking example of the meticulous reasoning that has made California jurisprudence a byword and a reproach," exclaimed the *Call*. When the Justices expressed resentment at what they deemed misrepresentation, Chief Justice Beatty was invited to restate the court's reasoning in language clear to the layman, and this Beatty did, in the form of an open letter which was published in the Sacramento *Bee*. Elucidating the technical argument, the Chief Justice wrote: "Though the facts that Schmitz was Mayor and Ruef the political boss of the city may have been as notorious in San Francisco as the fire or earthquake, no lawyer could contend for a moment that they were facts of which a court could take judicial notice in passing upon the sufficiency of the indictment."

This merely fanned the fire, and impelled the formidable Dean Wigmore to re-enter the lists with a dissection of the Supreme Court's reasoning which left that honorable bench with scarcely a rag of legal covering. Against this criticism the Justices and their partisans in the State bar strove manfully in surrebuttal and the epithets flew, until the public scorn was summed up by the *Call* in the bitter words: "Long ago the whole world passed judgment on the judges."

Schmitz accepted the decision loftily, saying it demonstrated that the high tribunal believed "what I have always claimed—that I was removed from office and railroaded to prison."

The next day, after nine months of confinement, he was released in $400,000 bail, which was posted by William J. Dingee and Thomas H. Williams, millionaire president of the California Jockey Club, operators of the betting operations at the malodorous Emeryville race track.

"God, it's good to be free again!" cried Schmitz as he whisked home to Presidio Heights. Entering the insurance business with his brother Herbert, he promptly sent out circulars announcing his new enterprise and soliciting trade.

The Pacific-Union Club, of which Rudolph Spreckels and James D. Phelan were coventried members, sometime thereafter named Williams to its board of directors.

3   Deadlock

Slowly, like a clawing, caterwauling cat being dragged by the tail across a carpet, Ruef was hauled nearer to trial. When his attorney, Frank Murphy, moved in Judge Dunne's court to dismiss indictment 305, citing the attitude of the Supreme Court and alluding to the asseverations of Kaplin and Nieto, the Judge interposed with abrupt severity: "Stop, Mr. Murphy! I want you to stop right there, and say that any person making such statements as that is telling a willful, vicious falsehood and a deliberate untruth, made for no other purpose than to interfere with the administration of justice and to assist the greatest criminal that has ever appeared before the bar of this court to escape his just deserts. Let me tell you again, all persons, no matter how high their station or respectable their calling, should be brought to the bar of justice, and the higher their station and the more respectable their calling, the more reprehensible their conduct and the more serious and severe should be their punishment. Motion is denied. Abraham Ruef, stand up."

For a moment the startled boss did not move. Then he arose, pale and agitated, expecting to hear his sentence.

Judge Dunne recited the history of the case and Ruef's plea of guilty, then proceeded: "Abraham Ruef, do you know of any legal ground why sentence should not be passed upon you?"

Murphy hastily intervened with arguments to arrest judgment, while Ruef sank back weakly in his chair, and reluctantly, Judge Dunne bowed to the rulings of the higher courts, but not until he had put into the records this dissent: "The defendant would be sent to Folsom [prison] for the maximum term permitted by the law, if the Supreme Court had not come to his relief. I see no other alternative than to grant the motion. But at this time I want to say here, both as a citizen and as a judicial officer, that in my opinion it is a matter to be regretted that the Appellate Court did not reach a conclusion, equally open to them, which would bring as much comfort and encouragement to the forces of good as the conclusion which they did reach will bring to the forces of evil."

Then gathering up his papers, he passed into his chambers, leaving Murphy still expostulating.

Ruef kicked up his heels in relief as he headed back to jail. "Well," he chortled, "here goes the greatest criminal of the age!"

But early in April, after all the technicalities in which Ach gloried (and defended by citing the most respectable precedents) and all the demurrers had been swept aside (Judge Lawlor disposing of fifty-five at one stroke), Ruef went to trial in Judge Dunne's department for bribing Supervisor Jennings Phillips in the Parkside deal. Dunne did not sit; he had left for a vacation in the East, and at his request Superior Court Judge Maurice T. Dooling, of San Benito County, presided in his stead.

Meanwhile, the prosecution's third attempt to convict Tirey L. Ford had got under way. In this trial Heney appeared only intermittently, the State being represented by John J. O'Gara, one of District Attorney Langdon's regular assistants; against this relatively obscure counsel were pitted some of the ablest lawyers in the West, captained by A.A. Moore. Ford had pleaded "twice in jeopardy" as well as "not guilty," but Judge Lawlor ordered the trial to proceed.

The utmost difficulty was encountered in securing a jury, venireman after venireman stating that he had become prejudiced in favor
of the defendant, that two trials on the same charge seemed enough,
and that they would not trust the prosecution or its witnesses any
longer, after the Ruef immunity affair.

"I have no faith in Mr. Spreckels, nor Mr. Heney, and I don't
care about Mr. Langdon," was one man's frank expression.

"I don't know that I would believe the evidence that is brought
up," was another.

"I wouldn't believe these supervisors, or people like that," said a
third.

Others thought the supervisors' confessions "sounded like a
novel," or that the prosecution was "hurting business." Repeatedly
the fixed opinion was expressed that "if Ford is guilty, the whole board
of supervisors is guilty and ought to be punished; the poor should be
treated just like the rich."

But at length a panel was sworn, and on April 21st Gallagher,
wheelhorse of the prosecution's witnesses, took the stand once more,
and after Heney had finished questioning him, and he had told of
receiving $85,000 in all from Ruef for distribution to the "good
dogs," was given an artful raking over by Ford's attorney. Moore
deftly played up to Big Jim's air of guilelessness, the witness's re-
sponses coming for the most part in monosyllables.

"Forty-three years old, you say?" Moore murmured innocently.
"Just in the prime of life, rotund and apparently cheerful? Is it your
expectation to resume the practice of law here? You were the head
of the Native Sons of the Golden West? You were once nominated
for Superior Judge?"

Gallagher shifted uneasily, but Moore jabbed again.

"But fortunately—or unfortunately—you were defeated? What
other positions of prominence have you occupied in the common-
wealth? Been a candidate for an appellate judgeship? How narrowly
did you escape that nomination? You aspired once to be governor?
Well, you had it in mind, anyway? If you were not a higher-up, you
were as high up as you could get?"

There was a sting in it, but Gallagher's attitude was that he
"just regretted it, that is all." To one question he had a forthright
reply. Moore had asked: "Did the rest of the board of supervisors

know that you were to get $15,000, while you were paying them only $4,000?"

"There was no concealment," came the blandly self-satisfied answer. "I simply didn't tell them. And they didn't ask. They knew better than that."

When the session ended for the day, Gallagher was still squirming on the seat of discomfiture.

At 7:30 o'clock that evening, A.A. Moore, dining in his home in East Oakland, heard a thud and felt the concussion from a powerful detonation not very far away. Half an hour later, he was astonished when reporters appeared to question him about the dynamiting of Gallagher's home, a dozen blocks from there, at a time when Gallagher, his wife, and six other persons, including three children, were inside it.

The wrecked building stood at 1370 19th Avenue in Oakland. It belonged to Gallagher's brother-in-law, W.H.H. Schenck, with whom Gallagher and his wife had been living since the San Francisco fire. The explosion ripped out the front of the two-story wooden house, knocked out basement walls, hurled a verandah pillar one hundred feet, and drove a piece of studding, with a fragment of a window casing and a lace curtain and shade attached, through the window of another house thirty feet off.

The Schencks, with their children and a visitor, were sitting in the dining room downstairs; they were thrown to the floor, but escaped serious injury because of the protection afforded by the solid chimney between them and the explosion. They groped through smoke and dust and got into the back yard. Gallagher and his wife were upstairs, and had just stepped out of the room directly over the explosion point; the floor of this room was blown clear through the roof. All lights were ripped out, and in darkness Gallagher felt his way down the splintered staircase to where it broke off in mid-air, dropped to the floor, helped his wife down, and with her took refuge in the yard.

A.A. Moore was dumfounded by the news.

"A most regrettable crime!" he exclaimed. "I cannot imagine who could be guilty of the attempt, or why it was committed."

Henry Ach and Frank Murphy scoffed at the supposition that the explosion was an attempt on Gallagher's life engineered by someone interested in the graft defense.

Ford was appalled. "None but an inhuman wretch could have committed such a dastardly deed," he said.

To Heney and Spreckels the explanation was clear: Gallagher was their mainstay in the trials, since only he could link Ruef and the supervisors in the passing of the bribes; his removal, therefore, would render proof of bribery almost impossible. The two men hurried across the bay and inspected the ruins. The dynamiting had been expertly planned: the entire contents of the house were smashed,—furniture, dishes, books torn to bits, the top of the heavy dining-room table split from end to end. Heney denounced the outrage as the work of "hired assassins in the employ of men interested in the outcome of the graft prosecution"; it was, he said, attempted murder, not the act of a crank or fanatic. Gallagher had no doubt that his death had been intended; recently, strange men had been following him in the street, and he had been warned by Heney and Burns to be on guard against danger.

Gallagher then revealed an incident not hitherto made public. When Luther Brown came to San Francisco, he opened an office for the Sierra Power Company, a bona-fide corporation that owned a small mountain power plant, in the building where Burns maintained his headquarters. Soon afterward, the United Railroads detective J.C. Brown approached Gallagher with an offer to him to become the company's attorney. Big Jim asked what the job would entail.

"Make a trip or two a year to our plant, for one thing. You may have to visit our new plant in Mexico."

Gallagher smiled and declined the employment.

At the time of the dynamiting, J.C. Brown had switched allegiance and was working for Burns, and he genially confessed: "If Gallagher had gone to Mexico, he would never have come back!"

Burns was out of the city when the explosion occurred, and upon his return, his attempts to investigate were hampered systematically by detectives in the employ of Patrick Calhoun. The latter volunteered that he was pushing his own investigation of the "un-American outrage" and resented Burns's interference.

Ford's trial was not interrupted, Gallagher resuming the stand the next day, and on May 2nd O'Gara summed up for the State, while Byington and Moore spoke briefly and bitterly for the defendant. At 11:57 A.M. the jury retired, and at 12:03 P.M. they returned,—having organized, elected a foreman, balloted, and reached a verdict in five minutes and forty-five seconds. Their verdict was "not guilty."

A cheer went up in the courtroom and was echoed by friends of the defendant in the street outside. Later, at a victory luncheon in Tait's restaurant, Ford and the other United Railroads officials received an ovation.

To Heney, Ford's acquittal meant no change whatever in the prosecution's plans for Ruef: if they failed to convict on the first three or four tries, he said, they were prepared to prosecute the boss one hundred and twelve times.

Even when the State Supreme Court dealt the graft investigators another stunning blow by setting aside the conviction of Louis Glass, on grounds so technical the man in the street made no pretense of understanding the tortured reasoning, the dogged little prosecutor refused to admit that he was discouraged. And a goodly portion of the public still backed him up.

The difficulties encountered in finding a jury to try Ruef were enormous. Here, Heney personally took charge, and his frequent clashes with Ach and Murphy soured the atmosphere. Even after the jurors had been tentatively agreed upon, there were further upsets and delays. One juror, already accepted, a dairyman, was found to have served a sentence in the house of correction for watering milk, and he was dismissed. The day after this happened, Burns received a telephone call from a tailor named Cohn who said another ex-convict was in the jury box, accepted by both the State and the defense,— Morris Haas, a small-time liquor dealer, who, Cohn said, had served time in San Quentin on an embezzlement conviction. Burns found a rogues-gallery photograph of Haas, and Heney confronted the juror with it in court, asking whether he recognized the man. Haas started a mumbled explanation, but Heney cut him off with, "We are not here for the purpose of trying you, Mr. Haas," and brought out that the man had been sentenced under a different name in 1888.

Interposed attorney Murphy: "You were pardoned for that offense?"

"Certainly I was!" cried the unhappy juror, and Heney snapped: "Did Mr. Murphy know about this?"

"No, sir; he did not know."

"Then how does he know about it now?"

"He didn't know about it!"

"Then," persisted Heney, "what was he coming over to me for, when this matter came up?"

Murphy flushed. "For the purpose of preventing this man from being publicly disgraced in this courtroom," he said. If Heney had told the defense privately of his discovery, Murphy added, the juror could have been excused quietly, without scandal.

"I have no doubt of that," flashed Heney. "But I do have doubt that if you knew of a former felon being in the jury box, and we did not know about it, that you would say anything about it."

Haas stumbled miserably out of the courtroom. The incident was the highlight of a dull day of wrangling.

Evidences of jury tampering were reaching the prosecution. In the last Ford trial, a Burns operative who had been assigned to advise O'Gara on the qualifications of prospective jurors was found to be giving false information. Burns suspected there was a leak in his office, and his suspicion was strengthened when one night his keys were stolen from his trousers in a Turkish bath, duplicates were made, and the originals were returned while he steamed. However, the thief blundered by putting a couple of the duplicates on the key ring and Burns spotted the switch. He had the locks on his office doors and files changed, but leaks continued.

Yet, in spite of all obstacles, a jury was selected who would decide the boss's innocence or guilt in the Parkside matter. A complication had arisen when the Oliver grand jury, upon winding up its work, voted a recommendation that the indictments against the three Parkside officials—Green, Umbsen, and Brobeck—be dismissed, because extortion would have been a more accurate charge in this case. Heney had pointedly ignored this recommendation up to the time he placed his first witnesses on the stand before Judge Dooling.

J.E. Green was called. He refused to testify. Heney thereupon asked the court to dismiss the indictments standing against the witness and the court granted the motion. Then Green talked without hesitation about his dealings with Ruef and the payment of the bribe to get the street-car franchise his company needed. Later, the indictments against Umbsen and Brobeck were dismissed in the same manner, and they became willing witnesses against Ruef.

On the day when "good dog" Gallagher took the stand, courtroom fireworks flashed. Murphy accused Heney of packing a gun, and Heney flung back a challenge to "take that gun out of your pocket and come outside,—I'll give it to you this minute!"

When Ach complained of such theatrics, the prosecutor flared: "Yes, I have a gun, and I propose to carry a gun! An attempt has been made to assassinate one man in this case, and I have been threatened with assassination! I don't propose to be done up by some of their hired thugs,—there are half a dozen in this courtroom right now!"

"Burns's thugs!" shouted Murphy.

"No, your thugs!" Heney retorted.

Later he apologized to the court for the outburst, explaining that he had been under a great strain, "trying cases for four years, here and in Oregon."

Former Supervisor Wilson (who at last had been ousted as State Railroad Commissioner, although it had taken a special session of the Legislature to do it) followed Gallagher; then Coleman, Boxton, and the rest. Boxton good-naturedly admitted that on the occasion of the "Black Flag Speech" he had imbibed considerable wine and he could not recall exactly what he did say. But Coleman, "the boy orator," remembered every word.

When the State rested, the defense elected to call no witnesses and proceeded at once with their summary for the jury. Ach held up Ruef as the victim of a hostile, unscrupulous press, and sneered that mention of Heney's serving as prosecutor out of pure patriotism "always makes me think of Spreckels sugar barrels"; the prosecution, he asserted, was dead, then and there. Ruef's father and sister sat close to Abe and wept.

The prosecution was not dead, Heney answered Ruef's attorney; "the wish is father to the thought in the mind of the man who pays your fee." But Heney's argument was ragged, not equal to those he had made against Glass and Ford; he sounded tired; the long struggle was telling on him.

When the jury retired at 9:00 P.M., an immense crowd gathered in front of the building near ruined City Hall, into which the courts had been shifted from Temple Sherith Israel, and many bets were laid regarding the verdict. But no agreement was reached by the jurors that night. The next day went by, and finally, after deliberating forty-three hours and voting thirteen times, the jurors reported they stood deadlocked at six to six.

When Judge Dooling dismissed the jury, both sides maintained they were disappointed; the prosecution at not obtaining a conviction, the defense at not winning a clear-cut exoneration.

Then the Appeals Court ordered Ruef's release on bail, and after much dickering the boss departed from jail under $1,560,000 bond, the highest ever posted in a criminal case in California. He was light-heartedly confident as he returned to his neglected law business and prepared to counter the prosecution's next move.

4   Pistols, Poison, and Slingshots

To many not unsympathetic onlookers, continuation of the graft prosecution seemed a hopeless cause, fraught with hazards, ill-omened, degenerating into futility. Schmitz freed, Glass freed, Ford acquitted, the Parkside magnates exonerated, Ruef successfully defiant, the boodling supervisors at liberty—unpunished, none of their pelf restored—the city infested with prying detectives and informers, prospective jurymen harassed, businessmen clamoring for settled conditions, a large section of labor inimical, more and more newspapers swinging to the defense,—what had all the wind and noble purpose accomplished? Miscreancy flourished, and since it could not be deracinated it must be endured. But Heney had no thought of retreat, and he could count upon a strong element of popular support; though this was less vocal than the defense's multiple, rumor-mouthed organs, it still held staunchly for a purge of all corruptionists.

Despite the setbacks, Heney set about trying Ruef again, and after that, he said,—Calhoun, the head and instigator, in the prosecution's eyes, of the stream of noxious "influence." Spreckels, seldom speaking, seldom ruffled, self-contained and stubborn, did not waver; he was becoming used to calumny.

Of course, the record was not as negative as the enemies of the prosecution pretended, and many men powerful in the community suddenly were walking in unaccustomed uprightness as a result of indictment or fear of incurring that fate. And in spite of all cynical disparagement of the prosecution and harping on its mistakes and shortcomings, the moral sense of San Francisco and California had been rekindled; sooner or later it would burst into purifying flame.

The day after the Ruef jury wrangled to a halt, Langdon and Heney appeared before the finance committee of the new board of supervisors in support of the District Attorney's request for a $150,-000 appropriation to meet some of the costs of the prosecution. The resources of the defense forces seemed to be limitless, Langdon stressed; the highest-paid lawyers in the West (at one time or another fifty-two of them) were arrayed against the District Attorney's meagerly budgeted staff. Pleading for means to continue the struggle, Langdon told the city fathers in all sobriety: "It is no longer a fight between grafters and honest citizens, it is anarchy against the law. We are hounded by day and we are hounded by night. We are fighting millions and all that millions can buy. But we are in the fight to stay."

Heney reinforced this plea, graphically picturing what the prosecution had to contend with. He said: "There are at the present time following William J. Burns and myself about this city armed thugs in the employ of Patrick Calhoun. These thugs have besieged the courtroom during the Ruef trial, have pursued us in automobiles, and have shadowed our homes. I can prove everything I say. Yesterday, in the Ruef case, attorney Frank Murphy said to Charlie Haggerty: 'Charlie, how many men have you here now?' And Haggerty replied, 'There are twenty, and the automobile has gone for others.' What did that mean? It meant that there were twenty armed thugs there prepared for anything. The courtroom was crowded with twenty as bad men as I ever saw in a penitentiary, and all were armed. One of them called aside one of my associates and advised him confidentially to keep away, if he did not want to be killed. Anarchy, the anarchy of organized wealth, reigns in this city. The Ruef jury was fixed: Tom Gibson, a United Railroads detective, admitted it several days ago.

I have given up two years of my time, worth more than $100,000, to fight corruption here. Rudolph Spreckels has not paid me a ten-cent piece for this work, and he doesn't owe me anything. I entered the struggle because of my love for my country."

At this point the president of the California Club, a women's organization, suggested that "it might be well to proceed with general business"; but several businessmen, clergymen, and others demanded an opportunity to speak in favor of the appropriation, and eventually the supervisors gave Langdon $70,000.

Sleepless vigilance was required of the prosecutors, for it seemed that their enemies found new outlets for the dissemination of libels and untruths daily. The reproach most persistently leveled against the prosecution was that it was "hurting business." Bankers used this plea to exert pressure on the commercial community and the borrowing public; to a merchant desiring a loan, for example, there might be insinuated that the graft trials were exposing San Francisco to the contempt and distrust of the whole world, ruining what little credit the city still had. Calhoun personally importuned advertisers to boycott the *Bulletin*. And against the asserted motives and objectives of the prosecutors, scurrilous aspersions proliferated in shadily financed publications which mushroomed overnight, the source of their instant prosperity seldom being difficult to trace. A few instances will illustrate the extent and intensity of this "poison pen" onslaught.

In January, 1907, the *Mission Times,* a nondescript neighborhood weekly in San Francisco, was sold to a man named Williams for $75,—assets, good will, everything. The buyer paid no cash, but gave his unsecured note for the full purchase price. Within one month, Williams had collected $500 from an agent of the United Railroads. Later, he received a regular subsidy of $250 a week, more than $1,000 a month, for thirteen weeks, when the subsidy was cut to $50 a week. Meanwhile, he was being favored with substantial payments for nebulous advertising. In all, Williams estimated that during 1907 he collected more than $7,000 of United Railroads money, in return printing gutter abuse of the prosecution, its aims, and its members. This was one example of a "boughten press," and it was duplicated many times.

On a large scale was the chain of newspapers which sprang up in 1908 through the populous Central Valley of California. These were owned by the Calkins Syndicate, a commercial printing firm. The string rapidly acquired the Fresno *Herald* and the Sacramento *Union,* both well-established, important dailies, and in San Francisco a new afternoon newspaper, the *Globe,* was launched to compete with the *Bulletin.* All the Calkins newspapers were frantically anti-prosecution. The Calkins Syndicate, it turned out, was receiving the entire printing business of the Southern Pacific Railroad and its subsidiary enterprises, an immense contract; yet after a year, the syndicate went bankrupt in a tangle of smelly financing, including large loans extended on flimsy or non-existent security by banks dominated by the all-powerful Railroad. Patrick Calhoun was said to have sunk large sums in the *Globe,* and so, according to rumor, had Harrison Gray Otis, the elderly, sour-tempered owner of the Los Angeles *Times.* Otis, who was cynical about his allegiances, once chuckled that he had been given $15,000 to print an especially virulent attack upon the graft prosecution which he would have printed anyway; the supplier of the $15,000 he would not identify, but the name Calhoun was mentioned.

This relentless press attack was damaging, and the most corrosive element in it was the stew of ridicule served up daily by the San Francisco *Examiner.* Hearst had hired away from the *Chronicle* a clever young cartoonist named Bud Fisher, and Fisher concocted a comic strip based on the absurd antics of a string-bean figure called "Colonel A. Mutt." (This was the genesis of the famous "Mutt and Jeff" strip of later years.) Into this ribaldry Fisher introduced the principals of the graft prosecution. Heney he made a cross-eyed cretin, a boob with a slobbering grin named "Beany," who kept falling into imbecilic scraps of his own devising. Burns was depicted as "Hot Tobasco," Spreckels as "Rudolph Pickles," James D. Phelan as "J. Tired Feelin," and Judges Lawlor and Dunne as "Judges Crawler and Finished." The slapstick humor was coarse but it was funny, and the town couldn't resist laughing.

Incensed by the vilification, some of the more ardent supporters of the prosecution retaliated by forming the Citizens League for Justice, militants all, pledged to uphold the trials in every way feasible. An elite corps was enlisted by Fremont Older for more aggressive action if the need should arise; these, known as Minute Men, were prepared to answer on the run any summons. Thereafter the badge of the Citizens League, prominently displayed on dress bosom or coat lapel, become a common sight in courtrooms, in spite of the injured complaints of nettled defense attorneys.

After Gallagher's home was dynamited, the prosecution moved to preserve his testimony in a form that could be used in future trials, should some further attempt against his life succeed. Under California practice, testimony given before a grand jury could not be used as trial evidence, but testimony given in a preliminary court hearing could be. Ruef had not figured in a preliminary hearing, and the prosecution set about correcting this omission. Upon application of the District Attorney, Judge Dunne dismissed one indictment against Ruef, who was then rearrested on a simple complaint charging the same offense. He was taken before a police judge for a preliminary hearing, and Gallagher testified through the resulting sixty-seven-day ordeal. Ruef's attorney in this side appearance was Adolph S. Newburgh, a police court practitioner close to Frank Murphy. Here again, thugs on the payroll of the United Railroads, detectives hired by Luther Brown, infested the spectators' benches, and the prosecutors were warned that there was a plan for Newburgh to goad Heney into some "shooting taunt," whereupon guns would bark and Heney would be cut down in the first volley.

Aware of his peril, Heney stepped up to Ruef in the courtroom one day and in a loud voice called attention to the presence of surly, armed hangers-on.

"If any trouble occurs here," he said distinctly, "I want to warn you, Ruef, that you will get yours first. You've hired thugs to assassinate me."

Ruef flushed and screamed that Heney was a liar, and those in the courtroom grew tense; but Heney controlled his anger and went on with questioning a witness. It was noticed that close to each Brown plug-ugly was stationed a Burns agent, who was under orders (it developed) that if gunplay started, he was to kill Ruef at once and take a chance on getting anybody else. At this time Heney ceased to attend night sessions of court as a precaution, admittedly apprehending that he might be shot down in some dark street.

Five days after Ruef's mistrial, two rental flats which Gallagher was building in Oakland were dynamited, at an hour when normally he would have been on the ground paying his workmen; because of rain, he had transferred that day's pay-off to a downtown office.

Then, in mid-July, a Greek named John Claudianes was arrested, and confessed having been an accomplice in the Gallagher dynamitings. Further, he revealed that the plot had been to kill not only Gallagher, but Heney, Burns, Older, and Rudolph Spreckels.

John Claudianes was young, poorly educated, unstable, a drunkard, a sexual pervert, and a liar. Nevertheless, his startling story was corroborated from other sources, even after he confessed and confessed and confessed again in several versions of the basic tale. He was a member of the colony of Greek contract laborers who had been brought into the city after the fire by the United Railroads to reconstruct its trackage. He was picked up when he tried to claim a $1,000 reward offered by the *Bulletin* for information leading to the arrest of the Gallagher dynamiters. Older had dismissed Claudianes as a crank, but a letter was found which the Greek had written to his brother Peter, in which he accused Peter of holding back money that had been paid for the dynamite attacks. The letter was addressed to Peter in Reno, Nevada, but before law officers there could be apprised, Peter had fled.

John Claudianes said that he and his brother had been hired by one Felix Paduveris to murder the members of the prosecution; Paduveris was a subcontractor of Greek labor gangs. The brothers had been promised $1,000 for the job, and the intention had been to use various methods of murder. Gallagher at first was to have been killed by shooting poisoned broken glass into his face with a slingshot; Heney was to be poisoned by the milk delivered to his home; the Spreckels mansion was to be dynamited, after the killers had gained entrance by bribing the gardener; Older had escaped dynamiting at the beach, where he often went to swim, only because, having received a warning from a friendly underworld source, he had brought along a police escort.

For one reason or another, these plans had been discarded, and dynamite then had been carried across the bay to blow up the Gallagher home. A barking dog frightened away the brothers on their first attempt, John Claudianes said, and he backed out; but Peter went ahead alone and set off the blast. Later, Gallagher's flats had been dynamited for good measure, and Paduveris was furiously angry when nobody was killed.

Felix Paduveris, it was established, had connections with both Ruef and Calhoun; a photograph of him in the uniform of a United Railroads conductor was found in his room, and for a while he had been employed as a spotter by the street-car company; he also had been dickering to sell to the United Railroads a pilfer-proof cash fare box which he had patented. Like Peter Claudianes, Felix Paduveris "flew the coop" when John Claudianes started talking, departing so hastily he did not even pick up his belongings. Paduveris never was found, and it was believed that he had returned to Europe and was living there under an assumed name.

The search for Peter Claudianes extended across the nation, while the anti-prosecution press howled in derision of the entire yarn, and Ruef sneered. But after months of tracking by Burns, Peter Claudianes was seized in Chicago. He was returned to California, confessed, was indicted, tried, and convicted, all in jig time. He declared he had been hired by Paduveris, whom he understood to be acting for the graft "higher-ups." He was sentenced to life imprisonment in San Quentin penitentiary. Ruef did not sneer at the sentence.

5 Bribing a Juror

For the third time Abraham Ruef was placed on trial, this time before Judge Lawlor, accused of bribing Supervisor Furey in the overhead trolley matter. Again, every ingenious device that legal cunning could contrive was deployed to hamper, delay, and jinx the proceedings, and acrimony between counsel reached new heights of intensity; talk of gun threats and accusations of tampering with jurors were of almost daily frequency. Henry Ach and Frank Murphy again appeared for Ruef, the two defense attorneys working as a team to ignite

Heney's flash-point temper. Burns was on edge lest some outburst occur in court, with fatal consequences.

"A man who carries his gun ought not to be afraid," Ach scoffed to Heney at one point, and the prosecutor roared back: "I'm not afraid of anybody except those who hide behind us, or blow up folks in their sleep!"

"I ask the court to disarm Mr. Heney," broke in Murphy. "We don't carry guns on our side."

"You don't have to," was Heney's retort, "because we don't hire people to kill anybody. You would never shoot anybody except in the back."

Murphy in turn flushed and his voice became menacing. "That is the only place you ever shot anybody!"

"That's a lie!" came Heney's shouted challenge; and Judge Lawlor was able to restore order only after the sternest dressing-down all around.

So it went, day after day, until September 4th. On that day, while Ach was questioning a talesman, a quiet-mannered, conservatively dressed man entered the courtroom and approached the bar.

At his appearance, Murphy sprang up, knocking over a chair in his haste, and asked permission to make a statement, hurrying on when Judge Lawlor paused in perplexity: "The charge of bribes or bribery has been heard a great deal, but the first real instance of it was made two weeks ago when John M. Kelly, a juror on the panel, made to me indirectly an offer to accept bribe money for his vote. I reported the matter to Presiding Judge Sturtevant two days ago, and I think an investigation should be made."

The man standing at the bar, listening courteously, was John Martin Kelly. Heney bounced to his feet. "This is the most audacious thing I ever heard!" he exploded. "I have in my pocket a statement from this prospective juror in which he says that a man was sent to him to offer him a bribe. He has since been acting under the instructions of Mr. Burns and reporting to him every day. E.A.S. Blake, the man who offered the bribe, was traced to Ach's office yesterday. Kelly was going to induce them to pay over the money. They had occasion to suspect something when they saw Kelly in court, and now they make this audacious statement. I never saw anything like it!"

Great excitement prevailed, and at Ach's suggestion the tentatively seated jurors were excused; then, at his own insistence, Murphy took the stand and made a sworn statement that brought A.S. Newburgh, Ruef's attorney in the preliminary hearing, into the picture.

Murphy said he had met Blake in Newburgh's office several weeks previously, and had showed him a typewritten list of the jurors drawn on the panel, remarking, "You may know some of them." Blake replied that he knew Kelly well; they had once worked together in Shreve's jewelry store, Kelly as sales clerk and Blake as an engraver. "And I," Murphy went on, "having in mind your honor's recent decision to the effect that one had a right to ascertain the mind of a juror . . ."

"Was that after my decision?" interrupted Lawlor.

"Well, no," Murphy conceded, "but I remembered that you had said so at some time. I asked Blake if he knew how Kelly stood on the graft prosecutions. He said Kelly was a liberal-minded man—a good fellow—and he thought he could give Ruef a square deal."

Later, in Newburgh's office, Murphy said, Blake reported that Kelly was demanding $1,000 for his vote, and Murphy said he answered, "There's nothing doing," and got Blake to make an affidavit recounting the bribe solicitation. This affidavit Murphy produced.

"Did you ever tell Blake that Kelly asked too much for his vote?" Heney prodded. "That you had been getting jurymen for $500 apiece? Did you tell him to tell Kelly not to be afraid?"

"No—and I didn't attach a great deal of importance to the incident."

"When did you change your mind about that?"

"When I began to suspect that it might be one of Burns's jobs. I came to the conclusion that it was, and that I should expose him."

"Is that the reason why you waited until Kelly came in here before you sprung it? Didn't you hear Ruef, or somebody at your table, say, 'There it goes!' when he came in?"

Murphy became greatly excited. "I believe both you and Burns are capable of putting up any kind of a job in a criminal case where you want a conviction!" he shouted. "You and your squint-eyed sleuths! But I haven't bitten at any of your bait!"

"Don't be too sure," responded Heney.

Ach asked Murphy to state when he first mentioned the matter to him. On September 1st, three days previously, Murphy replied, and Ach sat down with a contented air.

Judge George A. Sturtevant was called in, and he recalled that on that day Murphy had "said something about a $1,000 proposition having been made," but the Judge could not remember that any names were mentioned, and he had advised Murphy to inform Judge Lawlor, who was in charge of the case. Thunder sat on Lawlor's brow as he listened, and sternly he gave permission to the patiently waiting Kelly to take the stand and tell his story. This was circumstantial, and later was corroborated by several witnesses, all reputable.

Kelly said he had known Blake thirteen or fourteen years. Early in August, Blake had called at the office where Kelly was then employed as a real-estate salesman, and asked to speak with him alone. They went into a private room, where Blake, looking very nervous, said: "John, I've got a proposition. If you like it, all right. If you don't, just keep quiet. There is a chance for you to make a little money. You are drawn on the Ruef jury. There is $500 in it if you vote for acquittal."

"I was sitting in a swivel chair," Kelly continued, "and I swung around so as to look out the window, and I said to myself, 'Here is a man who is trying to bribe me and get me sent to San Quentin.' So I said to Blake, 'Give me until tomorrow.' He said, 'All right.'"

Kelly told his employer about the visit that same day, and the latter advised him to telephone to the District Attorney. Kelly did, and was referred to Burns, who urged him to play along, telling Blake $500 wasn't enough, that he wanted $1,000. When he did so, Blake promised to "take the matter up with the proper parties," Kelly testified.

"Did he say anything about the chances you were taking?" asked Heney.

"Yes. He said that jurors in former Ruef trials had been fixed and he didn't see why I should have any trouble."

Blake had held out for a payment to Kelly of $800, apparently hoping to pocket $200 himself; but a couple of days before, he had become suspicious and no further meeting had taken place. The prosecution had hoped to have Kelly accept the money and say nothing until Ach was questioning him on his fitness for jury service, and then to "blurt the truth right out." But Burns shrewdly guessed

that Murphy or Newburgh had tumbled to the trap, and the immediate appearance of Kelly in court was decided upon.

"Didn't it strike you as audacious," Heney asked, "that the
defense should be charging the prosecution with tampering with
jurors, when you knew that these very lawyers [Murphy and Ach]
had sent Blake to you?"

Ach sprang up and protested the "insult." Judge Lawlor silenced
the combatants. Then he listened with keenest attention while a
woman stenographer employed in Kelly's office and then Kelly's
employer confirmed Kelly's story. Attorney Newburgh was summoned
and denied everything.

"Did you offer Kelly $500?" said Heney.

"That is only an insult!" retorted Newburgh. "I don't like to be
insulted by a man like you!"

Ach, reading a newspaper, drily advised Newburgh to answer the
question.

At this point Judge Lawlor cut short the testimony and announced
that the grand jury would investigate the entire matter "to the bottom.
The court has very serious views on the situation that has arisen here.
The sort of malevolence exhibited between counsel suggests a condition of affairs in which ordinary crime fades into insignificance. This
charge made here falls on everyone connected with the case."

The grand jury did look into the matter (this was not the Oliver
grand jury but a new panel, the so-called McFarland grand jury)
and indicted Blake, Murphy, and Newburgh for attempted jury-
fixing. Blake was arrested on his way out of town and jailed. The
two attorneys were bailed pending trial.

September was proving a lively month, with events moving toward
a climax of which the prosecutors had been fore-warned again and
again.

6   A Bullet in Court

If Burns's ubiquitous operatives had chanced to drop into certain
bars near the place where Abe Ruef was on trial, during September
and October, they might have noticed a man on a spree, who with

barroom loquacity was boring everyone within earshot with his grievances. His life was ruined, he sniveled maudlinly; his family had been disgraced; he had lost his business,—all because of Francis J. Heney. The drunkard was Morris Haas, the ex-convict whom Heney had expelled from the jury box in Ruef's previous trial. Haas had found solace in alcohol since his humiliation; he had lost his little shop. He became obsessed with the fantasy that people leered at him in the street, and for hours he hid in darkened nickelodeon shows. Then back to the neighborhood bars, where certain strangers seemed prone to buy him drinks and encouraged him to dwell on his misery.

"If anybody did that to me, I'd kill him," one of these furtive Samaritans whispered. "A man who would do a thing like that doesn't deserve to live."

Haas told one friend, "That man did me out of $4,000."

The friend laughed.

Every morning Haas's youngest boy (he had four children) would fetch the *Examiner* from the doorstep and the family would laugh together over the funny "Beany" cartoons. Here was "Beany" as a chorus girl kicking up her skirts and warbling, "Everybody Knows My Number—23." And "Beany" and "Hot Tobasco Burns—the greatest special detective that ever did special detecting—" as slapstick comedians thwacking each other in the pants. Or "Beany" as a grinning, bespectacled magician, pulling out of a hat a bedraggled rabbit labeled "Judge Crawler."

Haas would laugh with his youngsters, and then weep over the disgrace and poverty that had been brought upon them by publication of his shameful past. Once he told his intimate friend, Mrs. Miriam Cohn, that he was going to turn on the gas and kill his family and himself, but she talked him out of that. Miriam, he said often, was the women he should have married. A little later he told her he was practising target shooting in the basement of his house, and showed her the pistol. He also showed her an old-fashioned, single-shot derringer, muttering that he could "always fall back on that." Mrs. Cohn coaxed him out of such wild ramblings, while her husband, the little tailor, listened and said nothing; he regarded the drunken failure of a man with contempt and some fear; but he had telephoned to Burns once, that was enough.

Meanwhile, in Lawlor's court the indicted Murphy was replaced as Ruef's assistant counsel by an expert legal quibbler from the northern end of the state, Thomas B. Dozier. The pressure on Heney intensified, and taunts of every sort were tossed at him: "Half-Irish, half-German, and God knows how yellow," Ach derided, and Heney returned the compliment by terming Ach "the shrewdest and most unscrupulous lawyer ever met in a courtroom."

Among spectators in regular attendance sat underworld thugs— "Butch" Bell, "Bunco" Kelly, "Kid" Nelson, all notorious hoodlums— "a typical graft courtroom," was the *Call's* impression.

Outside the courtroom, the abuse of Heney reached new heights: "bloody-handed, foul-mouthed Heney," the Oakland *Tribune* called him. In one tense clash, the prosecutor threatened to "rawhide half-a-dozen reporters of this city for writing lies,"—this after the *Examiner* had made a hullaballoo over its discovery that Heney had collected a $30,000 legal fee from an East Bay water company in June, 1905— months before he undertook the graft prosecution—and had drawn the most scurrilous inferences, publishing a cartoon showing two repulsive birds in one nest—Heney and Ruef—with the caption, "What's the Difference?" When a Justice of the Supreme Court publicly declined to shake Heney's hand, the *Examiner* gloated, "But there are others who will," and cartooned Heney surrounded by a border of outstretched hands marked: "Uriah Heap," "Benedict Arnold," "Baron Munchausen," "Boss Tweed," "Ananias the First," "Simon Legree," and "The Forty Thieves." An outrageous cartoon depicted a long-necked fatuously simpering "Beany" with "X" penciled over his jugular vein, just under the jaw, and the tag: "X Marks the Spot."

Heney fretted under the mud bath but kept at his duty, and at last, on November 5th, a jury was completed. More than 1,400 veniremen had been examined: the transcript of their testimony, running to 1,375,000 words, was sufficient to fill two books roughly the size of the English Bible. With the calling of witnesses, the shifty-eyed boss's trial finally got under way, and again Gallagher led off; it was his tenth trip to the stand.

Because of the sweltering heat, noise, and foul air which rendered his own courtroom insupportable, Judge Lawlor had procured the use of the auditorium of Carpenters Hall, a building just erected, located on Fulton Street below Van Ness (the site of the present magnificent

City Hall). The auditorium was half-finished, bare and draughty, the carpet was in process of being laid, but there was accommodation for the crowd bent on hearing the evidence against the defendant.

Examination of Gallagher proceeded with normal acerbity on both sides, and Big Jim was still in the chair on Friday, the 13th, when at five minutes after four o'clock Judge Lawlor called a recess and requested counsel to step into his chambers while the jury retired to their room on the floor above. When they were alone, the Judge opened his mind to the attorneys, saying he was gravely concerned with the intensity of public feeling against Ruef; he half-feared some accident, perhaps even an attempt at kidnapping by lynch-minded hotheads; and he wondered whether it might be possible to assign a trustworthy guard to watch over the defendant, without the jury or the public being informed. Ach undertook to look up the law on the subject; then he and Dozier strolled out to join Ruef on the sidewalk in front of the Hall for a smoke.

Heney wandered back into the courtroom and sat down at the counsel table. His bodyguard, John Foley, was seated at one side chatting with a police officer. In excellent fettle, Heney jokingly bragged to Al McCabe, chief clerk of the District Attorney's office, about his having correctly foretold the outcome of the municipal election held the day before on adoption of the Hetch-Hetchy water project. He leaned forward on his elbows as he chatted and laughed in his odd way, with his mouth open. Sitting or standing around the Hall were many persons; scattered on chairs lay copies of that afternoon's *Globe* containing this doggerel:

> *Francis J. Heney, sometimes called Beany,*
> *Cooked an immunity pie.*
> *When it turned out a hash*
> *With a flavor of Ach,*
> *He remarked, "What a Big Boob am I."*

No one paid much heed to a small, neatly dressed man who approached Heney from behind with one hand plunged into the pocket of his overcoat. Suddenly he withdrew that hand, which clutched a revolver, and before Foley could stir, he had fired, aiming at Heney's jugular vein, just below the jaw.

The prosecutor staggered to his feet and brought his hands up to his head; through the fingers dripped blood, spattering law books on the table. Then he pitched forward into McCabe's arms.

"They got me when I wasn't looking," he gasped.

The insignificant man who stood holding the smoking pistol was Morris Haas.

Ruef and his attorneys were on the sidewalk when they heard the shot. Running toward the door, they were crushed back by people pouring out. Somebody shouted that Judge Lawlor had been shot. Another man said it was Gallagher. Then a reporter, dashing for a telephone, yelled that it was Heney. Ruef's automobile stood at the curb and Abe ordered the chauffeur to fetch the nearest doctor. In a few minutes the driver returned with Dr. A.S. Tuschler, hurrying from his office just around the corner on Van Ness Avenue. The doctor went inside, leaving Ruef unnoticed in the excited throng; at his driver's suggestion, Abe slipped away to Tuschler's office and waited there for half an hour. Then, returning to the Hall, he was refused admittance by the policeman at the door until a Burns detective happened along and identified him.

Judge Lawlor was in his chambers with his stenographer and the porter of the building when the pistol shot was heard, apparently coming from the street. Lawlor went to the window, and seeing the crowd tumbling out, hastened to the courtroom, pushing past the porter when the latter tried protectively to bar his way. The Judge found Heney lying on the dusty floor, his head propped on a scrap of carpet. A physician who had happened to be in the room, Dr. H.A. Franck, was bending over the wounded man. Lawlor ordered the doors closed and no one be allowed to enter or leave, then knelt beside Heney, who looked up and mumbled: "Judge, they've got me at last."

Lawlor put a hand on Heney's forehead and replied, "You're not so badly hurt as that."

"Yes I am, Judge," Heney spoke with difficulty. "Tell my wife ... I love her better than anyone in the world."

"Yes, I will," the Judge interposed, and glanced at Dr. Franck, who shook his head, indicating that the wound was fatal. Lawlor instructed Assistant District Attorney O'Gara to take Heney's dying statement and turned to the business of re-establishing order.

O'Gara knelt and wrote down Heney's painfully articulated words: "I believe I am going to die. I wish to make a dying statement. I was sitting at my table when I felt what I thought was a blow. I do not know who shot me. I was doing nothing to anyone."

Dr. Franck signed to O'Gara to stop, and just then Dr. Tuschler came in. An ambulance had been called, and Heney was placed in it and carried to Central Emergency Hospital, four blocks away. He remained conscious all the while.

At 5:15 P.M., Judge Lawlor reconvened court in the jury's room, sitting on the stairs just outside the door. At the sound of the shot, the jurors had run toward the courtroom, but had been held back by bailiffs, although one juror did glimpse Heney on the floor. Lawlor sent the jury back to the St. Francis Hotel under strong guard, and ordered Ruef into protective custody to thwart any attempt at mob vengeance. The defendant was quickly removed to the county jail, where thirty extra policemen were posted, armed with rifles, to augment the Sheriff's force. Ach and Dozier lingered in the Judge's chambers for an hour, dazed by the event, both expressing abhorrence of the shooting.

"My God!" exclaimed Ach. "I wish I had never taken a criminal case in my life! I'll never take another when I get out of this one! This comes of having armed men in the courtroom!"

Finally they left by a side door, guarded by deputies.

A second too late, guard Foley and others had leaped on Heney's assailant and wrested the gun from his hand. He struggled, but was wedged into a corner of the jury box and ringed around by police officers, who held back the crowd. Burns, who was in Langdon's office when he received word, raced to Carpenters Hall, arriving almost as quickly as Police Chief Biggy and a swarm of uniformed and plainclothes police. Spreckels was right behind them.

Burns and Captain of Detectives Thomas Duke questioned Haas as he lay handcuffed on the floor, demanding the names of his accomplices. Incoherently, Haas protested that he had acted alone.

"I did it for humanity's sake," he babbled hysterically. "I'd be ashamed if I hadn't done it!"

"Why didn't you shoot Ruef for humanity's sake?" demanded Burns.

"Because he didn't denounce me that day. My boy was so proud when my name first appeared in the papers. He said, 'Why, Papa, your name is in the papers.'"

"Whom did you have a talk with about the matter before you came to shoot Mr. Heney?"

"Oh, not a soul! I kept it to myself. I talked to myself all the time. Oh, if Mr. Heney hadn't brought that picture! He showed my picture in stripes! I couldn't say a word!"

A stenographer took down the examination verbatim, and after nearly an hour of questioning Haas was removed to the county jail. Burns had taken charge of the revolver, and that evening Chief Biggy was furious that it had not been turned over to him. Biggy and Burns had been at loggerheads for some time, the Chief resenting what he believed to be Burns's attempts to override his authority in the police department.

News of Heney's shooting flashed through the city with amazing rapidity, and a crowd congregated at Carpenters Hall; within fifteen minutes, five hundred people had assembled, and in less than an hour, a thousand. Violence was in the air; that Heney was mortally wounded was all that was known for sure. The small army of police blocking every entrance to the building was tense.

At Central Emergency Hospital, meanwhile, the prosecutor was undergoing an hour-long examination with fortitude, once even managing to muster a grin and mutter: "I'm feeling pretty good for a fellow as badly done up as I am. I'll live to prosecute 'em yet."

The doctors were impressed by his refusal to die, for it was only by a hair's-breadth that he had escaped being killed outright. His odd habit of smiling with his mouth open, and the fact that he had been sitting down, forcing the assassin to fire from above, miraculously had saved him: the bullet, after ripping through the lower right cheek, had taken a downward-slanting path, barely missing the main arteries and the brain, and was lodged below the jaw on the left side.

The hospital corridors became clogged with persons of all conditions eager to hear the medical report. Mrs. Heney arrived quickly in the company of Spreckels and his wife, and after them, the high and the lowly,—students, politicians, fellow lawyers, workingmen, churchmen, businessmen.

At 9:00 P.M. Heney's condition was felt to be precarious, and it was decided to transfer him to Lane Hospital (today, the Presbyterian Medical Center) at Clay and Webster streets hard by Temple Sherith Israel, about a mile away. He was placed in a horse-drawn ambulance; as he was being carried out, he spoke to Dr. Beasley (the same Beasley who had called for hanging Ruef on "Black Friday") with unimpaired nerve: "Good night, doctor. I'll see you again."

Several hundred hushed sympathizers escorted the ambulance, and upon its reaching the foot of the slope leading up to the hospital, they insisted on unhitching the horses and pulling the vehicle gently over the uneven pavement, in order to spare the wounded man any unnecessary jolting. From then on until dawn, bulletins were issued hourly. These grew steadily more hopeful, and by morning it was estimated that Heney had a fighting chance to live. He had never asked for more.

7 Vigilantism Again

San Francisco did not sleep that night. Lynch fury gripped the city and crowds milled through the streets, howling threats. A mob surged around the *Examiner* building, where the lower floor was sandbagged and rifles were passed out to the staff; the *Examiner's* ridiculing of the martyred prosecutor was held responsible for directing the assassin's aim: the "Beany" cartoon was remembered,— "X Marks the Spot."

Two hundred members of the Citizens League for Justice met and demanded swift punitive action. Richard Cornelius, who had been president of the carmen's union destroyed by Patrick Calhoun, boldly asserted: "The time has come when there should be a Vigilance Committee to deal with the criminals in this city!"

Hiram Johnson spoke as forcefully: "This is the most dastardly thing that ever was done! I have no doubt that Haas was hired. It strikes me there is no use going on trying this rat three or four times more. He is the man who is back of this. He is the man who blew up Gallagher's house."

"Who is the rat?" called half-a-dozen voices.

"Why, Ruef!"

Several prominent attorneys volunteered to carry on for Heney without compensation, and Johnson, Matt I. Sullivan, and J.J. Dwyer were chosen. The League issued a summons to a mass meeting of protest to be staged in Dreamland Rink the next evening; everybody was urged to be there. Two other rallies were scheduled to be held in churches on the day after that.

Expressions of revulsion at the deed and of sympathy for the victim's family and associates poured in from societies and lodges, from university presidents and famous men and women at home and abroad, from the Attorney General of the United States, from the White House.

"Inexpressibly shocked," wired President Roosevelt to Rudolph Spreckels. "The infamous character of the would-be assassin no less than the infamous character of the deed call attention in a striking way to the true character of the forces against which Heney and you and your associates have been fighting." To Mrs. Heney, an equally forthright Presidential telegram expressed "horror and detestation of the deed" and praised Heney for "the absolutely fearless way he has attacked and exposed corruption without regard to the political or social prominence of the offenders or to the dangerous character of the work."

Almost without exception, the press of the nation condemned the murderous attack. In San Francisco the editorial outcry was stentorous.

MURDEROUS HIGHER-UPS! screamed the *Bulletin*.

"Will they stop at nothing?" despaired the *Call*. "Are not stealing, perjury, bribing, dynamiting, murder enough?... Who hired Haas to shoot Heney? There is no proof,—not yet. But those who hired him shall not be guiltless of his wrong!"

The *Examiner* suddenly fawned on Heney as "courageous," called his attacker "cowardly," and piously prayed for the prosecutor's recovery. And the *Chronicle* registered equal abhorrence of the "appalling crime," which "adds another to the long record of disasters which have befallen this unfortunate community."

But the Los Angeles *Times* could not forego its habitual venom-ousness. For immediate comment it hastily inserted at edition time an editorial headed, COURT OF JUSTICE NO PLACE FOR GUNS, which roundly denounced judicial laxity in San Francisco, by contrast held up Los Angeles courts as models of decorum, and contained not one word of regret that Heney had been shot or expression of hope that he might survive. Nor did a word of sympathy or sense of outrage emanate officially from San Francisco's fashionable clubs. And many labor groups also remained pointedly silent.

Saturday afternoon, Burns and Langdon went to the county jail to interrogate Haas. The two policemen on watch refused to let Burns enter the prisoner's cell, by order, they said, of Chief Biggy or a police commissioner or both; they seemed to be confused as to the order's source. Langdon angrily warned that Burns was his regularly deputized agent, and at last the policemen yielded. The visitors talked with Haas more than an hour, and Langdon professed to be amazed at the man's coolness.

"Haas displayed a cunning that convinces me that he is playing a deep game," he reported afterward. "He was as calm and as cool as I am at this moment, and when he didn't want to answer a question he didn't mind saying so. I am convinced that Haas was egged on to his crime by others."

Burns reported that Haas said he was urged frequently to kill Heney "by certain persons whose names I won't tell you, and I also talked to other people about killing Heney and was advised not to do it. In addition to that, certain persons approached me several times and referred to the time I was thrown off the Ruef jury, saying, 'I'd never stand that roast,' and, 'I'd kill a man who did that to me,' and similar things."

Further than to say that these unnamed persons had pestered him with murderous suggestions, Haas refused to be drawn out; but he did confess that these persons were interested in the outcome of the Ruef trial.

In direct contradiction, Chief Biggy published his own conclusion. "I am convinced that the shooting of Mr. Heney was the single act of the prisoner Haas. The evidence that the police department has obtained up to this time does not reveal any conspiracy, but strengthens the theory that Haas did the shooting without being influenced by others, and that the inciting cause was a personal grievance."

The antagonism between Burns and Biggy thereupon flared into the open.

On Saturday evening, an hysterical throng of five thousand persons jammed Dreamland Rink, and another five thousand collected in Steiner Street outside. Speaker after speaker assailed the graft "higher-ups," but pleaded with the crowd to let the law take its course; Mayor Taylor presided, and implored the assemblage not to revive San Francisco's tradition of vigilantism. Every mention of Heney's name brought the throng to their feet cheering, and again and again the shout was taken up, "Throw the *Examiner* out!" Phelan, Spreckels, labor leaders, clergymen of many faiths, attorneys denounced the "eatanswill gazettes" of the "gutter press," which were believed to have prompted the assassin.

"I will mention names," declared Phelan, deeply moved, and harshly he listed William H. Crocker, Drum, Glass, and Calhoun as corruptionists,—men of his intimacy, whose ways he knew. When Spreckels arose, the crowd went almost berserk with excitement, and the agitation continued while the financier expressed shame over Heney's shooting,—"shame that such an act should have been committed in the city of my birth, the city for which I am fighting and will continue to fight!

"The poisoned matter that has been printed concerning Francis J. Heney has weaned you away from the truth," he went on emotionally. "You have believed some of the charges that have been made against this little man [who] has been fearlessly fighting hundreds of millions of dollars of organized wealth! . . . I want to say to you, and it may be news, that Francis J. Heney has not accepted one dollar of compensation for his work in this prosecution, nor will he accept one dollar of compensation!"

Repeatedly the speakers called for orderly procedure,—against Ruef, against the "higher-ups," against Haas. "The prosecution will go on," Langdon pledged.

When finally the rally was with difficulty dispersed, after adopting resolutions demanding vengeance on Heney's enemies, the speakers were compelled to address the great overflow crowd outside.

In the midst of these speeches a message arrived from Ingleside jail. It was read aloud: at 8:40 that evening, Morris Haas had been found dead in his cell, slain by a single bullet fired into the center of his forehead.

Was it suicide? Or was it cleverly plotted murder?

8   The End of Biggy

Had Haas ended his life violently in remorse for his atrocious deed? Or had he been shot to seal his lips? If suicide, who had smuggled the death weapon into his double-guarded cell? By what means? With whose complicity? A furious controversy burst around Police Chief William J. Biggy, friends of the prosecution blaming Biggy for Haas's removal,—so opportune for his accomplices, if accomplices there were. Either the Police Chief was totally incompetent or Biggy had sold out to the "higher-ups," the cry echoed, and the latter theory was favored by a wide segment of people in the aroused city.

The inquest on Haas was thorough and developed irreconcilable contradictions. Haas had been shot with an antique pistol, a 41-caliber, single-shot derringer, about three inches long, an inch thick at the butt, and five-eighths of an inch through at the muzzle. Burns insisted that the unusual weapon, for which ammunition was difficult to procure, had either been slipped to Haas in jail in the hope that he might kill himself,—or that he had been murdered in a simulated suicide. Burns and Captain Duke, both experienced police officers, had searched Haas in Carpenters Hall before the prisoner was turned over to Biggy's custody, and they had found no weapon except the revolver used to shoot Heney. Two policemen searched the prisoner again upon his arrival at the jail, and no weapon was found by them, they testified. Biggy insisted that the tiny pistol had been concealed in Haas's elastic-sided high shoe and was overlooked by the searchers, although three of these were his own men. He preferred departmental charges of negligence against Duke and the others.

Mrs. Haas and Mrs. Cohn had visited Haas in jail and talked with him, in the presence of a policemen, a few hours before his death. Burns intimated that one of these might have conveyed the gun to the prisoner, but they denied it. Haas's wife said she had never seen the derringer before; Mrs. Cohn recognized it as the firearm Haas had shown her, muttering that he could "always fall back on that."

Haas had been under constant surveillance by two policemen stationed outside his open cell door all Friday night and Saturday. They testified that the prisoner had been wretchedly sick Friday night, vomiting repeatedly, but on Saturday he seemed composed and even cheerful. They said that both nights Haas had asked permission to sleep with his shoes on, and while they thought the request odd, they could see no harm in it and had consented. They had not examined his shoes, they admitted, but both were positive that they would have noticed the bulge caused by an inch-thick object tucked into either shoe.

Haas's body had been found on the floor of the cell—where it had rolled from the cot—shortly after he went to bed Saturday evening; he had pulled the blanket over his head at once to shut out the light. The guards had heard a shot; they ran in and found the man dead. One trouser leg was rolled up above the elastic garter, and they thought they detected an indentation in the flesh above the ankle, which might have been produced by prolonged pressure. In Haas's right-hand trousers' pocket was an extra cartridge for the derringer, although both Burns and Captain Duke were sure the cartridge had not been in the pocket when Haas was searched. There were almost no powder burns on the dead man's forehead, indicating, experts said, either that he had been shot from a distance greater than three feet or that the muzzle of the pistol had been pressed tightly against the skin.

When Chief Biggy appeared at the inquest with a lawyer to "represent his interests," Langdon was flabbergasted; by law, the District Attorney was legal adviser to the Chief of Police.

"Is it possible that Chief Biggy is trying to block this investigation?" Langdon questioned, and the coroner refused to let the lawyer participate in the proceedings.

The corpse was placed before the coroner's jury, the shoes put on the feet, and the derringer slipped inside one shoe; then each juror individually examined the body, looked and felt around the ankles and feet, and all agreed that they could not avoid noticing the bulge in the shoe.

The testimony of other witnesses proved to be vague and inconclusive. Mrs. Cohn confirmed that Haas had told her about people egging him on to kill Heney, but she maintained that she could not recall what names he had mentioned, although she was sure he did mention names.

The coroner's verdict was suicide, and immediately the organs of the prosecution turned on Chief Biggy viciously. Said the *Call:*

... Could Biggy have framed it better for the "higher-ups" if he had been directly in their pay? To relieve himself and further to comfort the murder conspirators, Biggy invents and springs the silly tale—a tale discredited by his own men—that Haas had the pistol and the cartridges in his shoes. If Haas did not kill himself, who did? Perhaps Biggy can point to the man.

Biggy, a literal-minded man and honest in his actions, once before in his career had demonstrated a propensity to override his associates and assert his prerogatives too officiously. His fitness to serve as Police Chief had come under fire before the Haas climax, and two months previously, Rudolph Spreckels had told him bluntly that he ought to resign, that the prosecution had lost confidence in him inasmuch as he was surrounding himself with "dishonest, grafting subordinates" just like the clique Jere Dinan had built up while Chief. Biggy bridled at this trespass by Spreckels upon his official dignity, and he had further come to believe that Burns was scheming to get his job,—a suspicion in which Biggy was encouraged by newspaper meddling. Now the prosecution press demanded that Biggy be dismissed, and denounced him as a menace to the peace of the city.

MAYOR TAYLOR—STOP BIGGY BEFORE HE TURNS THE POLICE FORCE BODILY OVER TO THE SERVICE OF THE MEN AND INTERESTS THAT HAVE SO OUTRAGED JUSTICE! STOP HIM *NOW!* So read a front-page headline in the *Call.*

"Biggy tried to keep Burns from getting to Haas," read another at-

tack. "Why? ... To crown his stupidity—is he really so stupid?—
Biggy lets the assassin kill himself."

This excoriation of the unhappy Chief kept up day after day.

. . . If Biggy had done half his duty, Haas would now be alive and would
be telling who prompted him to shoot Heney [ranted the *Call*]. Biggy is a
man of shame and no honor. He is not fit to be the chief of anything.
The whole currish pack of rich criminals whom Heney was driving toward
the penitentiary is on the trail again,—and Chief of Police Biggy hunts and
yelps with it. Nobody respects Biggy. Not even Biggy.

The harassed Chief became distraught, and his critics insinuated
that he was drinking immoderately and frequenting disorderly houses.
Someone (the *Bulletin* and Older received the blame) egged on his
long-estranged wife to invade his office and create a scene, to the
scandal of the police department. The *Call* maintained that the two
policemen Biggy had personally detailed to guard Haas had been
notorious Ruef placemen for years, with records of political skuldug-
gery. The Citizens League for Justice let it be known it was drawing up
a formal accusation of incompetency and dereliction of duty against
the Chief for submission to the police commissioners.

The furor was unabated when, on the last day of November—
two weeks after Heney had been shot—Police Commissioner Hugo D.
Keil, who lived at Belvedere, on the northern shore of the Golden
Gate opposite San Francisco, received a telephone call from a man
who would not give his name and whose voice Keil did not recognize,
saying that "the man you know" would be calling on Keil that evening.
Biggy had been confiding his troubles to Keil, a particular friend. Late
that evening, Biggy left his office at police headquarters; in his
pocket was his written resignation, and on his desk he left a letter explaining his reason for resigning, namely, that he was being "hounded
and worried to death."

On his way to the water front he stopped in a saloon, and purposely or by inadvertence left his service revolver in the washroom.
The police launch, *Patrol,* which would take him to Belvedere, was
moored at the Ferry Building at the foot of Market Street, with a
policeman on board. While waiting for the launch's civilian engineer,

William Murphy, to show up, Biggy invited the policeman to smoke a cigar with him in the cabin, which the man did, although smoking on duty was a breach of police discipline. When Murphy arrived, Biggy waved the policeman ashore, although police regulations required that more than one member of the force should be aboard the launch on all trips.

The half-hour run to Belvedere was made smoothly. Keil was awaiting his visitor, and in his home Biggy and he had a long conversation. At first, the Chief was much agitated, and declaring he could no longer endure the newspaper attacks, handed his resignation to Keil; but the commissioner refused to accept it and tried to talk him out of quitting, saying that only patience was needed, the tempest would blow out, given time. Gradually Biggy became calmer, smoked a cigar and drank a whisky congenially with his host, and when he arose to leave seemed quite restored again; he promised to do nothing about quitting for the present. But Keil was worried. Biggy had told him that he had been shadowed for days by men whom he knew to be in Burns's employ, for what reason he could only surmise. That the rival detective forces of the prosecution and the graft defense undoubtedly contained men of dubious and even desperate character, who might be capable of some violent action on their own account, both Keil and Biggy realized; upon learning, therefore, that Biggy was not armed, Keil insisted that he borrow his own revolver. Biggy laughed as he slipped the pistol into his overcoat pocket, but the commissioner watched the *Patrol* pull away into the darkness with foreboding.

At about 10:45 P.M., when the launch was passing Alcatraz island, Murphy, who was stationed at the helm forward, glanced around and saw the Chief leaning on the after rail, gazing intently at the water. Previously, Biggy had complained of feeling cold and had taken shelter in the cabin amidships. Murphy was occupied with the motor and steering and did not look around again until the *Patrol* was idling into the Ferry Building berth. Then he discovered that he was the only person aboard.

He notified the harbor police, and the launch was sent back over the route, but no trace was found. When word was brought to Commissioner Keil, the messenger found him pacing up and down in his

living room, greatly distressed, with all the lights in the house burning
brightly.

"I knew it!" Keil exclaimed, and told of the nocturnal visit.

Over this disappearance burst another furor, this time the prosecution forces under attack for supposedly having harried the Police
Chief to his death by suicide. Accidental drowning was ruled out, it
was believed, by a number of factors: Biggy was a strong swimmer,
and would at least have made some outcry if he had fallen over-
board, yet the engineer had heard nothing; also, although the *Patrol*
was notoriously crank, rocking at the slightest undulation of the
water, the bay was unusually placid that night, with almost no wind,
and Murphy had felt no sudden lurch at any time during the return
trip.

But against the suicide theory was Biggy's apparent cheerfulness
when he said good night to Commissioner Keil. Moreover, the Chief
was a devout Catholic and might be expected to have strong religious
scruples against self-destruction.

There remained the possibility of deliberate murder. But by
whom? Who feared betrayal or involvement by Biggy? The riddle of
Haas's equivocal death was spun again, with no solution forthcoming
satisfactory to everybody.

Two weeks after the disappearance, Biggy's body was recovered
from the bay, but neither it nor his clothing gave any enlightenment.
He was accorded a civic funeral, with a requiem mass in St. Mary's
Cathedral, and Father McQuade, delivering the eulogy, appealed for
charity in judging the manner of his death.

"For God's sake, and in the face of no evidence to the contrary,
give him the benefit of the doubt," the priest urged, averring that it
could have been nothing but accidental drowning.

At the embittered inquest two days later, the puzzle still was not
cracked. There were conflicts in testimony, recriminations from both
camps, charges and counter-charges, but no clear picture evolved: the
engineer, for example, could not even say exactly where his passenger
vanished; the events were shrouded in harbor mists. The jury returned a verdict of accidental death, and censured the prosecution
and its allies for having contributed to the tragedy.

Several years later, the engineer, Murphy, went insane. Often he was heard screaming: "I don't know who did it,—but I swear I didn't do it!"

9 A Plaque in the Bay

In Lane Hospital, the bullet was removed from Heney's neck muscles by delicate surgery (it had lodged about one inch below the left ear) and thereafter his recovery progressed rapidly. (On Heney's advice, Dr. Beasley locked the extracted bullet in the hospital safe and refused to surrender it to Biggy's police.) His mind never lost its clarity, while his physicial stamina and courage delighted the medical men. One week after the shooting, he was pronounced out of danger, and in a message of rededication to the public he indicated his conviction that he had been preserved by divine Providence for the accomplishment of a predestined task,—the regeneration of San Francisco.

Francis Heney was not a notably religious man, but first of all he gave thanks humbly to "Almighty God for my miraculous escape from death . . . Henceforth my life shall be consecrated to the just enforcement of the law and to the principle that no man shall be above the law. . . . If the assassin's bullet suddenly disclosed to the public the hideousness of the gigantic conspiracy to defeat the law, then I shall feel that . . . my poor efforts have met with immeasurable benefit to my beloved city and state. . . .

"Let us now highly resolve," he urged in a fervent exordium, in which his idealism, his strength, and his deficiencies all were plain, "that we shall not only not tolerate crime in any form, but that we shall likewise cast out and discredit the tolerators, the apologists, and the abettors of crime; that justice shall not be made a mockery in our courts. . . ; that the plausible shall not be accepted for the true, whether uttered by the higher-ups or the lower-downs, by honest-minded weak men or by designing trimmers."

Ten days after he was shot, Heney celebrated Thanksgiving Day by taking a ride in Golden Gate Park with his wife, Burns, and

Spreckels; his face was swathed in bandages, but to passers-by who waved a frantic welcome he returned his familiar, indomitable grin.

Meanwhile, the trials went forward. In Ruef's case, Judge Lawlor swept aside a mass of protests by the defense lawyers that their client could no longer get a fair trial, in view of Heney's shooting, and ordered the proceedings to continue with Hiram Johnson, Matt I. Sullivan, and J.J. Dwyer supporting Assistant District Attorney O'Gara.

And in Judge Dunne's court, E.A.S. Blake went on trial as the go-between in the attempt to bribe talesman Kelly. Blake was defended by two attorneys, who opened with the now routine challenge of the indictment, which they contended had been invalidated by the misspelling of the name of one witness. When Langdon cited decisions of the State Supreme Court holding that such minor clerical errors do not abridge the rights of a defendant, Judge Dunne purred concurrence; these rulings, he remarked, "seem to be based on commonsense,—something," he added with a winning smile, "which we do not always meet in judicial proceedings."

The jury box was filled quickly; Newburgh, Murphy, Kelly, Heney, and Judges Sturtevant and Lawlor were called as witnesses; and in one week Blake was convicted. He faced a maximum sentence of five years in prison and a $5,000 fine.

This *dénouement* brought into the District Attorney's office a sudden flood of evidence tending to show jury-tampering; the foreman of the jury which had disagreed in Ruef's Parkside trial even expressed contrition publicly for not having spoken up sooner.

"Had I known then what I have since learned about jury-tampering," he confessed, "I could have sprung a sensation in court. That jury was not an honest one."

He related how, during the course of the trial, three jurors who were contractors received mailed invitations to bid on various United Railroads construction projects, although none had ever done any work for the street-car company. With the court's consent, they submitted bids, and all three received contracts, one for a $50,000 job. The foreman also recalled that when the jury retired to ponder a verdict, two jurors had drawn apart and refused to discuss anything except outright acquittal; they had never budged from this obstinacy.

Arraignment of the attorneys, Murphy and Newburgh, followed Blake's conviction, and during a recess in the examination of the grand jurors who had had the temerity to indict them (these defendants, too, started the delays at the beginning), Blake exploded a bombshell. In court, before Judge Dunne, he confessed the plot to bribe Kelly. Any suggestion that he was buying immunity by this confession was nailed by both Langdon and Dunne in explicit preliminary questioning, during which Blake swore that he was motivated by a desire to ease his conscience, and had been offered nothing and promised nothing by the prosecution.

He revealed that he had become acquainted with Newburgh through a mix-up in their mail, Newburgh occupying an office across the hall from his own. "He introduced me to Murphy. He showed me a list of the prospective jurors and asked if I knew any of them. I told him I did, I knew Mr. Kelly very well."

At Murphy's request, Blake sounded out Kelly on his feeling toward Ruef, and "two or three days after I met them both at the office. They [Murphy and Newburgh] said they had $1,000 they would be willing to give to Kelly, provided he would vote 'not guilty' for their client. He [Murphy] asked me if I would submit that offer to Kelly, and I did. The first time I offered him only $500." Kelly's refusal, and his subsequent holding out for $1,000 were recounted. "I reported back to Murphy that Kelly would accept $1,000. That practically settled the matter."

After his arrest, Blake continued, an attorney whom he did not know appeared to defend him, saying he had been sent by a "mutual friend,"—who turned out to be Murphy and Newburgh. Blake had paid this attorney no fee. Neither did he know who his bail bondsmen were; they had been secured by his counsel.

After his arrest, Blake continued, Murphy and Newburgh had assured him that he need not worry, that they would do everything possible to help him, and should he be convicted would provide for his wife. Then, after his conviction, Murphy had reassured Blake that he possessed good grounds for a new trial. "They said, 'When we get up into the higher court, it will be thrown out,' or something like that." Murphy proposed to pay him $10,000 which would be handed over the day he was sentenced, and also would pay his wife $100 a month as long as he was in prison,—provided Blake would take the sentence and say nothing to implicate others. The $10,000 was to be deposited in advance with a trustworthy third party, chosen by Blake; and as proof of his ability to deliver, Murphy had flashed promissory notes in the aggregate amount of $7,500, all made payable to Murphy and signed by Abraham Ruef and endorsed by the latter's father and sister.

"I selected the third party," Blake concluded, "and they said he would be all right. He had the $10,000 and he told me the $10,000 would be paid to me on the day I was sentenced."

Blake was returned to jail, and Ruef and Murphy laughed heartily over his confession (after their dismay wore off) and branded everything he said a monument of lies.

"The whole thing is a farce," chuckled Newburgh.

Then amid the turmoil over Heney's shooting and Haas's death, Murphy was brought to trial. Blake took the stand and retold his story, while Murphy sat with bowed head. Blake added the piquant detail that while dickering over Kelly's vote, Murphy had told him (Blake) that he would be willing to pay Kelly as much as $5,000 if the jury should stand ten to two, or eleven to one, for conviction.

Toward the end of August, the witness continued, Newburgh began to suspect that Kelly had "snitched," warned that Burns detectives were shadowing Blake, and said the latter must make an affidavit right away charging Kelly with soliciting a bribe. Accordingly, Blake said, he went to an attorney and swore to the false affidavit,—the same affidavit Murphy had produced dramatically in Judge Lawlor's court. A few hours before his arrest, Blake recalled, Murphy and Newburgh had taken him to dinner in the new Pup restaurant and assured him that despite anything Kelly might say, he could never be convicted on one man's word; at that time Murphy had handed him $50 and promised he would receive $30 a week during the trial and $5,000 afterward with which to re-establish himself in the contracting business.

Blake's attorney was put on the stand and admitted that Murphy had sent him to Blake, and that Blake had paid him no fee. Then Heney was called as a witness. It was his first appearance in a court-room since he had been shot, and although he spoke with a slight impediment caused by the bullet, he testified firmly and clearly, de-scribing the scene in Judge Lawlor's courtroom when Kelly walked in: "As Kelly stepped up to the gate, Ach said to Murphy, 'There she goes!' Murphy was very excited and began addressing the court from his chair. He attempted to rise, stumbling against the chair occupied by Ruef. He finally came around the table, talking all the time."

Murphy glared and stirred uneasily while Heney testified.

Newburgh denied making any bribe overtures. Murphy took the stand and denied making any offer of a bribe, denied every charge made by Blake, except that of sounding out veniremen in a legitimate way.

A list of prospective jurors was shown to him, with "$1,000" penciled after Kelly's name; Murphy denied that he had made the mark.

The defense called nineteen witnesses who testified to the bad character of Blake and eleven who praised Murphy's reputation for probity, among these latter being gentle, kindly Father Henry H. Wyman, head of the Paulist Fathers at Old St. Mary's Church in Chinatown.

This resort to acquittal by compurgation caught the prosecution off guard; it had never occurred to them that Murphy's character might be invoked to establish innocence, and in summing up, District Attorney Langdon sought to retrieve his oversight.

"People have been brought into this court to shake hands with Murphy simply for effect," he cried scornfully. "They have asked us why we have brought no witnesses here to repudiate Murphy's character. We have one. Our greatest character witness against Frank J. Murphy is Frank J. Murphy. Is there any one of you twelve gentle-men who has been able to look him in the eye during this trial? Did you notice that on the witness stand his eyes were shifting con-stantly, unable to look straight into the face of any man? There sits our character witness! See him there,—fat, sleek, with his big jowls showing that he is well fed! Isn't criminality written all over his face? Murphy—the great lawyer—who has been defending bunco

steerers and yeggmen in the courts of this city, and who then undertook the defense of that arch criminal, Ruef! Murphy, just from the
hayfields of Watsonville some six or eight years ago, was taken in
hand by this buncoman, 'Emmons Arthur Show-em-up' Blake, and
was sold a gold brick! You know that jurors have been corrupted in
these graft trials before! You know why those two jurors tied up that
other Ruef jury!"

When Langdon closed, Mrs. Murphy was in tears, with her husband ostentatiously consoling her.

The jury retired at noon. On the first ballot they stood nine to
three in favor of acquittal, and on the tenth, taken at 11:35 that
night, they voted unanimously "not guilty."

Mrs. Murphy shrieked and fainted upon announcement of the
verdict.

Newburgh next was placed on trial, and again Blake—who meanwhile had been sentenced by Judge Dunne to four years in prison—
repeated his sordid story. This time the prosecution brought character
witnesses to testify against both Newburgh and Murphy, including the
Mayor of Watsonville, Murphy's home town, who stated that
Murphy's reputation was unsavory there. Newburgh wept on the
stand, spoke of his fourteen years practising law, and revealed incidentally that as a beginner he once had shared an office with Francis
J. Heney and R. Porter Ashe, the attorney under indictment for kidnaping Fremont Older; they had split the rent three ways. Newburgh's counsel assailed Blake as "a moral monstrosity, a monumental spectacle of human depravity, reeking with the slime and grime
of perjury," and after several hours of debate, the jury reported that
it was deadlocked at six to six. The panel was discharged, and two
months later Newburgh was brought to trial again. Blake, suffering
from erysipelas, was too ill to complete his testimony this time, but
Kelly was a witness, and Newburgh again repeated his denials under
oath. And the jury voted "not guilty."

Echoes of the case reverberated for months. The Paulist community at Old St. Mary's had become quite as divided in opinion re-
specting the graft trials as the rest of the city. The church, destroyed in
the great fire, was in process of rebuilding, and some of the Paulists
were scandalized when Father Wyman accepted the gift of a pulpit
from Frank Murphy and his wife. A silver plaque affixed to this gift

was engraved with the donors' names and a date: "December 14, 1908." This was two days after Murphy's acquittal. The offended fathers resented what they considered a *quid pro quo* for Wyman's testimony, and one night two of them stole into the church, unscrewed the plaque, and threw it into the bay. Then their consciences got the better of their indignation and they confessed to Father Wyman.

10 "Dare You Acquit This Judas?"

When Ruef's trial resumed, Henry Ach received the treatment that had been handed out to Francis J. Heney for month after irritating month: Heney's volunteer replacements—Johnson, Sullivan, and Dwyer—snubbed the defense counsel, declining even to exchange a "good morning," and throughout the witness-questioning goaded, taunted, and quibbled in the defense's best style, individually and as a team. Johnson excelled in guying and mimicry, Sullivan in explosions of scathing contempt, and Dwyer was a canny disputer of legalities. O'Gara, as Assistant District Attorney nominally in charge, scarcely counted.

Again and again Ach theatrically protested against being made the butt of "insults"; the court was equable, but hardly sympathetic. Again and again Ach met his match in Johnson, who aped his mannerisms, pacing up and down as Ach paced, flinging out his arms in Ach's stage-like gestures, echoing Ach's words.

"Submit it!" Ach would cry, and Johnson would repeat in the same tone, "Submit it!"

"I point to the whole record!" Ach shouted, and Johnson echoed, "I point to the whole record!"

And when Ach became offensive in pressing a witness, Johnson would bristle: "I won't tolerate having a witness sneered at! You will be interrupted every time you make one of your rotten insinuations! You may howl, but not without a protest from me!"

It was the game that had been played against Heney, but in reverse. In vain Ach appealed to the court for protection against such "unprofessional conduct."

"Counsel for the defense is gibing and jeering, snarling and sneering, not only at me but at the court," Johnson retorted hotly. "I am here performing one of the highest duties given to an attorney,—acting without compensation in place of a stricken brother."

Judge Lawlor did what he could to restrain the passages at arms, but refused to yield to Ach's innumerable objections, grimly reminding counsel that "such objections are well calculated to undermine the administration of justice. This trial must get along."

And get along it did.

Alex Lathan angered Johnson when the boss's former chauffeur balked at repeating the evidence he had given before the grand jury about the ride to Ford's office with the shirt box. Lathan had been traced to Seattle, arrested there, and brought back to testify, but he proved obstinate, wringing his hands, moistening his lips, wiping sweat from his forehead, glancing appealingly toward Ruef,—but refusing to testify. His indictment for perjury followed.

Outside the courtroom feverish excitement mounted amid an epidemic of arguments. The Haas inquest, Murphy's trial, the conviction of Peter Claudianes in the Gallagher dynamiting, Biggy's vanishing,—all these were proceeding concurrently with Ruef's trial, and the public's attention was torn ten ways at once. Interest was hectic, and Lawlor's courtroom in Carpenters Hall was thronged, many spectators wearing the badge of the Citizens League for Justice conspicuously, to the grievous distress of defense counsel laboring under the glare of hostile eyes.

While Biggy's body was still being sought, the prosecution rested its case against the boss. The defense called no witnesses. Then opposing counsel gave over three days to fiery summations.

Ach averred that Ruef was the "victim of a most dastardly, vicious, and outrageous plot.... Who made Rudolph Spreckels the god almighty of San Francisco? ... Andy Wilson comes here like a dude, jingling his ill-gotten gains in his pocket. With Gallagher it is ditto. Do you think Calhoun, too, is a silly ass who wouldn't know better than to draw criminal money from the Mint? Criminal money? Criminal fiddlesticks!"

But it was commented that at no time did Ach deny that Ruef had bribed the supervisors.

Dozier, in coarser vein, likened Gallagher to "a hippopotamus, sweating perjury from every pore. On the stand he had the easy nonchalance of a race-track tout. As for the supervisors, they went into the immunity bath in corruption and there were raised in glory,—the crooked made straight and liars truthful!" At 10:00 P.M., Lawlor shut off Dozier, and the next day Hiram Johnson spoke for the prosecution.

The courtroom was jammed with a brilliant audience—educators, politicians, clergymen, attorneys, social leaders, the pick of the community—when the prosecution opened what was to be the forensic masterpiece of his career. On the sidewalk stood another crowd in drenching rain. League for Justice badges were everywhere, for the fate of Abe Ruef, the *bête noire* of so many of the city's inhabitants for so many years was at issue. The mood of the crowd was determined.

As a virtuoso of invective, Johnson outdid himself; his excoriation of Ruef and his attorneys was the most blistering ever heard in a California courtroom. He had received a warning from Burns that four of the jurors had been "fixed," and took up this challenge, glaring into the faces of the jurymen one by one while he dared them to acquit "this Judas."

"Are you afraid to convict him?" he hissed. "Are you ready to turn him loose? If you are, by the gods we will know the reason why!"

His fists rose above the tossing forelock as he tore into Ach's pretense of the boss's innocence. Maybe the supervisors did lie, he conceded,—"but whose supervisors were they? Who was the blackest soul in all that black crew? Who was the captain of that pirate ship? Who selected and elected and bought and sold every one of these supervisors, not once, but many times? There he sits,—with a plea of guilty upon his lips,—and you are asked to acquit him! There he sits, Abraham Ruef! With a turn of his hand he upset the government of this city. With a turn of his hand he sold these men, and that's the way he gets his dirty money,—the money he depends upon to get some men to vote him not guilty!"

Under the tongue-lashing, Ruef sat pale and motionless; his aged father sat beside him with bowed head. Johnson alluded to the $50,-000 in small bills paid just after the earthquake and fire and cried: "Picture it! Picture the child and the widow with her mite! Picture the people all over the United States, who with arms outstretched sent this money to the relief of the suffering. Picture those torn and tattered bills, sent for a purpose so holy, and, oh, the irony of fate! Picture them going into the hands of Ford and Ruef, to become the medium of our betrayal in our great helplessness! History contains no instance so base and greedy and horrible as the conduct of this man! Nero fiddling while Rome burned and Caligula with his cruelties were no worse than him! There he stands among the ashes and debris, taking these torn dollar bills with the tears of the givers upon them, and selling his home, your home, my home!"

To the twelve men the issue was put plainly. "Stripped of the fog with which high-priced lawyers bought with stolen gold have tried to shroud the case, the question is this: has the administration of justice become so weak that a political boss, having stolen more than the twelve of you can earn in a lifetime, go unwhipped of justice? Ruef has taught a doctrine here which it will take a generation to unteach. But because he has sold himself for so high a figure, they want you to set him free! Are you going to do it?"

Some of the jurymen quailed and others fidgeted before the flushed face streaming perspiration. Hands clenched, collar wilted, Johnson poured out words torrentially: "Away with dynamiters! Away with assassins! Away with bribers of witnesses and jurors! It is an insult to our intelligence to talk about guilt or innocence! Every inhabitant of this state knows Abe Ruef to be guilty! We have been here for months,—thousands of dollars have been spent,—all this trial, tribulation, and all this blood! Dare you acquit this man? Dare you? If you vote him innocent, may God call upon you the consequences of your act! If you dare to violate your oaths, may that God in His infinite mercy deal with you, because, by heaven, the people of this community will not! For your own sakes, for you and yours, for all who live in this city, for all who rank themselves as patriots instead of thieves,—I demand a verdict of guilty at your hands! And when we have finished, I will ask you again, my friends! . . ."

The jurors paid attentive heed to Judge Lawlor's instructions. At 3:36 P.M. they retired. Just at that moment the rain slackened and a rainbow was seen arching above the ruins of the old City Hall,—an omen of hope?

For hours the jurors wrangled; from their room just above the courtroom came sounds of slamming chairs, loud voices, scuffling. The crowd remained in the Hall, tensely waiting. Ruef paced nervously inside the railing, stopping occasionally to speak to an acquaintance or to drop into his seat wearily. Ach was not present; he was ill, threatened with pneumonia; he had been on the verge of collapse for days. Even after the jurors had gone to dinner, hardly a person left the courtroom; people spoke in whispers instead of chattering; the prosecutors looked glum.

At 8:00 P.M., the jurors resumed. Ruef seemed to have relaxed, and spent most of the evening chatting with two young women stenographers employed by the defense. A rumor circulated that the jurors stood eight to four in favor of conviction, and that the four holdouts were not budging. Then the jury came into the courtroom to have some of the transcript read to them, and at 1:00 A.M., having reached no agreement, they were sent under guard to the St. Francis for the night.

The next morning the courtroom again was filled. As time went by the air grew electric with suspense, and hour by hour Ruef's hopes rose, for the deadlock obviously was holding. The jury went out to lunch and returned. All over the city a hush of expectation settled, and strong police forces were moved into the streets around Carpenters Hall. Detectives swarmed in the courtroom, scrutinizing every movement, listening to every word. The report persisted that the four holdouts for acquittal were still stubbornly resisting all arguments or threats.

Three o'clock came, and at half-past three word was passed that Frank Heney intended to pay a call on Judge Lawlor. At once Fremont Older went into action, telephoning to members of the Minute Men brigade, instructing them to hasten to the courtroom. Soon half a hundred were on hand, with more scattered through the throng outside.

When Heney's auto drove into sight a roar went up from the street. Gathering in volume, it was taken up inside the building. Heney alighted from the car smiling, waved his hat gaily and posed for photographers; then he was escorted into the Hall by Burns and O'Gara. When he appeared in the doorway of the courtroom the cheers were deafening; men and women stood on chairs, waving hats and handkerchiefs in frenzied welcome until the uproar shook the building. For ten minutes it continued,—ominously audible to the twelve jurors directly overhead.

Heney walked to the spot where he had been shot, sat down in the same chair; leaned across the table that had been reddened with his blood, and grinned at his associates. On his lower right cheek showed a livid, freshly healed scar; otherwise he seemed recovered, spirited and energetic, pugnaciously amiable as ever. But a twitching of the mouth muscles when he spoke showed a lasting effect of Haas's bullet. After a few moments he strode into Judge Lawlor's chambers, brushing past Ruef with a level stare; the boss colored. Ten minutes later Heney left the building, again amid a storm of cheers.

Inside the courtroom the air had grown stale, but the crowd sat on. Then, just before four o'clock, the jury reported it had arrived at a verdict.

There was a scramble for seats, and Judge Lawlor warned against demonstrations. In the stillness that followed, the trampling of the jurors' feet coming down the uncarpeted staircase was heard, and they filed into the box; several seemed to be in tears. As each entered, Ruef eyed him fixedly, his face taut and pale.

"We have reached a verdict," the foreman announced.

A sigh swept over the room. The foreman handed the slip of paper to the court clerk, who passed it to the Judge. Lawlor read it in silence, and returned it to the clerk to be entered.

Then the clerk read: "Guilty."

A newspaper reporter sprang up to signal to a confederate at the back of the Hall and six detectives leaped on him, while bailiffs bawled "Order!" But there was no demonstration. Ruef whispered consolingly to his father, asking the old man to break the news to his mother and sisters. The Judge polled the jurors and thanked them for their long service, some of them having been sequestered from families and personal affairs for seventy-six days, since the previous September. Leaving the bench and taking a seat near the jury-box rail, the Judge told them, in a voice trembling with emotion: "You have performed a public duty and performed it well. Your action has met with the warm approval of the court."

The jury was discharged, and Ruef was remanded to jail pending sentencing. Then the courtroom was cleared expeditiously. Ruef listened to expressions of regret from friends with his customary nonchalance. The two stenographers wept. Abe shook hands cordially with the detectives who had been guarding him and smilingly declined to comment on the jury's action. With hands in pockets he stood watching the crowd leave, and when all had departed he nodded to the waiting deputies and started toward the door.

A city welfare worker, a Miss Frye, chose that moment to step up and beseech Ruef to confess his sins and embrace Christianity. For once the boss's glib tongue was stoppered down, and he stared, at a loss. Then, recovering his aplomb, he murmured with a sarcastic smile that he might discuss the matter, at another time.

When he came down the steps toward the prison van waiting at the curb, a few jeers went up from a dense crowd held half a block away by double lines of police. But generally the crowd watched in silence as Abe stepped into the heavily escorted "Black Maria" and was borne away.

PART FOUR

"Let us hear the conclusion of the whole matter."

1 Calhoun on Trial

At the District Attorney's office, the conviction of Ruef came as a joyful surprise; the best they had hoped for was a hung jury. The jury foreman disclosed that the deadlock had lasted until 3:30 that afternoon, when two of the four holdouts swung over to a "guilty" verdict. The commotion caused by Heney's appearance in the courtroom, which the jurors had rightly interpreted, decided the remaining two.

"This is a victory for the entire United States!" Langdon exulted. "What was really on trial was the institution of the law."

Heney received the news by telephone. With his cackling laugh, he said: "Calhoun next."

Ruef was convicted on December 10, 1908, two years and twenty-five days after his initial indictment, and more than three years after Francis J. Heney had denounced him in Mechanics Pavilion and

promised to send him to prison. In the tumultuous interval much
had changed. Ruef was not in prison yet; there was the long gamut of
appeals to run through, but he had been found guilty of committing a
crime jointly with Patrick Calhoun, Tirey L. Ford, and others of the
United Railroads officials, and the target of the prosecution now was
the conviction of Calhoun. True, Ford had been acquitted of the very
offense of which Ruef had been adjudged guilty, and in which they
had acted jointly; but Ford, it was said in some quarters, had merely
carried out orders given by his superior. Now, with Ruef's conviction,
the prosecution hoped to make the count stick against the man who
had issued the order to bribe.

The opposition press stepped up its campaign against the "iniquity" of bringing Calhoun to trial at all, the Los Angeles *Times,*
for one, asserting that "Heney and his associates have indicated
several times their willingness to make any compromise and to sacrifice many other cases in order to 'get' Calhoun." This, of course, was
not the truth: the prosecutors simply had refused to be swerved from
the clear understanding that the only way to end the civic corruption
was to stop it at its source,—and Calhoun, they were convinced, was
the fountainhead of the system of bribery.

For the defense, Heney had become the target against whom their
hatred was concentrated, for all realized that on him depended the
conduct of the crusade. Of the prosecution group, Spreckels might
have been replaced, Burns's work was largely finished, Langdon was
an effective pleader but not indispensable; but nowhere, with Heney
gone, could be found the same combination of legal ability and fighting courage, joined to personal magnetism and dedication to the
cause. Had Haas's bullet gone an inch higher, no one doubted that
the graft prosecution would have ended then and there.

Heney's isolation was intensified when, on the day after Ruef's
conviction, Hiram Johnson and Matt I. Sullivan reported to the
League for Justice the successful termination of their task.

"We will not figure in the prosecution of any of the other graft
cases," Johnson said.

In order to gather strength for the coming climactic test, Heney
left on a tour of the East, where audiences in Philadelphia, New York,
and elsewhere heard him flay the San Francisco grafters with vim.

Meanwhile, the temper of San Francisco had changed. The spirit of the city was essentially volatile, and with Abe Ruef headed toward prison, with Schmitz dethroned, with the boodling supervisors only a memory of the "bad old times," many citizens were in a mood to abate the controversy and patch up a liveable truce. Maintenance of a high moral tone can become irksome, and while few persons troubled to contest the guilt of the highly placed corruptionists (and fewer still doubted it), the public's wrath had been expended and there was a desire for peace; the bowstring of civic revulsion had been stretched taut too long; even adherents of the prosecution were inclining to the belief that to prolong the struggle would be futile.

In a prodigious spurt of energy, the city had made fantastic progress in rebuilding; a visitor in January, 1909, marveling: "That this wonderful city could have been built in two years by men engaged in two hundred childish conspiracies strikes one as more remarkable than the feat itself!" There were, to be sure, citizens who believed the "conspiracies" were in no sense "childish," but involved the fundamentals of democratic government, and for these, Heney spoke with the voice of conscience and duty. But among others, who became more numerous every day, the long-continued dissension had become a bugaboo; openly or covertly they were inclined to let the whole matter drop.

Seizing upon this lassitude, the forces of the graft defense stepped up their efforts to displace Heney permanently. Among the bitterest assailants, the Los Angeles *Times* ranked foremost. At the time Heney was shot it had forborne to express concern whether he lived or died; and a mere week later, when his recovery seemed likely, had relieved itself of accumulated bile by publishing its candid appraisal of the single-purposed prosecutor:

...Well or ill, whole or wounded, we cannot modify in one jot our opinion of this man. He is ignorant of the law, violent in disposition, a bluffer by breeding and long practice. He is as tempestuous a blusterer as ever disgraced the practice of the law. He is a bundle of selfishness seeking after vainglory, merciless in his cruelty when he has some helpless wretch to badger.... We regret the elimination of Heney out of the [Ruef] case in the way in which it was done.... But desirous of the good name of the state, of the peace of San Francisco, and of the ends of justice, we cannot help rejoicing...

Rejoicing turned to rage when Heney, in bandages, announced: "Calhoun next."

Upon his return from the East, Heney was welcomed at the Ferry Building by an enthusiastic crowd, and in a humorously militant speech he promised that he would "rope and hog-tie Patrick Calhoun like a refractory Spanish cow,"—an inelegant simile that raised the hackles of the proud Southerner. Reporters employed by Calhoun took down Heney's words, and these were to be thrown at him in court time and again as an example of his coarseness and lack of all gentlemanly instincts.

Ruef's trial had shattered legal records: it had run for one hundred five days and had necessitated the summoning of one thousand four hundred fifty veniremen, of whom four hundred forty-five had been questioned individually on their fitness to serve. But Calhoun's trial was to exceed these statistics; beginning January 12, 1909, it was to continue for one hundred fifty-nine days, until June 20th; and two thousand three hundred seventy veniremen were to be called, of whom nine hundred ninety-two were examined by counsel,—seventy-seven for each juror accepted. Legal talent appearing for the defense included the two Moores, Earl Rogers, Byington, Barrett, and the Georgia attorney, Alexander S. King, while behind the scenes the giant of the California bar, Garret W. McEnerney, lent astute direction. Against this battalion were arrayed Heney and O'Gara, of the District Attorney's staff. An irony often commented upon was that O'Gara's salary of $300 a month represented less than the fee some of the defense attorneys drew for a single day in court.

For months Calhoun had been demanding trial, after having consumed several months in unsuccessful attempts to forestall even his arraignment. Now this reversal of strategy (which seemed to have coincided with the disappearance of the United Railroads treasurer and cash book from the jurisdiction of the San Francisco court) was cleverly manipulated to capitalize on the alteration in popular feeling: every device was seized upon to sicken the public further with the interminable quarrel.

Years of strain had frayed Heney's temper, never easygoing; and during the weeks of haggling over selection of jurors, when he was harassed and bullied in relays, he served notice more than once that he would stand on the niceties of professional usage no longer; his position was perilous and he would defend himself by all means available.

Taunted by Byington, he roared: "I won't stand that! I warn this man right now! If I am to be shot again, I will be shot from the front, and not from behind! I draw the line, over which no man dare step! For months I took all the vilification that could be heaped upon me, merely because I dared to do my duty, which someone had to do. I am through with it now, and I want this thoroughly understood!"

Upon A.A. Moore's wondering aloud whether "the learned gentleman is going to turn loose these gunfighters," Heney flung back: "Nobody has been dynamited and nobody has been shot on your side of the case, and nobody will be! We don't hire people for that!"

"Your honor," remonstrated Moore, "I think Mr. Heney should be instructed not to exploit this shooting matter!"

Judge Lawlor admonished Heney to "learn the art of patience," whereat the prosecutor replied: "I have learned the art of patience. But after a man has been shot through the head, he doesn't think so much of the art of patience!"

Lawlor then besought of the defense a little magnanimity, observing: "Mr. Heney was stricken down in this court while engaged in the performance of his duty, and resumed his activities at an early date. Mr. Heney is laboring under embarrassments which should appeal to the humanity of any individual. Moreover, there are times when Mr. Heney does retort when I think counsel on the other side are responsible for it. The remark made by Mr. Moore was calculated to cause an explosion."

"By me?" said A.A. Moore, all innocence. "I have scarcely said anything in the whole case."

And so it went, day after day. Talesmen evinced the utmost reluctance to be chosen for jury service. Businessmen and laboring men alike expressed suspicion of the prosecution; many confessed marked partiality toward the defendant. Now and then humor lightened the exchanges, as when one talesman was asked: "Have you ever had any business dealings with the former supervisors?"

"Thank God, no!" came the horrified answer, and laughter relieved the tension for a moment. But most of the sessions were grimly

contested, with Calhoun's lawyers working as a unit, resourceful and
tricky, to obstruct, confuse, and infuriate their opponents. Through it
all, Calhoun reiterated that all he wanted was a fair and fast trial.

Sensations were by no means ended. Burns produced one when, on
Saturday, March 27th, he arrested his secretary, Rex N. Hamlin, for
selling prosecution secrets to the Calhoun camp; Hamlin admitted that
he had been giving the opposition copies of confidential reports by
Burns agents for months. Burns next raided the legal offices of the
United Railroads at the Oak and Broderick streets carbarn and
arrested seven men as participants in the theft of documents, including
Luther Brown and William Abbott. The charges were grand larceny
and complicity.

Failing to find the desired evidence in the carbarn, where desks,
cupboards, and files were ransacked savagely, on the next day, Sunday, Burns raided the company's general offices in a downtown
building.

Calhoun was at his country estate in Burlingame when the carbarn
was raided, but he was on hand Sunday. Entrance being denied to the
raiders, a deputy sheriff broke the glass in the door and forced his
way in. When Calhoun refused to open his safe, a locksmith, brought
along for the purpose, drilled it open, and a second safe, also,—one
used by Thornwell Mullally. Policemen and Burns detectives, under
the supervision of an Assistant District Attorney, watched the safe-
cracking, while Calhoun sat at one side, conveniently within camera
range, uttering repeated protests against the "un-American outrage."

The contents of the safes were sifted through, two Burns men
turning over hundreds of documents and segregating a pile of yellow,
typewritten sheets which they identified as copies of their day-by-day
reports on prospective jurors.

"This is my interview with juror W.A. Knowles," exclaimed one
of the men. "I can identify two-thirds of them by my initials."

"That is absolutely news to me if those are your reports," said
William Abbott, watching the inspection calmly.

"Here is the 1908 jury panel," the Burns detective continued.
"Here is a man who was drawn in the Newburgh trial."

More than seven hundred of these reports were bundled up and carried away, after file cases, desk drawers, and closets had been painstakingly searched.

Calhoun, dignified but furious, dictated a statement to the reporters present:

You have been, gentlemen, witnesses of one of the most significant outrages ever committed on the American continent. Under our Constitution, and as part of the fundamental basis of American liberty, every man is protected against unlawful search and seizure of his papers.... The evident purpose of this search was not to obtain papers belonging to Burns; it was a fishing expedition for the purpose of looking into the private affairs of the United Railroads, and if possible gather from the files some evidence to support their charges of bribery against me.

A legal tug of war ensued over the legality of these raids, the defense contending—among other oddities—that the search warrant was invalid because it had been issued on a Sunday,—although a restraining order obtained by Calhoun from a judge while the raid was in progress, which the raiders refused to honor, on the contrary *was* binding *in spite of* having been issued on a Sunday.

The graft defense seized on the raids for propaganda purposes across the country, and the hue and cry became so effective that even the liberal, fair-minded magazine, *The Nation,* reprimanded the prosecution, saying:

...The impression is gaining ground that the effort is to "railroad" Mr. Calhoun to prison at any cost, and that the daring procedure of Messrs. Heney and Burns in obtaining evidence...is not justifiable even in the endeavor to free an utterly demoralized city from the toils of scoundrels and blackmailers.... Even a railway president is entitled to justice in court....

The Nation admitted its incomprehension of the complex situation:

...Never do we recall a more sensational trial or one more difficult for the outsider to understand. Indeed, we question whether San Franciscans themselves, who are not "on the inside," have a clear perception of all that is going on, or realize fully what everything means.... *The Nation* would welcome the conviction of Mr. Calhoun if the facts warrant it. But even a reformer cannot turn despot and run the machinery of government himself without provoking an immediate reaction....

The point that the raids on the United Railroads offices were made for the purpose of recovering stolen property, which stolen property was found in the private safe of the president of the company, was missed by *The Nation,* and ignored elsewhere.

Two weeks after the raids, on April 15th, a jury to try Calhoun was finally sworn, a thirteenth member being empaneled to provide an alternate against emergencies.

Calhoun was being tried for bribing Supervisor Ferdinand Nicholas, and in his opening statement Heney said he would prove that Ruef authorized Gallagher to bribe Nicholas; that Gallagher was given the money to bribe Nicholas by Ruef; and that Calhoun, either directly or through Tirey L. Ford, or both, had authorized Ruef to make the offer of a bribe to Nicholas in return for his trolley franchise vote.

Nicholas, perhaps the oldest of the boodle supervisors, testified that he received $4,000 from Gallagher for his vote. Gallagher repeated his testimony, long since grown stale; Wilson and the other supervisors corroborated him; Mint officials again told of remitting to Ford the $200,000 deposited in Calhoun's name, acting on Calhoun's written and telegraphic orders. The available ledgers of the United Railroads failed to show any record of this $200,000. Witnesses showed that Ford and Ruef were in frequent and close communication at that time. The web of circumstantial evidence was drawn tightly, and then, in an extraordinary display of candor designed to set at rest the hoary clamor that the prosecution was merely a commercial conspiracy against the United Railroads, was privately motivated, or had spent huge sums illicitly, Heney called to the stand Rudolph Spreckels.

"From the time we attempted to empanel this jury," Heney stipulated, "the attorneys for the defense have been attempting to try Rudolph Spreckels, James D. Phelan, and God knows who else. By insinuations they have been endeavoring to get into the minds of this jury the idea that Mr. Spreckels was back of this prosecution for malicious purposes and for gain, for profit, to get hold of the United Railroads. I told them when they were making those insinuations that

I proposed to throw down the bars to them; that I proposed to force them to the proof; that I would put the witnesses on the stand and would not object to a single question asked them. The witness Spreckels is now on the stand, and we won't object to their asking him anything on earth, from the time he was born down to the present minute."

It was a dramatic showdown that went far beyond any legal obligation, and the defense grasped at the opportunity eagerly. Earl Rogers pried, queried, fished, and prodded without gaining any substantiation for the defense thesis. Spreckels answered every question calmly, fully, and for the most part cheerfully. On the subject of expenditures, he volunteered to enter in the record an audited statement of all monies paid out in behalf of the prosecution. This he produced. The itemization was complete and minute, containing such details as "F.J. Heney—$23,823" and "W.J. Burns—$123,250," and also trivial outlays like "elec. buzzer—$1.35" and "incidentals—pens —$.40." The breakdown showed that not one penny of compensation had gone to Heney, the $23,823 total against his name covering office expenses, rent, salaries for clerical help and detectives, automobile hire, telephone, and other routine specific expenditures. Burns had been paid salary and subsistence, plus all his office expenses and the cost of his detective force; Hiram Johnson had been paid $11,000 and J.J. Dwyer $13,400, but not one penny had gone to Heney. Every name was given, every person who had received as much as a ten-cent piece was listed, but not one penny had gone to Heney. The grand outlay to date amounted to $213,391.50, of which Spreckels had contributed $138,478.05, and he was obligated, he indicated, for much more. His only reservation was his refusal to identify other contributors to the fund, "to protect those whom I promised to protect," he said; "outside of that, the matter is entirely an open matter; I have no concern in it." One exception he did make: James D. Phelan, he testified with a smile, would have no objection, he was sure, to having it known that he had contributed $10,000.

During four days, defense counsel fished and fished in vain, and at last, after incurring repeated reproofs from the bench for the far-fetched manner of their examination, they gave up. Phelan then stepped up to the stand and underwent a similar grilling, answering with the same candor and giving the defense no satisfaction. Then Heney issued a challenge.

"Will you," he confronted the defense attorneys, "produce an itemized account of monies expended in opposition to these prosecutions?"

"I beg your pardon?" Earl Rogers gulped.

"I say, will you produce an itemized account of monies expended in opposition to these prosecutions?"

This was a ready-made chance for the defense to clear itself of suspicion that money had been paid to influence witnesses, to bribe jurors, to subsidize the *Globe* (which in headlines called Rudolph Spreckels a "skulking blackmailer," a "slanderer," a "briber"), to subvert agents of the prosecution, to instigate murder and mayhem. But Calhoun's counsel expressed themselves as outraged by Heney's challenge, and Rogers excitedly urged the court to assign the prosecutor's proposal as "misconduct."

Heney called his law partner, Cobb, who revealed that the firm's flourishing law practice had dwindled to insignificance during the three years of the prosecutions. Still the defense sneered almost daily that Heney was the "paid hireling" of private interests seeking a private revenge.

Only one link was lacking in the chain of evidence tracing the unexplained $200,000 from Calhoun to Ruef, Gallagher, and the supervisors, and that was some direct corroboration that Ford had given the money to Ruef: nobody could swear positively to that except Ruef or Ford. Neither was called to testify, and Calhoun produced no witnesses.

On June 14th, five months after the trial started, the closing speeches began. Police reserves were required to handle the crowds inside and outside of Carpenters Hall. Among the excited throng were many persons fanatically loyal to the prosecution, and others equally biased in favor of the defense.

O'Gara led off for the State and hammered on Calhoun's failure to offer any explanation regarding the $200,000.

"Why did not Tirey L. Ford come here and hold up his right hand and swear that he was not guilty of paying this $200,000 to Ruef?" he demanded. "Why has he not appeared, to inform this jury that three juries failed to convict him, and say, 'I am an innocent man'?

Ford did not come forward because he could not,—he would have steeped himself further in crime."

Ford, seated beside Calhoun in a group including Abbott, Mullally, and other company officials, and Calhoun's wife and daughters, listened with a stony face.

The next day Alexander King talked five hours, played on the harp strings of friendship, mildly reproved his young opponent in style *arioso* ("Mr. O'Gara was ungenerous"), and made much of the prosecution's inability to produce any witness to the passing of the $200,000 to Ruef.

"Everything about the conduct of Ford, Ruef, and the defendant is consistent with the theory that the money went elsewhere," King declared blandly. Where else it went he did not venture to say. Calhoun listened to his friend with rapt benignity.

Then A.A. Moore took up the argument, and referred bitterly to "the hired prosecutor, who works for fame, or glory, or money, or all." Francis J. Heney was on the itemized account submitted by Spreckels as receiving some $23,000, Moore stressed slily,—"for office expenses if you like, but $23,000 is $23,000." The charge of bribery stood unproved, he contended. "There is no evidence that Ruef received a dollar from Ford for any purpose. Should we then be made to show what disposition was made of any sum entering into the transactions of the United Railroads?

"Suppose, for the sake of argument," he shifted ground, "that this money was shown to have been paid by Tirey L. Ford to Abraham Ruef. Could anyone here, called as a witness, say that this payment was anything more than a surety for peace? Ruef was known to be the omnipotent power, not only controlling the supervisors but also in connection with the entire labor element of the city. However, this is all speculation."

The supervisors' testimony Moore dismissed as palpable perjury. "Gallagher and Nicholas were swearing for their necks,—a sort of bunco game that nearly approaches bribery itself. Gallagher! The top of his head does not emerge from the pit of corruption he has digged for himself! Would you return a dog to the pound on his testimony?"

Interrupted by nightfall, Moore spoke all the next day, while courtroom excitement increased. And with this solemn exhortation he rested: "In a moment I shall leave you with the honor of Patrick

Calhoun. Life is not ours to keep. Each one of us knows that he nightly pitches his tent a day's march nearer to his last home. But a man's honor is his to keep, and life is nothing in comparison with honor. A man lies down with the innumerable caravan, but his honor goes down to his children and their children. So we want you to leave Patrick Calhoun's honor untainted. This has been a long war. We must end it. We leave you with the honor of Patrick Calhoun, persuaded that justice will be done, and that the great and good God, who regulates the course of the universe and watches the fall of the sparrow, will give the victory to Patrick Calhoun."

When Heney arose to conclude for the State, Tirey Ford was not in his usual seat. Heney spoke all day to a fascinated crowd. Again many notables were present; Ethel Barrymore, the actress, who was starring at a local theater, occupied a front seat and during a recess shook hands twice with Calhoun, who introduced her to his lawyers. During the noon break, a woman effusively handed a basket of roses to the defendant as he stepped into his car.

Heney was less ornate than A.A. Moore or Alexander King, and he lost no time in striking at the class-distinction chimera raised by his opponents: innocent rich men like Calhoun being hounded, while guilty poor men like the "good dog" supervisors were allowed to roam at liberty.

"It did not take three months to get a jury to try Michael Coffey, the supervisor," Heney reminded, "nor did it take two months more to convict him of accepting a bribe in this very trolley matter. That *was* a matter of class distinction. Coffey did not have money to obstruct justice. He was convicted on the same testimony offered here, including the testimony of James L. Gallagher..."

A chorus of protests from defense counsel interrupted him, the first of a stream of objections that chopped up his argument and butchered his eloquence. But he proceeded for twelve hours, studded with dramatic clashes. Discussing the activities of Abbott, Ford's legal assistant, he made clear: "I am talking about William M. Abbott, than whom no milder villain ever cut a throat or scuttled a ship. In appearance a Sunday School superintendent, he is yet one of the men who was responsible for this record of black iniquity!

"They have defied us to produce a witness who witnessed this bribery," he went on. "They have asked: 'Show us the man who saw

Ford hand the money to Ruef.' Well..." He walked over to where Calhoun and his coterie sat and scrutinized the faces there. "...I will show you the man who saw Ford give this money, if he is here. He was here yesterday, but he is not here today. His name is Tirey L. Ford,—and he is the man who saw his own hand pass this bribe money to Ruef!"

Turning to the contention that Ford had paid Ruef an attorney's fee of $200,000, and that Ruef had bribed the supervisors out of his own pocket, Heney scoffed at this "nonsense,—even a half-wit would know that for what it is! The fighting Mr. Calhoun,—who would not suffer the opposition of Mr. Spreckels,—would not allow the demands of the carmen and broke their union,—the fighting Mr. Calhoun did not allow that curly-headed rascal to hold him up! It was not in the proud spirit of Mr. Calhoun to do so. He is of the class that has for its motto, 'Millions for defense, but not one cent for tribute'—until they are indicted, and then the millions flow as they have flowed here."

He had been charged with ambition, Heney said, and confessed: "I do have an ambition; an ambition to free my city from the jury-fixers and witness-bribers; an ambition to clean out the filth that infests our public offices. And I will fulfill that ambition if God permits me to live!"

At 10:00 P.M. he was still going strongly, and the next morning he spoke for another hour, while outside the building, bricklayers and society women stood elbow to elbow in long lines, listening to his voice, although unable to distinguish the words. He spoke with undiminished power and fire, his tones quivering with wrath as he listed Calhoun's iniquities. The street-car magnate gave him undivided heed, while across the courtroom, also attentive, sat Rudolph Spreckels, erect and proud.

The jury retired and debated that afternoon and that evening, and then were locked up for the night. The next day they resumed, and at noon reported they were deadlocked at ten to two in favor of acquittal.

The wind-up came quietly. The clerk polled the jury, and Heney addressed the court: "In view of the fact that these jurors have been deprived of their liberty for three months, it seems apparent that they have fulfilled their duty. I believe they should be discharged."

His voice was hoarse, scarcely audible, his manner bespoke extreme fatigue.

The defense concurred, and the jury was dismissed. One hour after adjournment, Heney sent word to the public: "I am ready to try this case again, and I will go ahead tomorrow if necessary."

2   Prelude to Finale

The transcript of testimony in the graft trials ran to four and one-half million words, and the public's power of endurance, unlike Heney's, had become exhausted. A contributing disillusionment was the acquittal of Luther Brown in the kidnaping of Fremont Older; even the prosecution's bloodthirsty critic, the Los Angeles *Times,* damned that verdict as unwarranted, pronounced the evidence clear, and said the jury had simply voted its disgust with the whole, long-drawn-out muddle.

And again a municipal election was subjecting the graft issues to the deadly catalysis of political passion. In his speech to the Calhoun jury, Heney had alluded to his candidacy for the district attorneyship in the November voting. The decision to seek this office had been prompted by desperation. Langdon had had enough, he refused to run again; and loss of the District Attorney's office would foreclose the graft prosecution automatically. Other acceptable choices also had declined, and at length, with great reluctance, Heney had agreed to make the race in spite of his extreme mental and physical depletion. He was hampered by a recently enacted election law which by a technicality disqualified him for the Republican nomination, inasmuch as he had been registered as a Democrat; and his name was placed on the Democratic ticket only by resort to the device of a write-in preliminary vote. His opponent, running under the combined endorsements of the Republicans and the Union Labor Party, was a lawyer who had first been proposed by Supreme Court Justice Henshaw,—Charles M. Fickert. In the mayoral race, the Union Labor nominee pitted against Mayor Taylor was Patrick Henry ("Pin Head") McCarthy, the labor boss close to Eugene Schmitz.

Heney's words in announcing his candidacy turned out to be repercussive. Citing George Washington's rejection of the offer of a crown, he had continued emotionally: "Washington, as a reward for his sacrifice, was twice made President of the United States by a noble people, just as a noble people in this city may vindicate me by electing me district attorney."

This sentence his enemies pounced upon as proof of Heney's bombastic egotism, and from a distance the Los Angeles *Times* belched vituperation with a ferocity that startled even seasoned practitioners of the slimy art of mud-slinging. Eructed the *Times:*

> [Heney] is a busted stink-pot... an ignorant, noisy cow-puncher... a product of the slums of San Francisco... a public calamity.... His election would mean a long agony of spite persecutions and keep the city in a perpetual boil of passion.... Even San Francisco, the city that elected Gene Schmitz mayor three times in succession, will balk at Heney!

Organized labor lined up with entrenched wealth to stamp out this threat to their ill-assorted privileges. It was an ironic alliance: laboring men being assured that the fuss was "only a fight between millionaires, all of them grafters," so "stick to your class, let's keep the graft in our own hands"; while smooth-palmed millionaire sons of steerage immigrants who had struck it rich were denouncing any degree of approbation of Heney as "treason to our class."

Despite political preoccupation, Heney did bring Calhoun to trial again, whereupon the defense led off with a furious attack on Heney's right to prosecute at all, and Judge Lawlor's fitness to preside. Days were consumed in tedious, bitter-tongued argument, and before a jury could be agreed upon, Lawlor realized the impossibility of excluding the current campaign's animosities. Thereupon he suspended the trial until after the election.

Other crosscurrents were working against prolongation of the crusade. Ever since Rabbis Kaplin and Nieto had broken with the prosecution over immunity for Ruef, whispers of anti-Semitism had been rife, not only in San Francisco but in respectable Jewish circles throughout the nation; Ruef, it was inferred, was being persecuted because he was a Jew. A build-up of bias in favor of the boss resulted, although vigorous and authoritative dissent was voiced; Rabbi Stephen S. Wise of New York, for one, repudiating Ruef and his crimes as "a blot on Israel's record of good citizenship in America." Wise, who had gone to New York from Oregon, knew the West and its personalities thoroughly.

Rabbi Kaplin had become the editor of *Emanu-el,* a leading Jewish periodical in the West, and this influential weekly's tone had grown more and more hostile to the prosecution. By contrast, at Rabbi Kaplin's invitation Patrick Calhoun had figured as speaker of honor at cornerstone-laying ceremonies for a new synagogue.

Other religious factions were similarly riven. The Episcopalians had been conspicuously embarrassed because some of the indicted corporation executives and their close supporters occupied high positions in that church. William H. Crocker was senior warden of Grace Church, Calhoun and Ford were members of St. Luke's, Glass an official of St. Paul's; and their influence was potent. When Dr. David J. Evans, rector of Grace Church, from the pulpit condemned Heney's shooting and prayed for his recovery, murmurs of "No! No!" arose among the congregation; and the rector thereafter was subjected to petty spitefulnesses which eventually forced his retirement.

At the same time Dr. Bradford Leavitt, the respected minister of First Unitarian Church, was writing that "some ministers hereabouts have left their pulpits recently because they did not feel free to speak the truth as they saw it, and men have also left the pews because they suspected the ministers were muzzled and their sermons censored by those who paid the bills." Chronic dissension, he reported, was developing over the delicate issue of the "social reaches" of the corruptionist guilt, and the respective shares of labor, capital, politicians, corporations, and the churches themselves in bringing about "San Francisco's disgrace."

Catholics differed just as widely. Schmitz had campaigned ardently as a Catholic,—without scorning to frequent Jewish temples ("at the behest," it was sneered, "of his Jewish master") even on high holy days to woo votes; on one occasion, a synagogue's committee of elders welcomed him wearing Schmitz campaign buttons! Such pliancy had alienated both lay and clerical members of his own church. This division was illustrated by the Sacramento *Bee,* owned by one of California's foremost Catholic laymen, Charles K. McClatchey, and strongly in favor of the prosecution. When the *Bee* got wind of the ructions at Old St. Mary's caused by Frank Murphy's gift, Father Wyman implored McClatchey to suppress the story "for the good of the church"; but the publisher, who shared the indignation of the two priests who had removed the offensive plaque as a "brand of shame," printed the account. He received a disconsolate letter from Father Wyman stating that he would offer a Mass for McClatchey's forgiveness; to which the latter replied that in asking forgiveness where no wrong had been committed, Father Wyman was bearing false witness in heaven; he suggested instead that Masses be offered "for those who have outraged public integrity."

The city in truth was sick, and insidious whispers gained credence that the long struggle was no more a battle for righteousness, but a self-righteous vendetta, prolonged for no public good by Heney and Spreckels. Seldom was the phrase "the People of the State of California" heard in a courtroom; the complainant in common parlance had become "the prosecution," and that meant above all Francis J. Heney. His very fixity of purpose, linked with the vehemence and unrestraint of his emotions, were played up to disparage him.

"Look," his opponents cried "the man is obsessed. He cannot be satisfied with a legitimate triumph; he must rule or ruin. The crooks have been expelled or rendered harmless, honest officials govern our city; why continue to persecute men who, while they may have transgressed in one particular by accepting the code that has been accepted for decades, are otherwise useful citizens, men of worth and ability? Why keep up a hopeless fight? Millions cannot be whipped, and the city is purged."

It was a copperhead cry; but many voters were conditioned to be lulled. People were crisis-battered; trying to reweave the whole social fabric was too onerous a task. Shoals of special agents were irritating and inflaming the community, spreading suspicion and resentment by their snooping among neighbors, business associates, relatives, friends, church members, even long-forgotten acquaintances in other cities; ringing doorbells on strange missions; soliciting signatures to specious petitions, all designed to hamper or call off the graft trials. At one time it was estimated that half the adult males of San Francisco had been investigated by one side or the other, or both. No man knew whom to trust.

Beyond the metropolis, Californians implored San Francisco to be steadfast. But the outlanders had not been buffeted by natural

catastrophes and years of strife, their fortunes and their tranquillity
were not under the hammer. Besides, the tradition of San Francisco
had always been one of toleration for human frailties. Heney's call for
"moral stubbornness" found fainter and fainter response. Right up to
election eve, the prosecutors were confident; but when the ballots had
been counted, Fickert swamped Heney by a ten thousand-vote majority, while "Pin Head" replaced the poetical Dr. Taylor.

It was the knell of the graft prosecution. Only a handful of bitter-
enders refused to concede. Even the *Call* admitted the inevitability of
the verdict and withdrew its support; its proprietor, John D. Spreckels,
explaining that "Heney tried to do too much too fast." But the after
shocks of the city's moral earthquake were not to subside with such
rapidity.

3   Hasty Hands Make Heavy Work

One of Fickert's first actions upon assuming office in January,
1910, was to move for dismissal of the indictment against Patrick
Calhoun on the ground of insufficient evidence. When he took over the
District Attorney's office, Fickert informed the court, he found the files
stripped of material pertinent to the case; witnesses and evidence
scattered; Gallagher, the indispensable witness, unaccountably disappeared. Judge Lawlor denied the motion for dismissal and ordered
Fickert to make a vigorous effort to find Gallagher and bring him
back to testify.

Gallagher was located in British Columbia; he was undecided
whether he would ever return to San Francisco. In April, Fickert
joined Calhoun's attorneys in moving for dismissal of *all* the indictments outstanding against the trolley magnate. Hinting that Fickert
was not exerting himself unduly to get Gallagher back, Lawlor delayed ruling until August. Then, in a long decision, he imputed
Gallagher's continued unavailability to a clandestine understanding
with the District Attorney or with the Calhoun defense, or with both.

"At practically every turn the District Attorney has followed the
lead of the defense," the Judge made his meaning clear. "The law has
broken down."

Again he refused to dismiss the indictments.

A scene unparalleled in American courts ensued, as one by one Calhoun's attorneys assailed Judge Lawlor in terms of gross abuse, and one by one were consigned to jail for contempt. Stanley Moore first accused the Judge of "doing politics from the bench that you stultify by your occupancy"; and when the court attempted to silence him, shouted to be heard,—"a right which any court with a speck of fairness would accord!"

Lawlor told him to sit down, suggesting that he make his reply through the press.

"We assign that as the last word of your partisanship!" stormed Moore, and the Judge sentenced him to five days in jail and ordered him into custody at once.

A.A. Moore interposed that he heartily agreed with his son. "Your honor is a bitter partisan and doing politics from the bench," he said. The Judge held him in contempt, and when he was not arrested at once, the father protested, "I tried to line myself up here in thorough accord with Stanley Moore, holding your honor as I do in thorough detestation, believing you to be an abslutely contemptible man!"

A.A. Moore thereupon was taken into custody, but Barrett was on his feet registering "a most solemn and serious protest" on behalf of Calhoun, who "considers the proceedings of today infamous...the most unjust and oppressive ruling ever made in an American court of justice."

When Barrett was ordered to jail, the defendant arose and with patrician dignity himself addressed the bench: "May it please your honor: I have been educated, sir, to have respect for the courts. I have sat in your court under circumstances that would have tried the patience of any American. But, sir, I cannot sit quiet and listen to the vile insinuations which you yourself have stated there is no evidence before you to justify. There have been periods, sir, when the greatest honor that could come to a man was to go to jail; and as an American citizen I say to you that if you should send me there for contempt, it will be heralded all over this country as an honor. You have seen fit, sir, to send three of the most distinguished counsel of this state to jail. Why? Because they have sought to express, in terms of respect and yet in terms of strength, their protest against injustice..."

"Mr. Calhoun," the court interrupted, but Calhoun would not be curbed.

"There is a time—pardon me, your honor—when every man has a right to be heard."

"Mr. Calhoun!" repeated Lawlor sharply, and again was ignored by the haughty defendant: "Now before I take my seat, I desire further to say this, that any insinuation that implies that either I was a party to the absence of this witness [Gallagher] or that I have sought to control the District Attorney's office of this city is untrue. There is no evidence before this court. You yourself know it."

With that he sat down.

Judge Lawlor did not hold him in contempt.

The three attorneys served their sentences at Ingleside county jail with all the trappings of a holiday. They were permitted to receive visitors freely, among these Calhoun and other prominent clients, and had their food brought by their servants from the kitchens of the Fairmont Hotel.

Meanwhile, Abe Ruef, that diligent casuist, had not been idle. The day after his conviction his jauntiness returned, and he stood for an hour before Judge Lawlor, hands nonchalantly in pockets, while the history of his case was reviewed and motions were entered for a new trial. Judge Lawlor denied the motions and sentenced the little boss to fourteen years in prison, the maximum penalty for bribery.

Ruef was returned to jail and remained there a year, until December, 1909, when he was again released on bail pending disposition of his appeal. This had been six months in preparation and filled twenty-four printed volumes with two-and-one-half million words,—a five-foot shelf of sophistry. There were five hundred and forty-one pages devoted to "Misconduct of Judge"; and alleged misconduct by the District Attorney, and errors in the examination of witnesses and in the admission of evidence, figured almost as extensively. The transcript of his case from indictment to verdict also was incorporated.

After months of study, the Court of Appeals denied this petition for a new trial. This was in November, 1910, and on December 31st—the last day of the fourth consecutive year of the graft prosecutions—Ruef petitioned the State Supreme Court for a rehearing.

The chariot of justice then wobbled uncertainly to a cynical halt.

The Supreme Court comprised seven Justices, who decided by majority vote; Ruef needed four votes to obtain a rehearing,—the foreseeable outcome of which would be the quashing of his conviction and the granting of a new trial,—with Fickert as prosecutor. Should the court fail to act one way or another on his petition within thirty days after the Appeals Court ruling had become final, the appeal would be lost and the case could not be reopened. The last day on which the Supreme Court could register an opinion was January 22, 1911.

Justice Frederick Henshaw was preparing to take a trip, and on January 10th he signed his opinion, granting the rehearing. The next day he departed. Two more justices subsequently granted the petition, and on January 22nd—the last possible day—Chief Justice Beatty added his consent. This made a majority of four, and the boss was given another chance to wriggle free.

A howl of execration arose from end to end of California. In homes and hamlets everywhere, Hiram Johnson's words—"all this trial, tribulation, and all this blood!"—had struck root, and the people cried, in the words of one commentator, that California justice lay exposed "as devoid of honor and respect as a common strumpet."

Then a lawyer (several were to claim the credit afterward) detected a flaw in the Supreme Court's action. This was a technicality and tenuous, admittedly; but that a technicality should be invoked against that master juggler of technicalities, Abe Ruef, seemed merely deferred justice, and the point was brought to the attention of the State's Attorney General.

Under the law, a Supreme Court Justice became, in effect, legally dead the moment he left the territory of the state; he could exercise no function of his office during such absence. When the Supreme Court's decision was filed on January 22nd, Justice Frederick Henshaw was outside the boundaries of California; therefore, his opinion was inoperative, and only three—not four—Justices had approved Ruef's rehearing. In default of a majority, the appeal thus was rejected. And the thirty-day limit having expired, the case could not be reopened.

A final fillip was given to the farce when the record disclosed that Justice Henshaw, in his zeal to accommodate a friend, had signed his opinion *before the Attorney General had submitted his brief stating the reasons for opposing Ruef's petition.*

On February 28th, the Supreme Court, in a humiliating reversal, acknowledged its error, and the order for a rehearing was vacated. Abe Ruef had been "railroaded" into prison by the oversight of Justice Henshaw,—on a technicality.

On March 7, 1911, Ruef was taken across the bay and entered San Quentin prison,—five years and four months after a San Francisco audience had cheered Francis J. Heney's fervent pledge: "I will send Abe Ruef to the penitentiary where he belongs!"

One last resource Ruef had kept in reserve,—the possibility of an executive pardon. With Railroad influence to help him, expectation of clemency had seemed justified. But sitting in the Governor's chair in 1911 was Hiram W. Johnson.

4 "La Commedia è Finita"

"All this trial, tribulation, and all this blood! . . ." What had it come to?

The graft prosecution produced three hundred and eighty-five indictments. Ruef's commitment to prison left the slate still cluttered.

In September, 1910, Judge Dunne accused Theodore Halsey's doctors of misrepresenting the state of his health and ordered the telephone lobbyist to trial. Lackadaisically prosecuted by one of Fickert's assistants, Halsey was acquitted. Then in November, the State Supreme Court, on technicalities so abstruse the average citizen could not follow them, quashed the conviction of Louis Glass. The majority opinion was written by Justice Henshaw.

Abram K. Detwiler, the Home Telephone Company promoter who successfully eluded pursuit, reappeared in San Francisco after the election of Fickert and ultimately won dismissal of the indictments against him.

In August, 1911, with James L. Gallagher still absent, the Court of Appeals ordered Judge Lawlor to dismiss the indictments against Patrick Calhoun, Tirey L. Ford, William Abbott, and Thornwell Mullally in the trolley bribery. "The law," said the Appeals Court, "will not tolerate repeated postponements on the vague hypothesis that perhaps in the future a fugitive witness may return to the court's jurisdiction."

Judge Lawlor complied with the order, but prophesied: "I am more convinced now than I was a year ago that...when his importance as a witness in any of these cases has ceased, James L. Gallagher will again be in our midst."

At the same time, Judge Lawlor dismissed the indictments against the gas company directors, Drum, De Sabla, and Martin.

In December, 1911, the Supreme Court threw out the conviction of former Supervisor Michael Coffey, the hackman, on grounds almost identical with those which Ruef had advanced in his petition.

Early in 1912, Eugene Schmitz was brought to trial for bribery before Judge Lawlor. He seemed like a wraith from the past when he pleaded "not guilty," and the two key witnesses were wanting: Gallagher still missing, and Ruef, brought from San Quentin, refusing to testify unless all the indictments standing against him were dismissed. Some of these were in Judge Dunne's department, and Dunne refused. Under the circumstances, Judge Lawlor had no option but to instruct the jury to find Schmitz not guilty, with the comment: "It will be a source of shame to San Francisco that where the showing of great crimes was so formidable, the vindication of the law fell so far short of what was needed in the way of example."

In May, 1912, the Appeals Court ordered Judge Dunne to dismiss the one hundred twenty-three remaining indictments voted by the Oliver grand jury against Ruef, Schmitz, Halsey, Glass, the prize-fight managers, and a scattering of others. Dunne obeyed the order.

Then in June, James L. Gallagher returned to San Francisco.

But the sour after comedy remained to be played to its Gilbertian finish.

No man had toiled harder or longer to put Abe Ruef behind bars than Fremont Older: the *Bulletin* had attacked the boss in his heyday and had never yielded an inch.

On the day Ruef entered San Quentin, Older sat in his cubbyhole office and thought over the years of struggle, recalling Ruef in his glory lording it over the city, a sprightly, agreeable, debonair scoundrel surely, endowed with much ability, shaped by the standards and conventions of his time and place. Older had no doubt that Ruef had committed villainies, but for the first time he asked himself whether Ruef was a villain. With characteristic impetuosity, warm-heartedness, and illogic, he decided that Abe was not. Besides, Ruef was being punished, humiliated, disgraced, probably destroyed, while those who had utilized him as a tool—willing, but still an instrument to further their greedy interests—went free and unattainted. Without ado, Older started agitation to get Ruef out of prison by means of a parole.

The donnybrook precipitated by this defection of one of the prosecution's mainstays matched anything produced during the long warfare. Older bore with a shrug the reproaches of both camps and the odium of being stigmatized as a turncoat. He visited Ruef in prison, but the boss could not comprehend his motive. On April 6, 1912, the *Bulletin* announced that it would publish Ruef's memoirs as a case history of the causes of civic corruption. This step was calculated to enlist public sympathy.

"Solitude, restraint, confinement make for introspective thought," Ruef prefaced his narrative. "Since the heavy doors of the state prison closed behind me, I have given much consideration to the events and influences which ended so ignominiously a life full of hope. I have reflected; I have studied; I have considered the causes, the effects, the surrounding conditions, the inevitable consequences of the destructive social and civic forces which brought about that result. I believe much good can come from a straightforward statement of my experiences. I have determined to make such a statement. . . . I feel that the narration will have much educational value and will, in some degree, conduce to the benefit of society, of the city, of the state, and perhaps of the nation."

The author still cherished the large vision: the words echoed that guilty-plea exculpation made in Judge Dunne's court so long ago.

Several chapters recounting Ruef's early political adventures had appeared when the board of prison directors met in an extraordinary public session on June 8, 1912, to consider his application for a parole. One member of the five-man board was Tirey L. Ford,— who, the *Bulletin* said, but for Abe's silence would have been in a cell and Ruef free. The propriety of Ford's sitting under the circumstances was scathingly commented upon throughout the state, and

Epilogue

"Vanity of vanities, all is vanity."

"Let Us Hear the Conclusion of the Whole Matter"

The draft indictments were quashed. The heroisms and perfidies of that time were relegated to reminiscences, the mountainous transcripts gathered the mold of neglect and oblivion's dust. But the rancors engendered by the long civil strife were not dissipated or easily assuaged: a generation steeped in violence, suspicion, and discord was to bear indelibly the stigmata of that noble and ignoble conflict.

The victors, as victors will, took their revenges. Proclaiming themselves the "party of reconciliation," they called for harmony,—but harmony on their terms; and those who had been identified with the prosecution, and who could be reached, felt their spite.

Grand jury foreman Bartley P. Oliver was one of the first to be overthrown. Finding his real-estate business boycotted, in 1910 he

395

announced that he was leaving the city of his birth for involuntary exile. "I'm winding up my affairs and moving away," he told friends. "Maybe my partner can do better without me; he doesn't have anything to live down." Later he returned, acquired wealth, and became a noted philanthropist.

Golden M. Roy also was compelled to depart for several years, until resentments cooled.

Former Supervisor Rea tried persistently to give back the $1,250 bribe money he had taken, and several lawyers puzzled over the legal teaser without finding a means; Rea's reputation never was cleared. A grocer on the jury that convicted Schmitz suffered a permanent falling-off in business amounting to fifteen hundred dollars a week. Charles Boxton was relieved of his teaching position and saw his dental practice dwindle. These were a few of those who paid the price of the struggle.

On the other hand, none of the indicted corporation officials lost caste socially or forfeited the esteem of the commercial community. Louis Glass retained the vice-presidency of the Pacific Telephone & Telegraph Company until 1912, and thereafter was president of a company he had organized, the Philippine Telephone & Telegraph Company, with offices in San Francisco. Vice-president of this firm was Theodore V. Halsey; upon Glass's death, Halsey became president.

The enormous outlays in which the graft defense involved Patrick Calhoun, directly and indirectly, and his unsuccessful attempt to recoup by a bold land speculation, in 1913 resulted in his being squeezed out of the United Railroads by restive stockholders; in liquidation of his indebtedness to the company he gave his personal note for $1,096,000,—which the incoming president entered on the books at a valuation of one dollar. In 1916, Calhoun went through bankruptcy proceedings, stating that he was living on the generosity of his wife; but in the mid-Thirties, when he was eighty, he moved to Southern California and built up a new fortune in oil leases. In 1943, while crossing the street in front of his home in Pasadena, he was run down by two teenagers in hot-rod cars. Horribly mutilated, with one leg torn off, he retained consciousness until removed to a hospital, where he died, tenacious to the last. Admiring friends maintained that "they had to come up on the sidewalk to get him"; a statement not true in fact, but thoroughly expressive of his arrogant, unyielding spirit. Eighty-seven years old at his death, he was buried on the ancestral acres in South Carolina.

After 1909, Rudolph Spreckels ceased to expect that the public some day would do justice to his altruism, but he nursed no grudges. His Pacific Avenue mansion and princely estate at Burlingame continued to be the focus of a lively social set, and reverting to his vocation as a money-gainer, he piled up more millions in the Twenties; he estimated his profits in a single year as more than $18,000,000. Then the tide turned, and under repeated reverses he was ousted from the presidency of the First National Bank (which then was absorbed by the Crocker bank) and in 1934 filed in bankruptcy. This overthrow he accepted with the stoic phlegm he exhibited during the graft trials.

"Other financiers jumped out of windows when they found themselves penniless," he shrugged. "I never lost a night's sleep over it."

By his wife's will, he later inherited a competence, and (in 1958, at eighty-six years of age) he died in San Mateo, a suburb of San Francisco, where he had been living in a three-room flat. Youngest of the graft prosecution principles, he had outlived them all.

The fate of James D. Phelan was less burdensome. Although one of the city's foremost citizens, he was repeatedly passed over in the distribution of civic honors. However, he weathered the storm, and in 1915 became the first United States Senator to be elected by direct popular ballot. He served until 1921, being succeeded by Samuel M. Shortridge. Death came to him in 1930, when he was sixty-nine.

The judges who had borne the brunt of the graft furor—Lawlor and Dunne—were endorsed by the voters, Lawlor being re-elected to the Superior bench in 1912 and Dunne in 1914. Later, Lawlor was elevated to the Appeals Court and then to the State Supreme Court. Langdon became a Supreme Court Justice, and Matt I. Sullivan a distinguished Chief Justice of California. And Heney's partner, Charles Cobb, became an Assistant United States Attorney General.

Hiram Johnson was catapulted into the governor's chair by his record in the graft trials, serving two terms, during which California benefited by progressive legislation two decades in advance of the rest of the nation. He later was elected to the United States Senate, where he remained until his death in 1945; meanwhile, having been nominated for the Vice-Presidency on the "Bull Moose" ticket of 1912 with Theodore Roosevelt, and, subsequently, by a fluke of misjudgment, just missing becoming President himself.

A few years after the graft trials, Fremont Older was deprived of the editorship of the *Bulletin* because of his inveterate espousal of unpopular causes. After helping to secure Ruef's release, he spearheaded the agitation to free Thomas J. Mooney and Warren K. Billings, convicted of the 1916 Preparedness Day bombing in San Francisco. Older then became editor of the *Call,* which William Randolph Hearst had purchased, and had the melancholy satisfaction of seeing it absorb the *Bulletin.* In 1935, a Nestor among enthusiasts, he collapsed while driving along a country road and died, aged seventy-eight.

Eugene E. Schmitz did not prosper after his downfall. Several business ventures he tried petered out—real estate, mining, publication, music (his operetta, *The Maid of the San Joaquin,* failed in New York)—and in 1915 he attempted a political comeback, to the amusement of the public, announcing that he would run for Mayor against the incumbent, James Rolph, Jr., the most popular Mayor San Francisco ever had. Eugene pitched his appeal to women, who were voting for the first time that year, and astonished everybody by garnering 35,000 votes. Rolph, however, defeated him two to one.

In 1916, lawsuits and judgments forced the sale of Schmitz's prized Vallejo Street house to meet a $5,000 debt; the $30,000 mansion was knocked down for $2,500 cash. Once more he turned to politics, and in 1921 was elected a supervisor. The city re-elected him to a second term, during which he again became involved in an allegation of graft. Nothing came of this, but after 1925 he lapsed into obscurity, two attempts to start a boom for him as Mayor or Governor on an independent ticket meeting with no success.

In 1928, in his home at 3127 Franklin Street (still an address on the "right side of town"), he died, aged sixty-four. His funeral was held in St. Brigid's, his parish church, and drew an overflow crowd; standees lined the aisles during celebration of Requiem Mass by friends among the clergy. The floral tributes were innumerable, the police and fire departments provided a guard of honor, Mayor Rolph and the board of supervisors attended, while honorary pallbearers included Patrick Henry ("Pin Head") McCarthy and Jeremiah Dinan.

Obituary notices of the man varied widely. The *Examiner* recorded that Schmitz's friends had never ceased to number him in "the noble army of martyrs," victimized by a malignant press, and termed his life "as vivid, adventurous, and splashed with color as the beloved city in which he made his home." From New York came a telegram of condolence from Dudley Field Malone, a Democratic lawyer-politician, addressed to J.W. Ehrlich, San Francisco criminal lawyer:

> THROUGHOUT TWENTY-FIVE YEARS I HAVE NOT ONLY BELIEVED IN HIS COMPLETE PERSONAL INTEGRITY BUT I VALUED THE FRIENDSHIP OF HIM AND HIS FAMILY WITH ABIDING AFFECTION.... I KNOW WE ALL HOPE THAT IN HIS HAPPINESS NOW HE WILL FIND THE JUSTICE AND UNDERSTANDING WHICH DID NOT COME TO HIM IN HIS LIFE.

Against this was a contemporary dismissal of Eugene Edwards Schmitz as "the smallest man mentally and meanest man morally that ever occupied the mayor's chair."

Perhaps closer to the truth was the appraisal given by District Attorney Langdon in New York in 1907. Langdon had come East to speak in Carnegie Hall, and he was trying to explain to New Yorkers how Schmitz had got himself elected three times in a row.

"You have to give Gene credit," he said. "He is the king of bluffers. He is the most plausible man in the world. He could come into this room with evidence against him a foot high, and in ten minutes convince you that he was a wronged man. And he is the best poker player in California,—which is going some!"

Schmitz was survived by his wife, Julia, and two daughters, one of them a Dominican nun. His brother, Herbert, survived until 1953.

The man who convicted Schmitz, Francis J. Heney, lived out the years after 1909 in anti-climax. His defeat for the District Attorneyship proved a fade-out. Resuming law practice, he was shunned by important clients, and he had acquired a host of enemies politically; he was unsuccessful in his bid for a Senate seat in 1914 and the California Governorship in 1918. Physically, he was scarred and permanently deafened by Haas's bullet. In 1912, he became active in the "Bull Moose" movement, and was one of the first admirers of Theodore Roosevelt to advocate the formation of a separate Progressive Party.

But in many ways he remained under a cloud. He was never a party man: his flair and genius resembled those of a guerrilla fighter. In an independent command, defending a clear-cut issue, he was superb,—inventive, daring, tenacious, elusive of pursuit. And he loved a battle. To him each lawsuit was a fight, in which everyone who was on his side was a friend and everyone opposing him an enemy. He asked no quarter and gave none during the struggle. But he did not work well with a team, and party leaders never were sure what tack the thorny man might take next.

His generosity in personal life was not widely recognized. Yet, in 1923, when the widow and son of a half-brother, whom Heney had helped financially, accused Frank of fraud in settling the estate, Superior Court Judge J.A. Brown of San Jose, rendering his decision, not only exonerated Heney of the charges, but went out of his way to add that the latter had been actuated throughout the dealings with his family by "a spirit of generosity, fraternal devotion, and consideration almost unparalleled in the annals of kinship. He stood in the breach and put up not only the funds of his large earning capacity, but practically all he could borrow, until the brother's debt to him, mounting higher and higher, reached an almost stupendous sum. He seems never to have demanded or accepted anything for himself, but on the other hand consented and insisted that everyone else be taken care of while he waited for his due."

After the death of his wife, Heney cut his connections with San Francisco and moved to Los Angeles, where he married again and practised law until in 1931, Governor Rolph appointed him to the Los Angeles County Superior bench. The next year he was elected to a full six-year term. Irascible, unpredictable, still full of gusto ("combustible Heney," he was called), he often spoke about the stirring days of the graft prosecution and his shooting in court.

"The bullet struck me just below the right ear," he would say, then cackle with his odd grin; "but you know what a lawyer's jaw muscles are!"

When he died in Santa Monica in 1937, newspapers recalled him, some grudgingly; a few tributes were printed, one by Justice Langdon praising Heney as "a lover of justice, willing to fight and die for it, as exemplified by his lifelong activities in its behalf." But his true epitaph had been spoken nearly thirty years before.

On the day Heney was shot, when it seemed certain he had been killed, Hiram Johnson had said movingly: "When Frank Heney fell today while in the performance of his duty, decency and right were stricken. For two years this one man persevered in the right, for right's sake alone. Without compensation, sacrificing a great legal practice, giving without complaint the best years of his life, Francis J. Heney, facing all the combined forces of evil in this city and state, has stood unflinchingly at his post, making the fight that is the fight of us all. Daily abuse and vilification have been his portion and reward. In spite of it, where a weaker man would have faltered, Heney has persevered.... For generations his exposure of rottenness in San Francisco, his prosecution of the criminal rich, will live and make this city and state better. He has been shot simply because he was fighting for the right."

The life of Abraham Ruef after his release from prison was one of ostracism and obscurity. Disbarred from the practice of law, enjoined by the terms of his parole from re-entering politics, he was still wealthy. He opened an office in a building he owned at the corner of Kearny Street and Columbus Avenue, on the edge of North Beach, not far from where he had started his career,—but that had been in a previous century. There he managed his investments and toyed with bizarre promotions, which at one time included a process for removing the alcohol from wine without affecting the flavor. It was unsuccessful. A promotion that was successful was the world-famous tourist center at Fishermen's Wharf.

Now and then curious San Franciscans might climb the dusty stairs to the two-room, fourth-floor office occupied by the former boss to see whether the brass plate on the door really read: "A. Ruef, Ideas." It read: "A. Ruef, Ideas, Investments, and Real Estate." He advertised in the city directory in the same terms. Now and then his sarcastic wit would flicker in headlines, as when he threatened to build a tall apartment house that would cut off Rudolph Spreckels' view of the bay,—a project which did not materialize. But he was never restored to public favor. Even to have business dealings with him was considered compromising, and he made little effort to slough off the odium attached to his name.

Late in 1935, a reporter on the prowl for a feature article visited the aging former political overlord and found him a paunchy little man, talkative and placid. The curly locks, long grizzled, were almost gone, the flowing mustache was clipped to a stubble. He discussed the forthcoming mayoral election freely, analyzing the chances of the several candidates and correctly forecasting the winner; but his tone and manner were listless.

"You know," he mused, "all men like the honor of public office. They just can't resist it. Their friends get around them and tell them to run. And then they do."

Hooking a thumb in the armhole of his vest, he laughed mirthlessly.

He preferred to chat about college days, and his eyes strayed to the ceiling and glazed with far-away remembrance when he harked back to his part in helping to establish the students' co-operative at Berkeley.

"We started with a capital of eight dollars," he recollected. "I understand they have hundreds of thousands of dollars now. We started that store to give students cheaper textbooks. They were very expensive then."

His features lit up wanly. The reporter alluded to the graft prosecution, and Abe was not embarrassed.

"Laws are made by men. They got me."

There was no resentment in the tone; he sounded as matter-of-fact as a baseball player who had been tagged out while trying to steal second base.

On February 29, 1936, Abraham Ruef died in his home at 2819 Pierce Street. A few days previously he had taken to bed; he was seventy-one, and his heart had been weakening for some time. With him at the end were his sister, Mrs. Henrietta Sittenfeld (the "Miss Ruef" of the "law offices"), and other relatives. The funeral was private, and he was buried in Eternal Hope Cemetery, close by the city he had ruled.

One final irony was reserved: although he was believed to have left an estate of several hundred thousand dollars, when the tangle of obligations was balanced against the liabilities, it was found that Abe Ruef had died broke.

Today a bust of Edward Robeson Taylor, the Mayor of the prosecution, graces the lobby of San Francisco's Public Library; commemorative tablets and tributes to James D. Phelan abound; but there is no monument in San Francisco to the man who, "to save a city's honor, gave of his substance, 'without getting anything out of it,' " Rudolph Spreckels. The rotunda of the splendid new City Hall arches almost above the spot where Francis J. Heney's blood flowed in token of his contribution toward making San Francisco cleaner, brighter, and better, yet one seeks there in vain for a marker or memorial. But in encyclopedias there is an entry, "RUEF, ABRAHAM...," which stands as a testament and a reminder to the San Franciscans of today.

Acknowledgments

Source materials for the history of the San Francisco graft prosecution are voluminous and widely dispersed through newspapers, court records, official documents, magazine articles, and the pamphlets and miscellaneous publications which proliferated during the turmoil.

Wherever possible, contemporary, eye-witness, or participant accounts and expressions of day-to-day sentiment have been relied upon principally. Indispensable have been the complete files of the newspapers listed in the Bibliography. Other publications cited are a culling from among the many, many consulted.

Although annotated studies of the great controversy are available —chief among these being Franklin Hichborn's eyewitness book, *The System*, invaluable because of its contemporary viewpoint; and Walton Bean's excellent and authoritative *Boss Ruef's San Francisco*

405

—the method followed by the author has been to examine all primary sources independently, and thereafter compare the findings with previous studies. In this way, numerous gaps in the story have been filled in successfully from the original materials. During this process, Hichborn's skeletonized recounting of the entire development, from start to finish, has been of constant assistance as a factual guidepost.

In reconstructing so complex a cross section of history, so fiercely contested by the opposing partisans, some errors of detail or omission are bound to creep in despite all vigilance. For these, the reader's indulgence is bespoken; they are attributable to the author alone.

Bibliography

Altrocchi, Julia Cooley: *The Spectacular San Franciscans*. New York, 1949.

Anonymous: *The Complete History of the San Francisco Horror*. New York, 1906.

Asbury, Herbert: *The Barbary Coast*. New York, 1933.

Atherton, Gertrude: *California: An Intimate History*. New York, 1914.
　　　　　　　　My San Francisco: A Wayward Biography. Indianapolis, 1946.
　　　　　　　　Harper's Weekly, "San Francisco and Her Woes." November 2, 1907.

Bean, Walton: *Boss Ruef's San Francisco*. Berkeley, 1952.

Bonnet, Theodore F.: *The Regenerators: A Study of the Graft Prosecution in San Francisco*. San Francisco, 1911.

Bronson, John: *The Earth Shook, The Sky Burned*. New York, 1959.

Brice, John: *The Gaudy Century: The Story of San Francisco's Hundred Years of Robust Journalism*. New York, 1948.

Byington, Lewis F.: "Foreword" to *California's Diamond Jubilee*. San Francisco, 1925.

Byington, Lewis F., and Lewis, Oscar (editors): *The History of San Francisco*. San Francisco, 1931.

Caughey, John Walton: *California*. New York, 1953.

Cleland, John: *California in Our Time: 1900–1940*. New York, 1947.

Coblentz, Stanton A.: *Villains and Vigilantes*. New York, 1957.

Cohn, Alfred, and Chisholm, Joe: *Take the Witness*. New York, 1934.

Coleman, Charles M., *P.G.&E. of California, 1852–1952*. New York, 1952.

Report of Committee on the Causes of Municipal Corruption in San Francisco. San Francisco, 1908.

De Ford, Miriam Allen: *They Were San Franciscans*. Boise, 1947.

Dickson, Samuel: *San Francisco Is Your Home*. New York, 1947.

Dictionary of American Biography. New York, 1928–1936.

Dosch, Arno: *Overland Monthly*, "Rudolph Spreckels: The Genius of the San Francisco Prosecution." November, 1907.

Edholm, Charlton: *Traffic in Girls and Work of Rescue Missions*. Oakland, 1900.

Encyclopedia Americana: *Ruef, Abraham* (article).

Englehardt, Father Zephyrin, O.F.M.: *San Francisco, or Mission Dolores*. Chicago, 1924.

Gatlin, Dana: *McClure's Magazine*, "Great Cases of Detective Burns: How Abe Ruef Confessed." February, 1911.

Geberding, Elizabeth: *Delineator Magazine*, "Woman's Fight Against Graft in San Francisco." October, 1910.

Genthe, Arnold; text by Irwin, Will: *Pictures of Old Chinatown*. New York, 1908.

Hamilton, Edward H.: *Cosmopolitan Magazine*, "The Liberating of San Francisco." August, 1907.

                                       Cosmopolitan Magazine, "What San Francisco Has Done about It." July, 1911.

Hichborn, Franklin: *"The System," as Uncovered by the San Francisco Graft Prosecution*. San Francisco, 1915.

Holliday, Charles W.: *The Valley of Youth*. Boise, 1948.

Inglis, William: *Harper's Weekly*, "Celebrities at Home: Patrick Calhoun." November 21, 1908.

                                       Harper's Weekly, "For the Kingdom of California: The True Story of San Francisco's Civil War Between the Grafters and the Elaborate Forces of the Prosecution." May 23, May 30, June 6, June 13, 1908.

Irwin, Will: *The City that Was: A Requiem of Old San Francisco*. New York, 1906.

                                       American Magazine, "They Who Strike in the Dark." April, 1909.

Jewish Elite Directory and Society List of San Francisco. San Francisco, 1892.

Kahn, Edgar M.: *Cable Car Days in San Francisco.* Stanford, 1940.

Keane, George (attributed): *Overland Monthly,* "The Confessions of a Stenographer." August, 1907.

Keeler, Charles: *San Francisco and Thereabout.* San Francisco, 1912.
　　　　　San Francisco Through Earthquake and Fire. San Francisco, 1906.

Kemble, John Haskell: *San Francisco Bay: A Pictorial Maritime History.* Cambridge (Maryland), 1957.

Kennan, George: *McClure's Magazine,* "Criminal Government and the Private Citizen: A Study of San Francisco." November, 1907.

"Kew": *Outlook Magazine,* "San Francisco's Ferment." August 31, 1907.

"L.A.": *Outlook Magazine,* "Impressions of a Careless Traveler." September 17, 1904.

Lane, Franklin K.: *The Letters of Franklin K. Lane.* New York, 1922.

Langdon, William L.: *Cosmopolitan Magazine,* "The Story of the Great Struggle." August, 1907.

Latta, Estelle: *Controversial Mark Hopkins.* New York, 1953.

Lewis, Oscar: *Bay Window Bohemia.* New York, 1956.

Levy, Harriet Lane: *920 O'Farrell Street.* New York, 1947.

Macomber, Ben: *The Jewel City.* San Francisco, 1915.

Marx, Guido H.: *The Nation,* "Reform in San Francisco." July 1, 1909.

Mowry, George E.: *The California Progressives.* Berkeley, 1951.

Nation, The, "The San Francisco Trial," June 3, 1909.

Nunan, Thomas: *Diary of an Old Bohemian.* San Francisco, 1927.

O'Brien, Robert: *This Is San Francisco.* New York, 1948.

Older, Cora Baggerly: *McClure's Magazine,* "The Story of a Reformer's Wife." July, 1909.
　　　　　San Francisco, Magic City. New York, 1961.

Older, Fremont: *My Own Story.* San Francisco, 1909.

One Hundred Years of the First Unitarian Church of San Francisco: 1850–1950. San Francisco, 1950.

Palmer, Frederick: *Collier's Weekly,* "Abe Ruef of the 'Law Offices.'" January 12, 1907.

Phelan, James D.: *The Independent,* "The Regeneration of San Francisco." June 20, 1907.

Pringle, Henry F.: *Theodore Roosevelt: A Biography.* New York, 1931.

"Q": *Overland Monthly.* "Ruef, a Jew Under Torture." November, 1907.

Quiett, Glenn Chesney: *They Built the West.* New York, 1934.

"R.H.C.": *Harper's Weekly,* "Patrick Calhoun and the Carmen's Strike in San Francisco." December 21, 1907.

Riesenberg, Felix, Jr.: *Golden Gate: The Story of San Francisco Harbor.* New York, 1940.

Ross, Edward A.: *Sin and Society: An Analysis of Latter-Day Iniquity*. San Francisco, 1907.

Ruef, Abraham: *San Francisco Bulletin* (serially), "The Road I Traveled." 1912.

Schmitz, Eugene E. (purported author): *The Fate of the San Francisco Grafters: Benedict Arnold of His Native City*. San Francisco, 1908.

Steffens, Joseph Lincoln: *Autobiography*. New York, 1931.

> *American Magazine*, "Breaking Into San Francisco." December, 1907.
>
> *American Magazine*, "The Clash of Classes in San Francisco." November, 1907.
>
> *American Magazine*, "Heney Tackles the Oregon Land Graft." October, 1907.
>
> *The Letters of Lincoln Steffens*. New York, 1938.
>
> *American Magazine*, "The Making of a Fighter: How Frank Heney Prepared in Arizona for the Work He Is Now Doing in San Francisco." July, 1907.
>
> *American Magazine*, "Rudolph Spreckels: A Businessman Fighting for His City." February, 1908.
>
> *The Shame of the Cities*. New York, 1904.
>
> *The Struggle for Self-Government*. New York, 1906.
>
> *American Magazine*, "The Taming of the West: Discovery of the Land Graft System, A Detective Story." August, 1907.
>
> *American Magazine*, "William J. Burns, Intriguer." April, 1908.

Sunset Magazine (Files). 1906–1912.

Taylor, Edward Robeson: *Selected Poems*. San Francisco, 1907.

Todd, Frank Morton: *Eradicating Plague from San Francisco—Report of the Citizens' Health Committee*. San Francisco, 1909.

Wells, Evelyn: *Champagne Days of San Francisco*. New York, 1939.

> *Fremont Older*. New York, 1936.

Wendte, Charles W.: *Thomas Starr King, Patriot and Preacher*. Boston, 1921.

Wilson, Carol Green: *Chinatown Quest: The Life and Adventures of Donaldina Cameron*. Stanford, 1931.

Young, John P.: *Journalism in California*. New York, 1915.

> *San Francisco, A History of the Pacific Coast Metropolis*. New York, 1912.

Zarchin, Michael M.: *Glimpses of Jewish Life in San Francisco*. San Francisco, 1952.

Newspapers
    San Francisco *Bulletin* (complete files 1904–1910)
    San Francisco *Call* (complete files 1904–1910)
    San Francisco *Chronicle* (complete files 1904–1910)
    San Francisco *Examiner* (complete files 1904–1910)
    Los Angeles *Examiner* (complete files 1904–1910)
    Los Angeles *Times* (complete files 1904–1910)
    Also the files of the London *Times,* New York, *Times,* Sacramento *Bee,* San Francisco *Globe,* San Francisco *News,* and numerous other daily and weekly publications.
    Public documents
    Court records
    Trial transcripts
    Directories
    Pamphlets, letters, and personal reminiscences.

Index

Abbott, William M., 70, 200, 243, 285, 286, 287, 288, 296, 303, 306, 374, 379, 380, 390

Ach, Henry, 28, 61, 96, 98, 100, 104, 106, 110, 124, 125, 133, 135, 136, 137, 138, 140, 141, 145, 148, 149, 150, 152, 153, 156, 159, 166, 185, 215, 216, 218, 225, 227, 229, 234, 235, 285, 316–17, 321, 324, 327, 334, 335, 336, 338, 340, 341, 343, 361–62, 365

Adler, N. Max, 118, 119, 121, 138

Aetna Indemnity Company, 152, 155

Altmann, Aaron, 146, 212

American Federation of Labor, 20

Andrews, Thomas P., 81, 109–10

Andrieu, Alfred, 124–25, 126

Aoki, Viscount, 146

Ashe, R. Porter, 292, 293, 294, 297–98, 360

Associated Press, 247, 261

Atherton, Gertrude, 67, 130, 246

Bachman, Joseph, 139

Barbary Coast, 10

Barrett, John J., 133, 135, 136, 137, 138, 141, 143, 149, 249, 255, 372, 387

Barrymore, Ethel, 380

Bassity, Jerome, 85

Bay Cities Water Company, 95, 205, 248

Beasley, Shadworth S., 104–05, 107, 345, 355

Beatty, William H., 86, 319

Bell, "Butch," 340

415